Group Leadership:
A Training Approach

Richard Nelson-Jones

Royal Melbourne Institute of Technology

Brooks/Cole Publishing Company
Pacific Grove, California

A CLAIREMONT BOOK

Brooks/Cole Publishing Company
A Division of Wadsworth, Inc.

Printed in the United States of America

10   9   8   7   6   5   4   3   2   1

Library of Congress Cataloging in Publication Data

Nelson-Jones, Richard.
    Group leadership : a training approach / Richard Nelson-Jones.
       p.   cm.
    Includes bibliographical references and index.
    ISBN 0-534-17010-2
    1. Leadership.   2. Work groups—Management.   I. Title.
HD57.7.N45   1991
658.4'036—dc20   91-25842
                                                                                    CIP

Sponsoring Editor: Claire Verduin
Editorial Assistant: Gay C. Bond
Production Editor: Linda Loba
Manuscript Editor: Lorraine Anderson
Interior Design and Cover Design: Lisa Thompson
Art Coordinator: Cloyce Wall
Typesetting: Shepard Poorman Communications Corporation
Printing and Binding: Arcata Graphics-Fairfield

THIS BOOK focuses on the central skills needed for leading training or lifeskills groups. Training groups are time-limited, structured, psychological education groups focused on helping participants develop one or more lifeskills—for example, parenting, stress management, or assertion skills. Training groups are now perhaps the most common way that helpers work in groups.

This book is intended for group leaders who either will be or are in roles where they train others in lifeskills. Such people may be in numerous areas: counseling, teaching, parent education, marriage guidance, social work, nursing, health care, rehabilitation, career work, youth work, correctional work, community relations, personnel work, and working as training officers in business, industry, and public service. The book can be used to train such people as part of group leadership courses at undergraduate, community college, and postgraduate levels. Trainers forced to acquire training skills on the job also may find the book useful. And with its comprehensive detail, the book can be used as a reference by trainers and others.

A number of assumptions underlie the book. First, my theoretical position integrates both cognitive-behavioral and existential-humanistic insights. Second, lifeskills are self-help skills. Lifeskills training groups teach participants to manage on their own. Third, effective training involves both teaching and group interaction. Consequently, lifeskills group leaders require both facilitative and didactic skills. Fourth, I take an optimistic approach to the human condition. Though all of us to a greater or lesser degree have acquired some lifeskills weaknesses, we can choose not to sustain them. Well-led training groups help people reclaim and develop more of their human potential.

This is a practical handbook or training manual designed to build a comprehensive range of group leadership skills. It spends time on basic skills for the simple reason that training-group leaders too frequently hamper their effectiveness by getting the basics wrong. Chapter 1 places training groups in the context of different kinds of groups and further clarifies their characteristics. Chapter 2 gives an overview of how people not only acquire, but also maintain both lifeskills strengths and weaknesses. Eleven "how-to" chapters follow, describing how to prepare for a training group; design lifeskills programs; assess participants and help them do self-assessment; facilitate training groups; speak in public; demonstrate lifeskills; manage structured activities; prepare and lead sessions; consolidate trained skills and end groups; evaluate and research training groups; and maintain and develop your group leadership skills.

This book views group leadership skills as choices that can be made either well or poorly. Sometimes the book presents trainer choices in list form to highlight different options. The book's learning-by-doing or "hands-on" emphasis is reinforced by the inclusion of numerous exercises. Readers will be more likely to develop skills if they will work through these exercises. Session outlines, program outlines, and training examples also illustrate skills. Each chapter starts with a list of questions, to let readers know what lies ahead, and ends with a summary of chapter highlights, for purposes of review. Throughout, I have attempted to use simple, clear English.

I want to express appreciation to the following people: Claire Verduin, for commissioning the book and for making helpful editorial comments in the nicest possible way; Gay Bond, for her encouragement and empathy; and the following reviewers for their helpful suggestions: Dr. Cheryl Bartholomew, George Mason University; Dr. Mary Lou Cormier, University of Maine; Dr. Michael Dougherty, Western Carolina University; Dr. Robert Frank, University of Northern Iowa; Dr. Sam Gladding, Wake Forest University; Professor Stephen A. Haberman, North Harris County College; Dr. Jean Macht, Montgomery County Community College; Dr. Kenneth R. Newton, University of Tennessee; Professor Kathleen M. Ritter, California State University-Bakersfield; Professor Steven Rollin, Florida State University; and Dr. Elizabeth Van Dalsem, San Francisco State University. Last but not least, my thanks to all those practitioners, theorists, and researchers who have written about groups and whose names constitute an honor roll in the bibliography.

I hope that you find working through this book an interesting and rewarding experience. I wish you good skills when you lead training groups.

Richard Nelson-Jones

C O N T E N T S

v

7   **How to Speak in Public   149**

8   **How to Demonstrate Lifeskills   187**

9   **How to Manage Structured Activities   219**

10   How to Prepare For and Lead a Session   251

11   How to Consolidate Self-Help Skills and to End a Group   275

12   How to Evaluate and Research a Training Group   299

13   How to Maintain and Develop Training-Group Leadership Skills   313

L I S T   O F   E X E R C I S E S

1

An Introduction to Training Groups

Give people a fish, and you feed them
for a day.
Teach people to fish, and you feed them
for a lifetime.

Chinese proverb

Chapter Questions

How do training groups differ from other groups?

Why the growth of training groups?

What sorts of training groups are there?

What are lifeskills?

What is the leader's role in training groups?

What are some criticisms and reservations about training groups?

Introduction

As we approach the twenty-first century, leading training groups is likely to become an increasingly large part of the work of many helpers. Attempts to help people acquire the skills to manage their lives better are nothing new. However, as psychological knowledge has developed, so have systematic attempts to use psychological insights and principles to train people to be more effective in all aspects of their lives. Terms like *psychoeducation* (Ivey, 1976), *human resource development* (Carkhuff, 1971a), *lifeskills teaching* (Hopson & Scally, 1981), *lifeskills training* (Gazda, 1989), *deliberate psychological education* (Mosher & Sprinthall, 1970; Sprinthall & Scott, 1989), and *developmental education* (Nelson-Jones, 1988a) have been used to describe this movement.

However, the growth in the training function of group helpers has not been paralleled by a growth in books about how to train. The major focus of most books on group leadership is still on interactional groups rather than training groups (for instance, Corey, 1990; Corey, Corey, Callanan, & Russell, 1988; Gazda, 1989; Jacobs, Harvill, & Masson, 1988; Ohlsen, Horne, & Lawe, 1988). There were no books with the word *training* in their titles or subtitles found in the content area of group theory and practice in a recent survey of the leading textbooks used in counselor education programs throughout the United States (Sampson & Liberty, 1989). This book attempts to redress the imbalance by taking group-leader-as-trainer skills as its major focus.

How Do Training Groups Differ from Other Groups?

Many kinds of groups are available to people seeking psychological support and information. Here I'll list and describe some of the main kinds of groups. Though an oversimplification, this listing may help you place training groups within the broad context of other kinds of groups. Needless to say, overlap exists between the different kinds of groups.

Discussion Groups

Discussion groups focus on specific topics, such as how to deal with AIDS sufferers, whether or not to legalize pot, and whether or not religion is helpful or harmful. Discussion groups are topic-centered rather than centered either on the relationships between discussion group members or on the systematic development of specific life-skills. Discussion groups aim to get participants involved and to broaden their knowledge and understanding of stipulated topics.

Information Groups

Information groups impart specific information. Though information may be provided by members to each other, usually the group leader is the main source of information. Information groups cover such areas as occupational information, sex education, and drug and alcohol education. Information groups have the educational purpose of helping people acquire specific knowledge. Such groups tend to have developmental and preventive rather than remedial goals.

Task-Oriented Groups

In task-oriented groups, the task rather than the topic is the group's major focus. Task groups go beyond talking to action, or at least to deciding on and planning proposed courses of action. Usually task-oriented groups have specific and clear goals. Examples of task-oriented groups include groups to decide on the rules in a nursing home for the elderly, groups to plan how to market a new product, research teams, and social club committees. The personal development of task group members is tangential to performance of the group's tasks. If and when these tasks are completed, such groups are likely to disband.

Growth Groups

Growth groups come under many different titles: encounter groups, sensitivity groups, T-groups, experiential groups, human relations groups, and so on. Rogers defines an encounter group as follows: "This tends to emphasize personal growth and the development and improvement of interpersonal communication and relationships through an experiential process" (Rogers, 1970, pp. 4–5). Central values for growth groups include dropping social facades, cultivating openness and honesty, working in the "here-and-now," getting in touch with and expressing feelings, and working through blocks to making genuine person-to-person contact with other members. Yalom observes that the goals of such groups are often vague (Yalom, 1985). Participants in growth groups tend to be self-selected and tend not to view themselves as clients or patients, but rather as people in search of higher levels of self-actualization. Growth groups are often time-limited: for instance, a weekend marathon group.

Counseling Groups

In counseling groups, group interaction and relationships are used by leaders to help members attain personal goals. Members of counseling groups tend to be clients who use group counseling after, concurrently with, or instead of individual counseling. Ohlsen (1977) views group counseling as enabling clients to (1) discuss what really worries them, (2) define desired new behaviors, (3) practice essential interpersonal skills, and (4) implement new behaviors. Though group counselees undoubtedly have their anxieties and personal difficulties, there is a basic assumption that these concerns are not so debilitating as to require extensive personality change (Gazda, 1989; Ohlsen, Horne, & Lawe, 1988). Counseling groups are frequently time-limited; however, they tend to last for months rather than for either days or weeks. For instance, Mahler (1969) suggests that about ten sessions should be the minimum for most group counseling programs held in schools.

Psychotherapy Groups

Psychotherapy groups tend to be distinguished from counseling groups and encounter groups along a number of dimensions. First, the purposes of therapy groups are almost invariably remedial rather than developmental or preventive. Second, the clientele tends to be "relatively seriously emotionally disturbed" (Gazda, 1989, p. 45) or "persons who are in need of or desire a personality restructuring, who are so debilitated as not to be able to function effectively in their day-to-day lives" (Ohlsen, Horne, & Lawe, 1988, p. 14). Yalom observes that therapy groups are often composed of people who cannot cope with minor everyday stress without discomfort (Yalom, 1985). Basic interpersonal competencies and the ability to send and receive messages without much distortion cannot be assumed. Third, because of their lower self-esteem and self-awareness, therapy group members are more closed, defended, and concerned with their psychological survival. Especially at the start of psychotherapy groups, members are less open to questioning themselves and less willing to learn from new experiences. Fourth, the training of psychotherapy group leaders tends more to be "intensive psychological and/or medical at the doctoral level" (Gazda, 1989, p. 15). Fifth, the distortions contained in members' transference relationships with the leader are likely to be explored in greater depth than in counseling or encounter groups, where they may not be explored at all. In sum, psychotherapy groups are intensive and often long-term group experiences, frequently held in psychiatric inpatient and outpatient settings, for people with highly debilitating emotional problems and interpersonal skills weaknesses.

Self-Help Groups

Self-help groups go by other names, such as peer support groups, mutual support groups, and mutual sharing groups. Huge numbers of self-help groups exist. For example, around 1980, there were approximately half a million self-help groups in the United States, with a total membership of 15 million (Katz, 1981; Riordan & Beggs, 1987). The range of self-help groups is vast, and includes women's groups, men's groups, gay groups, Alcoholics Anonymous, widows' groups, bereaved parents' groups, groups for relatives of people suffering from schizophrenia or senility, Overeaters Anonymous, and Mended Hearts (for coronary surgery patients). Self-help groups often evolve their leaders from within their own membership, but may still have experts on call as consultants. Self-help groups place a heavy emphasis on sharing and mutual support.

Support Networks

People exist with various degrees of connectedness to others who can support them (Acock & Hurlbert, 1990). In reality, individuals' support networks comprise participation in many different networks: family, friends, work colleagues, clubs, church, school, and so on. When people seek help from professionals, it is often a sign that their own helping or support networks are inadequate (Murgatroyd, 1985). In a sense, support networks are informal rather than formal self-help groups. People of varying degrees of disturbance may need to appreciate more the importance of support networks and may need to develop their skills of expanding, participating in, and using their networks (Conn & Peterson, 1989).

Training Groups

Training groups, lifeskills groups, or lifeskills training groups are time-limited, structured groups with specific and predetermined learning goals and programs. There often is no assumption of mental unwellness for participation in a training group. Social skills are perhaps the most common focus of training groups—for example, assertiveness, managing anger, or managing conflict—but training groups can also focus on many other areas of living, such as health, studying, or work. Training group leaders use both didactic and facilitative skills to help participants develop skills and then transfer and maintain them after the program's end.

Following are some examples of people participating in training groups.

- ▼ Inez, 43, goes along to a weekend workshop, run by a social worker in private practice, on assertiveness skills.
- ▼ Leon and Margie, both in their early 30s, attend weekly sessions in effective parenting at their local community mental health center.
- ▼ Paco, 9, participates in a class at his primary school to develop friendship skills.
- ▼ Julie, 17, has a class at her high school on career decision-making skills.
- ▼ Gene, 63, attends a series of seminars, offered by his company's personnel department, on preparing for retirement.
- ▼ Leroy, 18, attends a skills group at his university counseling center on managing test anxiety.
- ▼ Connie, 21, attends a course in human relations skills as part of her teacher training.

To reiterate, we can define training groups for this book as follows:

> Training groups are time-limited, structured groups in which one or more leaders use a repertoire of didactic and facilitative skills to help participants develop and maintain one or more specific lifeskills. Important features of training groups include: no assumption of psychological disturbance, systematic instruction, experiential learning-by-doing, and a high degree of participant involvement.

Why the Growth of Training Groups?
▼ ▼

Several reasons can be given for the growing emphasis on training groups. Perhaps the most obvious reason is that problems of living are widespread, and the world is full of people failing to maximize their human potential. The statistics on marital breakdown provide one indication of this. In the early 1980s the divorce rate for first marriages in the United States was 49 percent (Glick, 1984). In the period from 1971 to 1985 the number of divorces per year in England and Wales more than doubled, from 75,000 to 154,000 (Office of Population Census and Surveys, 1987). In Australia, the percentage of marriages ending in divorce increased from 14 percent in 1971 to 35 percent in 1986 (McDonald, 1988). These figures partly reflect the facts that obtaining a divorce has become easier and that divorce is less socially stigmatized than it once was. Nevertheless, the figures underestimate the extent of marital breakdown. If the figures for the separated population were added to those for the divorced population to form a "dissolution index," the rate of marital breakdown would be considerably higher. Add the many couples who remain neither separated nor divorced, but unhappy, and the extent of marital distress, with its repercussions for children, becomes even greater. Keeping relationships happy and intact is just one among many possible areas where numerous people experience problems of living.

Training groups have both developmental and preventive objectives. You do not have to admit to mental disturbance to participate in a training group. The goal of lifeskills training in an ideal world would be to teach everyone the requisite skills to meet all developmental tasks throughout their lives. Distinctions between remedial, preventive, and developmental emphases are seldom clear-cut. Daws (1973), writing of the need for preventive work in schools, argues that the strongest expression of the preventive principle is work devoted to the personal and social education of *all* students in such a way that it anticipates their developmental needs. Drug and alcohol education and AIDS education are further examples of preventive training.

Increased pressures for helper accountability provide another impetus for running training groups. Some helpers consider that their cost-effectiveness is much greater if they actively engage in developmental and preventive interventions, like training groups, rather than passively wait in their offices for clients requiring remedial help. These helpers seek ways to benefit as many people as possible. Also, they wish to better justify to budgeteers and other influential people the services they offer.

Successful training groups can both save and make money. Poorly functioning people cost money, while well-functioning people can make money. For instance, good communicators in business and commerce are more likely to contribute to income and profits than poor communicators. Skilled supervisors and managers are conducive to developing and maintaining competitiveness (Goldstein & Gilliam, 1990). On the other hand, employees whose functioning is impaired through stress-related, substance abuse, or other emotional problems are often costly.

The increased influence of cognitive-behaviorism has been a major stimulus for people to run training groups. The theoretical foundations for training groups rest on the behavioral (actions-focused) revolution in helping of the 1960s and the cognitive (thinking-focused) revolution of the 1970s. The cognitive-behavioral model is basically a lifeskills training model. Many, if not most, training groups now focus on both thinking and action skills.

What Sorts of Training Groups Are There?

The scope of lifeskills training is vast. Training groups can be run both with clients of helping services and with those who are not clients. We can differentiate among training groups on the basis of (1) the broad areas addressed, and (2) the settings for the groups.

Broad Areas for Training Groups

Four broad areas can be identified in which training groups can be fruitfully conducted with nonclient participants. First, there is the area of developmental education. Developmental education entails training people, from children to the elderly, in the psychological lifeskills appropriate to their developmental stage (Havighurst, 1972). The second broad area is that of training specific clienteles to handle better their problems of living. Examples of this include training in coping with dual careers for married couples (Amatea & Cross, 1983), emotional expressiveness for men (Moore & Haverkamp, 1989) and assertiveness for women (Butler, 1981), and coping with unemployment for the unemployed and those facing job loss (Azrin, Flores, & Kaplan, 1975).

The third broad area for lifeskills training groups is that of work-related training. Work-related training groups can be run on either a preservice or an in-service basis. In-service training programs include those on relationship skills for teachers and doctors; anger management skills for police officers; and supervisory skills for newly promoted supervisors. Helper training is a fourth broad area for training groups. Much training in practical skills for helpers takes place in groups—for example, training counselors and social workers in listening skills.

Settings for Training Groups

Lifeskills training groups are run in many different settings. Following is a description of some of the main settings, with examples of the skills areas addressed.

Elementary and High Schools

Lifeskills training takes place in both elementary and high schools. Training groups can be run both within and outside the formal curriculum (Martin, 1983). Morgan (1984) describes a kindergarten-to-sixth-grade guidance curriculum in an Oregon school district. The program's objectives were clustered into such skills areas as awareness of feelings, valuing, listening, cooperation and conflict resolution, and occupational and educational decision making. Another program attempted to train visually impaired elementary school children in social skills (Sacks & Gaylord-Ross, 1989).

Four of the main areas in which training groups can be conducted in high schools are study skills, relationship skills, career education, and staff development. Study skills groups cover both study techniques and managing test anxiety. Illustrative relationship skills groups include Mosher and Sprinthall's seminar and practicum format for teaching empathy in high schools (Mosher & Sprinthall, 1971; Sprinthall, 1973, 1980) and Hatch and Guerney's (1975) pupil relationship enhancement program (PREP). PREP focuses on training pupils to enhance their skills as speakers (expressive mode) and as listeners (responder mode) in two-person relationships. Some life-skills training groups have focused on control of anger and aggression both in the classroom and toward teachers (Huey & Rank, 1984; Pentz & Kadzin, 1982). Other topics for relationship skills groups in schools include overcoming shyness and making friends, assertiveness, managing conflict, cross-cultural communication skills, integration of sexuality, and sex-role education. Such training may be aimed at either pupils in general or at specific groups—for example, gifted and talented adolescents (Barnette, 1989). Adolescents also have been taught stress-reduction skills to raise their self-esteem and lower their proneness to anxiety and anger (Hains & Szyjakowski, 1990) Other training groups relevant to relationships include drug and alcohol education (Dorn & South, 1986; Wragg, 1986), AIDS education, and groups for children and adolescents whose parents are getting divorced.

Career education training groups in schools can have a number of objectives, including self-awareness, opportunity awareness, decision making (Savikas, 1990), information-seeking skills, interview skills, and learning how to cope with transition (Amatea, Clark, & Cross, 1984; Roessler, 1988). Additional objectives of career education groups include handling unemployment, leisure skills education, and helping disabled students make a successful transition from secondary programs to employment and independent living (Brolin & Gysbers, 1989).

Staff development training groups in schools can cover such areas as counseling skills, relationship skills, and classroom and behavior management skills. Some staff may also gain from training groups to reduce stress and avoid burnout.

Colleges and Universities

Training groups in colleges and universities can be designed for at least three groups: students, staff, and helping services trainees. Training groups aimed at students include remedial, preventive, and developmental interventions across a number of lifeskills areas. Sometimes these are taught by faculty within the curriculum—for instance, relationship skills programs. Often training groups are run by counseling center staff outside the curriculum. The range of training groups includes those on study skills, managing test anxiety, relationship skills, career development skills (Garis & Niles, 1990; Swain, 1984), anxiety and stress management skills (Romano, 1984), and effective thinking skills (Barrow & Moore, 1983; Heppner, Neal, & Larson, 1984). Specific training groups also are aimed at the problems of new students, minority groups, females, males, homosexual or bisexual students, and singles or couples, among others. Some training interventions, such as drug prevention courses (Gonzalez, 1990) and seminars on date rape, may be targeted at large numbers of students.

Training groups for staff include those in helping and tutoring skills (Ratigan, 1986; Thorne & Da Costa, 1976). Sometimes these groups go beyond training staff for their faculty roles to assist them in becoming counseling service paraprofessionals. Staff can also be trained to identify their own self-defeating attitudes and behaviors. For instance, Thurman (1984, 1985) ran a training group to reduce coronary-inducing Type A thinking and behaviors among university faculty. He focused both on altering irrational beliefs and on anger management. Relationship skills and retirement planning are further areas for staff lifeskills training groups.

Helping services trainees include those in courses for counselors, social workers, applied psychologists, pastoral carers, personnel managers, community health workers, doctors, nurses, health paraprofessionals, rehabilitation workers, career officers, youth workers, and teachers. Training groups for such people can focus on skills in counseling and helping, group facilitation, relationships, behavior management, team building, and leadership. In addition, helping services trainees can be trained as training-group leaders.

Medical Settings

Training groups in medical settings are conducted with two main categories of participants: patients and their families, and health professionals and paraprofessionals. Patient groups can be run in hospitals and outpatient clinics in numerous skills areas, including anxiety management, stress management, heart attack prevention and management, headache management (Martin, Nathan, Milech, & van Keppel, 1989; Murphy, Lehrer, & Jurish, 1990), pain management (Keefe et al., 1990; Turner & Clancy, 1988), relationship skills; social phobia management (Heimberg, Dodge, Hope, Kennedy, Zollo, & Becker, 1990), alcohol and drug rehabilitation, overcoming obesity (Kalodoner & DeLucia, 1990), coping with depression (Brown & Lewinsohn, 1984), coping with physical disabilities, overcoming insomnia (Morawetz, 1989; Morin & Azrin, 1987), and making the transition back to the community after hospitalization. Training groups can also be conducted with family caregivers (Abramowitz & Coursey, 1989; Lovett & Gallagher, 1988). Groups on death and dying can be run for relatives of terminally ill patients, and on how to cope for relatives of patients who have illnesses such as schizophrenia, Down's syndrome, or Alzheimer's disease. Sometimes, as in the case of coping with AIDS, the scope of training groups is extended beyond blood relatives to include lovers and friends.

Lifeskills training groups can be run on both preservice and in-service bases for health professionals and paraprofessionals. One-to-one helping skills can be taught to a range of personnel, from medical residents to support staff—for instance, hospital receptionists. There is a widespread need for relationship skills training for health workers. Training groups can be run in hospitals and nursing homes to sensitize staff both to each other's and to residents' needs (Allred, 1988). Additionally, medical staff can be trained to recognize patients who should be referred to psychologists or psychiatrists. Furthermore, training groups can be run to help health workers cope with work-related problems and stresses—for instance, on how to avoid burnout and how to work through feelings about being with badly disfigured or dying patients.

Business and Industry

Lifeskills training groups in business and industry are big business. Toomer (1982) writes of the American scene: "It has been suggested that industry spends more money on education and training than the public service does on educating and training students in elementary and secondary school" (p. 20). Much of this training is in nonpsychological work skills. However, there is still a considerable amount of psychological lifeskills training, aimed both at improving efficiency and morale and at preventing psychological health problems.

Three broad areas for lifeskills training groups in business and industry are career development, communication skills, and mental wellness. Training groups in the career development area can be on such topics as career planning, job enrichment, preparation for transfer to a new location, coping with job loss, and retirement skills. Effective communication is important both within organizations and with customers (Georges, 1989; Goldstein & Gilliam, 1990). Lifeskills training groups to build intraorganization communication skills encompass management and leadership, supervision, team building, negotiation, managing conflict, assertiveness, cross-cultural communication, counseling, expressing appreciation, creative problem solving, conducting effective meetings, and public speaking. Training groups for delivering customer services can focus on the skills of listening, negotiating, sending clear messages, and managing anger and conflict.

The cost both to business and industry and to individuals of psychological problems is substantial. For the employer the negative effects include absenteeism, industrial accidents, underachievement, and interpersonal conflict. Such problems can involve the costs of underutilization of the plant, medical and worker's compensation, absenteeism/overtime, and replacement training (Osipow, 1982). A high proportion of those fired by business and industry are terminated because of communication, substance abuse, and other psychological problems. Training groups for mental and physical wellness include those focusing on stress management, weight control, smoking cessation, alcohol and drug education, marital and family relationship skills, and physical fitness (Blanchard, 1989; Wilbur & Vermilyea, 1982). These groups can be aimed at all levels—for instance, managers, supervisors, production-line employees, and sales staff.

Marriage and Family Agencies

Lifeskills training groups for marital and family competencies do not fit neatly into any single setting. Partner relationship skills and parenting skills are the two main emphases. Such groups may be run in outpatient clinics, counseling centers, churches, voluntary agencies, parent-child education centers, and private practices. Nowadays numerous people live in de facto relationships, either temporarily, or prior to or instead of marriage. Consequently, partner relationship skills are important for both unmarried and married people. Such skills include listening, self-disclosing, asserting oneself and helping one's partner do likewise, expressing caring, identifying and engaging in joint rewarding activities, cooperative decision making, building trust, managing anger, managing conflict, and relating sexually (Nelson-Jones, 1990b). Also, sometimes training groups focus on the sex-role expectations and behaviors of partners and on the problems of dual-career couples (Amatea & Cross, 1983).

Numerous training groups exist to teach effective parenting skills. A prime example is Gordon's parent effectiveness training (Gordon, 1970). This program focuses on the skills of active listening and sending "I" messages, and on his "no-lose" method of resolving conflicts. Other skills for parent training groups include skills to increase the exchange of rewarding behaviors in parent-child conflicts (Raue & Spence, 1985), assertiveness (Clifford, 1987), anger management skills (Nomellini & Katz, 1983), behavior management skills for dealing with children (Webster-Stratton, Hollinsworth, & Kolpacoff, 1989), fathering skills (Resnik, Resnik, Packer, & Wilson, 1978), and sexuality education skills (Bundy & White, 1990).

Miscellaneous Settings

Other than those already listed, there are many further settings for lifeskills training groups. These include the following:

Voluntary agencies: Voluntary agencies cover an enormous range of activities. Examples of training groups run in voluntary agencies include groups focusing on coping with grief and bereavement, coping with homosexuality, and providing care in a church community.

Government agencies: Many of the lifeskills training groups run in business and industry are also relevant for people in local, county, state, and national government. They are also pertinent to armed forces personnel of all ranks.

Career and employment services: The kinds of lifeskills training groups run in career services include those aimed at improving knowledge of the world of work, decision making, information seeking, and interview skills.

Prisons: Training groups can be run for prison guards—for instance, on managing stress or anger. Groups can also be run for adult inmates and juvenile delinquents—for example, on relationship skills (Sarason, 1976), anger and aggression management (Schlichter & Horan, 1981), and finding and keeping employment (Weissman, 1985).

Private practices: Professionals in the helping services often provide consultation and training groups for social service agencies, schools, courts, clergy, police, and other community service agencies. Private practitioners may also, on their own premises, run training groups for the public—for example, on relationship or stress management skills.

Retirement communities and senior citizen centers: Quality of life is a very important issue for old people. Training groups can focus on such issues as adapting to a retirement or nursing home community and making friends (Plesma & Flanagan, 1986); assertiveness, sometimes in relation to dealing with grasping offspring; use of leisure skills; values clarification; coping with physical changes; and dying and survivorship.

What Are Lifeskills?

The meanings of the word *skill* include proficiency, competence, and expertise in some activity. However, the essential element of any skill is the ability to make and implement a sequence of choices to achieve a desired objective. For instance, if you are to be good at asserting yourself or managing stress, you have to make and implement effective choices in these lifeskills areas. Also, if you are to be good as a training-group leader, you have to make and implement effective choices in skills areas such as facilitating groups, speaking well in public, and demonstrating skills clearly.

The concept of skills is best viewed not as an either/or matter in which you either possess or do not possess a skill. Rather, it is preferable to think of yourself as possessing *skills strengths* or *weaknesses* or a mixture of the two. If you make good choices in a skills area, this is a skills strength. If you make poor choices, this is a skills weakness. Put simply, the criterion for good or poor choices is whether they help or hinder you in assuming personal responsibility for your happiness and fulfillment.

In all lifeskills areas you are likely to possess both skills strengths and weaknesses in varying degrees. For instance, in the skills area of listening, you may be good at understanding talkers, but poor at showing them that you actually have understood. The object of lifeskills training groups is to help participants to shift the balance of their strengths and weaknesses in one or more skills areas more in the direction of strengths. The object of training lifeskills group leaders is the same, but in regard to training skills rather than lifeskills. In both instances, those being trained are helped to affirm themselves and others by becoming *better choosers*.

Defining Lifeskills

There are a number of ways to approach a positive definition of *lifeskills*. Some of these are explored in the following paragraphs.

Lifeskills entail *personally responsible choices*. When people are being personally responsible they are in the process of making the choices that maximize their happiness and fulfillment. Personal responsibility is a positive concept whereby people are responsible for their well-being and making their own choices. Lifeskills are the component skills by means of which people assume rather than avoid personal responsibility for their lives. Lifeskills are also *self-help skills*. Lifeskills are competencies that enable people to help themselves. As such they empower rather than disempower or weaken people (Hopson & Scally, 1981).

Lifeskills are conducive to *mental wellness*. People who are limited in their possession of lifeskills are less able to fullfill their potential and meet their needs than those more skilled. Psychological distress both reflects and results from deficiencies in lifeskills. However, this is less true for biologically influenced disorders, such as schizophrenia (Lazarus, 1989). Lifeskills possess a *psychological component*. Virtually any skill—for instance, tying a shoelace—might be viewed as a lifeskill. However, almost all the lifeskills mentioned in this book have a large "mind" component in them. Thus, even though many lifeskills are stated as specific observable behaviors, they usually also heavily involve people's thoughts and feelings.

Lifeskills are not static, but are *processes* requiring effective sequences of choices. Throughout their lives people are choosers. Humans can never escape their mandate to choose among possibilities (Frankl, 1969). People who possess a lifeskill choose to make the choices involved in implementing that lifeskill. To attain their full human potential, people require a *repertoire* of lifeskills in a number of different areas. These lifeskills need to be appropriate both to their developmental tasks at any particular stage of their life span and to any special problems of living, challenges, or transitions they may face.

We can draw these threads together into the following definition of *lifeskills*:

> Lifeskills are personally responsible sequences of choices in specific psychological skills areas conducive to mental wellness. People require a repertoire of lifeskills according to their developmental tasks and specific problems of living.

Attitude, Knowledge, and Skills

It can be helpful to think of specific lifeskills as comprising three dimensions: attitude, knowledge, and skills.

Attitude: An appropriate attitude to any lifeskill is that you assume personal responsibility for acquiring, maintaining, using, and developing it. You may lose some or all of a lifeskill if you fail to work at using and developing it. A personally responsible attitude is the motivational or "wanting to do it" dimension of a lifeskill.

Knowledge: Any lifeskill involves knowledge concerning the best choices to make. People who have been exposed to good examples— for instance, by their parents' behavior—may possess the required knowledge implicitly rather than explicitly. People with skills weaknesses are likely to need to have the relevant knowledge clearly spelled out so that they can instruct themselves. Knowledge is the "knowing how to do it" dimension of a lifeskill.

Skill: The skill dimension entails the application of attitude and knowledge in practice. Skills can be the "inner game," focusing on feeling and thinking, as well as the "outer game," focusing on observable actions. In appropriate circumstances, you translate your "wanting to do it" and "knowing how to do it" into "actually doing it."

Some Specific Lifeskills

In the section on sorts of training groups, many different lifeskills areas were identified. Other writers have attempted to divide lifeskills into different categories. For instance, Egan and Cowan (1979) have identified six categories of skills, relating to (1) physical development, (2) intellectual development, (3) self-management, (4) value-clarification, (5) interpersonal involvement, and (6) small-group involvement. Hopson and Scally (1981) discuss lifeskills training in relation to five specific situations: (1) education, (2) work, (3) home, (4) leisure, and (5) the community. In Exercise 1 we categorize lifeskills into seven areas: (1) feeling, (2) thinking, (3) relationships, (4) study, (5) work, (6) leisure, and (7) health. The feeling and thinking categories contain the fundamental psychological skills, while the other five categories represent areas of human functioning.

Exercise 1 provides a list of central lifeskills and asks you to rate yourself on these skills. The idea behind the exercise is to create interest by encouraging you both to look at your own lifeskills and to identify lifeskills areas in which you might lead groups.

Exercise 1 Assess Your Lifeskills
▼▼

The questionnaire that follows lists a number of lifeskills in seven broad areas. Rate how satisfied you are with your lifeskills by using the following rating scale:

3 *much* need for improvement
2 *moderate* need for improvement
1 *slight* need for improvement
0 *no* need for improvement

Put a question mark (?) rather than a rating by any lifeskill whose meaning is not clear to you. If a lifeskills area is not relevant to you—for example, study—you can choose not to respond in that area.

*Your
rating*   *Lifeskill*

1. *Feeling*

_____   Acknowledging the importance of your feelings

_____   Being aware of and open to your feelings

_____   Being aware of your wants and wishes

_____   Possessing inner empathy/ability to tune in to and explore feelings

_____   Being aware of your body sensations

_____   Being able to experience your sensuality

_____   Being able to be spontaneous

_____   Being fully aware of the parameters of existence—for example, death, suffering, fate

2. *Thinking*

_____   Possessing a realistic conceptual framework

_____   Assuming personal responsibility for the choices that make your life

_____   Using coping self-talk

_____   Choosing your personal rules

_____   Choosing how you perceive

_____   Attributing cause accurately

_____   Predicting risk and reward

_____   Setting personal goals

_____   Visualizing

———— Making decisions

———— Managing problems

3. *Relationships*

———— Owning your thoughts, feelings, and actions in relationships

———— Disclosing personal information

———— Expressing feelings appropriately

———— Sending good voice messages

———— Sending good body messages

———— Sending good touch messages

———— Overcoming your shyness

———— Making initial contact

———— Using conversational skills

———— Using good listening skills

———— Responding helpfully

———— Asserting yourself

———— Showing caring

———— Relating sexually

———— Managing anger

———— Managing conflict

———— Being aware of sex-role issues

———— Being aware of cross-cultural issues

———— Possessing skills for specific roles—for example, parenting, dealing with elderly relatives (stipulate role and skills) ————————

4. *Study*

———— Making educational choices wisely

———— Setting goals

———— Managing time effectively

———— Meeting deadlines

———— Reading effectively

———— Possessing writing skills

———— Coping with achievement/examination anxiety

———— Coping with math/statistics anxiety

———— Being creative

———— Thinking critically

———— Participating in groups

———— Speaking in public

5. *Work*

_____ Accurately identifying your values
_____ Accurately identifying your interests
_____ Realistically appraising your abilities and skills
_____ Being aware of opportunities
_____ Gathering information
_____ Making decisions
_____ Presenting self in writing
_____ Interviewing for jobs
_____ Constructively evaluating feedback
_____ Preparing for and handling transitions
_____ Being able to develop/make the most of your work setting
_____ Using teamwork skills
_____ Managing money
_____ Possessing skills for specific roles—for example, managing, supervising, providing customer services (stipulate role and skills)

_____

_____

6. *Leisure*

_____ Valuing leisure time highly
_____ Being aware of personally rewarding interests and activities
_____ Gathering information
_____ Making decisions
_____ Being willing to develop skills in specific activities
_____ Being able to relax passively
_____ Having adequate and enjoyable holidays

7. *Health*

_____ Assuming responsibility for your health
_____ Eating nutritionally and in moderation
_____ Adequately controlling alcohol consumption
_____ Avoiding smoking
_____ Avoiding addictive drugs
_____ Keeping physically fit
_____ Managing stress well
_____ Observing a good balance between work, relationship, family, and recreational activities

Conclude the exercise by writing out a summary statement that identifies as specifically as possible the areas in which you might (1) develop your own lifeskills, and (2) be a lifeskills trainer.

Leadership Role and Style
▼▼

As the name suggests, the leadership role in training groups is that of trainer. Though lifeskills groups may involve releasing participants' existing potentials, their major emphasis is on systematically instructing them in skills. The word *trainer* is used because it has stronger connotations than the word *teacher* in three important aspects of acquiring and developing lifeskills. First, training emphasizes learning practical rather than intellectual skills. Second, training suggests experiential learning or hands-on learning-by-doing. Third, training entails participatory learning—the learner is an active participant in setting and achieving goals. Throughout this book, to emphasize the importance of participatory learning, members of training groups are called *participants*.

Despite the wide variety of group approaches, there are basically two main styles of leading groups. Each style consists of a cluster of leadership skills. Stating the two extreme positions, the leader can be either didactic or facilitative. Let us look in turn at each of these extreme leadership styles.

The adjective *didactic* means instructing or having the manner of a teacher. Didactic group leaders are highly task-oriented. Achieving the teaching or training goals of the group comes first, with the fostering of group interaction and relationships coming in a poor second. Didactic leaders are the experts who know best how to impart knowledge and skills. They take the jug-and-mug approach to group work— that is, they keep control of what is poured into participants, how, and when. Didactic group leaders develop or decide upon the content of their programs in advance and do not allow participants to share in decisions on goals and methods. What experiential component they allow in their groups involves coaching, rehearsal, and feedback, with little time for discussion. At all times, teacher knows best.

The adjective *facilitative* means making easy or easier, assisting, or helping. Facilitative group leaders are more concerned with the quality of relationships in the group and with helping participants explore and experience their feelings than with any systematic training in specific skills. Much time is spent working to improve the here-and-now relationships in the group and on trying to release the group's healing potential. The facilitative leader shares responsibility with the participants for how the group develops. Though the leader may give feedback, this is more in response to material generated in the group than any systematic attempt to impart skills. Participants are free to accept or reject the leader's comments. A major agenda of the facilitative leader is helping participants drop their social masks and thus engage in genuine encounters both with themselves and with each other.

Plotting the way a leader works on a simple two-dimensional continuum like the following is an unsatisfactory way to look at group leadership style.

Didactic ------------------------------ Facilitative

Most training-group leaders use both didactic and facilitative skills. In any group a tension almost invariably exists between how much the leader emphasizes one cluster of skills as opposed to the other. Training-group leaders may alter the balance in response to either the particular needs of different clienteles or the particular needs of a group at any given moment. Skilled training-group leaders possess both good didactic skills and good facilitative skills that they use flexibly to attain group goals. Figure 1-1 provides a four-dimensional framework for looking at training-group leadership style.

| High facilitative skills | Low facilitative skills |
| High didactic skills | High didactic skills |

| High facilitative skills | Low facilitative skills |
| Low didactic skills | Low didactic skills |

Figure 1-1 A four-dimensional framework for viewing training-group leadership style

The probability is that training-group leaders possessing and using both high didactic and high facilitative training skills are generally more effective. Nevertheless, leaders exhibiting one of the two crossover styles, high facilitative–low didactic and low facilitative–high didactic, may also do good work. For instance, leaders may have much scope for using didactic skills and little scope for using facilitative skills in large lifeskills training groups that, by force of numbers, are heavily focused on imparting information. On the other hand, leaders exhibiting high facilitative and low didactic training skills may be good at helping participants to learn from one another, if less good at helping participants learn from them. Leaders combining low didactic with low facilitative training skills are almost certain to be ineffective.

This book heavily emphasizes the notion of *training-group leaders as choosers*. Leaders must try to make the choices that best meet their goals and those of the group's participants. To do this adequately, leaders require a repertoire of skills.

Some Criticisms and Reservations
▼▼▼

Lifeskills training groups are not magic. They are open to criticism from both professionals and participants. Much of this criticism relates to inadequate leader behavior rather than to training groups as such. In this section some criticisms that might be made of lifeskills training groups are responded to.

Effectiveness

Criticism: Training groups vary in their effectiveness.

Response: Many considerations determine how effective a training group is: leader skills, the state of readiness and degree of motivation of participants, the time available, and so on. Systematically run training groups, based on theory and research, are still a relatively recent development. Furthermore, there has been a dearth of skilled leaders. One reason for this is that helping services training programs, when they teach group work, are more inclined to focus on leading counseling groups than on leading training groups. Unfortunately, some leaders have made exaggerated claims for lifeskills groups. This may partly reflect ethical shortcomings—for instance, wanting to "make a quick buck." Also, some leaders inadequately acknowledge that lifeskills training is not just a matter of participants learning new skills strengths, but also of unlearning old, and sometimes rigidly held, skills weaknesses.

Leading a training group is difficult, not easy. Lifeskills training requires more work on its theoretical underpinnings: for instance, psychology is weaker on theories of optimum as contrasted with abnormal functioning (Maslow, 1962, 1970). Further development and research validation of training skills is also desirable. Particular attention should be paid to considerations related to assisting the transfer and maintenance of lifeskills to real-life settings. Furthermore, potential training-group leaders require systematic training by skilled trainers rather than being left to "fly by the seat of their pants."

Trainability

Criticism: People vary in their suitability for participating in training groups.

Response: This is correct. Joining a lifeskills training group is not a universal panacea. Some people, particularly those who have been unfortunate enough to have received a severe lack of nurturing when growing up, may be better off in individual counseling. Either concurrently or later they may join a training group. Others may resist joining training groups or not commit themselves to them if they do join. Some people are threatened by any group approach to helping. Others may find the concept of lifeskills hard to grasp. They may consider that lifeskills are inherent rather than learned. Also, some may find it difficult to admit that they require lifeskills training. It means acknowledging that they have room for improvement.

Another problem, common to much of education, is that lifeskills training groups may insufficiently take into account individuals' needs and states of readiness. A further problem where training groups are prescribed—for instance, as part of a school curriculum—is that not everyone wants to be there. For instance, some boys may think it "sissy" to be trained in relationship skills and may disrupt the class in ways that interfere with the learning of interested peers (Nelson-Jones, 1986). In short, the issue of trainability is a complex one. The improvement of both training-group content and leaders' skills may make it less of a problem in the future.

Depersonalization and Superficiality

Criticism: People are more than skills and just focusing on their lifeskills is superficial.

Response: Arbuckle (1976) observes that the history of trying to teach a person to be a more effective human being is about as dismal as the history of traditional psychoanalysis to cure a person of sickness. He adds that he has known many ineffective people who have possessed many of the mechanical skills of being an effective person. On the other hand, there are innumerable people who fail to actualize their human potential because they mechanically repeat learned patterns of ineffective behavior. Poorly designed and led training groups can be superficial and can depersonalize. However, well-designed and well-led training groups are advocated here. As much as possible, these groups should be based on good theory, take into account their participants' states of readiness and stages of psychological development, and focus on feelings as well as on thinking and acting. Poorly functioning people, possibly unawares, can depersonalize both themselves and others by being highly manipulative. Well-designed training groups can help give them skills to meet their needs without resorting to mechanical and superficial manipulation.

Conformity

Criticism: Training groups insufficiently prize participants' individuality.

Response: There can be a danger in moving away from a counseling model, with its emphasis on uncovering and bringing out people's existing potentials, to a training model, with an emphasis on skills education. This danger can be represented by words like *brainwashing* and *conformity*. There is the risk that instead of encouraging personal responsibility and autonomy, training-group leaders will tell people how they should be. Consequently, participants may replace one set of externally based *must*'s, *ought*'s, and *should*'s with another. This may pose a special risk in areas where there can be a deep sense of injustice—for instance, in some women's and homosexual groups. An answer to this is better selection and training of leaders. Because sometimes training groups are poorly conducted is not a reason for abandoning them altogether. Effective training groups can provide people with the skills both of getting more deeply in touch with what they think and feel and of expressing this assertively. Fostering such skills is the opposite of encouraging conformity.

Your Group-Leader-as-Trainer Skills: Initial Assessment
▼ ▼

This chapter ends with an opportunity for you to do an initial assessment of your skills strengths and weaknesses as a lifeskills training-group leader. You will be asked to reassess yourself with the same questionnaire at the book's end. The initial presentation of this questionnaire is meant to get you thinking in a self-referent way about the central skills of a training-group leader.

Exercise 2 Assess Your Skills Strengths and Weaknesses as a Training-Group Leader
▼ ▼

Using the following format, make a worksheet for assessing your skills strengths and weaknesses for leading lifeskills training groups. Answer as best you can at this time.

Skills Area	My Strengths	My Weaknesses
Preparing training groups		
Designing lifeskills programs		
Assessing and helping self-assessment		
Facilitating training groups		
Speaking in public		
Demonstrating lifeskills		
Designing and implementing structured activities		
Preparing and managing individual training sessions		
Consolidating self-help skills and ending training groups		
Evaluating and researching training groups		

Make a list of your main skills strengths and weaknesses. The intention of this book is to help you shift the balance more in the direction of skills strengths. You may wish to refer back to your initial assessment when at the book's end you reassess your group-leader-as-trainer skills.

▼ Chapter Highlights

▼ Terms like *psychological education, human resource development, lifeskills teaching,* and *personal and social education* have been used to describe lifeskills training.

▼ The scope of training groups is vast. Settings for training groups include elementary and high schools, colleges and universities, medical settings, business and industry, and marriage and family agencies, among many others.

▼ Training groups are time-limited, structured groups in which one or more leaders use a repertoire of didactic and facilitative skills to help participants develop and maintain one or more specific lifeskills. Important features of training groups include: no assumption of psychological disturbance, systematic instruction, experiential learning-by-doing, and a high degree of participant involvement.

▼ Lifeskills are personally responsible sequences of choices in specific psychological skills areas conducive to mental wellness. People require a repertoire of lifeskills according to their developmental tasks and specific problems of living.

▼ Categories of lifeskills include feeling, thinking, relationships, study, work, leisure, and health.

▼ The group-leader-as-trainer requires both didactic and facilitative skills.

▼ Reservations about training groups relate to their effectiveness; the degree to which lifeskills are trainable; whether they are superficial and depersonalize participants; and whether they erode personal responsibility and encourage conformity.

Acquiring and Maintaining Lifeskills: An Overview

If we do not change our direction, we are likely
to end up where we are headed.

Chinese proverb

▲▲

Chapter Questions

How do people learn lifeskills strengths and weaknesses?

How do some become successful in coping with life's tasks, while others
lead stunted and unproductive lives?

What inner and outer factors influence how people acquire lifeskills?

What inner and outer factors influence how people maintain lifeskills?

Introduction

Given that we humans are only weakly programmed by our instincts
(Maslow, 1962, 1970), what are the processes by which we acquire
lifeskills? In this chapter some factors influencing how people acquire lifeskills strengths and weaknesses are suggested. However, it
is insufficient only to discuss how people learn lifeskills in the first
place, because they may either maintain or fail to maintain what they
have learned. There is an important distinction between *acquisition*
and *maintenance*. Consequently, this chapter also discusses how people maintain their lifeskills strengths and weaknesses. More often
than not, as a lifeskills group leader you will work with people who
already have skills weaknesses that they maintain. Thus, lifeskills
training partly helps people unlearn skills weaknesses as well as
learn different and better skills strengths.

This overview does not claim to be a comprehensive presentation of personality and developmental psychology. Nevertheless, focusing attention on how people acquire and maintain lifeskills serves
a number of purposes. First, highlighting the processes by which people acquire and maintain lifeskills before they enter training groups
suggests processes and practices that leaders might either encourage
or avoid in such groups. All leaders operate from theoretical assumptions, whether explicit or implicit. They possess models of how people can be trained. Ideally, their models of how people learn and
maintain skills strengths and weaknesses before training cohere with
their models of how they can use training to help people develop
different and better skills. Second, the discussion in this chapter indicates the integrative theoretical position taken in this book. This position does not restrict itself to cognitive-behavioral theory, but also
draws upon humanistic and existential insights (Nelson-Jones, 1984).
Third, raising awareness about the learning histories that people
bring into training groups can protect leaders against a naive Polly-
annaism. People who enter lifeskills groups at 10, 30, and 50 years of
age have had, respectively, 10, 30, and 50 years of prior living. In
varying degrees they will have built up a pattern of skills strengths

and weaknesses. Leaders need to work from "where people are at." Participants' starting points can include considerable lack of awareness, faulty prior learning, and resistance to change.

Some Factors in Acquiring Lifeskills
▼▼▼

A number of factors influence whether people acquire lifeskills strengths or weaknesses. These factors include supportive relationships, role models, rewarding consequences, instruction and self-instruction, information, opportunity, challenge and confrontation, peer group interaction, thinking skills, anxiety management skills, sex-role considerations, culture, and social class. We'll briefly examine each of these factors.

Supportive Relationships

People are active explorers of their environments, not just passive receptacles. Bowlby (1979) writes of the concept of a secure base or attachment figure. He observes that there is accumulating evidence that humans of all ages are happiest and able to function most effectively when they feel that a trusted person will come to their aid should difficulties arise. Rogers also stresses the importance of supportive relationships for releasing people's "actualizing tendency" (Raskin & Rogers, 1989; Rogers, 1959, 1980) or inherent capacity to maintain, enhance, and develop themselves. In particular, Rogers has focused on supporting others through empathy. Empathy entails not only sensitively and accurately understanding the inner worlds of others, but also communicating your understanding back to them so that they feel understood. Empathy helps others listen better to themselves and get more in touch with their wants and wishes, and it may enable them to become freer to manifest lifeskills previously latent in their repertoire.

The role of supportive relationships in the life of the growing child goes far beyond enabling the acquisition of specific lifeskills. The presence or absence of supportive relationships can either affirm or disconfirm people's core of personhood. Children may either feel themselves of value and possess the confidence to interact with the world or they may become inhibited, withdrawn, and afraid to take risks. This lack of self-esteem may block them from both learning and using lifeskills.

Role Models

Bandura has been a prominent psychologist drawing attention to the power of learning from observing others' behavior (Bandura, 1969,

1977, 1986). Skills weaknesses as well as strengths are frequently learned this way. Learning from observing others is pervasive and is potentially insidious because much of it is unconscious. You learn and yet remain unaware that you have learned. Here are some instances of learning from others' examples:

▼ Meryl, 23, grew up in a home where many significant feelings were neither acknowledged nor openly expressed. Now she has a boy-friend, Todd, who says he would prefer it if she would let him know when she is angry rather than bottle it up.

▼ Melanie, 15, observes her parents arguing a lot. Each parent is quick to blame the other. When someone criticizes Melanie, how-ever gently, she bristles and gets defensively aggressive.

▼ Emilio, 43, had a dad who was a workaholic and who died of a heart attack in his mid-50s. Recently, Emilio, who has similar work patterns to his dad, has been having chest pains. Emilio wonders if he should ease up before it's too late.

▼ Nita, 36, worked for a supervisor, Maggie, who was good both at making her supervisees feel understood by her and also getting good work out of them. Nita thinks that by observing Maggie she has picked up some effective supervision skills—for instance, ac-tive listening and giving clear instructions.

Skills strengths and weaknesses in the areas of feeling, thinking, and action can be learned from observing role models. For instance, Meryl was helped to acquire the skills weakness of having trouble acknowledging her feelings from the absence of demonstration in her family. Her parents' examples also helped her to acquire the thinking skills weaknesses of thinking that she would never gain ap-proval if she were to be more open. Furthermore, by not expressing some of her feelings, she acts in a closed way that mirrors her par-ents' behavior.

Rewarding Consequences

Learning lifeskills from observing role models is often intermingled with learning from rewarding or unrewarding consequences. For in-stance, in the preceding example, Meryl's family, in addition to not disclosing their own feelings, may have sent unrewarding verbal and/or nonverbal messages that discouraged her from talking about her feelings to them. One of the factors affecting the influence of models is whether their behaviors bring about consequences per-ceived by observers as rewarding (Bandura, 1977).

Rewarding consequences can be either primary or secondary. Primary rewarding consequences are those that people find reward-ing independent of their learning history—for instance, food, shel-ter, sex, and human warmth. Skinner (1971) considers that all rewards eventually derive their power from evolutionary selection and that it is part of human nature to be rewarded by particular things. However, he considers that only a small part of behavior is immediately reinforced by rewards of evident biological significance. Most behavior is emitted in response to secondary rewards—for example, approval or money—that have become associated with or conditioned to primary rewards.

The role of rewarding consequences in helping or hindering people in acquiring lifeskills is immense. Virtually from the moment of birth, humans are given messages about how "good" or "bad" their actions are. Usually, with the best of intentions, adults try to reward children for developing the skills necessary to cope with the world. However, often the rewards they provide are deficient in various ways. For example, most people learn their relationship and thinking skills from a mixture of observing others, unsystematic feedback, and trial-and-error. Rarely, either inside or outside the home, are people systematically rewarded as they develop these lifeskills. Furthermore, sometimes children are rewarded for exhibiting skills weaknesses rather than strengths. For example, they may find that they are more likely to get their way if they shout aggressively rather than take a more reasonable approach.

Another major problem in the use of external rewards is that people may continually look outside for a locus of evaluation rather than think through and get in touch with what they themselves think and feel (Raskin & Rogers, 1989; Rogers, 1959). Consequently, they may lack a secure sense of their own identity. An associated complication is that those receiving positive or negative rewarding consequences from others may sometimes fail to make the distinction between their specific behaviors' being good or bad and their whole personhood's being good or bad. Failure to make this distinction can undermine their self-esteem in at least two ways. On the one hand, because someone else thinks they have behaved badly, they may wrongly perceive themselves as bad. On the other hand, because someone else thinks their behavior is good, they may become dependent on that person's approval to maintain their fragile self-esteem. However, despite these pitfalls, provision of rewarding consequences by others is central to how people learn to provide rewarding consequences for themselves.

Instruction

Much instruction in lifeskills is informal and takes place in the home. Some of this is very basic—for instance, asking children to say "please" and "thank you." Children are often told by their parents and others how to relate, how to study, how to look after their health, and so on. There are three important issues here. First, do the people doing the informal instruction have an adequate conceptual framework and understanding of the skills that they are attempting to pass on? It is possible to misinstruct as well as to instruct. For instance, children may be misinstructed both to be prejudiced against people who differ from them on various characteristics and to deal with all perceived provocations on the basis of "an eye for an eye, a tooth for a tooth." Second, do the instructors have an adequate model of instruction? Children are notorious for not listening to their parents. Attempts to impart lifeskills may falter either because children feel talked down to or they do not see the relevance of the instruction. Third, to what extent are children then able to instruct themselves in the lifeskills that others have attempted to impart? Arguably, if learners do not know how to talk themselves through the sequences of choices involved in the skills, many lifeskills have been inadequately learned. Much instruction falls far short of this self-instructional objective.

In Chapter 1 mention was made of some systematic attempts in schools and colleges to train people in lifeskills. To date, these kinds of lifeskills groups are probably the exception rather than the rule. Inside and outside education there is still a widespread assumption that the main role of educational institutions is academic rather than practical. Allied to this is the assumption that the home is the main arena for acquiring lifeskills. Some parents may see attempts to teach lifeskills in the schools as usurping their roles. Furthermore, conflicts can arise between lifeskills taught in schools and colleges and those espoused in the home. For instance, argumentative parents may not like being told by their children that in school they are being taught the best way to handle conflicts is by assuming a cooperative rather than a competitive attitude. Doubts about the effectiveness of lifeskills training and about the skills, qualifications, and experience of leaders also work against the adoption of lifeskills groups in schools and colleges.

A further problem in lifeskills instruction is that the idea of skills in certain areas is alien to many. For instance, it is common for people to talk about work skills, study skills, or even health maintenance skills. However, it is much less common for them to talk about feeling, thinking, and relationship skills. Difficulties in instructing people in lifeskills are created when they fail to acknowledge that the concept of skills is applicable and provides them with tools to use in many important areas of their lives.

Self-Instruction

Self-instruction is another important way in which people acquire lifeskills. Self-instruction can help people consolidate lifeskills in which they may have received either formal or informal instruction. For instance, people who have received instruction in interview skills can then rehearse and practice them by instructing themselves as they visualize using the skills in an imaginary interview. Another way in which self-instruction helps consolidate skills entails drawing conclusions from their application. As a result of learning from practice, people can instruct themselves to apply the skills in better ways to particular situations they confront.

Many people try to improve their lifeskills through reading self-instructional books. Popular examples of such books include Norman Vincent Peale's *The Power of Positive Thinking* (1953), Wayne Dyer's *Your Erroneous Zones* (1976), and Alberti and Emmons's *Your Perfect Right: A Guide to Assertive Living* (1986). These self-instructional books can help people acquire a richer conceptual framework for understanding the skills they need for their lives. However, sometimes the understanding of lifeskills acquired from books falls far short of that required to apply the skills. Also, self-instructional books may insufficiently motivate people to use and practice the skills.

Information

People need adequate information if they are to develop lifeskills. For instance, keeping them in ignorance about basic facts of death and sexuality impedes their self-awareness and capacity for emotional responsiveness. Human beings often relate to their children on the basis of lies, omissions of truth, and partial truths (Steiner, 1974). Adults may protect themselves in the eyes of their children in ways that blunt their children's awareness of the world. Also, children are heavily dependent on the amount and accuracy of information available from significant adults. For example, an adult who does not understand the concept of anxiety may mislabel a child's social anxiety as "wimpishness" or "being difficult," thus blocking the child's self-understanding and harming his or her self-esteem.

Opportunity

Children, adolescents, and adults alike need adequate opportunities in line with their maturation to test out and develop their lifeskills. However, many people's chances of exploring themselves and developing a sense of their own competencies in areas such as relationships, study, work, or leisure are restricted, as in the following examples.

▾ Kasra, 17, is very worried about his dating skills. He has had little experience with girls because he has three younger brothers and no sisters and because his parents sent him to a single-sex boarding school out in the countryside.
▾ Marquita, 25, thinks that she lacks public speaking skills. She has just been appointed as a lecturer at a community college after completing graduate school. She has never taken a class in public

speaking and admits to having been very nervous on the few occasions when she was asked to give seminar papers as a student.

▼ Art, 39, would like to develop his leisure skills by taking up golf. However, there are no public courses where he lives and the private golf clubs in his area are far beyond his budget.

▼ Carlos, 16, would like to acquire gourmet cooking skills. However, there are no cooking classes available in his high school.

▼ Kerryn, 17, never received help for her test anxiety in high school because no one knew how to help her. She hopes that in college she can learn better skills for coping with her debilitating test anxiety.

Challenge and Confrontation

People are challenged by life to develop skills. Challenge is implicit in any learning. Learning entails risking giving up the safety of the known to acquire better skills. Transition points in people's lives, such as moving to a new area, school, or job, or having one's first child, frequently act as a stimulus for skills development. However, sometimes these challenges are met in ways that reactivate previous skills weaknesses, like social withdrawal, rather than in positive ways. Adversity and pain can also help people acquire lifeskills. Though adversity can erode some people's confidence, others rise above it. The breakup of a relationship, unexpected loss of a job, or coming to terms with an illness or injury can each be opportunities for personal growth. Frankl (1959) writes of how, even in Nazi concentration camps, some people were able to use their suffering as an opportunity for personal growth.

People exist in the world of their perceptions (Beck & Weishaar, 1989; Combs, Richards, & Richards, 1976; Ellis, 1962, 1980, 1989). These perceptions are of varying degrees of accuracy. For instance, parents may assume that all is well in the family yet suddenly be confronted with the acute distress of one of their children—for instance, by a suicide gesture. One response to such a confrontation is to externalize it, by perceiving that the child is the problem. Another response is to use the confrontation as an opportunity to explore their behavior toward the child. Where this degree of openness exists, confrontations can not only enlarge people's perceptions, but also provide them with the opportunity to develop their lifeskills. There are many instances in most people's lives of being confronted with negative or positive feedback that, for good or ill, they can use to develop their skills.

Peer Group Interaction

Peer groups provide one of the main avenues for learning lifeskills strengths and weaknesses. Peer groups can provide supportive relationships, role models, rewarding consequences, instruction, information, opportunity, challenge, and confrontation. Following are some examples of people acquiring lifeskills through social interaction in a peer group.

▼ Sally and Greg are parents of two preschool-age children. They mix a lot with parents of other preschoolers and find it mutually helpful to exchange information on how best to deal with their children.

▼ Thuc has just been appointed a bank manager. He has made friends with a number of other bank managers so that they can learn from each other's experience.

▼ Ayana was blinded in an industrial accident six months ago. She meets weekly with a self-help group of other recently blinded people both for emotional support and to exchange coping strategies.

▼ Michele is part of a group of medical school students who discuss how best to survive the onslaught of an extremely heavy workload.

▼ Felicia's husband died recently. Felicia belongs to a support network whose other members have also had to cope with the death of a loved one. Felicia has learned from her friends many skills for both coming to terms with grief and surviving on her own.

Learning from peer group interaction can be for good or ill. Every peer group has its rules or norms of varying degrees of explicitness concerning appropriate behavior on the part of its members. In each of the preceding examples, the peer groups probably taught more skills strengths than weaknesses. However, other peer groups may have norms—for instance, hatred of people who are racially different or heavy participation in substance abuse—that are lifeskills weaknesses. Also, there is the danger that participants in any peer group, whether its norms are constructive or destructive, will allow the other members to do their thinking for them. Insufficient autonomous thought is a major lifeskills weakness.

Thinking Skills

Thinking skills are important lifeskills to be acquired both in their own right and because they contribute to learning and using other lifeskills (Beck & Weishaar, 1989; Ellis, 1989; Nelson-Jones, 1990a). Mention has already been made that people who do not realize that skills are involved in various areas of their lives—for instance, in their relationships—are less likely to have tools for developing competencies than those who acknowledge that specific skills are desirable. Also, the idea that skills are sequences of choices can help people to work on developing them. They can identify the choices involved in the skills and then choose whether or not to make them.

The idea that you are personally responsible for developing and using the lifeskills conducive to your survival, happiness, and fulfillment is a thinking skill as well as an overriding lifeskill (May & Yalom, 1989; Nelson-Jones, 1984). The extent to which people acquire this habit of assuming responsibility for their lives influences how motivated they may be to acquire and develop lifeskills. Assuming personal responsibility goes deeper than verbal acknowledgment of it. Your feeling, thinking, and action choices need to be clearly based on this assumption, too. You have to not only "talk the talk," but also "walk the walk." Following are examples of people either assuming or avoiding personal responsibility for acquiring and developing their lifeskills.

▼ Ari has an unhappy relationship with his 12-year-old son David. Ari locates the problems in David and thinks "David has to learn to grow up before we can be happy together." Ari's inability to assume responsibility for acquiring better parenting skills helps keep both David and him stuck in their repetitive cycles of negative behavior.

▼ Celia is manager of a shop selling office equipment. A year ago she became aware that many of the thirty employees who worked in the shop were unhappy in their work. Celia had a series of conversations with her staff to find out the reasons for their dissatisfaction. Feedback about her behavior included that some staff found her brusque and that she rarely expressed appreciation to anyone. Celia accepted these criticisms and worked on avoiding put-downs and expressing appreciation. Once Celia acquired better managerial skills, both morale and sales in the shop noticeably improved.

The capacity to be realistic about the role of mistakes and setbacks during the process of acquiring a lifeskill is another important thinking skill. The assumption that acquiring a lifeskill involves continuous improvement is erroneous, causing people to become discouraged when inevitable mistakes and setbacks occur. Sometimes when initially acquiring a skill, learners may appear to get worse before getting better. For example, shy adolescents starting dating may be highly conscious of their inadequacies. If they tell themselves, "Mistakes and setbacks are terrible and I will never be any good," they may give up. However, if they tell themselves, "Mistakes and setbacks are uncomfortable, but I'm learning all the time and starting to do better," they are more likely to help themselves through the sometimes awkward period of trying out new behaviors. Usually, the process of acquiring lifeskills is best represented by a jagged rather than a smooth learning curve.

Another important thinking skill relevant to acquiring lifeskills is the ability to perceive your behavior accurately. In the earlier examples of Ari and Celia, Celia was able to perceive her behavior accurately and, hence, to initiate learning, whereas Ari was able to do neither. Perceiving your behavior accurately is also important during learning. You can erode your confidence if you selectively focus on your weaknesses and difficulties at the expense of acknowledging your strengths and successes. On the other hand, you can erroneously think that you are making better progress than the facts justify.

Anxiety

Thinking skills are also highly relevant to managing unhelpful as contrasted with helpful anxiety. In his book *The Inner Game of Tennis* (1974), W. Timothy Gallwey observes that every game is composed of two parts: the outer game of playing your opponent and the inner game that takes place in the mind of each player. This inner game "is played against such obstacles as lapses in concentration, nervousness, self-doubt, and self-condemnation. In short, it is played to overcome all habits of mind which inhibit excellence in performance" (p. 11). Similarly, acquiring and maintaining lifeskills involves an inner game to deal with thinking skills weaknesses that threaten to interfere with learning and performance. Gallwey focuses on teaching people the art of "relaxed concentration." Learning any lifeskill is best achieved when the mind is alert yet relaxed enough to devote all its energies to the task at hand.

Children grow up having both helpful and harmful experiences with respect to their self-esteem. The fortunate ones acquire a level of anxiety that acts both as a protection against actual dangers and also as a motivator to realistic levels of achievement. Unfortunately, adults, through their role modeling and the faulty consequences provided for children's behaviors, often pass on and contribute to significant, debilitating anxieties. These anxieties can be both cause and effect of children's—and later adults'—thinking skills weaknesses. These weaknesses include reluctance to assume responsibility for their lives, difficulty facing reality, low tolerance for mistakes and setbacks, and inability to evaluate performance accurately. Other ways in which anxiety can interfere with skills acquisition and performance are in causing you to not hear instructions clearly, insufficient awareness of significant information from practical learning situations, difficulty concentrating, thought blocking, feeling confused, and mentally and emotionally freezing. Since people's inner mental game is disrupted by anxiety, their outer game of observable behavior tends to suffer correspondingly. Deficient behaviors resulting from as well as manifesting anxiety include unwillingness to take realistic risks, tense and nervous rather than relaxed skills performance, a heightened tendency to say and do the wrong things, unnecessary aggression, excessive seeking of approval, and a combination of overstriving and underachieving.

Learning lifeskills entails learning not to let anxiety get in the way of acquiring and using the skills. People who either are helped to or who help themselves to acquire anxiety management skills may learn other skills more easily than people without anxiety management skills. Some anxiety management skills—for instance, tensing and relaxing one's muscles or breathing slowly and regularly—help people to manage the physiological arousal associated with anxiety. Many anxiety management skills entail learning to think more effectively.

These thinking skills include choosing personal rules for one's own and for others' behavior that are realistic rather than perfectionistic (Ellis, 1980, 1989); using coping rather than anxiety-engendering self-talk (Meichenbaum, 1983; Meichenbaum & Deffenbacher, 1988); not jumping to unwarranted perceptual conclusions (Beck & Emery, 1985; Beck & Weishaar, 1989; Emery, 1982); and using good visualizing skills (Lazarus, 1977; Nelson-Jones, 1990a).

Acquiring and using good lifeskills builds confidence and lowers anxiety, which in turn may help future lifeskills learning. Conversely, being highly anxious may impede the learning of some lifeskills and lead to poor performance in them. This poor performance may further raise anxiety and make future lifeskills learning even more difficult.

Sex-Role Considerations

This is a period in which traditional sex roles are being challenged and changed. Nevertheless, often males and females are still brought up with different emphases in their lifeskills. In Western societies, certain psychological characteristics have traditionally been viewed as either feminine or masculine. Feminine characteristics have included being affectionate, gentle, sensitive to the needs of others, tender, and warm. Masculine characteristics have included being aggressive, ambitious, assertive, analytical, and dominant (Bem, 1974). The predominant traditional roles of women have been those of nurturers and social harmonizers. Men's traditional roles have focused on being breadwinners and disciplinarians.

Because of differing views about their psychological characteristics and sex roles, males and females have been encouraged to develop different lifeskills strengths and weaknesses. In regard to relationship skills, Argyle (1984) states that the research evidence suggests that there are a number of areas where females may be more socially competent than males. These areas include being better at sending and receiving body language, being more rewarding and polite, and disclosing more and forming closer friendships. On the other hand, Argyle notes that assertiveness is an area in which women appear to have more problems than men. Other areas where males and females may have been brought up with different lifeskills include the following:

Sexual relationships: The male has traditionally been expected to be more of the initiator and to be more open about acknowledging and expressing sexuality than the female (Alberti & Emmons, 1986; Masters & Johnson, 1975).

Parenting: Child care has been mainly the responsibility of the female and hence it has been less important for the male to learn parenting skills.

Home maintenance: Females traditionally have developed more skills to look after the inside of the house, whereas males have developed more skills to look after the outside of the house, including the garden and the car. Purchasing and preparation of food has been mainly a female responsibility.

Education: Where funds were limited in a family, it was sometimes considered more important to educate males than females since homemaking was traditionally a female's main role. Male educational achievement was sometimes more valued than that of females.

Work: The idea of having a career traditionally has applied more to males than females. Certain traditionally feminine occupations— nursing, teaching, secretarial work—have been thought to reflect women's nurturing nature, while entrepreneurship and senior management have been thought to require "masculine" skills.

Leisure: Female leisure interests traditionally have centered more around the home and family than those of the male with his pubs and clubs. In some respects, the female was once the social secretary to the male, doing much of his private and business entertaining.

Currently there are huge changes under way in how sex roles are defined, negotiated, and end up in practice. There has been an increase in talk about psychological androgyny. The androgynous male or female "is flexibly masculine or feminine as circumstances warrant" (Bem, 1981, p. 362). Thus, males and females can be brought up with a range of lifeskills, including both those traditionally regarded as masculine and those traditionally regarded as feminine.

There also have been considerable changes in how people, perhaps especially females, behave in practice. For instance, between 1948 and 1985, women's share of the U.S. labor force grew from 29 to 45 percent and their participation rate from 33 to 55 percent (Bloom, 1986). In 1985, 42 percent of U.S. families had two wage earners, with an additional 14 percent having three or more wage earners (Russell & Exter, 1986). Additionally, the role of women in the work force is changing, and hence their need for different work and life skills. In the United States, the proportion of female managers rose from 27 percent in 1972 to 36 percent in 1986. Additionally, more women are becoming entrepreneurs. In 1960 women started one in ten new American businesses; in 1985, one in five; by 1995, it is projected to be one in two (Bloom, 1986).

Perhaps enough has been said to indicate that in the past people's acquisition of lifeskills has been heavily influenced by their biological sex. Though sex roles are changing, there are still numerous areas in which, subtly or not, males and females learn lifeskills differently.

Culture

Lifeskills learning is heavily influenced by the culture in which it takes place. Culture refers to the predominant patterns of behavior and rules for living of a given group during a given period. Here are a few examples. Argyle (1986) conducted a study of the rules for social relationships in Britain, Italy, Hong Kong, and Japan. He found that in the Eastern cultures, especially in Japan, there were more rules about obedience, avoiding loss of face, maintaining harmonious relationships in groups, and restraining emotional expression. Gaze, or looking at other people in the area of their faces, is perceived differently according to culture. In the "contact" cultures of the Arab world, Latin America, and southern Europe, the amount of gaze is high. Too little gaze is seen as impolite and insincere. However, in "noncontact" cultures like those of North America, northern Europe, and Asia, too much gaze is seen as threatening. Gestures have different meanings in different cultures, so misunderstanding body language can lead to embarrassing cross-cultural misunderstandings. In Greece, people toss their heads back to say no. The "A-OK" sign in North America of thumb and forefinger in a circle means in France and Belgium "You're worth nothing," and in southern Italy either means "You asshole" or signifies that you desire anal sex (Ekman, Friesen, & Bear, 1984). Level of self-disclosure may also differ according to culture. For example, British female undergraduate students have been found to disclose less than their American counterparts (Jourard, 1971). Language is an obvious manifestation of culture. For instance, though bilingualism is increasing in Canada, French Canadians have French as their primary language and English Canadians have English.

The United States and Canada are huge cultural melting pots. The 1980 U.S. census found that 83 percent of Americans identified with at least one ancestral group, the four largest being English, German, Irish, and African. Nearly seven million Americans claimed some American Indian ancestry, though only one million identified themselves as Indian on the census race question. Hispanic and Asian are increasingly prominent ancestral groups. In the 1980 census, 31 percent of Americans identified with two or more ancestral groups (Robey & Russell, 1984).

The 1981 Canadian census showed that almost 16 percent of Canadians were born outside Canada, whereas the corresponding figure in the United States was 6 percent. Among those reporting a single ethnic background, British was the largest group, comprising over 40 percent of the total population, followed by French, 27 percent; German, 5 percent; Italian, 3 percent; and Ukranian, 2 percent. Over 80 percent of the population of Quebec identified French as their single ethnic heritage. Only 8 percent of Canadians identified with more than one ethnic group (Pryor & Norris, 1983).

Cultural and racial diversity increases in the United States. The 1990 U.S. Census showed a population gain of nearly 100 percent for Asians and Pacific Islanders, whose numbers grew from about 3.5 million in 1980 to 7.3 million in 1990. In the same period, the number of Hispanics increased from 14.6 million to 22.4 million, while blacks increased from 26.5 million to just under 30 million. Those identifying themselves as American Indians grew to nearly 2 million. The white population increased by more than 11 million to 199.7 million, but the white share of the total U.S. population dropped from 83 percent in 1980 to about 80 percent in 1990. More than a third of America's population growth over the decade—from 227 million to 248 million—came from migration (Vobiejda, 1991).

These statistics indicate that for the United States, within an over-riding American culture there are numerous cultural variations and interminglings. In Canada, there are two main subcultures, the English-Canadian and the French-Canadian, within an overall Canadian culture. However, there are many other ethnic groupings, including a large number of recent Asian migrants. Additionally, Canadian culture is subject to media bombardment from its more populous southern neighbor. In short, the lifeskills of individual Americans and Canadians are likely to be influenced both by their national cultures and by one or more ancestral cultures.

Social Class

Lifeskills learning is also heavily influenced by social class considerations. Income, educational attainment, and occupational status are three of the main ways in which social class is measured in North America. Other indications of social class include where you live, what school you went to, and how you speak. Poverty, overcrowding, disease, lack of educational opportunity, and lack of support for educational aspirations work against people's breaking out of lower-class constraints. The lifeskills needed in urban ghettos are more those of physical and emotional survival than of so-called civilized living. These ghetto-dweller skills are very different from those required for being a "preppie." Also, the skills required by blue-collar workers in relating to their colleagues are different from those required by white collar workers. Communication tends to be more blunt and direct among blue-collar workers.

All people are shaped by their learning histories. They bring their learning histories into training groups. Though we have considered fourteen factors that influence how people acquire lifeskills, this listing is far from exhaustive.

Some Factors Maintaining Lifeskills
▼▼

There is an old story about a person asking for a pay raise on the basis of nineteen years' experience and being told, "You have had one year's experience, which you have repeated eighteen times." Once acquired, lifeskills strengths can be maintained and developed. Alternatively, these strengths can degenerate into weaknesses. Lifeskills weaknesses, once acquired, can also be maintained, sometimes at great personal cost. Paradoxically, people frequently choose to repeat behaviors that are unrewarding for themselves and others.

The challenge to maintain lifeskills strengths will be addressed at many points in this book. This section focuses on how people maintain lifeskills weaknesses. Especially for children, acquiring lifeskills strengths and weaknesses is more a matter of what the environment does to them than what they do to themselves. Young people are frequently at the mercy of their elders. However, maintaining lifeskills strengths and weaknesses into adulthood is a different matter from acquiring them initially. The balance of attribution of cause shifts more in the direction of what people do to themselves than what the environment does to them. The buck stops much more with the individual.

What People Do to Themselves

We will now consider some of the processes by which people maintain their lifeskills weaknesses. These processes center around thinking skills weaknesses.

Attributional Deficiencies

How people assign cause greatly influences the degree to which they maintain lifeskills weaknesses. Earlier, mention was made that assuming responsibility for developing and using lifeskills was an overriding lifeskill. Assuming this responsibility consists of at least two areas: first, overall responsibility for making your life (Frankl, 1959; May & Yalom, 1989); and second, responsibility in specific situations.

Attributions of responsibility and cause are explanations that people give themselves to make sense of what happens in their lives. Faulty attributions are those that explain responsibility and cause inaccurately. Following are some potential attribution errors that people may use to sustain lifeskills weaknesses.

"It's my nature": People may block themselves from change by saying that characteristics like laziness or excessive anger are their nature. They fail to realize that such lifeskills weaknesses are learned and then maintained.

"It's my unfortunate past": People may blame their parents and others in their past for the fact that they are not as they would like to be now. These attributions to an inadequate upbringing may or may not be accurate perceptions of how their skills weaknesses were initially acquired. However, for people who have left home, upbringing

is largely irrelevant to how they maintain their skills weaknesses in the present.

"*It's my bad luck*": People often make their luck. For example, a woman who keeps choosing inadequate partners may erroneously attribute her difficulties to bad luck rather than to her failure to develop skills in choosing partners.

"*It's my poor environment*": Undoubtedly, adverse social conditions like poverty, overcrowding, and poor housing make it more difficult to develop certain lifeskills. However, many people have learned to overcome the skills weaknesses contributed to by their poor environments.

"*It's all your fault*": This absolutistic attribution of blame to someone else is possibly the most common reason why people stay stuck with skills weaknesses, particularly in the areas of managing anger and conflict. Why bother to develop your lifeskills when it is always someone else's fault? Responsibility for negative events is conveniently externalized.

"*It's all my fault*": Blaming oneself all the time can also interfere with overcoming lifeskills weaknesses. Quite apart from the fact that cause is inaccurately identified, self-blame may erode the confidence people require to deal with the realistic difficulties in their lives. Guilt can be a constructive emotion if it leads to better lifeskills. However, guilt also can be destructive if it brings about self-disparagement rather than self-improvement. Overinternalizing responsibility for negative events is a characteristic of very depressed people (Weishaar & Beck, 1986).

Unrealistic Personal Rules

Personal rules are the *do*'s and *don't*s by which people lead their lives. Each person has an inner rulebook of standards for himself or herself and for others. Sometimes these standards are realistic and appropriately flexible. On other occasions the standards may be unrealistic and inappropriately rigid. Ellis has coined the term *mustabation* to refer to rigid internal rules characterized by *must*'s, *ought*'s, and *should*'s (Ellis, 1980, 1989). Following are illustrations of "mustabatory" personal rules in different lifeskills areas. These unrealistic rules are not only lifeskills weaknesses in themselves, but maintain other lifeskills weaknesses. For example, the feeling area rule that "I shouldn't have negative feelings about other people" may interfere with the open and honest communication necessary for intimacy.

Thinking: "I must not think for myself."
Relationships: "I must always be liked by everyone."
Study: "I must always learn without making mistakes."

Work: "I must always feel fulfilled in my work."
Leisure: "Work must come before leisure."
Health: "I must not acknowledge when my body feels stressed."

Faulty Self-Perceptions

People can maintain lifeskills weaknesses if they erroneously think their skills are adequate. Here are some examples:

▼ Boris used to think that he looked after his health adequately until one day he had a heart attack. He then realized that he had adopted an "It can't happen to me" attitude that had allowed him to keep smoking and eating too much.

▼ Aretha thinks that she is a very affectionate person, though others do not find her so.

▼ Whenever her daughter Leanne says that she is unhappy with their relationship, Melinda says that she has done everything she can for her.

▼ Bruce thinks of himself as an adequate public speaker. He does not seem to notice how bored his audience becomes when he speaks.

▼ Ricardo sees himself as a good lover who does not need to develop his skills. Others tell a different tale.

▼ Anita sees herself as an inadequate student, despite getting high grades. She is afraid to go on to graduate school, though her teachers tell her she has the ability to do well there.

In each of the preceding illustrations, people were seeing only what they wanted to see. They were giving way to the Nelson-Jones Reality Principle: "If you cannot accept reality, create it" (Nelson-Jones, 1990a). *Defense mechanisms, defenses,* or *security operations* are terms for the ways that people operate on incoming information that differs from their existing self-pictures (Arlow, 1989; Freud, 1936; Maslow, 1962, 1970; Sullivan, 1953). As in the case of Anita, it is possible to operate on positive feedback to sustain a negative self-picture as well as on negative feedback to sustain a positive self-picture (Rogers, 1959). In either instance, the faulty self-perceptions are likely to contribute to the individual's maintaining lifeskills weaknesses.

Defensive perceptions involve people in diminishing their awareness of life in order to remain more psychologically comfortable in the short term. Following is a list of some defensive processes.

Denial: Totally warding off from conscious awareness feelings, thoughts, and behaviors regarded as too frightening or threatening—for instance, homosexual feelings or clear evidence of your own hypocrisy.

Distortion: Altering feedback that you do not like to make it more acceptable to you—for instance, perceiving that you would have received a higher grade if your teacher had read your paper more thoroughly when all the evidence points to the teacher's being conscientious.

Rationalization: Providing excuses when your behavior causes you anxiety—for instance, making out that the reason that you have never developed adequate parenting skills is that you have always been too busy at work. Rationalizations differ from excuses in that rationalizers do not have full insight into their behavior. In short, they deceive themselves as well as attempt to deceive others.

Avoidance: Avoidance is a common manifestation of denial—for example, by remaining unaware that you avoid developing lifeskills in areas, like confronting people, that you find difficult.

Externalizing responsibility: Blaming other people rather than acknowledging your own responsibility for failing to develop your lifeskills.

Attack: "Attack is the best method of defense." Attacking and intimidating others who either provide or might provide negative feedback about one or more of your lifeskills; going for their jugular vein or disparaging their personality; making up stories about yourself and others that make you seem in the right and them seem in the wrong.

Projection: Externalizing something that is internal—for instance, experiencing difficulty in the lifeskill of controlling your sexuality and setting yourself up as a guardian of public morality. In such instances, people would do better to work on their own lifeskills.

Defenses against the good: Blocking off and diluting both the awareness of and also the manifestation of positive qualities such as generosity and concern for others. Being out of touch with prosocial feelings maintains egocentricity. Possibly humans are just as threatened by acknowledging their altruistic feelings as their less altruistic ones.

Negative self-labeling is another way in which people may sustain lifeskills weaknesses. Instead of perceiving themselves in a balanced fashion, they overemphasize their negative points and underemphasize their positive points. The outcome of negative self-labeling may be twofold. First, people may undermine their overall level of self-esteem. Second, they may erode their confidence and motivation to overcome specific lifeskills weaknesses.

Negative Self-Talk

Negative self-talk can be contrasted with coping self-talk (Meichenbaum, 1977, 1983, 1985, 1986; Meichenbaum & Deffenbacher, 1988). Coping self-talk has two main functions: calming and coaching yourself. A sample calming self-instruction might be: "Keep calm." A sample coaching self-instruction might be: "Break the task down and take one step at a time." Here are some illustrative negative self-talk statements:

"I'm never going to be able to do it."
"If I make a mistake it will be terrible."
"I'm starting to feel anxious and this is a signal that things may get
out of control."
"The future is hopeless."
"I can't stand setbacks."
"I've tried before without success."

These negative self-talk statements can inhibit people working on a
range of lifeskills weaknesses. Negative self-talk can also refer to specific lifeskills weaknesses—for example, "Learning to control my
anger is far too difficult a task."

Fear of Change

Once acquired, lifeskills weaknesses can become well-established
habits, and people can become very resistant to giving them up (Ellis, 1985, 1987; Grieger, 1989). We can identify seven possible components of fear of change First, there is fear of the unknown.
Changing a lifeskills weakness into a strength requires risking new
behaviors. There is no longer the safety and certainty of the old habits. The unknown becomes a negative consequence in its own right,
even though a realistic appraisal would indicate otherwise. Second,
there is fear of making an effort. Changing some lifeskills weaknesses
may be perceived to require the discomfort of effort. It may seem
easier to stay as you are rather than make this effort. Third, there is
fear of losing payoffs. There may be rewards and payoffs to maintaining lifeskills weaknesses. For instance, you may get your way if you
are violent in the home and perceive that you will lose your influence
if you take a more reasonable approach.

Fourth, there is fear of others' disapproval. Giving up lifeskills
weaknesses may bring you into conflict with other people. For instance, others may prefer you to be quiet, docile, and "nice" rather
than assertive. Fifth, there is fear of inner conflict. Overcoming lifeskills weaknesses may create an inner conflict between how you
were and how you are becoming. During the transition you may experience a painful conflict between your previous and emerging self-
pictures. Sixth, there is fear of failure. Failure can be defined in many
ways, both objectively and subjectively. Fear of failure can consist of
two elements: fear of the occurrence of negative consequences and
fear about your ability to cope with negative consequences if they
occur. Seventh, there is fear of success. People who succeed in overcoming lifeskills weaknesses have to face the consequences. For example, they may have to handle the consequences of obtaining a
promotion, being asked out a lot, or getting high grades. They may be
fearful about their ability to cope with their new status.

What the Environment Does to People

Lifeskills weaknesses are usually maintained both by what people do to themselves and by what the environment keeps doing to them. Many of the factors mentioned in the section on how people acquire lifeskills can help them to maintain their lifeskills weaknesses. For example, people may continue to have inadequate supportive relationships; lack good role models; receive inappropriate rewarding consequences from others; lack sound instruction in specific lifeskills; have insufficient or faulty information; lack suitable opportunities to develop their skills; not receive appropriate challenges and confrontations; belong to unhelpful rather than to helpful peer groups; be restricted by sex-role expectations and rules; possess cultural blinders; and undergo socioeconomic and social-class deprivations.

People have varying degrees of choice about how they can cope with and, if possible, overcome these external factors. For example, it may be possible to find good role models, to choose friends who offer more appropriate rewarding consequences, and to create opportunities for learning that might not seem immediately apparent. But sometimes external factors are relatively immutable, perhaps especially for young people living at home. Even so, there may be some lifeskills they can develop to survive living in what may be an emotionally inclement environment.

Concluding Comment
▼▼

Trainers in lifeskills groups cannot change how participants originally acquired their lifeskills weaknesses. To change direction trainers must help participants alter the thinking and action skills weaknesses that presently maintain their ineffective behaviors. Also, at risk of repetition, trainers need to realize that participants entering training groups often have had years of faulty learning and self-instruction.

> **▼ Chapter Highlights**
>
> ▼ All training-group leaders work on theoretical assumptions of varying degrees of explicitness.
> ▼ Participants entering lifeskills groups have built up patterns of skills strengths and weaknesses. Consequently, leaders need to guard against a naive optimism concerning change.
> ▼ An important distinction exists between how people initially
> *(continued)*

▼ **Chapter Highlights** (continued)

acquire lifeskills strengths and weaknesses and how they maintain them.

▼ Factors influencing initial acquisition of lifeskills include supportive relationships, role models, rewarding consequences, instruction, self-instruction, information, opportunity, challenge and confrontation, peer group interaction, thinking and anxiety management skills, sex-role considerations, culture, and social class.

▼ Lifeskills strengths and weaknesses are maintained both by what people do to themselves and what the environment does to people.

▼ The inner processes by which people maintain their lifeskills weaknesses include attributional deficiencies, unrealistic personal rules, faulty self-perceptions, negative self-talk, and fear of change.

▼ Many external factors influencing the initial acquisition of lifeskills weaknesses continue to influence their maintenance. These factors include insufficient supportive relationships, inadequate role models, inappropriate rewarding consequences, inadequate instruction, insufficient information, insufficient opportunity, peer group interaction, and sex-role, cultural, and social-class considerations.

3

How to Prepare a Training Group

In all things success depends upon previous
preparation, and without such preparation
there is sure to be failure.

Confucius

Chapter Questions

▼▼

What are the stages of a training group?

How can you find time to lead training groups?

What skills do you need in order to work with your environmental context?

How do you state goals and subgoals for training groups?

What choices should you be considering when preparing a training group?

What are some of the ethical and cross-cultural issues in running training groups?

Introduction

▼▼

This chapter looks at many of the choices that leaders make when they prepare training groups. The importance of preparing thoroughly for a lifeskills group cannot be emphasized enough. A leader who foolishly rushes in unprepared courts disaster. The following limerick tries to make this point:

> A training-group leader from Yale
> Had leadership skills that were frail
> He gave little care
> When he came to prepare
> So his sessions were boring as jail!

Stages of a Training Group

▼▼

A training group can be viewed as having four main, albeit overlapping, stages:

1. The preparatory stage
2. The initial stage
3. The working stage
4. The ending stage

The *preparatory stage* is what goes on before the group meets. This starts with either the creative glint in the leader's eye or with an external request for a lifeskills training group. Numerous leader choices exist at this stage. These choices include whether or not to have a co-leader; goals for the group; length of program and frequency and duration of sessions; location, physical setting, and facilities; resource material to be used; group composition; advertising; and whether or not and how to make a contract with group participants. Often a further set of choices involves how best to work with the group's environmental context. Last, but not least, leaders have to design the training programs they offer.

The *initial stage* starts when the training group first meets. This stage may last for the whole of the first session and sometimes extends into subsequent sessions. The initial stage has both relationship-building and task-orientation functions. The participants start getting to know the leader and each other. The leader requires initial structuring, ice-breaking, and group facilitation skills to help along this process. Participants can be oriented to the tasks of the group in at least two ways. First, the training program can be further outlined to them, elaborating on the idea of it that they are likely to have already when they enter. Second, participants can be encouraged to assess their skills strengths and weaknesses in the areas covered by the group. Initial self-assessment and setting of personal goals may not only motivate participants, but also provide them with yardsticks for assessing subsequent progress.

The *working stage* covers most of the remainder of the group sessions. Though the participants may engage in social relationships outside, inside the group they are encouraged to engage in working relationships. The leader uses facilitation skills to help participants learn from each other both by talking about themselves and by giving feedback. Additionally, the leader attempts to attain specific training goals by using didactic skills such as presenting carefully designed individual sessions; giving lectures; coaching, rehearsal, and feedback; using different group formats creatively; using exercises and games; and assigning and reviewing homework.

The *ending stage* focuses on issues of closure of the training group and on the transfer, maintenance, and development outside the group of the lifeskills learned inside it. Most training groups run for fixed terms, so participants have few illusions about when the group will end. Nevertheless, leaders may need to help participants handle feelings concerned with the breakup of the group. Above all, leaders need to focus on the consolidation of the lifeskills learned in the group as self-help skills for afterward. From their inception, well-designed training programs are sensitive to issues of transfer of learning. Ways of consolidating self-help skills at the end of a group include ensuring that participants have an adequate grasp of the self-talk necessary to guide their behavior in the skills areas; helping them assess their strengths and weaknesses; developing action plans for maintaining and developing their skills, including anticipating setbacks; and, where appropriate, arranging for one or more booster sessions.

A journey of a thousand miles must begin with a single step.

Lao-tse

Helpers and other potential lifeskills group leaders are always being confronted with role decisions about how best to spend their time (Morrill, Oetting, & Hurst, 1974; Watkins, Lopez, Campbell, & Himmell, 1986). Those considering leading training groups require the skills of making good role decisions. Helpers must be clear about both their objectives in regard to their overall role and about the objectives of their specific interventions. Three aspects of helper interventions are their clientele, their objectives, and their method. The clientele for an intervention can be an individual, a group, or an institution or community. The objectives of an intervention can be remedying moderate to severe psychological disturbance, preventing disturbance, or developing the lifeskills of "normal" people. The method of an intervention can be individual counseling, group counseling, training, or consultation.

Some helpers are appointed to positions in which their training function is primary. Others may have the opportunity to develop their helping or other roles to include lifeskills training interventions. Such training may be in one or more skills areas and may be aimed at one or more clienteles. Figure 3-1 shows simplified pie diagrams of the ways in which two different helpers might distribute their time among individual counseling, group counseling, training groups, and consultation. Time spent on administration, which may take as much as a quarter of total helper time (Troy & Magoon, 1979), is excluded here. Helpers may have more scope than they acknowl-

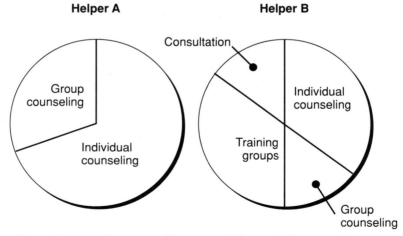

Figure 3-1 Pie diagrams of how two different helpers might distribute their time.

edge to develop their roles to encompass lifeskills training groups. If helpers can develop a vision of how they would like to perform, they may then be in a stronger position to achieve their goals. Helpers may still need to negotiate their roles within their institutions.

Exercise 3, on making role decisions, has been included because this is an important practical skill for people considering conducting training groups. If you have not thoroughly thought through your role, you may miss the opportunity to lead lifeskills training groups.

Exercise 3 Make Role Decisions: Allocate Your Time
▼ ▼

The first part of this exercise is for loosening up, so try and get as many ideas down as possible. Make up a worksheet with the following three headings:

Clienteles	Objectives	Methods

In regard to your present or future work role, fill in your worksheet indicating the following: (1) the possible clienteles for your work; (2) the kinds of objectives you might have for each clientele; and (3) the methods you might use with each clientele. In particular, take into account any opportunities you may have for leading lifeskills training groups; be specific about the skills focused on in possible training groups.

The second part of this exercise is for tightening up. Based on your responses on your clienteles/objectives/methods worksheet, (1) make a listing of your priorities among the activities you might realistically do; and (2) indicate how much of your time you might spend on each of these activities.

To what extent has this exercise altered your perception of how you might perform your role to include more of a focus on training groups? If you are part of a work team, this can be done as a group exercise.

Working with Your Environmental Context
▼ ▼

All lifeskills training groups, with the exception of those within private practices, are planned and led within institutional or agency settings. Consequently, it is critical that you show sensitivity to the institutional or agency perspective. One reason for showing such sensitivity is to avoid unwanted interference in what you try to do.

Brown (1986) cites the example of how correctional officers tried to thwart a group that was run within a prison wing. For instance, on arrival to start the first session, the leader found that the officers "didn't know" about it. During the session, correctional officers opened the door from time to time and stared through the window. At the end of the session, both members and leader heard a senior officer remark in a voice easy to hear, "You're wasting your bloody time with these buggars, they'll never change." Perhaps the leader might have spent more time preparing the ground with the correctional officers to prevent them from trying to sabotage the group. The same type of sabotaging may take place in other institutions, such as hospitals, schools, and businesses. For example, if some teachers feel that their "turf" is being infringed upon, they may try to block a lifeskills group from getting started or, once started, make derogatory remarks about it to pupils and parents.

Quite apart from heading off sabotage attempts, positive reasons exist for gaining support within your institution. If, as is likely, you work in a hierarchy, it can be diplomatic to let your superior(s) and colleagues know what you plan to do and address any reservations they have. You can develop a one- or two-page typed outline clearly communicating what you have in mind. Institutions have their codes of etiquette, which, if violated, can create problems. On the other hand, following etiquette can engender goodwill. Furthermore, your efforts at consultation and securing the necessary permissions may help you identify supporters as well as gain their support. Benefits of institutional support can include being allocated resources, whether time, money, access to participants, or physical facilities; having your work affirmed by others' making positive rather than negative comments about it to participants and potential participants; being supported in the event of misunderstandings over your group; and feeling that you are appreciated for what you do.

Institutions and agencies may have hidden agendas for their interest in training groups. These agendas can either work to your advantage or place you in a position of role conflict, or a mixture of the two. Costley and Moore (1986) provide the following examples of organizational hidden agendas: conducting stress management training to provide protection against legal liability arising from stress-related accidents; running women-in-management seminars "to project a positive image of equal rights for women in this organization and to get women's groups off our back" (p.102); and teaching employees communication skills in such a way that they know that if they continue to receive customer complaints they will be forced to attend more training programs on their own time. In business and industry, training groups can be tools for easing out poor employees.

Consultation skills for gaining institutional support include the ability to analyze the environmental context and to identify where best to look for support; sensitivity to institutional practices and codes of etiquette; the ability to communicate in a clear and non-threatening way regarding what you wish to do; showing that you understand others' viewpoints and reservations and, where feasible, will address them; and taking the time and effort to prepare the ground as a team member who works with the institution rather than a "lone ranger" who can all too easily be seen as a threat. A further consultation skill is that of finding out what training groups other people in the institution may want to see run. If others request your group leadership services, you start off from a position of support.

There is also an "inner game" to working within an institutional or agency context. It is very easy to get paranoid and to overreact to any perceived resistance to what you want to do (Whitaker, 1985). Some otherwise talented people in the helping professions sabotage their work by inadequately coping with their own thoughts and feelings. Here are two examples of potential lifeskills group leaders' not handling their inner game as well as they might:

▾ Kaya is an elementary school counselor who has proposed a lifeskills group on making friends to her school principal. When the principal expresses misgivings over how some parents might react, Kaya misperceives this as an unnecessary objection rather than a genuine reservation that she could help her principal work through.
▾ Joe is a social worker in a psychiatric hospital. He wants to run a transition skills group for adult patients who have recently returned to the community. His hospital sees his role as dealing with inpatients rather than outpatients. Joe gets extremely angry over his superiors' not seeing things his way. Joe cannot take no for an answer and meets increased resistance when he persists in pushing aggressively to fill a need that he thinks should be clear "even to a 7-year-old."

Some of the inner game thinking skills that might help you to work effectively within an institutional context include formulating realistic personal rules. You can avoid making self-defeating "mustabatory" demands both on yourself and others (Ellis, 1980, 1989). For instance, you can catch yourself when you think "If others do not give me what I want straight away, then they are unreasonable and I am a failure." Joe is an example of someone who translates unrealistic inner demandingness into counterproductive outer demands. Kaya is an example of someone too quick to attribute negative intentions to another. Jumping to perceptual conclusions before checking out whether there are more accurate ways of viewing others' positions is another thinking skills weakness to avoid (Beck & Weishaar, 1989).

You can learn to talk to yourself in ways that help you to stay calm and focused on achieving what you want (Meichenbaum, 1977; Meichenbaum & Deffenbacher, 1988). For instance, you may be nervous about going before a management group to present a proposal for a training group and then make matters worse by using anxiety-engendering rather than calming self-talk. Your obvious anxiety weakens your presentation's effect.

Exercise 4 Explore Your Skills in Working with the Environmental Context
▼▼▼

Think of a specific lifeskills group that you might offer in an institution or agency of your choice. Write out your answers as you complete each of the following tasks:

1. Perform an environmental context analysis that, as specifically as possible, identifies (a) where and in what form you are likely to find support for your group; (b) where and in what form you are likely to find resistance to your group; and (c) institutional practices and codes of etiquette that you need to take into account in planning and running your group.

2. Assess your own skills in dealing with the environmental context regarding your proposed lifeskills group. Such skills might include (a) relationship and communication skills: for instance, clearly expressing what you want to do, understanding others' perspectives, and responding adequately to their reservations; and (b) thinking skills: for instance, perceiving others' concerns accurately and not jumping to unwarranted conclusions about their motivation; possessing realistic personal rules; and using coping rather than anxiety-evoking self-talk.

3. Develop a plan for working effectively to have your lifeskills group accepted and supported within your institution or agency. Your plan should specify your goals and how you intend to attain each one of them.

Further Preparatory Considerations
▼▼▼

Further preparatory considerations for training-group leaders include knowing the subject matter, clarifying goals, and making choices about a range of issues from a number of group leaders to format, length, and setting of the group. We will examine each of these considerations briefly.

Know the Subject Matter

A distinction exists between training-group leaders' knowledge of subject matter and their delivery skills. Though it may seem obvious, if you are going to run a successful lifeskills program it is essential to have a good grasp of your subject matter. For example, a study conducted for the British Manpower Services Commission asked trainers and managers in large organizations with training programs which characteristics they would expect an effective trainer to have (Leduchowicz & Bennett, 1983). The three characteristics most associated with trainer credibility were, in rank order, knowledge of subject matter, good communication skills, and good planning and preparation.

It is unethical to run a training group if you are unfamiliar with your subject. In reality, there are degrees of familiarity with subject matter. Many leaders have a good working knowledge of a lifeskills area, but still need to update their information from time to time. Other leaders may originally have obtained a reasonable working knowledge of a lifeskills area, but have failed to keep up with its relevant research and practitioner literature. Still others may be reaching beyond their grasp since they have never adequately mastered the area in which they attempt to train.

There are three main kinds of subject matter knowledge that lifeskills group leaders require. First, there is *theoretical* knowledge. Theoretical knowledge involves familiarity with explanations of how people acquire, maintain, and can change their lifeskills both in general and in any specific lifeskills area. Second, there is *research* knowledge. What relevant research has been conducted in the lifeskills area of interest to you, and what is its relevance to designing and leading your training group? Third, there is *experiential* knowledge. For example, a leader running a training group for parents and adolescents on managing parent–adolescent conflict may have a fund of "case knowledge" derived from working with such problems both in family counseling and in previous groups. Additionally, that leader may have received initial training in running training groups plus further supervision.

Apart from the obvious point that if you do not know your subject, you are unlikely to be able to train people in it well, there are a number of other reasons for possessing a good knowledge base. First, knowing your subject releases time and energy for concentrating on how best to put it across. Second, you are more likely to be confident if you know your material. A side-effect of this confidence is that you handle the relationships in the group better. Third, you are more likely to be a source of influence for participants if they perceive you as having expertise (French & Raven, 1959). As a leader trying to develop participants' lifeskills, you are in the influence business. You cannot afford needlessly to erode your influence base. In Leduchowicz and Bennett's study (1983), the two items mentioned most frequently as characterizing noncredible trainers were being pompous and seeing oneself as superior, and lack of subject matter knowledge. Perhaps being pompous and seeing oneself as superior is a compensatory defense for inadequate knowledge of the subject.

Clarify and State Goals and Subgoals

A distinction can be made between the overall goal or goals for a lifeskills group and its cognitive-behavioral or operational subgoals. The overall goal is the focus of the group stated in broad terms, while the subgoals form a "how-to-do-it" working definition of the goal. Training groups that do not have clear goals and subgoals are at risk from many directions. These risks include lack of specificity in program design; wasting participants' time; and lowered motivation on the part of both leader and participants due to lack of a clear sense of direction. Successful training groups set out clearly both their overall goal and their specific subgoals.

Many considerations—from the perspectives of the leader, the potential participants, and the institution—can influence the overall goals leaders set for their lifeskills training groups. Practical considerations, like the amount of time and resources that can be devoted to the group, also apply. Defining the overall scope of a lifeskills group involves becoming more specific as to its content. For example, a leader may have eight weekly two-hour sessions to run an assertiveness group. However, this begs the question of what he or she means by assertiveness in this context. Possible meanings of assertiveness include training participants in the skills of expressing wants and wishes, taking initiatives, showing appreciation, stating their opinions, handling aggressive criticism, setting limits and saying no, standing up for their rights, and making assertive requests for behavior change. From these and other possible goals in the broad area of assertiveness, the leader needs to choose specific goals for the lifeskills group. At the preparatory stage, it is the leader who chooses goals. However, once the group meets, these goals can be modified in light of participants' feedback.

Having set out the broad skills focus of the lifeskills group, the leader still needs to break these skills down into operational or working subgoals. Say the overall goals of an assertiveness group are to develop participants' skills in setting limits, saying no, and making assertive requests for behavior change. Participants still do not know how to work toward these goals. Consequently, the leader needs to identify what thinking and action skills are relevant to attaining them. Basically, when leaders state subgoals in working terms, they state the specific steps in helping participants acquire the overall goals. Trainers in business and industry often use the term *task analysis* for the process of reviewing each task selected for training. Cook (1986) observes, "The output of this process is a list of the steps required to perform the task" (p.106). An example of how to state goals and subgoals is provided in the next chapter on designing training programs.

Choose the Number of Leaders

You can conduct lifeskills training groups on your own or with others. If you choose to work with another leader or leaders, all preparatory-stage considerations listed in this chapter should be discussed together. The size of training groups can vary, thus affecting the number of leaders desirable. Four ways in which you can lead training groups with others are as follows:

Co-equal leading: You work with one other leader on an equal footing. You share responsibility for the success of the group fairly evenly. Neither leader feels that he or she has to defer to the other one.

Supervisory co-leading: This is an unequal, apprenticeship model where one leader learns leader skills from another who acts in a supervisory role.

Team leading: More than two leaders are involved in running the group.

Using leaders' aides: One or more people are brought in to support the leader—for instance, the leader might give a presentation to the whole group, followed by skills-building subgroups led by leaders' aides. Leaders' aides can also be used where there are two or more leaders. Sometimes leaders' aides include technicians who work the audiovisual equipment.

Some of the potential advantages for participants of having more than one group leader include the following. Leaders may differ on basic characteristics—for instance, age, sex, and race. In lifeskills areas such as managing marital conflict, participants may benefit from having both female and male leaders. Co-leading also allows for differences in leader personality, thus increasing the likelihood that participants will feel comfortable with at least one leader. Further reasons for having more than one leader are that it increases the range of available resources, especially where leaders have different training strengths, and that individual participants may get more leader attention.

There are also potential advantages to working together for group leaders. Working with another, you can offer lifeskills programs to larger groups of participants than if you were training on your own. Some leaders prefer working with another leader. Co-leading can lessen feelings of isolation, both within the training group and within the institution or agency. Leaders can support each other both emotionally and in the mechanics of planning, designing, and running their group. Mutual support may lessen the chances of burnout where leaders carry a heavy training load. Leaders can also decide to perform different functions within the group—for instance, one may be more task-oriented while the other is more sensitive to relationship issues and to individual participants' anxieties and difficulties in acquiring skills. Either as co-equals or in the apprenticeship model, leaders can learn from each other. This learning can take place both by observing and also from discussion and feedback between group sessions.

The issue of whether co-leading is more expensive from an institutional perspective, is not clear-cut. On the surface, it seems that if two leaders are allocated to train the same number of participants as a single leader, running the group is roughly twice as expensive. However, this does not take into account the group's outcomes, which may justify some, if not all, of the extra expense. Economies of scale are possible from co-leading or team leading. For instance, where leaders take turns in giving presentations, they save preparation time. However, ultimately participants are likely to require some degree of individual attention as they develop their skills, thus placing limits on the possibilities for economies of scale.

There can also be problems and conflicts in leading training groups with another or others. Whitaker (1985) observes, "There is little else so unpleasant as trying to work with an uncongenial co-leader" (p. 95). However, differences of opinion can be handled constructively as well as destructively.

Following are some guidelines for effective co-leading:

1. Work with other leaders who have theoretical positions and values compatible with your own.
2. Work with other leaders whose training skills and experience you respect.
3. Work with other leaders with whom you feel you can engage in frank discussion and with whom you can have a collaborative rather than a competitive relationship.
4. Share with each other in all aspects of the planning and running of the group, even if you decide on a division of labor.
5. Commit time and energy to working with each other both before the group starts and between sessions.
6. Clearly understand each other's status and role. If you each wish to perform different functions in the training group, you should agree on this. If one of you is to exercise more power and authority, the other should be comfortable about this.

Decide on Group Size

Many considerations are relevant to group size. First, what is an optimum size for didactic training purposes? Second, what is a good size for participants to learn from and receive feedback and support from each other? Third, what are the practicalities of the training situation, including the resources available to the group?

From four to eight members is a good size for a training group. The group is small enough so that leaders can give time and attention to building the skills of individual participants. For instance, a training sequence may include coaching, video-recorded role playing, and playback accompanied by participant and trainer feedback. In a large group, going through this experiential learning sequence with individual participants would be far too time-consuming and repetitious. Because experiential learning is difficult to arrange, there can be a pressure in large groups for the leader to lecture about a lifeskill rather than to impart it in a practical, "how-to" way. Also, in settings such as schools, large groups may be more prone to disruption from participants not feeling actively involved.

Four to eight participants is also a good size for learning from interacting with other members. Yalom (1985) observes, "My own experience and a consensus of the clinical literature suggests that the ideal size of an interactional therapy group is approximately seven or eight, with an acceptable range of five to ten members" (p. 283). If the group becomes too large it is hard for individual participants to have their say, especially the shyer ones. Since the scope for person-to-person interaction is reduced, developing relationships may also be more difficult. Consequently, the cohesiveness of the group and its attraction to participants may be lessened.

In reality, practical considerations often determine the size of lifeskills training groups. For instance, if the group is being run for a school class or an army platoon, its numbers could be in the region of thirty. If a business organization is prepared to allocate only limited resources to the training function, this may create pressure for training groups larger than eight participants. On the other hand, if an institution or agency is prepared to offer sufficient resources to allow for co-leading, team leading, or using leaders' aides, the overall size of an effective lifeskills group could even be upwards of thirty, with individual attention to building skills and to small group interaction taking place in subgroups. Another set of practical considerations influencing group size has to do with the leader's confidence and skills. For example, a confident leader who knows how to run a group creatively through various forms of subgrouping may be better able to take on more than eight participants than someone less confident and skilled.

Decide on an Open Versus a Closed Group

An open group is one that may take in new participants during its life, whereas a closed group will not. The vast majority of lifeskills training groups are closed, for two main reasons. First, training groups are usually time-limited, say six to ten weeks, rather than being spread out over a longer period of time, say six months to a year. Consequently, there is less likelihood of the group's losing many participants. Second, participants in training groups, unlike those in interactional counseling groups, receive cumulative instruction in specific skills. Participants usually are not allowed to enter late, because they have missed out on earlier steps.

Decide on Group Composition

In almost all textbooks on group counseling, the issue of whether to have a heterogeneous or a homogeneous group is raised and debated. The participants in heterogeneous groups differ on such characteristics as styles of relating, age, sex, and presenting concerns. Homogeneous groups are characterized more by the similarities in their participants than by their differences. There is a much stronger emphasis on homogeneity in lifeskills training groups than in interactional counseling groups. Lifeskills training groups, which invariably include their specific skills focus in their titles, by definition have a high degree of homogeneity. Training groups often target specific clienteles—for example, stressed executives or prospective fathers. A further way in which training groups can be homogeneous is in the level at which they are offered—for example, training in public speaking skills can be either basic or more advanced. Entry into the more advanced program might be conditional on successful completion of the less advanced program.

Some training groups are more likely to attain their goals if their participants are somewhat heterogeneous. Examples include a dating skills group composed of both females and males; a cross-cultural awareness and communication group composed of participants from different cultures; an interracial communications group composed of participants from different races; a coping with death and dying group composed of those dying as well as those in good health; a hospital group on interprofessional communication composed of participants from different professions—for example, doctors and nurses; and a managing conflict group in industry composed of representatives from unions and management.

Decide on Group Participant Selection

Group member selection and group composition are interrelated in that participant selection is made according to the criteria for group composition. There are five main and sometimes interrelated ways of selecting participants for lifeskills training groups. First, there is *self-selection*. A training group can be advertised and filled on a "first-come-first-served" basis. Participants have decided of their own accord that they need to develop their skills and that they have sufficient finances to pay for the group.

Second, there is *leader selection*. Leaders have their own criteria for inclusion and exclusion. They may conduct intake interviews in which they and potential participants can assess their mutual suitability. Third, there is *third-party selection*. An example of selection by a third party is that of salespeople sent to effective communication courses by their sales managers. Third-party selection is common in business and industry and may be viewed as either reward or punishment.

Fourth, there is *compulsory whole category selection*. Sometimes training is required for whole categories of people—for example, a company may have a policy that all newly appointed supervisors must attend supervisory skills training groups. Fifth, there is *compulsory whole group selection*. An example of this would be career education lifeskills groups offered to all students as part of a secondary school curriculum.

A number of these methods of selection contain elements of compulsion. Though it is possible to select people to be physically present in training groups, they select themselves to be psychologically present. Many leaders would much prefer not to have unwilling participants in their groups. However, often the leaders too are part of systems that restrict choice.

Conduct Intake Interviews If Feasible

Intake interviews are individual interviews conducted by the leader with prospective participants prior to starting a group. The main disadvantage of conducting intake interviews is that they are time-consuming. However, especially where the group size is not going to be large, intake interviews have advantages that may outweigh their disadvantages. First, intake interviews allow the leader to apply criteria for inclusion and exclusion. Leaders can increase the chances that those joining need to improve their skills in the areas of their groups and at the levels at which they are offered. Potential participants either too advanced or not ready can be excluded. The motivation of participants to work hard can be assessed. Also, decisions can be made about whether to exclude participants with characteristics likely to be disruptive to the group—for example, monopolizing and excessive hostility. Second, intake interviews are a two-way process that allow potential participants to ask questions and to decide whether the training group is going to meet their needs.

Third, intake interviews allow leaders and participants to get to know one another. Leaders may get a clearer idea of individual participants' skills strengths and weaknesses. Additionally, intake interviews allow participants to feel that they have a relationship with leaders. This feeling may make joining the group a less threatening experience and possibly contribute to participants' "staying the course." Fourth, intake interviews allow leaders to orient prospective participants. For instance, leaders can clarify expectations by discussing the group's formal or informal contract. Also, participants may be encouraged to engage in pregroup preparation. Such preparation may include doing relevant reading; keeping a daily record monitoring their skills; answering a pregroup questionnaire; and watching a videocassette demonstrating desirable participant behaviors.

Decide How to Advertise

Advertising is not required for those lifeskills training groups that either are compulsory or whose participants are known to the leader—for instance, previous or current counseling clients. Leaders whose theoretical position is built around a single lifeskill may find it particularly easy to compose a training group from counseling clients: to a large degree, they operationalize all their clients' problems the same way. For instance, group rational-emotive therapy is essentially lifeskills training in the central skill of identifying and disputing irrational beliefs. Minimal advertising is required when leaders can obtain sufficient participants by notifying colleagues that they will be running a specific kind of lifeskills group. The nature and duration of such lifeskills groups may even have been joint decisions among colleagues, such as staff in a college counseling center.

Sometimes more extensive advertising is necessary to attract members for lifeskills groups. Methods of advertising training groups include the following:

Word of mouth: Letting your group be known to colleagues and other relevant people in an institution or agency. This can be done on a one-to-one basis or by giving talks about it.

Satisfied customers: Getting people who have received benefits from previous lifeskills groups to tell others about your group.

Referral networks: Over a period of time, getting to know people who might refer participants to you as and when you notify them you intend to run a training group.

Brochures and handouts: Compiling and disseminating appropriate literature about your proposed group.

Posters: Displaying well-designed posters that provide stimulating and interesting information about your proposed group.

Advertising in professional journals and newsletters: This kind of advertising is especially relevant if you wish to target professional and paraprofessional participants.

Advertising in institutional newspapers and newsletters: For example, college counseling services might advertise their lifeskills training groups in campus newspapers.

Advertising in the public press: Since advertising in the public press is likely to be expensive, the advertisements need to more than pay for themselves in terms of participants' fees.

Radio advertising: Sometimes this can be free—for instance, if there is a talk-show host interested in the area of your lifeskills group.

Running outreach programs: Running lifeskills groups on participants' "turfs" rather than in central training locations. Such groups may engender local interest both when first being run and, if successful, subsequently.

Successful training-group leaders may need to develop marketing skills in the best sense. Even though they may not charge money, if leaders believe in their product they should devise ways of bringing it to the attention of those who might benefit from it.

Settle on Format and Length of Group

Leaders have to make choices concerning the format and lengths of their training groups. Writing of developments in social work, Brown (1986) observes that in recent years, the shift in casework to brief task-focused interventions has also taken place in group work, "from groups that last for years, to ones that are much briefer in duration (say six to twelve sessions over a three- to six-month period) and specific in intent" (p.41). Though longer-term group counseling and therapy is still practiced and may be valuable to some, the shift to briefer and more focused groups is much more widespread than just within social work.

Though issues of format and length of lifeskills groups and of frequency and duration of sessions overlap, here the former will be discussed first. Basically, there are three main formats for training groups: massed, spaced, and massed-spaced combinations. Issues of postprogram follow-up and support are relevant to each of these formats. *Massed* lifeskills training groups are intensive in that all the sessions are massed together over a relatively brief period of time. Participants attend full-time. Sometimes massed training groups are called workshops. Examples of massed training groups include a two-day workshop on public-speaking skills run by a large corporation; a one-week training course on leadership skills for newly appointed supervisors; and a two-week training course on counseling and helping skills for health paraprofessionals.

In *spaced* lifeskills training groups, the individual training sessions are spaced out. For example, sessions may be held biweekly, weekly, bimonthly, or monthly. Because they are less intensive, spaced groups tend to take place over a longer time period than massed groups: say, from a month to six months. Examples of spaced training groups include a one-session-a-week group on parenting skills lasting for three months; a twice-weekly career education course for high school students lasting one semester; and a training group on assertiveness skills for women that lasts for eight weekly sessions.

In *massed-spaced combinations*, the massed element may come either at the start of or during the training group, but rarely comes at the end. The massed section gives participants an intensive exposure to skills that then get consolidated and developed in spaced sessions and practice. Examples of massed-spaced programs include a weekend workshop followed by once-weekly sessions for six weeks for training telephone counselors for the suicidal and depressed; a ten-week lifeskills group for young people, run by a church minister, on relationship skills, with sessions held one weekday evening per week and a weekend retreat halfway through the program; and a one-week intensive course on people-management skills for bank managers followed by four sessions at monthly intervals.

The dividing line is not always a clean one between a lifeskills training group and provisions, if any, for follow-up and support. A major theme of this book is the need for leaders to pay great attention to issues of transfer and maintenance of skills. Booster sessions, say three months after the group ends, may not only help participants' motivation but also assist them to overcome difficulties in implementing their skills. Additionally, the environments from which participants come can reinforce their skills development. For instance, participants in a corporation who have been to a public-speaking course can be given managerial support and opportunities to use and develop their speaking skills.

Both practical and teaching considerations influence the length of training groups. Practical considerations influencing length include the availability of participants. For example, a group run in a prison on skills for making the transition to the community must take into account the remaining jail terms of participants. Other practical considerations include the cost of sending participants to the training group; the time framework in which participants are available—for example, school semesters; the urgency of acquiring the skills—for example, job-seeking skills for the short-term unemployed; and the availability of leaders. Teaching considerations influencing the length of lifeskills groups center on whether the group can achieve its goals in the time available. Related considerations include the complexity and difficulty of these goals; the starting points of participants; and whether or not the group is part of a sequence of groups.

Practical and teaching considerations also determine the format of training groups. Many leaders do not have a choice of format: they work in environments geared to either massed or spaced training. For example, schools and colleges may lend themselves to spaced training, whereas business and industry training groups are often massed, with participants being taken out of their normal work settings. The main teaching consideration related to massed or spaced groups is to determine which format is most conducive to skills acquisition, maintenance, and development. Massed groups may give participants a thorough introduction to the skill and the chance to get to know each other in a brief period of time. However, unlike spaced groups, massed groups can have the major drawback of allowing participants insufficient time to learn and practice the skills so that they become part of their daily living. Also, massed groups may be too intense for the motivation and attention spans of some categories of participants, such as elementary school children. Though generalizations are risky, a massed-spaced combination format often has much to recommend it.

Settle on Frequency and Duration of Sessions

Even for massed groups, leaders must make choices concerning frequency and duration of sessions. For example, in a two-day workshop on public-speaking skills, how many periods should there be? Should they all be the same length, despite some sessions having different objectives? When and how long should the breaks be? Sessions in which participants acquire skills by means of an initial leader presentation that includes demonstration of skills, followed by coaching rehearsal and feedback, are time-consuming. Such practical training sessions may last two to three hours. Usually the final choice concerning length of sessions represents a compromise between practical and teaching considerations. For instance, despite the advantages of flexibility, there may be limits to the extent to which breaks can be altered.

For spaced groups, a number of practical and teaching considerations may influence the frequency and duration of sessions. Ideally, the length of the session should take into account such factors as the purposes of the session and the motivation and attention span of participants. However, such flexibility is not always possible. For instance, lifeskills groups that are run in schools and colleges as part of the formal curriculum may need to adhere to the normal length of classroom periods. Practical considerations may also influence frequency of sessions. For example, educational institutions may only be willing to allocate one period a week to a training group, or the leader may only be available weekly. Participants' ability to pay may also affect how many sessions they want to afford in a given period. Teaching considerations relevant to frequency of sessions include the need to maintain momentum (this may be easier if sessions are biweekly rather than weekly or longer) and the need to allow participants realistic opportunities for between-sessions homework (biweekly sessions may leave insufficient time for homework). Leaders make trade-offs and compromises all the time in deciding both on format and length of training groups and on frequency and duration of sessions.

Decide Location, Physical Setting, and Facilities

Where are you going to run your training group? If you are in private practice you can either use your own facilities or rent them elsewhere. Here the focus is on running lifeskills training groups in institutional, organizational, and agency contexts. There are at least four principal locations for such groups. First, there is the no-choice or limited-choice setting. In this case leaders have to work with the facilities they have whether they like them or not. For instance, school teachers may have to run lifeskills groups in the classrooms allocated to them. In running a relationship skills group for twenty-five undergraduates as part of my college's general education program, I was once assigned a classroom where the desks had to remain in rows at the departmental chairman's decree! His big concession was that students might turn their chairs toward each other. Since flexibility of space was important, I looked for and happily found a more congenial environment.

Second, the institution or agency may have its own training facility. For instance, a large corporation may have both a central training facility downtown and a further facility in the countryside. Colleges and schools may have specially designed areas for lifeskills training groups; so may other organizations such as hospitals. Central institutional training facilities tend to mean that participants leave their own "turf" and, by doing so, mix with participants from other parts of the organization. For instance, secretaries from different parts of a company may be brought together to acquire assertiveness skills. Traveling "abroad" in this way may free them to take more risks than they might if they had stayed in their work setting.

Third, there are outreach settings. In this case, leaders who may or may not possess their own training facilities go out to run "on-the-spot" lifeskills groups to meet local needs in different parts of an institution. Following from the previous example, the training of secretaries in assertiveness skills may take place in the various parts of the company in which they work. Outreach lifeskills groups can have the advantage of being more readily tailored to meet local needs. Also, outreach groups are more visible than groups run in central settings. Furthermore, once the group ends, it may be easier for participants drawn from the same setting to support each other in maintaining and developing their skills.

Fourth, training groups may be run outside institutional settings. Leaders may choose to organize lifeskills training groups in locations that have no connection with their employing institutions, organizations, or agencies. Such groups may be run in hotels and training facilities that are either local or distant—even overseas. The advantages of moving outside of organizational "turf" include the long hours that participants are able to spend without home and work distractions; the opportunity to develop social relationships and to improve morale; the increased possibility for fresh thinking in a different setting; and the chance for fun and a holiday.

Where they have a choice, leaders might ask themselves a number of questions regarding the location, physical setting, and facilities options that they consider. Following is a simple twelve-point checklist of relevant questions.

1. If necessary, can I obtain permission to use the location?
2. Will I be able to use the same location for the whole of my training program?
3. Is the location easily accessible?
4. Are the physical facilities the right size?
5. Does the location offer suitable privacy?
6. Is the location free from undue noise and other unnecessary distractions?
7. Is the heating, cooling, lighting, and ventilation adequate?
8. Is the decor pleasant?
9. Can the space be used flexibly?
10. Are the audiovisual facilities good?
11. Is the furniture conducive to the tasks of my group?
12. If necessary, are there adequate refreshment, toilet, and parking facilities?

This checklist is illustrative rather than exhaustive. Many training-group leaders are forced to accept physical facilities that are far from ideal. In this case, you can only hope that the quality of your work shines through!

Decide on Training Methods and Materials

The design of lifeskills programs and of individual sessions is covered later in this book. Suffice it for now to indicate that leaders in their preparation need to take into account what training methods and materials they will use. For example, if leaders intend to use demonstrations, are these going to be live or prerecorded? If the demonstrations are prerecorded, does the recording already exist or will the leader have to make it up? The main methods used in systematic lifeskills training include lecturettes, facilitated self-assessment, demonstrations, coaching, rehearsal and feedback, worksheets, exercises and games, group discussion, graduated practice, and homework.

Lifeskills training groups may involve extensive use of audiovisual aids. For example, audiocassettes may be used to present information and to demonstrate skills. Furthermore, audiocassettes may be used to develop participants' skills in self-instruction—for instance, in the skills of problem solving or progressive muscular relaxation. Visual aids include whiteboards, blackboards, flip charts, posters, prerecorded training videos and films, and live video recording and playback. Additionally, leaders may wish to record sessions on audiotape or videotape for supervision purposes.

Lifeskills training groups can also involve extensive use of written aids. Written aids for assessment and self-assessment include questionnaires, standardized tests, and behavior-monitoring sheets. Written aids for training include books, training manuals, training packages (for instance, a trainer manual, manuals for participants, and audiovisual aids), and handouts. A basic choice for leaders is whether you build your group around an existing training manual or package, or independently or collectively design your own material. Numerous commercial training manuals and packages exist. Leaders should familiarize themselves with the existing training materials in the areas of proposed programs. This does not mean that you have to adopt them either in whole or in part. There is much to be said for the freshness and extra relevance that comes from creating your own material.

Decide Whether or Not to Use Contracts

A number of different kinds of contracts are relevant to lifeskills training groups. First, there is the pregroup contract that ideally states clearly what the group offers and what is expected from participants. Second, there are the working agreements made between leader and participants during the life of the group. Unlike the pregroup contract, such agreements can be negotiated. Third, there are individual learning contracts in which participants set themselves personal goals for all or parts of the group (Corey & Corey, 1982; Wehrenberg, 1988). Fourth, there are contracts of varying degrees of explicitness that leaders may have about a training group with representatives of the institution or agency in which it is to be held.

The focus here is the pregroup contract or working agreement between leader and participants. Many advantages accrue from having clear pregroup contracts. Participants know what they are getting into. Consequently, they are more likely to be motivated and less likely to drop out. Employers and others who send participants to groups also know the skills they can expect their people to develop. This knowledge both helps them select participants and increases their understanding of the experience of those attending training groups. Pregroup contracts can be a good marketing and public relations strategy. Clear pregroup contracts also force leaders to think through issues connected with offering training groups. Such contracts also minimize the chance of unfortunate misunderstandings with participants in regard to matters such as workload or fees. Furthermore, clear contracts help leaders fulfill their ethical obligation to obtain informed consent from participants.

What might the contents of a pregroup contract be? Areas requiring clarification include the following:

1. What the training group offers participants
   a. The goals and subgoals of the group. "At the end of this training group participants should have the following skills . . . ."
   b. Brief biographies of leaders. What is their relevant background and experience?
   c. Structural details. These details include format and length of group, and frequency and length of sessions.
   d. Location.

  e. Group size and composition.
  f. Training methods. These may include demonstrations, lec-
     turettes, role playing, video feedback, and so on.
  g. Training materials. Key learning resources, such as a particu-
     lar training manual, might be indicated.
  h. Confidentiality. Any limitations on confidentiality should be
     stated—for instance, communication about participants with
     sponsoring employers.
  i. Release arrangements. Within an organization, it can be im-
     portant to know how being sent to a lifeskills group affects job
     and income.
  j. Certificates and such. Does participation in the lifeskills group
     lead to any formal recognition such as a certificate?
2. What the training group expects from participants
  a. Attendance requirements
  b. Outside-of-session commitment. For example, will weekly
     homework be assigned and, if so, how much time is it likely to
     take?
  c. During-session participation. For example, active participation
     in working at personal goals and helping others is frequently a
     requirement.
  d. Fees. Details of any fees and when they are due.

   This list of suggestions for a pregroup contract is not exhaustive.
Also, the list assumes that leaders are working with adults. Each
pregroup contract requires careful drafting in light of local needs
and circumstances. Leaders are more likely to achieve their objectives from using pregroup contracts if they have clear writing and
presentation skills.
   Sometimes the word *contract* is implicit rather than explicit in
pregroup contracts. For instance, a handout or brochure may state
what it calls expectations for leaders and participants. On other occasions the handout or brochure may use the word *contract* and resemble a legal contract. Some leaders may even get such contracts signed
and countersigned by both parties. There can be various levels at
which expectancies and working arrangements get clarified. For example, at a preliminary level a brochure suggests what the broad outline of a lifeskills training group might be, but then this may get
further clarified and codified for those joining the group. My preference is for expectations to be stated clearly without requiring signa-
tures. However, leaders who earn their livings by running training
groups may think they need the extra protection of signed contracts.

Review How to Assess and Evaluate the Group

   Since issues of assessment and evaluation are covered in some detail
later in this book, the topic is only briefly mentioned here. Many

areas exist in which you can make evaluation choices prior to starting your lifeskills training group. These choice areas include how to assess participants' skills before, during, and at the end of the group and how to help participants assess their own skills. Additionally, you may wish to assess the effectiveness of individual sessions and of specific training interventions. If you are under supervision, you also need to work out with your supervisor how best to assess your training skills. A further assessment consideration is whether you are required to submit grades or reports to third parties. For instance, if you run a training group as part of a formal school or college curriculum, you may need to decide how to assign grades.

Make a Time Commitment

Especially with groups being run for the first time, preparing for lifeskills training can be very time-consuming. A number of tasks take up much group leader time both individually and collectively: (1) gaining permissions and engaging in the negotiations to run the group; (2) designing the overall program; (3) designing individual sessions; (4) creating your own training materials; (5) obtaining and selecting participants, and (6) reviewing participants' self-assessments and worksheets. In addition, there are likely to be further tasks and commitments. Also, you can conduct training groups either in the evenings or on weekends, so you need to take into account the impact of these hours on you. In sum, an absolutely fundamental preparatory consideration for leaders is whether you are prepared to commit the time to run your proposed lifeskills training group properly.

Exercise 5 Prepare a Lifeskills Training Group
▼▼

For a lifeskills training group you may wish to lead, write out the choices you make concerning each of the following preparatory considerations. Refer back to the text if you are in doubt about the meaning of any of the categories.

Number of leaders
Group size
Open versus closed group
Group composition
Group selection
Intake interviewing
Advertising
Format and length of group
Frequency and duration of sessions

Location, physical setting, and facilities
Training methods and materials
Contracts
Assessment and evaluation
Time commitment
Other considerations

Summarize what seem to be the major considerations in preparing your lifeskills group.

Ethical Issues
▼▼▼

As with group counseling and psychotherapy (Corey, Corey, & Callanan, 1988), there are numerous ethical issues connected with running lifeskills training groups. Professional associations to which group leaders belong are likely to have their own codes of ethics. For example, the American Psychological Association has published a series of ethical guidelines and principles (American Psychological Association, 1973, 1981, 1987, 1990). The American Association for Counseling and Development has published its own ethical standards (Allen, Sampson, & Herlihy, 1988; American Association for Counseling and Development, 1988), and the National Board for Certified Counselors (1987) also has a code of ethics. Leaders are encouraged to familiarize themselves with the relevant sections of codes of ethics put out by associations to which they belong.

What are some of the many ethical issues that might be pertinent to lifeskills training groups that you run? Here are some suggestions:

Leader competence: Leaders should possess the personal maturity, psychological knowledge, training skills, and experience to be effective in the role. Where leaders are learning group-training skills, it is important that they work under adequate supervision.

Leaders' personal agendas, needs, and values: At all times leaders must show respect for the personal integrity of participants. They should refrain from imposing their own agendas, unfinished business, needs, and values on participants.

Assessment and diagnostic labeling: Training-group leaders operating within a cognitive-behavioral lifeskills framework are likely to share their assessments with clients. Ethical issues surround the degree of accuracy of such assessments and the extent to which they are imposed on participants. In general, an assumption of skills training groups is that leaders should refrain from applying psychiatric diagnostic labels to clients. However, in certain inpatient and outpatient hospital settings, this assumption may be untenable: participants may fit into psychiatric diagnostic categories and also have their skills strengths and weaknesses assessed in targeted areas.

Emotional and sexual relationships: Leaders should endeavor to pay equal attention to each participant. Emotional and sexual relationships with participants are unethical. Corey, Corey, and Callanan (1988) observe, "Most of the ethical codes caution against dual relationships and point to the need to avoid exploitation of clients out of the therapist's needs" (p. 173).

Informed consent: The importance of a clear contract for potential participants has already been stressed. Also, during training groups, leaders should endeavor to ensure that participants are clear about the activities in which they will engage prior to engaging in them.

Advertising: Advertising should accord with the rules of professional associations to which you belong. Overselling of program content and outcomes is to be avoided.

Psychological risk: Though lifeskills training groups, because of their focused and time-limited nature, tend to be less emotionally charged than psychotherapy or counseling groups, participants may still require leader protection from certain psychological risks—for example, excessive group hostility or inappropriate group pressure. Additionally, where necessary, leaders should arrange appropriate psychological support for people whose coping resources are being overwhelmed either inside or outside the group.

Termination issues: Issues involved in the ethical termination of training groups include adequate preparation of participants to handle setbacks and relapses; arranging for follow-up support, possibly including booster sessions; letting participants know where and how they might further develop their skills; and deciding to what extent and how to evaluate the group's processes and outcomes.

Confidentiality: Where there are limitations on confidentiality, participants have a right to this knowledge. In specific instances that cannot always be anticipated in advance—for instance, physical danger to third parties—leaders may have a duty to warn and protect. Such decisions may be based on legal requirements and not just on ethical considerations. Participants' records should always be kept secure.

Audio or video recording of sessions: Leaders may want to record sessions on audiotape or videotape for their own feedback, training, and supervision purposes. Where possible, participants should be informed of this wish before or during the initial session. Leaders should be honest about why the recordings are being made, who will have access to them, where they will be stored, and how they will be used.

Undue pressure: Leaders should respect the rights of participants not to disclose themselves more than they want to. Also, leaders should refrain from forcing participants to do exercises and games with which they are uncomfortable.

Issues regarding minors: There are numerous ethical issues regarding minors—for example, whether or not parental consent should be required for children to participate in a lifeskills group;

the reporting of alleged sexual, physical, or psychological abuse committed on children outside the group; and children's rights to confidentiality.

Financial exploitation: If there is to be a training-group fee, on what basis should it be set? There should be no hidden costs.

Rights of employing agencies: What rights do organizations and agencies employing the leader have? How should group leaders behave where there are conflicts of interest?

Rights of other professionals: If a participant or potential participant is receiving related services—for example, psychotherapy—from another professional, how should the leader behave?

These are just some of the ethical issues pertinent to leading life-skills training groups. You may be able to think of other important issues. From the moment you start preparing for your group, you must be sensitive to the ethical implications of your choices. If necessary, talk these through with either trusted colleagues or a supervisor. Some ethical issues may be emotionally and intellectually difficult for you. Nevertheless, you must confront these issues.

Cultural Considerations
▼▼

Sue and Zane (1987) observe that "The research and clinical literature on the delivery of mental health services to ethnic-minority populations has been quite consistent in drawing attention to inadequacies in the provision of services" (p. 37). Group leader behavior toward people from different cultures may be viewed as an aspect of professional ethics as well as an area in its own right.

Increasing Cultural Diversity

In Chapter 2, cultural origin data were presented from the 1980 and 1990 United States and the 1981 Canadian censuses. Existing data point to growing cultural, racial, and ethnic diversity. Between 1980 and 1990, blacks increased from 11.7 to 12.4 percent of the total American population, while Hispanics increased from 6.4 to 7.9 percent (Allen & Turner, 1990). During the 1980s, the number of Asians, Pacific Islanders, American Indians, Eskimos, and Aleuts in the United States grew by 65 percent, primarily the result of Asian immigration. These races' share of the U.S. population rose from 2 to 3 percent (Waldrop & Exter, 1990). Allen and Turner (1990) observe that "in the 21st century, one-quarter to one-third of all Americans will belong to racial or ethnic minority groups" (p. 34).

Cultural diversity exists not only within but between racial and ethnic groups. For example, the Hispanic group includes 12 million

Mexicans, 2.5 million Puerto Ricans, 2 million Central and South Americans, and 1 million Cubans. Furthermore, each of these subgroups has its own cultural and linguistic differences (Swensen, 1990). Cultural differences also exist among white Americans—for example, Italian-Americans or Irish-Americans. In addition, cultural differences interact with socioeconomic differences—for example, affluent versus nonaffluent whites, Indians, blacks, Hispanics, and Asians (O'Hare, 1989, 1990; Waldrop, 1990a, 1990b).

Within the United States, cultural diversity is unevenly spread and made up of different ethnic and racial mixes. The four most ethnically diverse counties in the United States are San Francisco, Manhattan, the Bronx, and Los Angeles (Allen & Turner, 1990). The least culturally diverse region is a broad area stretching from northern New England through the Midwest and into Montana.

Culture-Deficit Versus Culture-Sensitive Training Models

The area of cultural issues in lifeskills training is complex. However, a simple and useful distinction exists between culture-deficit and culture-sensitive training models. The culture-deficit training model assumes that the rules and values of the dominant or mainstream culture are normal. According to this model, variations observed in minorities are deficits; consequently, training programs should be designed to provide minority groups with experiences to make up for their assumed deficits (Rogoff & Morelli, 1989). The culture-deficit training model incorporates oppression even by those trying to "help" minorities. For example, patronizing attitudes and "missionary zeal" are two kinds of majority group helper insensitivity experienced by many American Indians (LaFromboise, Trimble, & Mohatt, 1990).

The culture-sensitive training model avoids the assumption that dominant group practices are proper and superior. Respect is shown for cultural differences, and the positive features of cultural variation may be emphasized. Whether culturally similar or dissimilar to participants, leaders attempt to prepare and conduct training groups in ways that acknowledge the different perceptual realities and skills of minority group members. Leaders understand that different behaviors may have different meanings for minority groups. For example, Ivey (1987) gives the example that the mainstream American way of showing attention by sitting opposite and leaning forward may be inappropriate in the Arctic, where it is best to sit side by side. Furthermore, leaders show sensitivity to minority group members' differing levels of and wishes for acculturation (LaFromboise, Trimble, & Mohatt, 1990; Spindler & Spindler, 1958). In addition, where appropriate, leaders use overt skills to improve cross-cultural understanding and communication—for instance, openly giving permission to discuss cultural differences.

Cultural Agendas in Lifeskills Training

Whether or not they are the focus of training groups, cultural agendas are almost always present in lifeskills training. The following are examples of lifeskills groups in which cultural issues are central:

▼ Training helpers in cross-cultural sensitivity and skills (Merta, Stringham, & Ponterotto, 1988).
▼ Training lay people—for instance, students and managers—in cross-cultural sensitivity and skills.
▼ Transition training for migrants in the skills of adjusting to their new cultures.
▼ Training minority groups in skills of racial and cultural identity development, including developing a bicultural identity, and in skills of coping with oppression and discrimination (Christensen, 1989; Fukuyama, 1990).

The following are examples of cultural agendas that may be present, if not always acknowledged, in lifeskills training groups:

▼ *Cultural mistrust*: leaders and participants may mistrust people from other cultures.
▼ *Differences in verbal and nonverbal behavior*: Within training groups, leaders and participants may have different communication styles depending on their cultures that impede messages' being sent and received accurately.
▼ *Differences in the meaning and application of lifeskills*: Lifeskills need to be learned in the context of cultural rules—for instance, the value attached to assertiveness and ways of being assertive may vary across cultures.

Cross-Cultural Skills for Leaders

Group leaders need to translate their cultural awareness and sensitivity into observable skills. A debate exists over whether helpers need to acquire culture-specific or culture-universal knowledge and skills. The approaches are not mutually exclusive, and each has its advantages and drawbacks. A risk of training-group leaders' adopting a culture-specific approach is that they may fail to adequately take into account within-group differences among minority-group participants (Lloyd, 1987; Sue & Zane, 1987). For example, leaders running college study skills groups should not automatically assume that all Asian-American students are achievement-oriented and want a highly directive trainer. A culture-universal approach aims to identify the knowledge and skills common to working with training groups whatever their cultural origins. In this approach, there is a risk of underemphasizing useful knowledge and skills for working with specific cultural groups.

Reasons for and against cultural matching of group leaders and participants vary according to the skills focus of the group. Groups of recent migrants with poor language skills obviously require bilingual trainers. However, in a culturally diverse country, cultural matching of leaders and participants is not always possible. Culture-sensitive skills that leaders need to develop if they are to prepare and run training groups include developing training materials and programs that acknowledge cultural issues; facilitating participants in disclosing and working through cultural mistrust and culturally based resistances; giving participants permission to talk about cultural variations in the meaning and applications of targeted skills; speaking in ways easily comprehensible to minority-group participants; giving skills demonstrations that use minority-group models; and using structured activities and assigning homework relevant to participants' cultural contexts.

▼ Chapter Highlights

▾ Lifeskills training groups require thorough preparation.

▾ Training groups have four major, albeit overlapping, stages: preparatory, initial, working, and ending.

▾ Helpers and others incorporating lifeskills training groups into their work require good skills at defining their roles and allocating their time.

▾ Leaders require adequate knowledge of the subject matter of any training groups they run. There are three main kinds of subject matter knowledge: theoretical, research, and experiential.

▾ Training-group leaders require both sensitivity to and skills at working with their environmental contexts.

▾ Goals for lifeskills groups should be stated first in broad terms and then operationalized into clear and specific subgoals. These subgoals should focus on the specific thinking and action skills required for attaining overall training-group goals.

▾ Preparatory choices for lifeskills training groups include number of leaders; group size; open versus closed group; group composition; group participant selection; whether or not to conduct intake interviews; format and length of group; frequency and length of sessions; location, physical setting, and facilities; training methods and materials; contracts; assessment and evaluation; and time commitment.

▾ Group leaders must always be conscious of the ethical and cross-cultural implications of their training-group choices.

4

How to Design a Lifeskills Training Program

There is always an easy solution to every human problem—neat, plausible, and wrong.

H. L. Mencken

Chapter Questions

What approaches are there to designing a training program?

What are some of the main program design considerations?

What is a good format for outlining a training program?

Introduction

Program design is always a major task of the preparatory stage of lifeskills training groups. Many of the component skills of designing and leading individual lifeskills sessions are described in much more detail in later chapters. Here we focus on the fact that in designing lifeskills training programs, leaders are hypothesis makers and testers. Each lifeskills program represents a series of "If . . . then . . . " statements relating process and content to desired outcomes. Most lifeskills group leaders do not evaluate their hypotheses by means of rigorous research designs. Nevertheless, leaders always need to be conscious that in designing and running their training groups, they are practitioner-researchers conducting behavioral experiments.

Approaches to Program Design

Training-group leaders have the final responsibility for putting their lifeskills training programs together and implementing them. Different approaches can be taken to constructing programs. For instance, leaders can design lifeskills programs around existing training manuals and packages. Usually it is worth researching what, if any, training manuals and packages already exist in your lifeskills area of interest. If you can locate suitable training materials, some of the work of designing a program will be done for you. However, you must still adapt existing material to the specific needs of your group. Another option is for leaders to design lifeskills programs by working closely with those requesting or paying for the programs. Leaders may do this either within their organizations or as outside consultants. In both instances leaders require consultancy skills such as clarifying others' goals and then formulating program outlines and content with them.

As a training-group leader you may design all aspects of your lifeskills program on your own. This model is assumed in this chapter. However, leaders can also design lifeskills programs working as part of a team. The team approach to lifeskills program design may range from working with co-leaders to large-scale curriculum design projects. Another possibility is to design your lifeskills program in consultation with participants. Such consultation may take place at the start of and during your training group. One approach is to design the whole program as a group exercise. Here, the leader acts as a resource person helping the group construct a curriculum geared to attaining participants' personal and collective goals. Another approach is to allow for flexibility within a program designed by you in advance. For example, a program may be altered after feedback and consultation with participants. Furthermore, in most lifeskills programs there is a role for individuals working toward personal goals as well as toward group goals. Hence, some degree of latitude is required to cater to individual needs.

Program Design Considerations
▼▼

Many considerations relevant to designing a training program are discussed in greater detail elsewhere in this book. Consequently, the present discussion is restricted to an overview of program design considerations. The following are some questions that leaders might ask themselves when designing lifeskills training programs.

What Are My Goals?

Training-group leaders require goals stated at three levels of specificity: overall program goals, broad skills goals, and skills subgoals. Lifeskills groups have overall or program goals expressed in general terms—for example, for delinquent boys to enter the work force and keep out of jail; for women to develop assertiveness skills; for drug addicts to get off and stay off drugs; or for psychiatric outpatients to develop social skills.

Overall goals then must be broken down into the broad skills goals targeted by the program. For example, a lifeskills program on anger management may have as an overall or program goal to help participants manage their anger better. This program goal says nothing about what skills the leader intends to train to help participants manage their anger better. The leader then decides that the broad skills goals are as follows (Nelson-Jones, 1990b):

Thinking skills	*Action skills*
Owning responsibility for anger	Using assertiveness skills to express anger constructively and request behavior changes
Choosing realistic personal rules	
Perceiving provocations differently	Handling aggressive criticism
Using coping self-talk	Using relaxation
Using visualization	

This list of broad skills goals may be sufficient to enable the leader to start outlining a program. However, even more detail is required of the component subgoals of each of the broad skills goals before the leader can decide how much time is necessary for training each skill and what each session's content should be.

For example, subgoals for the broad anger-management *thinking* skills goal of choosing realistic personal rules might be as follows:

Understanding how thinking influences feeling and action
The ability to identify unrealistic personal rules that generate anger
The ability to dispute unrealistic rules
The ability to reformulate self-oppressing unrealistic rules into self-supporting rules

Subgoals of the broad anger-management *action* skills goal of using relaxation might be as follows:

Understanding that relaxation may be used as an anger management self-help skill
Developing the skill of progressive muscular relaxation
Developing the skill of using visual images to relax
Developing brief relaxation self-help skills, such as controlled breathing
Developing relaxing recreational outlets

Depending on the length and complexity of the program, leaders may end up with a long list of goals and subgoals. Then leaders may be faced with the choice of how many skills they can train for in the group's life. A little, done thoroughly, tends to be preferable to too much, done superficially.

What Is the Knowledge Base for My Program?

Earlier it was mentioned that there are three main kinds of knowledge that lifeskills group leaders require: theoretical, research, and experiential. Leaders need to know the relevant theoretical and research literature for their skills groups. For instance, the preceding example of broad goals and subgoals for managing anger were derived from interventions described in the managing-anger literature (for example, Deffenbacher, Story, Brandon, Hogg, & Hazaleus, 1988; Feindler, Marriott, & Iwata, 1984). Also, if available, a further useful source of ideas is programs designed by others. For instance, Glick and Goldstein (1987) outlined three ten-week aggression replacement training programs entitled "Structured Learning Training," "Anger Control Training," and "Moral Education." Leaders who are open to their experience and who have previously run similar lifeskills groups can learn from what happened.

What Are the Structural Parameters of My Program?

Training-group leaders, though they sometimes have little choice when designing programs, always have to take structural parameters into account. Structural parameters described in the previous chapter include whether or not to have an open or closed group; group composition; the group's format and length; the frequency and duration of sessions; and the group's location, physical setting, and facilities.

What Environmental Considerations Must I Take into Account?

Leaders may design programs in consultation with third parties sponsoring or paying for programs. In designing programs, leaders must be mindful of how the content is likely to be perceived by significant others in their environments—for example, with training groups run in schools, principals, other teachers, and parents. In some instances, even if others are not actively involved, it may pay you to check out your program's content with them. Constructive suggestions and support may be positive outcomes. Unwanted pressure to edit your program may be a negative outcome.

What Management-of-Learning Considerations Must I Take into Account?

Most, if not all, of the considerations relevant to planning individual lifeskills group sessions are relevant to planning whole programs. As a designer and manager of lifeskills group learning, you should take into account clearly articulated initial, working, and ending stages; the sequencing of content across sessions; starting from where participants are; self-referent learning; involvement through participation; learning by hearing, observing, and doing; balancing facilitation with didactic input; adequate variety; realistic homework; availability of audiovisual materials and equipment; and suitable written training materials.

How Does My Program Help Participants Consolidate Trained Skills as Self-help Skills?

Ultimately, the effectiveness of a training group is what happens afterward. The crucial issue of how to consolidate the skills that your program targets as self-help skills for afterward is explored in some detail in Chapter 11.

How Am I Going to Evaluate My Program?

Leaders should always evaluate their training programs. Suggestions for evaluating lifeskills programs are provided in Chapter 12.

How Much Time Do I Have for Developing This Program?

Leader commitment of time can be a critical variable in designing training-group programs. Preparing written, verbal, and audiovisual materials consumes time. What you can do is heavily determined by the time and energy you either have or make available for this purpose. For example, if you lead any lifeskills group for the first time, you are going to have to commit much more time if you develop your own material than if you use existing materials. You may even have to exclude topics that you neither have time to develop nor can find suitable existing material for.

Outlining a Lifeskills Training Program
▼▼

Everybody who is incapable of learning has taken to teaching.

Oscar Wilde

Designing a training program is a journey from the general to the specific. A design for a program can start with one-sentence descriptions of each session, which are then developed into detailed session plans. Along the way there is much trial and error. As with many acts of creation, designing a lifeskills training program can be a messy business. However, ideally, at some point order emerges out of chaos. Leaders require the confidence and persistence to work through the inevitable problems that arise. Mustabatory fantasies about designing the perfect training program are very much discouraged.

When designing a lifeskills program, you make trade-offs and compromises all the time. Questions you may ask yourself include: How can limited time best be divided among the skills I want to train? What is a good balance between didactic and facilitative input? What is a good balance between working with the whole group and breaking down into pairs or subgroups? How can I best incorporate structured learning activities? and How can I make allowance for individual needs within the context of a group approach? Rarely are the answers to these questions straightforward. Try not to get discouraged if your program does not fall neatly into place at your first design attempt.

Let's take as an example outlining eight weekly two-hour sessions plus a three-month follow-up session for a training group in assertiveness skills to be run in a college counseling center. There is one leader. The mixed-sex group comprises eight participants who have either volunteered themselves or been referred by counselors. All participants are in the 18–22 age range.

The overall goal of the training group is to help participants become more assertive. The leader operationalizes being assertive into the following broad thinking and action skills areas:

Thinking skills	*Action skills*
Attributing cause accurately	Using "I" statements
Choosing realistic personal rules	Initiating
	Requesting changes in behavior
Using coping self-talk	
Realistically predicting gain and loss	Giving and receiving positive feedback

The leader decides to encourage self-assessment before the first session. During an intake interview, participants are asked to answer an assertiveness questionnaire in their own time. They are to bring their completed questionnaire to the first session. In addition, during the intake interview, participants are notified that they will be asked to complete the assertiveness questionnaire again at the group's end. Furthermore, participants will be requested to complete a three-month follow-up questionnaire focused on how well they have maintained their skills. Figure 4-1 provides an outline of the assertiveness program.

Figure 4-1 is an introductory overview of the structure and content of a lifeskills group. Ultimately, leaders require much more information—for example, detailed session outlines and well-developed training materials. Detailed session outlines are not provided here for our example assertiveness group for two main reasons. First, constructing session outlines gets reviewed later. Second, readers who have interest in other lifeskills might be bored with details of individual assertiveness sessions.

Exercise 6 is designed to give you an introductory opportunity to develop your skills at constructing a lifeskills group program. You may wish to return to Exercise 6 when you have worked through the book.

Exercise 6　Design a Lifeskills Training Program
▼▼

This exercise is probably best done on your own so that it forces you to think through some of the numerous issues in designing a lifeskills training program. However, the exercise can also be done in either pairs or small groups.

Design a training program for a lifeskill and a participant group of your choice. Assume that you have eight two-hour weekly sessions plus a three- to six-month follow-up session. You are the only leader. Your group consists of eight participants. Formulate and write out your plans in the following areas:

1. The overall goal of your group
2. The broad areas of thinking and action subskills for your group

3. A session-by session outline of your training program, using Figure 4-1 as a model
4. Detailed outlines for how you would distribute the time in each session (optional)

Session	Goals	Illustrative Content
Pregroup	Screening Assessment Facilitating self-assessment	Intake interview Assertiveness questionnaire

1	Getting acquainted
	Enhancing motivation
	Increasing awareness of what
	   assertiveness means
		Ice-breaking exercises
		Outline of program
		Lecturette on nonassertiveness,
		   aggression, and assertiveness
		Review of questionnaire answers/
		   setting personal goals
		Homework:
		Monitoring assertive and nonassertive
		   actions

2	Increasing awareness of
	–influence of thinking on feelings and
	   actions
	–owning responsibility for choosing
	–attributing cause accurately
		Discussion of homework
		Lecturette: ABC framework
		Exercise: being a chooser
		Exercise: attributing cause
		Group discussion
		Homework:
		Thinking-related exercises and self-
		   observation

3	Consolidating choosing and attributing
	   skills
	Developing skills of choosing realistic
	   personal rules
		Discussion of homework
		Lecturette/demonstration on
		   unrealistic rules
		Self-assessment exercise
		Group discussion
		Lecturette/demonstration on choosing
		   realistic rules
		Exercises and rehearsal
		Homework:
		Thinking-feeling-actions log
		Personal rules exercise

4	Consolidating rules skills
	Increasing awareness of sending
	   messages
	Developing initiating skills
	Developing realistic predicting skills
		Discussion of homework
		Lecturette/demonstrations on sending
		   messages and making "I"
		   statements
		Exercises and rehearsal
		Lecturette/demonstrations on taking
		   initiatives and predicting gain and
		   risk
		Group discussion
		Exercises and rehearsal
		Homework:
		Practicing "I" statements
		Initiating experiment
		Monitoring own and others' initiating
		   behaviors

Figure 4-1 An outline for an assertiveness training group.

Session	Goals	Illustrative Content
5	Consolidating "I" statements and initiating skills Developing skills in requesting behavior change	Discussion of homework Lecturette/demonstration on behavior change requests Self-assessment Group discussion Video role playing *Homework*: Monitoring own and others' behavior change requests Behavior change request experiment
6	Consolidating skills in requesting behavior change Developing coping self-talk skills Developing skills for coping with difficulties and setbacks	Discussion of homework Lecturette/demonstration on coping self-talk Exercises: coping self-talk Rehearsing behavior change requests and self-talk Rehearsing facing difficulties Group discussion *Homework*: Coping self-talk exercise Visualized rehearsal of facing difficulties Practicing all skills trained to date
7	Consolidating skills in requesting behavior change Developing skills in giving and receiving positive feedback Perceiving others' strengths	Discussion of homework Lecturette/demonstration on positive feedback skills Self-assessment Group discussion Rehearsal of positive feedback skills *Homework*: Positive feedback experiments Assessment questionnaire including coping with postgroup difficulties Practicing all skills trained to date
8	Consolidating trained skills as self-help skills Self-assessment Setting goals for future Evaluating program	Discussion of homework Summarizing of learnings by leader and participants Exercise: personal assertiveness goals Discussion/rehearsal of maintaining skills Lecturette: developing skills after the group ends Program evaluation questionnaire Group discussion/goodbyes *Postgroup homework*: Rehearsing, practicing, and developing assertiveness skills
Three-month follow-up	Consolidating trained skills as self-help skills Enhancing motivation Giving mutual support	Progress questionnaire Group discussion Discussion/rehearsal of maintaining and developing assertiveness skills

Figure 4-1 *(continued)*

▼ **Chapter Highlights**

    ▼ In designing lifeskills training programs, leaders are hypothesis makers. Each program represents a series of "If . . . then . . ." statements relating process and content to desired outcomes.

    ▼ A lifeskills program can be designed around existing training manuals and packages; in consultation with third parties; on your own; and in consultation with participants in your training group.

    ▼ Considerations in designing lifeskills programs include stating goals in skills terms; possessing an adequate knowledge base; knowing the group's structural parameters; acknowledging environmental considerations; managing learning considerations; consolidating trained skills as self-help skills; doing an evaluation; and working within the time the leader has.

    ▼ Designing lifeskills training programs is a journey from the general to the specific. Drawing up a moderately detailed session-by-session outline is a useful intermediate step.

5

How to Assess and Help Self-Assessment

Please listen carefully and try to hear
What I'm not saying
What I'd like to be able to say
What for survival I need to say
But what I can't say

Anonymous

Chapter Questions

Why is assessment in lifeskills training groups important?

What are some methods of assessing participants' lifeskills?

How can participants assess themselves?

How can group leaders devise their own assessment measures?

How might participants specify personal goals and subgoals for developing their skills?

Introduction

Assessing participants' skills is an important process that requires delicate handling throughout all four stages of a lifeskills training group. Although as a leader you may have your own valid reasons for assessing participants' lifeskills, ultimately what counts is that participants acquire the "take-away" skills of how to assess their own lifeskills. Consequently, right from the start, assessment is a means of helping participants assume more responsibility both for learning lifeskills and for maintaining, developing, and using them afterward. Clumsy assessment can do more harm than good. For instance, it may threaten participants, create expectations of excessive dependency on your expertise, and obscure their skills strengths by focusing too much on their skills weaknesses.

A simplistic distinction can be made between a medical and a lifeskills model of assessment. In the medical model, physicians are the experts who collect relevant information about patients to make diagnoses and prognoses that lead to treatment interventions, such as medication, bed rest, and surgery. The role of patients is not to play an active part in the diagnostic process but rather to speak when spoken to and follow their physicians' advice. In the lifeskills model, leaders collaborate with participants to identify their strengths and weaknesses so that participants may better understand both how they sustain their current level of functioning and how they can work for change. This model of assessment encourages self-help rather than reliance on external experts. In reality, the two models of assessment overlap. There can be numerous agendas, both overt and hidden, for conducting and participating in lifeskills group assessment. Also, skilled physicians encourage patients to play active roles in understanding and managing their health.

Can assessment be overdone? The answer is most definitely yes. Leaders need to be clear about their purposes for engaging in assessment and the likely impact that their assessment behaviors are going to have on participants. Also, leaders conducting either group or individual assessments require sensitivity to when "enough is enough." Furthermore, partly to overcome resistances, leaders require the ability to establish rapport when assessing.

Purposes of Assessment
▼▼▼

Training-group leaders, participants, and third parties may each have their own agendas and purposes for conducting and participating in assessment.

Leader Purposes

Leader purposes in conducting assessment procedures include the following. First, assessment may be used for *selection*. Leaders may wish to ascertain whether participants meet the criteria for inclusion in or exclusion from their proposed lifeskills group. Where space is limited, a further purpose of assessment may be prediction of those most likely to gain from the group. Second, assessment may be used to *improve program design*. Initial assessment of skills can provide valuable information for leaders to alter and fine tune programs to meet the needs of each participant group rather than assume that the same program is right for all groups. Third, assessment can *motivate* participants. By breaking skills down, assessment can make their attainment seem more manageable. Assessment can help participants acknowledge their strengths as well as identify their weaknesses. Furthermore, assessment can provide the information on the basis of which participants can set their personal goals.

A fourth reason why leaders focus on assessment in lifeskills training groups is to *encourage participant self-assessment*. Lifeskills are for life, not just for the duration of a lifeskills group. Consequently, leaders always need to be mindful of ways to encourage transfer and maintenance of skills. An essential ingredient of skills transfer and maintenance is participants' ability to engage in the self-talk of monitoring and, where necessary, changing their behaviors. Fifth, skilled assessment can help leaders *state working definitions of participants' problems*. Frequently, lifeskills group participants will describe problems in their personal, work, or leisure lives, but show little insight into how to manage them. Participants may make remarks like: "We always seem to end up arguing," "I just don't know what to do with my time now that I'm unemployed," and "I'm lonely and wish I had more friends." Competent training-group leaders are able to take these descriptive statements and assist participants in arriving at working definitions of their problems. Working definitions identify the skills weaknesses that sustain problems. To take a simple example, the descriptive statement of a problem "I am lonely and wish I had more friends" might be broken down into thinking skills weaknesses, such as having unrealistic personal rules about rejection, and action skills weaknesses, such as poor skills at initiating relationships and conversing. A working definition of a problem gives the participant a set of keys with which to open the door to change.

Assessment is also necessary for *monitoring the progress of individuals and the group*. Individual assessment can range from feedback during the initial acquisition and rehearsal of a skill to monitoring success in homework assignments and attempts to transfer skills into daily life. Group assessment can be either getting an overall impression of the individual assessments or systematically assessing all participants in the same way. Assessment can play a critical part in *consolidating participants' self-help skills*. Assessment at the end of a training group focuses on helping participants transfer, maintain, and develop their skills on their own. Participants' skills strengths and weaknesses require reassessing so that participants can acknowledge progress and identify areas for further work. Additionally, potential barriers to transfer and maintenance of skills, both on the part of participants and also of their environments, require assessment to develop appropriate coping strategies.

A further purpose of training-group assessment may be to *fulfill obligations to third parties*. Leaders may be required to provide assessments to third parties, such as businesses, government agencies, and other sponsoring organizations. This information may be used in decisions covering such matters as selection, promotion, salary increase, transfer, and even termination. Other instances of providing assessment data to third parties include assisting in parole decisions for juvenile delinquents, discharge decisions for psychiatric hospital inpatients; and providing grades in educational institutions where a lifeskills program forms part of a formal curriculum.

Assessment by leaders can also be used to *evaluate training groups*. Such evaluations can serve longer-term purposes outside of the immediate interests of the group. Evaluation that assesses both processes and outcomes may improve future groups. If this evaluative research is of publishable quality, others may learn from it too. In addition, evaluations can help training-group leaders demonstrate accountability to their paymasters. Demonstrating accountability may engender goodwill, be good publicity, lessen the likelihood of budget cuts, and increase the possibility of budget increases.

Participant Purposes

Participants may have their own purposes when it comes to assessment. Some of these purposes may match those of their leaders, but others may differ. "Legitimate" purposes that motivate participants to take part in assessment are those destined to help them achieve the stated goals of their groups. Participants wishing to improve their

lifeskills cooperate in assessment for reasons that include getting selected, better understanding their strengths and weaknesses, setting
personal goals for themselves, monitoring their progress, and consolidating their self-help skills at the end of a group. In addition, participants sent on training programs may wish to demonstrate that
they have met the expectations of their sponsors.

Sometimes participants may have reasons for engaging in or re-
sisting assessment that diverge considerably from those of their
group leaders. Consciously or unconsciously, participants may have
their own separate agendas. Here are some examples:

▼ Annie is a delinquent teenager in a remand home. The staff have
  nominated her for a training group on controlling aggression and
  learning to become more assertive and cooperative. Annie resists
  the notion that she needs these skills and does everything she can
  to frustrate the leader's efforts at assessment.
▼ Lily thinks of herself as the golden girl among the up-and-coming
  young managers in her company. Lily's boss recognizes her
  strengths, but also thinks she is far too hard on those who work
  under her. The leader's attempts to get Lily to honestly assess her
  people skills are hampered by three of Lily's other agendas: her
  desire to be seen in the best possible light by the leader; her wish to
  maintain her picture of herself as having superior people skills;
  and her fear of a negative report being sent back to her boss.
▼ Bernardo takes part in a human relations training course as part of
  the general education program at his college. Bernardo is not interested in improving the way he relates, but he is very motivated
  to attain good grades. Consequently, in the assessment exercises in
  the course he plays a game of trying to provide the answers that are
  likely to obtain him a high grade rather than making a sincere
  effort to appraise his skills strengths and weaknesses.

Even at the best of times, participants are likely to bring resistances and fears when it comes to assessing their lifeskills. Many may
be unfamiliar with thinking of themselves as needing lifeskills as contrasted with just doing what comes naturally. Assessment implies the
possibility that participants may be inadequate in some ways. These
inadequacies may be difficult to admit. Also, identification of weaknesses means that participants may have to leave the safe ways of the
present and change their behaviors. Added to this, some participants
may be genuinely disadvantaged if they are assessed and found wanting—for instance, those being considered for promotion in business
and industry.

Third-Party Purposes

Third parties may also have interests in the assessment of participants' lifeskills. Frequently people are assessed by others as being

ready for or needing to go to training programs to improve their skills. In business organizations, sometimes the suggestion that someone attend a training group is intended as a reward—for instance, for an employee who is being considered for a supervisory or managerial promotion. Sometimes the suggestion is intended to improve another's performance, without casting any negative aspersions on her or his abilities. On other occasions, there may be a clear message that the individual sent to attend training is required to perform better in the area in question or negative consequences will follow. In educational institutions, administrators may recommend teachers for training groups, and teachers and parents may recommend students for them. Other instances of third parties assessing people as needing to attend lifeskills training groups include therapists for their clients, nurses and physicians for their patients, ministers for people intending to get married or in marital difficulty, career workers for the unemployed, and social workers for people with substance abuse problems.

Leaders require sensitivity to the interests of those who have recommended participants for a lifeskills training group. Sometimes third parties can be actively supportive of participants' attaining training objectives. In such instances there may be no conflict of interest between assessments conducted for the participants' purposes and those required by third parties. Indeed, third parties such as teachers may be asked to provide feedback on how participants are using their skills in their natural settings. On other occasions, leaders may be in the much more difficult position of being contracted to provide reports to a third party that may not always help participants attain their personal goals outside the group.

Methods of Assessment and Self-Assessment
▼▼

Assessment can be either leader-centered or participant-centered. In leader-centered assessment, the source of power and control is in the leader. It is the leader who decides what assessment takes place, when and, how. In participant-centered assessment, participants discuss with the leader those methods of assessment that are most likely to be of value to them. Participants then make the final decisions as to which assessment methods are used. The dividing line between leader-centered and participant-centered assessment is not exact. Leaders can establish expectations that are conducive or run counter to participants' assuming responsibility for their learning. In practice, the difference may be more in how an assessment method is used than in the method itself. Also, it may be in the best interests of participants to trust leader assessment choices rather than to get bogged down in discussing them at the expense of time spent developing their skills. Nevertheless, the fundamental point remains: participants will not have their leaders around after the group ends, so both they and their leaders must collaborate to develop their self-assessment skills.

In counseling and psychotherapy, it is important that counselor and client form a working alliance to attain therapeutic objectives. Similarly, in lifeskills groups, it is important that leader and participants form a working alliance to attain training objectives. Therapeutic working alliances are more likely to occur where the counselor offers empathic understanding, genuineness, and respect to the client. The emotional climate should be task-oriented, yet at the same time relaxed and friendly. The same holds true for training groups. Leaders can introduce the idea of assessment in ways that enlist the interest of participants and make them feel that the findings may be of value to their attaining their personal goals. On the other hand, leaders can introduce assessment in ways that threaten and distance participants and make them feel that the lifeskills group is a waste of time.

Leaders have to design assessment procedures that are appropriate for their specific training goals. In the following pages, different methods of assessment and of encouraging self-assessment are reviewed.

Interviews

Interviews in lifeskills training groups can be conducted by either leaders or participants. Formal leader assessment interviews tend to take place, if at all, in the preparatory stage of training groups. At other times during their groups, leaders may ask a series of assessment questions that constitute a more informal kind of interviewing. However, this is likely to be done with other group participants present, whereas intake interviews are conducted one-to-one. Leader purposes in intake interviews can include helping potential participants assess whether the program is right for them as well as helping them understand better their strengths and weaknesses in the targeted lifeskills area.

Areas for Assessment

In an intake interview for a lifeskills training group, areas for leader assessment and participant self-assessment may include the following: reasons for wanting to join the lifeskills group, including whether a referral was involved; knowledge and expectations about the training group; motivation for change and ability to handle setbacks; level of functioning in the skills area—behavior, thinking, feelings, and physical reactions in specific situations; the length of time the skills area has been a problem and brief details of the problem's history; perceived strengths both in relation to the targeted skills and also in other relevant areas; the degree of interference of the skills weaknesses with the participant's well-being; factors maintaining the skills weaknesses—antecedents and payoffs of problematic behaviors; past coping strategies and their consequences; the nature of the participant's other problems; support factors for attaining training objectives; environmental barriers to attaining training objectives; and current life stresses and demands.

Assessment Interview Skills

A few assessment interview skills are briefly mentioned here. Most of these skills can fruitfully be adapted to leading training groups. For a more detailed discussion of the skills of individual interviewing, might wish to consult Brammer (1985), Cormier and Cormier (1985), Egan (1990), or Nelson-Jones (1988b).

Attention to physical setting. Attention should be paid to the environment and seating arrangements. Quiet, privacy, absence of interruption, and pleasant decor are each important. Chairs should be of the same height, possibly with a coffee table between them, and placed at a slight angle to avoid the impression of a face-to-face interrogation.

Empathic understanding. Leaders need to show that they are interested in the perceptions and personal meanings of participants and that they value and respect them as unique persons. Leaders require the skills of both understanding and also showing that they have understood what participants try to tell them. This understanding entails creating a safe emotional climate and having good skills at decoding verbal, vocal, and body messages. A useful skill is to reflect what the participant has just said and pause to see if he or she wants to continue before asking your next question. By doing this you show that you have heard, check out the accuracy of your understanding, give yourself more time to formulate your next question, and help prevent participants from feeling interrogated.

Use of questions. Various kinds of questions help assessment and self-assessment. Open-ended questions, unlike closed-ended questions, allow participants much choice in how they wish to respond. An example of a closed-ended question is: "Is your boss good or bad?" whereas an open-ended question might be: "What do you think about your boss?" Open-ended questions can be helpful at the start of interviews to encourage participants to tell their stories in their own words. They can be useful later to help participants share personal meanings without your putting words into their mouths.

When conducting thorough assessments, leaders require detailed information. Questioning for specifics helps participants work on their problems by understanding them more specifically and clearly. These kinds of questions include: "Can you give a specific example?" "How did you and the other person actually behave?" and "What were your thoughts in the situation?" Leaders often need to clarify that their own and participants' understanding of words and phrases corresponds. For example, participants who say they feel low, might be asked: "When you say you feel low, what do you mean?"

Reality-testing questions can also help clarify skills strengths and weaknesses. Examples of such questions are: "You say that you have no friends; where is the evidence?" or "You say you are poor at public speaking; where is the evidence that you are poor and is there any evidence that you may have some strengths as well in the area?" An advantage of such questions is that they encourage participants to confront themselves with the evidence rather than having the confrontations coming from the leader. Leader confrontation may be more threatening and less useful in helping participants to perceive the evidence accurately.

Use of experiential information. Leaders may learn much about participants' skills strengths and weaknesses through observing body and voice messages. Skilled interviewers "listen with the third ear" and learn to trust their inner experiencing of the client. Sometimes the voice and body messages that may be indicative of skills strengths and weaknesses are sent clearly. For example, people may or may not take care of their physical appearance, look as though they are on drugs, attend the interview on time, maintain a reasonable level of eye contact, talk about their feelings in ways that show they feel them too, and so on. On other occasions, the cues that the participant is anxious, economizing on the truth, confused, or something else may be much more subtle. Leaders may choose to stay within the participant's frame of reference and just reflect the messages they receive, and possibly ask for clarification. Alternatively, leaders may go further and gently or more forcibly confront participants, not only with how they experience their behavior but also with its possible significance for their lifeskills difficulties.

Use of role playing. Especially where relationship skills are involved, valuable information may be provided by leaders' doing assessment role playing with participants. Lifeskills entail sending voice and body as well as verbal messages. Leaders are limited in their ability to assess if they restrict themselves to verbal descriptions of behavior. At its simplest, an assessment role-play might entail asking a participant to imagine you are someone with whom they experience difficulty. Then they are instructed to speak to you with the voice and body as well as the verbal messages that they would use in real life. Elaborations of this can include more effort in setting the scene and coaching you in how to respond. You can also mirror their behavior or reverse roles to help them assess how they communicate. Participants may need encouragement to overcome their anxiety about engaging in role playing. You can explain to them that you are more likely to be able to help them if you observe how they actually behave rather than just hear their descriptions. You understand that they may feel uncomfortable at first, but this should pass.

Summarizing. Summaries can be used at various stages of the assessment interview. They can perform a bridging function between the different sections of the developing session. Summaries can also be very useful at the end of assessment interviews when they can give the session closure, ensure that leaders have accurately understood participants and provide feedback to participants on skills strengths and weaknesses. Participants should always be asked both their reactions to leader end-of-session summaries and also whether or not they wish to add anything. Sometimes it is a good idea to have the participant summarize the gist of the session in his or her own words to check out how much he or she really has understood. If relevant, it is important at the end of an assessment interview to communicate whether or not the participant has been admitted to the group. Also, you should check out whether or not he or she understands the group's administrative details.

Exercise 7 Practice Self-Assessment and Assessment of a Specific Lifeskill
▾▾

1. Self-assessment
   Select a specific lifeskill that you wish to improve. Write out an analysis of your strengths and weaknesses for this lifeskill. Cover each of the areas for assessment mentioned in the text, starting with "motivation for change and ability to handle setbacks."
2. Conducting an assessment interview
   Acting as a training-group leader, conduct an interview with a partner in which together you assess a specific lifeskill that he or she wishes to improve. Pay attention to the areas of assessment mentioned in the text. Select a suitable physical setting for your interview and try to use the following skills:

Empathic understanding
Good use of questions (open-ended, inviting specifics, reality-testing)
Use of experiential information
Use of role playing
Summarizing

Afterward discuss with your partner and then reverse roles so that your partner acts as the training-group leader interviewing you about a specific lifeskill that you wish to improve.

Peer Interviews

Peer interviews in which participants help each other assess lifeskills can be interspersed throughout training groups. For example, participants can be asked to pair off and to spend ten minutes each way, with one acting as interviewer and the other as interviewee. Interview tasks can include initial assessment of a skills area, monitoring progress and homework, and end-of-lifeskills-group assessment. During a group, the leader cannot afford to spend much time with any single participant in comparison to the others. Consequently, one of the most effective ways of encouraging assessment and self-assessment is to make time for brief participant interviews. Helping others often helps participants with their own self-assessment. Furthermore, participant interviews get everybody in the group involved. A variation of interviewing in pairs is to have triads in which the third participant acts as either an observer who later makes comments or acts as a coach for the interviewer.

Group Interaction

Participants can learn much about their lifeskills through interacting in groups as well as in pairs. A skilled leader facilitates participants' learning from each other. Some of these leader skills are presented in the next chapter. Ways that group interaction helps participants assess their lifeskills include discussing the purposes of assessment, discussing problems of mutual concern, obtaining feedback from others, learning from others' experiences inside and outside the group, and observing how others behave. If the numbers in a training group are large, assessment through group interaction can be encouraged by subgrouping. Sometimes audio or video recording and playback of group interactions provides participants with valuable self-assessment information.

Observation in Natural Settings

Assessment information can be obtained about participants through observations made about them in their natural environments. Often participants are recommended for lifeskills training groups on the basis of observations by others—for instance, managers by senior managers, workers by bosses, patients by doctors, teachers by administrators, pupils by teachers, and clients by counselors. Sometimes either verbal or written reports will be sent to leaders explaining the referral. Referral information may be useful in helping leaders assess both participants' lifeskills and their degree of environmental support. However, referral information requires cautious treatment since it may be heavily influenced by referees' personal needs and biases.

Observational assessment information about behavior in natural settings can come from many sources and be collected either systematically or otherwise. Teachers, parents, spouses, friends, bosses, and colleagues can each be sources of such information. However, such people may require instruction in what to look for. Additionally, leaders can spend time observing participants in their natural settings and seeing how they exhibit lifeskills strengths and weaknesses. For instance, leaders may observe in action either managers unskilled at conducting meetings or people unskilled at making requests in shops. Collecting information from natural settings can take place before, at the start of, during, at the end of, and after training groups. Such information may be especially useful in assessing the extent to which lifeskills are transferred to everyday life.

Behavior Rating Forms

Systematic collection of observational information involves the use of behavior rating forms. The simplest way of recording behaviors is quantitative—namely, counting the number of behaviors in each category that occur in a given period of time. Figure 5-1 is an example of a behavior rating form that might be used to assess conversational skills,

Initiates topic	
Maintains conversation	
Reveals personal information	
Asks for personal information	
Gives opinion	
Asks opinion	
Listens	
Agrees	
Disagrees	
Interrupts	
Shows aggression	
Shows support	
Shows appreciation	
Uses humor	

Figure 5-1 A sample behavior rating form for verbal conversational skills.

say talking to friends or interacting with family members at dinner. If this form is being used to collect initial or baseline data, the subject should be asked to behave as closely as possible to normal.

This behavior rating form can be filled out quantitatively by marking each time the subject engages in a category of behavior. A qualitative dimension can be built into the assessment by putting a minus sign (−) for each inappropriate behavior and a plus sign (+) for each appropriate behavior. Filling in the form might be made even more qualitative by using a five-point scale of appropriateness for each behavior, ranging from 1 for very inappropriate to 5 for very appropriate. If the rater wishes to assess more than one person's behavior, each person can be assigned a column with her or his name at the top. Behavior rating forms can focus on voice and body as well as verbal messages. Because there are many issues connected with what actually is a unit of behavior and what each category measures, leaders have to think carefully before using such rating forms. Also, untrained raters may require training. If correctly used, behavior rating forms filled out in natural settings can provide a useful record of both initial baseline behavior and of transfer of training and change over time.

Observational behavior ratings may be made on how participants handle situations simulated from their natural settings. For example, managers can be given tasks such as either counseling underperforming workers or taking part in group discussions on marketing initiatives (Gratton, 1985). Behavior rating forms can also be used during lifeskills training groups. For example, in a program on conversational skills, the group can be divided into a "goldfish" format with an inner and an outer circle. Participants in the inner circle are instructed to converse with each other; participants in the outer circle rate the behaviors of one or more of their peers in the inner circle.

Sociometric Measures

Moreno (1934) developed the sociometric method to establish patterns of feelings of acceptance and rejection and of like and dislike among members of groups. Sociometric ratings can be made in participants' natural settings to ascertain how they behave and are perceived to behave. For example, a leader running a team-building course for a group of workers in a company may assess such matters as patterns of like and dislike, of respect and disrespect, and of frequency of contact in the group. Teachers who run lifeskills programs to develop pupils' making-friends skills may trace the patterns of interactions within a class group by gathering information about whom the children consider their friends, to whom they feel they can disclose personal information, and whom they would invite to activities such as birthday parties.

Sociometric data can be collected by means of interview schedules, questionnaires, or direct observation. Circle diagrams provide a simple way of collecting sociometric information. For instance, a classroom group of children might be given a rating form with a series of four concentric circles of increasing size. They could be asked to put the name of their best friend or friends in the inner circle, their good friends in the next circle, their acquaintances in the next, and the names of those people whom they dislike in the outer circle. Another example is that sociometric data are often presented by allocating a numbered circle to each member of a group and then drawing lines with arrows between the circles indicating contact and either like (a straight line) or dislike (a broken line). Sometimes, in depictions of patterns of family interaction, females are depicted as circles and males as squares (no offense meant!).

Participants may have mixed feelings about being observed in their natural settings. Some may welcome it as a means of improving their lifeskills. Others may see it as an invasion of privacy that interferes with the building of trust with their leaders. Furthermore, collecting information in natural settings may threaten participants. For instance, evidence of unpopularity may cause pain. In addition, some participants may fear that assessment information collected in natural settings—for instance, at work—will be used against rather than for them. Leaders require sensitivity to participants' feelings regarding both whether and how they collect this information. Furthermore, leaders require skills at giving what may be unwelcome feedback.

Participant Self-Observation and Monitoring

At every stage of a training group, participants can collect their own self-observation data. Self-observation and monitoring takes place both inside and outside scheduled group sessions. Participant self-observation has many purposes for both leaders and participants, including initial assessment of skills strengths and weaknesses, establishing a baseline against which to measure change, testing out accuracy of perceptions regarding behavior, monitoring progress, monitoring homework assignments, collecting data on the consequences of trying out changed behaviors, providing information on transfer of skills to real-life settings, and contributing to end-of-group assessment of strengths and weaknesses.

Diaries and Journals

With the growth of cognitive-behavioral approaches to training, increasingly participants are being encouraged to monitor not only their actions, but also their thoughts and feelings. Keeping a diary or journal is one way of monitoring and recording observations in a lifeskills area. Special attention can be paid to writing up critical incidents where skills may have been used well or poorly. The learnings for the future from different experiences can be recorded. Although diaries and journals may be useful, some participants find this approach too unstructured and too easy to ignore. A further drawback is that the collection of information may be insufficiently systematic. Nevertheless, occasions may occur where the freedom allowed by choosing what one writes in a diary or personal journal has much to recommend it. Also, participants have different learning styles and some may work hard and profitably on this method of self-assessment.

Thinking, Feeling, and Behavior Logs

Based on the work of cognitive psychologists and psychiatrists like Albert Ellis (1962, 1980, 1989) and Aaron Beck (Beck & Emery 1985; Beck & Greenberg, 1974), there has been a trend toward self-observation and monitoring using an A-B-C format. In the A-B-C format,

A = the activating event or stimulus,
B = the individual's beliefs, thoughts, and visual images about the activating event, and
C = the individual's feeling and behaviors as a consequence of the activating event; may be extended to include the consequences provided by others for the individual's behaviors.

What cognitive therapists try to do by means of the A-B-C format is to go beyond description of behavior to show clients how their thoughts, feelings, and behaviors are interrelated. The idea is that how individuals feel and behave at C is heavily influenced by how they think at B about A, the activating event. Figure 5-2 shows entries for one day in a thinking-, feeling-, and behavior-monitoring log for a

A (the activating event, starting with date, time, and place)	B (beliefs and thoughts)	C (consequences, feelings, behaviors, others' reactions)
July 14, 8 a.m., home Wife comes to breakfast in curlers.	Why can't she make more effort to please me?	Resentment, made sarcastic comment, stormed out of house.
July 14, 1:15 p.m., work My secretary is late back from her lunch break.	She is ripping the company off and does not respect me.	Very angry and tense, made no comment, gave her extra task, tension between us.
July 14, 7:45 p.m., home Read son's average report card.	I'm paying for him to go to a private school, he should work harder.	Got mad, told son to shape up or else, son withdrew to his room.

Figure 5-2 Sample thinking, feeling, and behavior log in the A-B-C format.

man entering a managing-anger lifeskills group. Often such a log is kept for one or two weeks.

The following guidelines may help you in using thinking, feeling, and behavior logs:

1. Always supply the log yourself. Do not expect participants to make up their own logs. They may not do so in the first place, and even if they do, they may get them wrong.
2. Keep your log simple and in line with participants' capacities to understand and complete it.
3. Provide participants with a rationale for why it is important to fill in the log. You need to motivate them to do so. You can say something like, "Filling in the log conscientiously will help both of us understand your difficulties and thus make better decisions about how to handle them."
4. Give clear instructions on how to fill in the log, and make sure participants are capable of following them.
5. Reward participants for filling in their logs by showing an interest in their answers and praising them. This guideline is based on the basic behavioral principle that actions that are rewarded are more likely to be repeated.
6. Encourage participants to use their logs as a way of building their self-assessment skills. Try to get them to take an active role in analyzing the significance of the findings. Get them to share their assessment of what their logs communicate to them about their patterns of thinking, feeling, and behaving.
7. Do not expect participants to change their behavior on the basis of self-observation alone. They are likely to need assistance, work, and practice to build their skills strengths.

Audiovisual Feedback

Participants may learn much by observing how they actually behave in various lifeskills areas. For example, a couple who join a managing-conflict lifeskills group can be videotaped after being given the instruction: "Show us how you behave when you have a good fight at home. Do not hold back and be polite—try to make it as real as possible." Another example is that of employees sent to a public-speaking course who can be videotaped showing how they currently speak before an audience. In each of these instances, participants can be shown the playback and asked to evaluate their skills strengths and weaknesses.

Audiovisual feedback can also be used during a lifeskills program to encourage participant self-assessment. A couple who are learning managing-conflict skills can be asked to show how they might use their new skills in a difficult area for them. At the playback, they might be asked to identify which of their own and their partner's behaviors they thought were helpful or harmful. Sometimes participants may fill in a yes-or-no checklist when they watch the playback (Saskatchewan Newstart, 1973). For instance, items on a checklist for someone learning public-speaking skills might include, "I talked directly to the audience," "I gave a clear introduction," "I avoided a large number of *um*'s" and "My voice could be heard easily."

Psychological Tests and Lifeskills Inventories

▼▼

Numerous psychological tests and skills inventories are available for leaders to choose from. Anastasi (1988) writes, "A psychological test is essentially an objective and standardized measure of a sample of behavior" (p. 23). "Objective" means that the test has been constructed to measure and score the behavior under consideration without interpretation by the tester. "Standardized" means that the test will be administered in the same way to all participants and scored so that an individual's score can be compared with the scores of a group of similar people. Traditionally, psychological tests have been developed to gather information in the following areas: mental ability, aptitudes, achievement, personality, and interests and values. Sometimes psychological tests are designed to be self-administered rather than administered by a professional person—for example, Holland's Self-Directed Search (Holland, 1987).

Although they overlap, a distinction is made here between psychological tests and skills inventories. Skills inventories are self-report measures designed to elicit participants' perceptions of their behaviors and cognitions in different skills areas, such as assertiveness. Clearly, leaders have to choose skills inventories that meet their assessment purposes for any lifeskills group they run.

Who Can Use Psychological Tests and Lifeskills Inventories?

Leaders need to be competent in the three major aspects of using tests and skills inventories: selection, administration and scoring, and interpreting results. Test publishers and distributors may apply user qualification criteria before making tests and inventories available. In all events, there is an ethical obligation for lifeskills group leaders to be trained and competent in the use of any test or skills inventory they select.

Sources of Information About Tests and Skills Inventories

Leaders may find information on tests and measures in sourcebooks, publishers' catalogs, and research articles and books.

Sourcebooks

A very important source of information is the series of Mental Measurements Yearbooks compiled by the Buros Institute of Mental Measurement at the University of Nebraska. The introduction to the most recent yearbook states, "The *Ninth Mental Measurements Yearbook*, like the eight earlier yearbooks in the series, is designed to assist test users in education, psychology, and industry to choose more judiciously from the many tests available" (Mitchell, 1985, p. xiii). The yearbooks are comprised of reviews of tests published during a specified period; thus, each yearbook supplements rather than supplants previous yearbooks. The Buros Institute has also compiled *Tests in Print 111* (Mitchell, 1983), which is an index to tests, test reviews, and the literature on specific tests.

Test Critiques (Vols. 1–6) is another series of test review books (Keyser & Sweetland, 1984–1987). Instituted in Volume 3, each volume has a cumulative subject index incorporating the tests reviewed in all editions to date. A further valuable source of information is *Tests* (Sweetland & Keyser, 1986). The introduction to the second edition states, "*Tests*, a reference guide containing information on thousands of assessment instruments, is designed especially for psychologists, educators, and human resource personnel who search for tests to satisfy assessment needs" (p. ix). Readers are advised to check out the most current editions of each of these sourcebooks.

Publishers' Catalogs

Test publishers' and distributors' catalogs provide another source of information about which tests are available. A comprehensive directory and index of North American test publishers, with their addresses, is provided at the end of the latest *Mental Measurements Yearbook*. Anastasi (1988) provides a listing of the names and addresses of some of the larger American publishers and distributors of psychological tests.

Important test publishers and distributors outside North America include the National Foundation for Educational Research—Nelson (Darville House, 2 Oxford Road East, Windsor, Berkshire SL4 1DF, England); the Australian Council for Educational Research (P.O. Box 210, Hawthorn, Victoria 3122, Australia); Harcourt Brace Jovanovich, Australia (Locked Bag 16, Marrickville, New South Wales 2204, Australia); and the New Zealand Council for Educational Research (Education House, 178–182 Willis Street, Wellington, New Zealand). Quite apart from publishing and distributing local instruments, these organizations are often distribution agents for North American test publishers.

Research Articles and Books

Research articles evaluating training in specific lifeskills areas can be a good source of information about tests and skills inventories. Also, books that summarize research and practice in different skills areas can provide leaders with helpful ideas on assessment measures. Additionally, leaders can keep abreast of developments in testing by reading measurement journals such as *Educational and Psychological Measurement, Measurement and Evaluation in Guidance,* the *Journal of Personality Assessment,* and the *Journal of Applied Measurement.*

Assessing Psychological Tests and Skills Inventories

Leaders always need to evaluate the information provided in the manual of any test they consider using. *Standards for Educational and Psychological Testing* is a comprehensive guide to the evaluation of psychological tests (American Psychological Association, 1985). Additionally, leaders are well advised to look at the individual items in, if not to actually complete, any assessment instrument they seriously review.

The following are some important considerations in reviewing a psychological test or lifeskills inventory manual:

Rationale: Review the constructor's purpose in devising the instrument. Also, look for the date when the instrument and its manual were first published and for any subsequent revisions.

Who can take the instrument? Carefully examine the population for which the instrument is intended.

Administration details: Administration details include difficulty of administration from the leader's viewpoint; whether any special training or professional qualifications are needed; the time the instrument takes to complete; whether it is for group or individual administration; the format or formats in which the instrument is available; whether there are practice items; whether the administration instructions are clear, including allowable variations in administration and their likely consequences; and whether the instrument is machine- or hand-scored and the ease with which scoring can be performed.

Reliability: Reliability refers to the consistency of an instrument. Different ways of assessing reliability include the same instrument taken at two different times, test-retest reliability; two different forms of the same instrument, alternate-forms reliability; and measuring internal consistency on comparable halves of a test from a single administration, split-half reliability. Usually reliability is expressed in terms of correlation coefficients indicating the extent to which two measures are related, with test-retest and internal consistency coefficients possibly being most common. High reliability is not in itself a measure of high validity.

Validity: Validity, a central concept in measurement, means how well an instrument measures what it sets out to measure. The three main kinds of validity are predictive, content, and construct. Predictive or criterion-oriented validity refers to the soundness with which predictions can be made on the basis of a test score against some future criterion, such as the future performance of a task. Content validity refers to how well the instrument samples the behaviors it seeks to measure. Construct validity involves setting up a number of hypotheses about the test variable as a construct or concept and then examining the evidence relative to these hypotheses (Professional Affairs Board, 1980). When assessing the validity of a measure, leaders need to be clear about their own purposes, since the kinds of validity that are important for them relate to their purposes.

Item analysis and scale development: Test items can be analyzed qualitatively, in terms of their content and form, and quantitatively, in terms of their statistical properties, such as item difficulty and item validity. Some manuals provide details of how the items for a test were selected and analyzed. Furthermore, many tests add the scores on groups of individual items to form scales. A manual may provide details on the rationale, statistical and otherwise, for the selection of items to form a test's scales.

Norms: Psychological tests are generally interpreted with reference to norms. These norms illustrate the performance on the test of the population or populations for which the test was intended. Norms enable the test score of an individual to be related to the distribution of scores of a suitably large and relevant reference group.

Interpretation: The psychological test or skills inventory constructor's intentions for interpreting results should be clearly indicated. Information should be provided on common interpretive errors and on any other special factors that might affect interpretation.

Choosing Psychological Tests and Skills Inventories

Since there are both a multiplicity of group leader, participant, and third-party assessment purposes and a wide variety of lifeskills areas, generalizations about choosing psychological tests and skills inventories should be made and treated with caution. An instrument may be useful for training purposes if it fulfills some of the following criteria. First, there should be a considerable amount of evidence about just what lifeskill it measures. At best, most psychological tests and skills inventories are self-report measures rather than objective measures of observable behaviors. Second, the instrument should lend itself to being used for self-assessment and not just for leader assessment. Third, using the instrument should fit into the lifeskills learning process rather than disrupt it. Such disruptions may be either practical, in terms of time and inconvenience, or emotional, in terms of generating resistances, or both. Leaders should avoid saturation testing, involving the "buckshot" use of a comprehensive battery of tests and skills inventories. They should beware of testing for testing's sake. Instead, leaders should aim for precision testing, using only an instrument or instruments appropriate to the specific needs and states of readiness of a particular group of participants.

A further issue in selecting psychological tests and lifeskills inventories is the extent of participant involvement in their choice. If participants do not see the relevance of instruments, they either may refuse to complete them or complete them in invalid ways. Some leaders consider that participant completion of any assessment measures should be voluntary (Priestley, McGuire, Flegg, Helmsley, & Welham, 1978). However, the voluntary versus compulsory participation issue is not so simple where participants are being sent on training programs at the expense of their employers. It may be more important for participants to be helped by leaders to see the relevance for improving their lifeskills of any psychological test or skills inventory they are asked to take than for them to have a say in the selection of these instruments. Participants have a right to know the purposes for which the information is being collected and the degree of confidentiality they can expect.

Administering Psychological Tests and Lifeskills Inventories

Already stress has been laid on the importance of leaders' forming a working alliance with participants in regard to any assessment procedures used in a training group. This rapport should help participants take the procedures seriously. Psychological tests and lifeskills inventories must be administered and scored in a standard way or else they lose their statistical meaning. Leaders can contribute to ensuring standardization before, during, and after the testing process. Before the session, they can ensure that the test materials are suitably prepared and that they themselves are fully versed in how to administer them. In addition, they can see that the testing conditions are as adequate as possible. During the session, they can follow any psychological test or lifeskills inventory manual precisely. Additionally, in a group administration, leaders can make periodic visual checks to ensure that the participants are completing each instrument properly. After the session, leaders can see that the scoring instructions are followed as intended. Needless to say, the safe transit and storage of participants' responses to instruments is vital.

Interpreting Psychological Tests and Lifeskills Inventories

Many lifeskills inventories do not require scoring by third parties; rather, participants can score and evaluate their own answers. Participants can assess the meaning of their answers either on their own or in conjunction with their group leaders and other participants. Sometimes the leaders may need to score and feed back the findings of instruments. Although each participant may be given information in written form, leaders may have to discuss the meaning of findings in the group. Here it is important that leaders do not overinterpret the significance of the data, but discuss them as clearly and objectively as possible. Participants should be allowed to share their reactions to the findings. The information provided by psychological tests and lifeskills inventories may threaten participants. Despite the validity of instruments, it is still possible for participants to distort findings to meet their psychological needs. Consequently, to minimize this risk, leaders need to provide a safe emotional climate for the discussion of findings.

Some Problems in Using Psychological Tests and Lifeskills Inventories

We will mention here just a few of the many considerations leaders need to bear in mind about using tests and lifeskills inventories. Some respondents may respond in set ways. The concept of *response sets* implies that some people have tendencies to answer items in fixed ways that do not truly represent their behavior and perceptions. For instance, certain participants may have an acquiesence response set— that is, they tend to answer yes to questions. *Faking* implies conscious misrepresentation. Faking is especially likely to take place where participants have external reasons for doing well or badly, such as obtaining or not obtaining a promotion. Some participants may let their need for *social desirability* or to be seen by the leader in an approved light interfere with the accuracy of their responses. *Test anxiety* may distort some people's test scores. Psychological tests and lifeskills inventories can threaten participants. Test anxiety may debilitate rather than facilitate their performance. Leaders who are good at establishing rapport with participants may lessen test anxiety.

Resistances to taking psychological tests and lifeskills inventories may stem from fears about *invasion of privacy*. Anastasi (1988) observes that protection of privacy involves two key elements: relevance and informed consent. Relevance means that the information participants are asked to reveal must be relevant to the stated purposes of assessment. Informed consent refers to agreement by participants, after being adequately briefed about the nature and purposes of the assessment procedures, to take part in completing them. An obvious and extremely serious invasion of privacy occurs when a leader breaks a verbal or written contract involving not divulging test findings. *Test and lifeskills inventory bias* may be introduced, albeit unknowingly, into developing, selecting, administering, and reporting the results of instruments. Reasons for bias may include sexism, racism, ageism, and insensitivity to socioeconomic and cultural differences. For instance, although it is increasingly unlikely, tests and inventories may still use sexist language.

Exercise 8 Think About Using
Psychological Tests and Lifeskills Inventories
▼▼

Write out your answers to the following questions:

1. Finding out about tests and inventories
   Think of a specific lifeskill around which you might build a training group. Assuming that you are so inclined, what are some of the psychological tests and lifeskills inventories that you might consider as part of your assessment procedures? To answer this question you are encouraged to look up some of the sources of test information mentioned in the text.
2. Assessing your skills strengths and weaknesses
   Make up a worksheet similar to the following. Use the worksheet to assess your skills strengths and weaknesses in each of the three major aspects of using tests and inventories as a lifeskills group leader.

Use of tests and inventories	Skills strengths	Skills weaknesses
Selection		
Administration		
Interpretation		

3. Problems associated with using tests and inventories
   What are some of the main problems that might be associated with using psychological tests and lifeskills inventories in any future lifeskills training groups you may choose to offer?

Devising Assessment Measures
▼▼

The earlier discussions of behavior rating forms and of thinking, feeling, and behavior logs assumed that as a leader you might want to devise your own assessment measures. You cannot always assume that existing psychological tests and lifeskills inventories are suitable for your purposes. For example, you may want something simpler, shorter, more focused on a specific set of skills, more tailored to the language ability and to the age range of the groups with whom you work, and cheaper and more available than assessment measures already on the market. The following are some formats you can use for developing your own assessment measures.

Sentence Completion

You can ask participants to complete sentences that elicit information about how they think, feel, and act. Let us take the example of unemployed teenagers who join a lifeskills group in job-seeking skills. Sample sentences that these teenagers might be asked to complete include:

My biggest problem in getting a job is . . .
My other problems in getting a job are . . .
The skills that I have to offer an employer are . . .
The sorts of things that I want out of a job are . . .
When I go for a job interview, I feel . . .
When I go for a job interview, I think . . .
When I go for a job interview, I act . . .

An advantage of the sentence completion method is that it taps into participants' personal meanings with open-ended rather than closed-ended sentences. Furthermore, your ability to develop sentences focused on feeling, thinking, and action allows you a high degree of flexibility in what you focus on. Sentence completion may seem simple and naive, but then in lifeskills training groups simple is often smart and leader naivety may show up in trying to be too sophisticated.

Posing Problem Situations

Leaders can assess participants' current skills levels by asking how they might behave in specific problem situations relevant to the focus of a lifeskills program. You may seek responses to the problems in either open-ended or closed-ended ways. In an open-ended format, you may describe a scene and ask a question to find out how participants either currently behave or would like to behave. For example, an assessment problem in a dating skills program for college students might be as follows:

"You are five minutes early for class and a guy/girl that you have been interested in for the past few weeks, but never spoken to, comes and sits next to you. How would you behave (like to behave)?"

Nelson, Hayes, Felton, and Jarrett (1985) used a similar question in their research on ways of assessing social inadequacy. They developed the following criteria as indicative of socially skilled performance: (1) the person must introduce himself/herself; (2) the person must make small talk before specific invitation is made; (3) a specific invitation must be made; and (4) specific information must be given concerning the invitation (where, when, what, and such). As a leader, you may go beyond posing problems, to devising criteria whereby you assess whether participants show skills strengths or weaknesses in their responses.

With the closed-ended format, you pose a problem with alternative answers, as in a multiple-choice test. Let us take an example from a lifeskills program focused on training ten- to eleven-year-olds in assertiveness and social problem-solving skills.

"You are standing in line in the school cafeteria waiting to be served lunch when another student roughly your own size pushes in front of you. Mark the answer below that most represents how you would likely behave."

_____ I would push him/her back hard and tell him/her to get the hell out of my way.

_____ I would pretend that I had not noticed and do nothing.

_____ I would firmly say that I was in line first and would he/she please go to the end of the line.

In this example, each of the answers represents a different kind of behavior: namely, aggressive, nonassertive, and assertive. Consequently, participants' answers categorize them in terms of this particular question.

Checklists

Checklists can focus on virtually any aspect of a lifeskills area that you want. Many psychological tests are checklists in which respondents are asked to check behaviors that, unbeknownst to them, the test constructor has grouped into various categories for scoring purposes. You can devise your own checklists to suit your assessment purposes. Following is a simple checklist that a leader running a lifeskills group on overcoming shyness has devised to help participants identify specific categories of people with whom they feel shy.

"What people are associated with any feelings of shyness that you may have? Please mark those categories of people with whom you feel shy."

Mother _____	Same sex _____
Father _____	Opposite sex _____
Aunts _____	Children _____
Uncles _____	Friends _____
Grandparents _____	Neighbors _____
Boyfriend/girlfriend _____	Marital partner _____
Mother-in-law _____	Unmarried partner _____
Father-in-law _____	Strangers _____
Authorities by virtue of knowledge _____	People of higher status _____
Authorities by virtue of role _____	People of lower status _____

Checklists can provide more information if they provide multiple boxes in which people can tick. For instance, a question on a checklist for a stress management program might be: "I worry about my physical fitness," with participants having the option of placing a mark in one of three boxes: often, sometimes, never.

Card Sorts

Card sorts are another way of collecting assessment and self-assessment information. Instead of being in a paper-and-pencil questionnaire format, the items are printed on individual cards that the participant sorts into piles. For instance, in a lifeskills group on developing leisure skills, a number of different leisure activities might be listed on different cards. Participants could be asked to sort these cards into piles in various ways—for example, by whether they currently engage in the activities often, sometimes, or never, or by whether they like, dislike, or are indifferent to the activities.

Rankings

Rankings provide another source of evaluative information. Rankings can be helpful in providing positive and negative information: what a participant likes and wants or dislikes and does not want. For example, in a job-search lifeskills group, participants might be given a list of twelve characteristics of jobs, such as wages above a certain figure, brief travel time to work, and opportunity to meet people, and asked to rank them from 1 to 12 in terms of importance in choosing a job. Other uses of rankings are for finding out which of their problems participants consider most important to work on, and sociometric rankings in which participants rank which of the other group members they like, might want to spend time with, and so on.

Rating Scales

Rating scales provide another way of obtaining evaluative information, either quantitative or qualitative, concerning various items. For example, in an initial assessment as part of a training program on supervisory skills, a leader could request that participants complete a questionnaire with the following instructions:

"The questionnaire below lists a number of supervisory skills in five broad areas. Using the following scale, rate how satisfied you are with your specific skills in each of the five areas:

3   Much need for improvement
2   Moderate need for improvement
1   Slight need for improvement
0   No need for improvement

Put a question mark (?) rather than a rating by any skill whose meaning is not clear to you at this stage of the training program."

Another format for a rating scale is to ask participants to circle which of the numbers is nearest to where they think they are for individual items. For example, following are two items on an initial assessment measure for a program on managing test anxiety.

"When you take a college test, how do you feel? For each pair of adjectives, circle the number that best describes you."

| Anxious | 3 | 2 | 1 | 0 | 1 | 2 | 3 | Relaxed |
| Organized | 3 | 2 | 1 | 0 | 1 | 2 | 3 | Disorganized |

Perhaps enough has been said to show you that there are many ways in which you can devise your own measures for assessing participants' lifeskills strengths and weaknesses and helping them to assess themselves. Already you may know other ways. Later, when faced with a real-life assessment challenge, you may become creative in finding different ways—for instance, devising a game or some form of group task. Exercise 9 is designed to build your skills and confidence at devising your own assessment measures.

Exercise 9 Devise Your Own Assessment and Participant Self-Assessment Measures
▼ ▼

Think of a specific lifeskill around which you might wish to build a training group (this can be the same lifeskill that you selected for Exercise 8). You may need to refer back to the text to complete the following tasks, each of which may help you both to assess participants and to help participants assess themselves in regard to the lifeskill you have chosen.

1. Design a behavior rating form to measure observable behaviors.
2. Design a thinking, feeling, and behavior log for participants to monitor themselves.
3. Formulate at least three sentences for participants to complete.
4. Pose two problem situations, one in an open-ended format and the other in a closed-ended format.
5. Design a checklist to assess some aspect of the lifeskill.
6. Design a card sort having at least fifteen items that participants might sort into at least three categories.
7. Design a question asking participants to rank at least eight items.
8. Design a rating scale to go at the front for participants to use in rating each item in a questionnaire.
9. Design a questionnaire made up of at least five pairs of adjectives, with the members of each pair separated by the following

rating scale: 3 2 1 0 1 2 3. Ask participants to circle one of the numbers between each pair of adjectives.

10. Summarize which of the preceding ways of assessment and of helping participants assess themselves you might want to use for
    a. initial assessment of the lifeskill either before or at the start of your training group;
    b. monitoring the lifeskill during the training group; and
    c. end-of-training-group assessment of the lifeskill.

Encouraging Participants to Set Personal Goals
▼ ▼

Having worked with participants to collect assessment information, how do leaders then use it to help them improve their effectiveness? A major theme of this chapter is the importance of building participant personal responsibility by developing their skills at self-assessment. However, self-assessment is not an end in itself; rather, it is the stepping-stone to setting personal goals. In the previous two chapters, mention was made of the need for leaders to clarify and state goals and subgoals for their lifeskills programs. Similarly, it can be helpful for participants to have overall goals that they wish to attain by the end of a program, as well as subgoals that involve acquisition of the specific skills that will enable them to attain their overall goals.

State Overall Goals

Participants can set overall personal goals at any stage of a lifeskills training group, as suggested in the following incomplete sentences:

By the end of this group, my goal is to be able to . . .
By the end of the month, my goal is to be able to . . .
By the end of this session, my goal is to be able to . . .
By the end of this homework assignment, my goal is to be able to . . .
In the three months after the lifeskills group has ended, my goal is to . . .

Participants may require help in stating their overall goals. Considerations for good statements of overall goals include the following:

Realism: Participants' goals are realistic when they adequately acknowledge the constraints of their emotional resources and personal skills. These constraints should be neither overestimated nor underestimated. Goals should reflect realistic and potentially attainable standards.

Specificity: Participants should state their goals specifically. Ideally, goals should be stated so that participants can easily measure the success of their attempts to attain them. For instance, "I want to make more friends" is not as good as "I want to have a minimum of four new friends by the end of the group."

A time frame: Participants should state the time frame in which they want to accomplish each goal. Vague statements of intention are insufficient.

Leaders should encourage participants to keep written records of their personal goals. These goal statements can be placed in prominent positions at home or at work to act as reminders and motivators. At the end of the stipulated time frame, written statements of goals provide a yardstick for participants to use to measure how well they have done. A more formal approach to written statements of goals is to make them constitute all or part of learning contracts that participants make with either themselves or their leaders (Wehrenberg, 1988).

State Subgoals

At the start of a lifeskills program, participants may have insufficient insight into their skills weaknesses to be able to state subgoals well. For instance, a participant in a public-speaking program may have as an overall goal: "By the end of the program I want to be able to address my fellow sales representatives in a calm and relaxed way, yet make all my points clearly and cogently." At the start, this participant is likely only to have a vague idea of the specific thinking and action skills needed to attain this overall goal. As the program develops, the participant is likely to gain the required knowledge to state his or her specific subgoals. The following is a format that leaders can use for helping participants state goals and subgoals:

By the end of . . . [stipulate period], my goal is to be able to . . . [stipulate overall goal].

To attain my goal(s), the specific *thinking* skills I need to develop are: [state specific thinking skills in 1, 2, 3 fashion].

To attain my goal(s), the specific *action* skills I need to develop are: [state specific action skills in 1, 2, 3 fashion].

▼ Chapter Highlights

▼ Assessment and self-assessment of lifeskills can take place at each of the four stages of a lifeskills training group: preparatory, initial, working, and ending.

▼ Training-group leaders should always help participants acquire the "take-away" skills of how to assess their own lifeskills.

▼ Leaders, participants, and third parties may each have their own agendas for conducting and participating in lifeskills assessment. Sometimes there are conflicts of interest between these agendas.

(continued)

▼ **Chapter Highlights** (continued)

▼ Methods of assessment and self-assessment include interviews, group interaction, observation in natural settings, participant self-observation and monitoring, psychological tests and lifeskills inventories, and leader-devised assessment measures.

▼ Leaders require the skills of choosing and devising assessment measures that are tailored to the needs of specific lifeskills training groups. "Buckshot" approaches to assessment are to be avoided.

▼ Assessment and self-assessment measures that leaders can devise include behavior rating forms; thinking, feeling, and behavior logs; sentence completion questions; posing problem situations; checklists; card sorts; ranking questions; and questions using rating scales.

▼ Lifeskills assessment and self-assessment is not an end in itself; rather, it should help participants clarify and state personal goals and subgoals.

▼ Three important considerations in participants' effectively stating personal goals are realism, specificity, and a time frame.

6

How to Facilitate a Training Group

I pay the schoolmaster, but 'tis the schoolboys
   that educate my son.

Ralph Waldo Emerson

Chapter Questions

▼▼

Why do training-group leaders require good facilitation skills?

What are the main ways in which group leaders send messages?

What facilitation skills might a leader use in a training group's initial, working, and ending stages?

What thinking skills weaknesses might interfere with how well a training-group leader uses facilitation skills?

Introduction

▼▼

Following are some examples of situations where leaders can use and have used facilitation skills to help attain training-group lifeskills goals:

▼ In an employability skills group for incarcerated youth, helping participants assess their employability and communication skills (Weissman, 1985)

▼ In a Job Club group for the handicapped, both supporting participants and helping them support each other as they seek employment (Azrin & Philip, 1979)

▼ In a problem-solving skills group for shy adolescents, helping participants verbalize how they would apply the skills to a range of interpersonal problems (Christoff, Scott, Kelley, Schlundt, Baer, & Kelley, 1985)

▼ In a pain-management group, assisting participants to share their experiences in using cognitive-behavioral skills to make the most of their lives despite their pain (Turner & Clancy, 1988)

▼ In a parent effectiveness training group, getting parents to be open about their weaknesses and misgivings about how they relate to their children (Gordon, 1970)

▼ In an assertiveness training group for black high school students, helping participants discuss their experience of practicing the targeted behaviors outside the group (Stewart & Lewis, 1986)

▼ In a dating skills program for college students, helping participants overcome their anxieties about participating in role-plays in front of the group

▼ In a psychoeducational group for adult children of alcoholics, helping participants talk about growing up in a chemically dependent family and, where necessary, assisting them in confronting and diminishing denial (Downing & Walker, 1987)

▼ In management training workshops on a range of topics, such as interpersonal communication and making speeches, helping managers to participate actively (Zelko, 1986)

Though there is overlap, group leaders differ in how they use facilitation skills in training as contrasted with counseling groups. Training-group leaders require both the skills of facilitating interactional groups and the skills of facilitating focused learning.

Purposes of Facilitation
▼▼

Friends show their love in times of trouble, not in happiness.

Euripides

The overall purpose of facilitation is to create a climate in which participants can develop the targeted lifeskills. Specific purposes of facilitation vary with the stages of the group. Here we'll explore the purposes of facilitation both in general and at specific stages.

Creating the Proper Climate

Some insight into the role of facilitation in lifeskills training groups may be gained from Yalom's research into therapeutic factors in group psychotherapy (Bloch & Crouch, 1985; Yalom, 1985). Therapeutic factors are factors that patients regard as most salient to their improvement. Yalom acknowledges that a number of studies by himself and others have differed in their rank orderings of the value of the therapeutic factors. Yalom's twelve therapeutic factors are as follows:

1. Altruism—thinking of and helping others
2. Group cohesiveness—a sense of belonging to, feeling accepted by, and finding the group and its members attractive
3. Universality—learning that others have the same thoughts and problems, too
4. Interpersonal learning (input)—learning how I come across to others and why
5. Interpersonal learning (output)—the opportunity to be more trustful and to work on how I relate to others
6. Guidance—either the group leader or group members making suggestions or giving advice to me
7. Catharsis—being able to ventilate and to learn how to express my feelings
8. Identification—finding role models in the behavior of either the group leader or other group members
9. Family reenactment—being in a simulated family that helped me understand the influences on me of my original family
10. Self-understanding—learning about how, through the influences of my childhood and development, I distort my perceptions of myself and of others

11. Instillation of hope—seeing other group members improve and solve their problems
12. Existential factors—learning to acknowledge more fully the existential parameters of death, freedom, responsibility, and isolation and to make the most of my life

Though training groups have the added agenda of a specific skills focus, many of Yalom's therapeutic factors are highly relevant to why training-group leaders require good facilitation skills. Training-group leaders use facilitation skills not just to work with individuals, but also to create a climate in which participants help each other. A willingness to work on real rather than surface issues may come about through the climate of cohesiveness, safety, trust, and acceptance that leaders are able to foster in groups. Leaders seek to create norms or rules conducive to the group's work—for instance, honesty, openness, and willingness to assume personal responsibility for changing skills weaknesses. Much of the learning in lifeskills training groups takes place between participants. Universality, instillation of hope, and identification may come from other participants' disclosures. Interpersonal learning and self-understanding come from sharing and feedback within the group as well as from the advice and suggestions of the other participants. In addition, altruism is more likely to be experienced if leaders are skilled at releasing the group's healing potential than if not.

A further set of reasons why good facilitation skills are important for leaders is that they help build leaders' influence base. Leading lifeskills groups may be viewed as a social influence process in which trainers use their facilitative and didactic skills to help participants develop targeted behaviors (Brehm & Smith, 1986; Corrigan, Dell, Lewis, & Schmidt, 1980; Strong, 1968, 1978). A distinction can be made between possessing power, being able to force participants to do something whether they like it or not, and having influence, being able to affect participants' feelings, thoughts, and actions without having control over them (Steiner, 1981). At best, most training-group leaders possess influence. Good facilitation skills are likely to help participants feel understood and thus may enhance participants' perceptions of their leaders as expert, trustworthy, and attractive. These perceptions enhance the influence base of leaders when facilitating both group discussion and also didactic learning.

Facilitation Skills in Different Stages of Lifeskills Training Groups

Mention has already been made of the use of facilitation skills, such as empathy, in the *preparatory stage* when conducting intake interviews and initial assessments. Preparing participants well for entering a training group may also help leaders attain some of their later purposes when they use facilitation skills. Some leaders encourage interaction among members by asking participants to commit themselves to group contracts stressing such skills as self-disclosure, honesty, and listening to others. Also, leaders may ask participants to watch pregroup training videos in which these interpersonal skills are demonstrated.

In the *initial stage* of a lifeskills training group, leaders use facilitation skills to help participants get to know one another and manage their anxieties about being in the group. Especially if attendance is involuntary, leaders need facilitation skills to help participants verbalize and explore their resistances to being in or working in the group. If the participants in the group have characteristics different either from their leaders or from each other—for instance, culture, race, sex, status, age—the leader can use facilitation skills to help members work through any initial sense of isolation they may have from perceiving themselves as different (Moracco, 1981). A further use of facilitation skills is in helping participants to assess their skills strengths and weaknesses and set personal goals.

Facilitation skills in the *working stage* of a training group are used to foster both individual and interpersonal learning. Some participants may require help in overcoming self-consciousness about participating in structured activities before others, for instance roleplays. Facilitation skills are useful for debriefing participants after coaching and rehearsal sessions as well as for getting participants to offer feedback. Also, leaders need good facilitation skills to help participants describe their outside group and homework experiences in using the skills. Leaders who demonstrate and use facilitation skills can help participants support each other as they experience the inevitable setbacks and difficulties in developing their skills. In addition, good facilitation skills can help participants to share and express pleasure in each other's successes.

In the *ending stage* of a training group, leaders can use facilitation skills for a number of purposes. Participants can be assisted in assessing their end-of-program skills strengths and weaknesses and in helping others to do likewise. Leaders can help participants set personal goals and develop programs for consolidating and maintaining their trained skills as postgroup self-help skills. Leaders can help participants to acknowledge and deal with feelings about the group's end. In addition, leaders can help participants set up peer support networks on either a buddy or a support-group basis.

Group Leaders as Senders of Messages
▾▾▾

Whether they are being didactic or facilitative, training-group leaders are always sending and receiving messages. Sending and receiving messages are interlinked. People who receive others' messages poorly lack a good information base for sending appropriate messages. On the other hand, even people who receive others' messages well can still possess poor sender skills.

There are five main ways that humans send messages (Nelson-Jones, 1990b). In varying degrees, each of these ways is relevant to the leader's role.

Verbal messages: Messages expressed in words—for example, what you say in response to participants or what you say about yourself

Voice messages: Messages conveyed by how you talk—for example, quickly or slowly, loudly or quietly, with or without emphasis, in a high-pitched or deep voice

Body messages: Sometimes called body language or nonverbal communication, messages that you send with your face, with other parts of your body, and by how you dress and are groomed

Touch messages: Special kinds of body messages involving physical contact with another, sometimes indirect—for example, a group leader may rest an arm on the back of someone's chair rather than touch her or him directly

Action messages: Messages conveyed by *what you do* as contrasted with *what you say* or *how you say it*—for example, do you start and end your training sessions on time?

Whatever training interventions they use at any given moment, skilled training-group leaders make appropriate choices in each of these five message areas. Genuineness becomes an important issue when leaders can send messages in so many different ways. Rogers was a prime advocate of the importance of genuineness in working with groups as well as in other personal and helping relationships (Raskin & Rogers, 1989; Rogers, 1957, 1961, 1969, 1970, 1980). Are the messages that you send as a leader congruent or do you seem confused and insincere because you send mixed messages? You always need to be aware of not only what but also how you communicate. Also, do your actions match your words?

Facilitation Skills for the Initial Stage

▼ ▼

Some facilitation skills for starting lifeskills training groups are now discussed. Although they overlap, the leader skills mentioned here focus more on facilitating group discussion than on supporting structured learning experiences.

Arrange Seating

Leaders who are serious about the value of group interaction do not arrange the seating in rows with the trainer up front. This "jug and mug" seating arrangement (the leader is the jug containing the waters of wisdom, which she or he pours into each participant's mug) can lead to most comments being directed to and from leaders. Counseling and psychotherapy groups use a circular seating pattern with each chair being evenly spaced from the others. There is a clear message in this democratic seating arrangement about the value of group interaction. On the other hand, circular seating arrangements may also send a message that the group leader is not going to emphasize teaching. A horseshoe seating pattern has many advantages for training groups. A horseshoe allows the leader to operate both as a facilitator and teacher without having to keep rearranging the furniture. However, where appropriate, the leader can still use other seating patterns—for instance, either a circle or pairs.

Open the Group

Rogers used to start his encounter groups in an extremely unstructured way. He would make comments like: "Here we are. We can make of this group experience exactly what we wish" or "I'm a little uneasy, but I feel somewhat reassured when I look around at you and realize we're all in the same boat. Where do we start?" (Rogers, 1970, pp. 46–47). Rogers's opening remarks are too unstructured for life-skills training groups. Leaders would lose credibility by opening groups this way. Participants might rightly think, "If he/she doesn't know where to start, why should I be here?"

You need to tailor your opening remarks to the goals of your group. You have the twin goals of setting a safe emotional climate and a task-oriented climate. Further structuring can take place throughout the life of a group both by means of specific statements intended for that purpose and also by your voice, body, and action messages. In addition, you set the climate by the way you instruct and respond to participants. The following areas can be included in your opening remarks:

Calling the session to order
Introducing yourself
Welcoming participants
Communicating the time limits both of individual sessions and of the life of the group
Stating your purposes for the group
Clarifying your own role
Indicating participants' roles
Encouraging active participation and personal responsibility for skills development
Communicating an agenda for the remainder of the first session

Your voice and body messages are important accompaniments to your opening remarks. Your voice messages need to show commitment to the task. Even if you do not feel particularly confident, try not to appear diffident and uninvolved. Speak with a clear and firm voice and at a comfortable speed for your listeners. Speak directly to your audience in "you-me" language and try to join with each participant by looking in his or her direction. Under no circumstances read your opening remarks.

Following is an example of a possible opening statement:

> Hello, I would like to start the session now. As you know I'm [state name]. I have talked with each of you individually but this is the first time we are meeting as a group. We plan to meet every Tuesday from 4 to 6 p.m. for the next ten weeks. The group's purpose is to help you to develop [identify focus] skills. My role is both as a trainer and as someone who enables you to learn from one another. In this group you help yourself and each other by participating actively and by working hard to attain your own and the group's goals. The remainder of this session will be spent as follows: first, introducing ourselves; second, outlining the work of the group; third, clarifying personal goals; and fourth, assigning a homework task of monitoring your behavior.

Decide About Getting-Acquainted Exercises

Many training-group leaders use getting-acquainted exercises to speed up the self-disclosure and trust-building process between participants. There seems much less risk in using such exercises in lifeskills groups than in counseling or psychotherapy groups, where they may lead to pseudo-authenticity. Some leading writers on encounter and therapeutic groups do not favor using such exercises (Rogers, 1970; Yalom, 1985). Even in lifeskills training groups, getting-acquainted exercises can be gimmicky and demeaning to participants (Whitaker, 1985). However, well-chosen getting-acquainted exercises can shorten the acquaintance process in ways that, unlike in therapy groups, do not impede the group's task.

Following is a list of some ways leaders can approach the task of getting acquainted. Leaders always have to take into account the practical realities of any group with whom they work—for instance, group size and participants' age range—in choosing getting-acquainted exercises. Sometimes the participants in a training group will have had prior contact—for instance, as classmates or workmates. Even in such instances, leaders should not assume that participants know each other well: they may have been acquaintances relating in ritualistic ways.

Introduce oneself: Participants can be asked to introduce and say a few words about themselves. A variation on this is to have participants start by saying their name and then repeating the names of all those who have introduced themselves already before saying something about themselves (Corey, Corey, Callanan, & Russell, 1988).

Sometimes the leader may ask participants to cover specific topics in their statements—for instance, what they want to get out of coming to this lifeskills group or how it feels right now to be joining this lifeskills group. The order of introductions can be either as participants choose to speak up or starting with one person and then going around the group. Especially when groups are large, name tags often help members learn names.

Give a brief introductory speech: A variation on introducing oneself is to get participants to stand up in front of the group for a set period of time, say for ninety seconds or two minutes, and introduce themselves. You can allow them the last fifteen to thirty seconds for answering questions. This method lends itself to programs where public speaking is the major or one of the main skills being taught.

Use a ball or cushion: Here the participant to whom the ball is thrown thanks by name the person who has thrown the ball, says his or her own name, self-discloses while holding the ball, and then throws the ball to another person, and so on. For some groups and individuals there may be at least three advantages to this approach: the element of playing a game lessens anxiety; participants have something to do with their hands when it is their turn to speak; and the uncertainty of not knowing who will be next keeps participants awake. As with all introductory exercises, leaders can ask participants to cover specific topics. For example, I have asked undergraduate participants to describe their cultural background and to identify specific difficulties they have faced in cross-cultural communication. There can also be risks to using a ball or cushion—for example, some adult groups may consider it childish and some school groups may take it as an excuse either to break a window or to throw the ball hard at an attractive classmate.

Introduce a partner: Another getting-acquainted exercise is to divide the group into pairs. Partner A self-discloses to partner B, who listens and may ask a few questions. After a set time period, say two or three minutes, the partners reverse roles. This pair's work is followed by the partners' introducing each other in a plenary session. There are a number of drawbacks to this method. First, participants are not speaking for themselves when they get introduced to the group. Second, participants may forget salient information about the person they introduce. However, the partner being talked about may be given the opportunity to add missing information. Third, especially if their introductions come at the end, participants may be so busy remembering information to disclose that they do not listen properly to all the other introductions. A possible advantage of this method is that some participants may find it easier to break the ice by talking to the group about someone else rather than directly about themselves.

Use triads or small groups: Participants can be divided into threes or into small groups. Members of these groupings can be instructed to introduce themselves to each other during a set time period. Either alternatively or in addition, the subgroups can be asked to discuss a self-referent topic pertinent to the work of the group—for example, difficulties in either being assertive or managing stress. Where appropriate, subgrouping can be followed by either putting participants into different subgroups or holding a whole-group sharing and discussion session.

Discuss self-assessment exercises: Prior to the initial session, participants may have been asked to fill out a self-assessment questionnaire in regard to the lifeskill(s) targeted by the group. Participants can share their responses to the questionnaire either in pairs or in subgroups. Even if they have not filled out a questionnaire, participants can be divided into pairs or subgroups and asked to share their assessments of their strengths and weaknesses in the targeted lifeskills area(s). Such self-assessment exercises can be followed by whole-group sharing and discussion sessions.

Circulate with personal information visible: Participants can be asked to fill out either an index card or a yellow "post-it" sheet with information about themselves. For instance, in the top left-hand corner they can put what they like to be called; in the top right-hand corner they can put a couple of pieces of biographical information, such as age, place of residence, birthplace, marital status; in the bottom left-hand corner they can put three adjectives to describe themselves; and in the bottom right-hand corner they can put three hobbies. The information requested can vary with the purposes of the group. Participants then pin or stick their information on their fronts. They are then asked to circulate and hold brief conversations with as many new people as they can within a set time period. Some participants like this exercise because it both allows them to meet whomever they want and more closely resembles real life, where people relate to individuals rather than to whole groups. Furthermore, moving around sometimes helps energize participants.

Form a continuum: Another getting-acquainted exercise is to set participants the task of forming a continuum on some basis—for example, supervisors or managers can be asked to sort themselves into a line based on how long they have worked for a company, how tall they are, or how dark their hair is. Such tasks, without creating much threat, get participants interacting with each other.

Use movies and videos: Movies and videos can be used to facilitate self-disclosure and sharing of experiences. For example, Downing and Walker (1987) describe how they used the movie *My Father's Son: The Legacy of Alcoholism* (Rogers, 1984) as an icebreaker in the first session of their psychoeducational program for adult children of alcoholics.

A few closing points about using getting-acquainted exercises. First, leaders can use more than one. Second, many of the later learning experiences of lifeskills groups, for instance, role-plays with other participants, have an element of getting acquainted in them. Third, leaders can bring about a greater sense of group cohesion if they participate actively by introducing themselves in some of the exercises than if they sit on the sidelines in an "expert" capacity. Fourth, the getting-acquainted exercises can be used to make the existential point that participants are always choosers and thus need to take responsibility for the outcomes of their choices—for example, when introducing themselves participants choose what to conceal and what to reveal.

Exercise 10 is designed to get you thinking about the advantages and disadvantages of using getting-acquainted exercises when leading lifeskills groups. In addition, where possible, the exercise encourages you to experience the different approaches.

Exercise 10 Use Getting-Acquainted Exercises
▼▼▼

1. Make up a worksheet with three columns, headed *Exercise, Advantages,* and *Disadvantages.* Discuss the advantages and disadvantages of using each of the following getting-acquainted exercises in the initial session of a lifeskills training group.

Introduce oneself
Give a brief introductory speech
Use a ball or cushion
Introduce a partner
Use triads or small groups
Discuss self-assessment exercises
Circulate with personal information visible
Form a continuum
Use movies and videos

2. If you are in a group practicum, try out as many of these getting-acquainted exercises as you have time for and interest in so that you can get the feel of them. You may wish to defer discussing the advantages and disadvantages of the getting-acquainted exercises until after you have had the opportunity to experience them firsthand.

Encourage Participation

When leading groups, it is vital that you do not dominate, but rather encourage participants to make it their group as well. There is a Chinese proverb: Beneath a great oak tree, nothing grows." Even though in lifeskills training groups your task is to be more didactic than in counseling groups, you still want to convey a clear message to participants that their contributions are welcome. The previous section focused on getting-acquainted exercises that foster later interaction. Following is a list of some further skills that you can use, both in the initial and subsequent stages of training groups, to encourage participation.

Give cues in your opening statement: You can include in your opening statement comments that indicate that participation in the group is desirable. For instance, the earlier example of an opening statement included the comment, "My role is both as a trainer and as someone who enables you to learn from one another."

Encourage self-referent talk: You encourage participants to own and talk about their thoughts, feelings, and actions by means of "I" statements. Where appropriate, you encourage them to give concrete examples of their experiences. You discourage them when they intellectualize and generalize. Even early on, but using tact, you encourage participants to own rather than to distance themselves from their problems and skills weaknesses.

Encourage talking to each other: Ways by which you can encourage participants to interact with each other and not just with you include asking them to do this and using body messages, such as an arm gesture or turning your gaze in the direction of the group.

Make linking statements: You can find ways of relating what one participant has to say to what other participants have said—for example, in an overcoming shyness group for adolescents, "Mandy has just said something that many of you have also been saying one way or another, that it can be very scary meeting people for the first time."

Invite participation: You can give an invitation to participate to the whole group, with questions like "Does anyone else have anything they would like to share about what Rico has been saying?" Alternatively, you can give an invitation to a specific member who may have trouble contributing without your encouragement—for example, "Di, I've been watching your expression as Rico has been talking and wonder whether you would like to say something."

Give permission to discuss differences: If you think members of the group might feel excluded because of age, race, culture, sex, socioeconomic status, rank, or other differences, you can make comments that show you are sensitive to this possibility. Such comments function as permissions to air feelings of difference as well as indicate that difference does not have connotations of inferiority as far as you are concerned.

Give permission to discuss fears: Both participants and leaders are inevitably going to have anxieties about starting a new group. Leaders can acknowledge that this will be the case, disclose their own anxieties, and encourage participants to do likewise. For instance, in lifeskills training groups participants may have fears about starting off further behind in the skills than others, making mistakes, being slower learners, and admitting difficulties in public. Leaders who early in training groups facilitate a sense of acceptance of others and of universality, make an invaluable contribution to group participation and cohesiveness.

Offer support: Always support genuine attempts to participate by showing good attending behaviors, such as slight forward trunk lean, gaze, and head nods (Egan, 1990; Ivey & Authier, 1978). You can choose whether either to add verbal encouragement—as with a reflective response—or to leave it to the group to respond. If necessary, you should support participants in coping with negative reactions from others.

Foster group rules conducive to participation: Any group develops implicit and explicit rules or norms that constitute the *do*'s and *don't*s about how participants should behave. As leader, you can influence the development of norms that are helpful rather than harmful to participating. Whitaker distinguishes between groups that find either restrictive or enabling solutions to the tasks and problems they face (Whitaker, 1985). As leader, you have to decide whether to let the group work through problems with minimum assistance from you or whether to take a more active role in bringing about enabling rather than restrictive solutions. For example, if the group is just focusing on the problems of one participant, do you intervene? If you sense that fears of confidentiality are an issue in the group, do you either leave it to the group to do something about it or make sure the issue is discussed and, if possible, worked through satisfactorily? If you want a group rule about openness, do you wait for this to happen or do you actively try to influence the process by saying that this is what is best for the group and then rewarding participants who take risks? Training-group leaders are likely to be more active than counseling-group leaders in openly influencing group rules. The briefer length and more structured nature of lifeskills training groups pressures leaders to intervene rather than to observe the group constructing its own norms at its own pace.

Be a role model: Use "I" statements yourself and be direct and open with the group. In this way you help participants to feel that you are involved in the group as a person and not just as a technical expert.

Assist Self-Assessment and Stating Personal Goals

Training-group leaders need to be active in encouraging participants to engage in an ongoing process of assessing their skills strengths and weaknesses. Related to this, leaders encourage participants to define and redefine their personal goals in the targeted skills areas. Mention has already been made of intake interviews and getting-acquainted self-assessment exercises, with or without prior questionnaires. In the initial stage of a group, training-group leaders may actively establish self-assessment and goal-setting agendas rather than wait for agendas to emerge as in group counseling. Leaders then facilitate the ensuing sharing and discussion. As the group develops, participants should achieve a clearer understanding of how they sustain their skills weaknesses. Nevertheless, even in the group's initial stage, participants can start gaining more insight into their behavior and into what specifically they want to get out of the group.

The skills mentioned in the previous chapter for individual assessment interviews are also relevant for assessment and goal-setting discussions in groups. For instance, leaders may use questions that encourage participants to be more specific both about their experiences and about what they want to achieve. Sometimes leaders may choose to work on breaking down the problems of one participant into component parts as a way of demonstrating to other participants how to break down their own problems. Leaders can also help participants to develop the skills of setting goals that are realistic, specific, and have a time frame.

Some leaders encourage participants to go beyond self-assessment and goal setting by making learning contracts (Wehrenberg, 1988). Corey and Corey (1982) write: "Basically a contract is a statement by the group member concerning what he or she is willing to do during a group session or outside of the group meeting" (p. 110). Mention has already been made of contracts that set out appropriate behaviors for participating in lifeskills groups. The contracts envisaged here are specific to individual participants. These personal contracts outline actions to be undertaken and behaviors to be changed. Their time frame may be a session, a between-session break, or a longer period. Such contracts aim to encourage participants to assume responsibility for their learning by committing themselves to specific behaviors.

Handle Resistances

There are numerous reasons why people participate in lifeskills training groups. Some may be sent by third parties, such as their managers, or attend because they are institutionalized—for instance, juvenile delinquents. There may be varying degrees of involuntary participation in training groups. How can leaders attempt to cope with participants' resistances and, at the very least, try to prevent them from interfering with the motivation of the rest of the group? Leaders need to avoid pressuring or selling reluctant participants on the group's value. Pressure like this risks heightening rather than diminishing their resistances. Following is a list of suggestions for dealing with involuntary or reluctant participants.

Conduct intake interviews: Personal meetings between leaders and participants prior to training groups can perform a number of functions in lessening resistances: building rapport, diminishing anxiety, clarifying the group's purposes, and exploring whether there might be anything in the group for the participant.

Give permission to verbalize reservations: Training-group leaders can show sensitivity to participants' feelings about not wishing to be in groups by encouraging them to verbalize their reservations. Leaders may facilitate a sharing and discussion of reservations and correct any inaccurate fantasies about being in the group, such as "my defenses will be stripped away" or "they are collecting information to use against me." Resistant participants who see that leaders have bothered to understand their positions may feel less hostile to the group because of this. Leaders can also self-disclose with "I" statements about how participants' resistances affect them. Reluctant participants may appreciate this genuineness.

Facilitate assuming personal responsibility: After participants have had a chance to air their reservations, leaders can attempt to help them move on. There are various techniques for doing this. You can encourage questions about the purpose of the group and what participants might expect to get out of it. You can confront participants with their current existential predicaments of not particularly wanting to be in the group but having to be there, and ask, "How can you best make this situation work for you?" You can encourage participants to clarify and formulate personal goals. With some groups, you may choose to go further and adopt the approach Glasser has used in his reality-therapy groups with juvenile delinquents. Glasser confronts participants with the fact that much of their behavior to date has not been particularly helpful for them, that they have basic needs for love and worth, and that together they can work to help meet their basic needs more successfully (Glasser, 1965, 1984a, 1984b). This "tough love" approach has much to recommend it as long as leaders convey to participants genuine concern and commitment.

Control damage: Sometimes the best that leaders can do is to try to limit the damaging effects that resistant participants may have on the rest of the group. You can acknowledge their reluctance to participate and ask them to at least give the group a try. You can request that they do not interfere with the work of other participants. You can also support other participants in having the courage to speak up and give the same message. If you face continuous disruption, for the sake of the whole group you may have to exclude certain participants from attending future sessions. Exclusion is not always an easy option where, as in a school, all pupils may be expected to attend all classes.

Further Facilitation Skills

All of the facilitation skills you use in working with individuals are helpful for performing the leadership role in a lifeskills group. However, you need to adapt your use of individual helping skills. Also, you always have to weigh carefully whether you should allow space for participants to respond to each other rather than respond yourself.

Empathic Understanding

Though you may choose to respond empathically to individual members, there are at least five ways in which empathic responding may be different in group than in individual work. First, you may wish to respond empathically to an interaction between two or more members. One way to do this is to clarify what each has said. Another way is to summarize themes in the interaction. Second, you may respond to the group as a whole. For example, you may reflect anxiety at participating in self-assessment and in meeting a group of strangers. Third, you may respond to the unspoken needs of members who are not participating overtly and/or who may feel particularly vulnerable. Fourth, you may try to release the helping and healing capacity of the group by encouraging members to respond empathically to each other. Fifth, you may identify empathic responding as a useful self-help skill and encourage members to use it not only inside but also outside the group.

Use of Questions

Some of your questions may be addressed to the group as well as to individuals. Examples of such questions include: "Hannah has raised the issue of confidentiality. What does the group think?" "Do Joanne's experiences trigger any thoughts and feelings in any of you?" and "It seems to me that Dino would like some feedback or help from the group. Is anyone willing to provide this?"

Facilitative Confronting

Confrontations are challenges either to individuals or to the group as a whole that invite them to assess some aspect of their functioning. Often confrontations are focused on highlighting inconsistencies, such as between either what participants say and how they say it or what they say and what they do. An example of the latter inconsistency is agreeing to come to sessions on time and then coming late. Sometimes confrontations aim to challenge possible distortions of reality—for example, "You say you have no friends; where is the evidence for this perception?" (Beck & Emery, 1985; Nelson-Jones, 1990b). Sometimes you may choose to confront the whole group, such as when they use the restrictive solution of focusing excessively on one participant's concerns as a way of avoiding dealing with their own anxieties.

How you confront is as important as what you confront. You can soften your confrontation if you begin with a reflective response that shows you have heard and understood a speaker's message. Then build on this with your confronting response. This way you are more likely to keep the speaker's ears open to what comes from your viewpoint. Only confront as strongly as is necessary to achieve your goal. Heavy and insensitive confrontations create resistance. Also, try not to overdo confrontations. Nobody likes being persistently challenged. You can help participants move forward with skilled use of confronting responses. On the other hand, you can block and threaten participants as well as harm your relationship with them if you confront too often and too clumsily.

Self-Disclosure

An issue in lifeskills training groups is how much of a participant leaders should become. Leader self-disclosure can be for good or ill. At best, leader self-disclosure can contribute to an honest person-to-person working climate. Training-group leaders always send messages about themselves. If leaders send congruent messages they are perceived as authentic or genuine. However, if leaders say they are committed to the group, but do not indicate this with voice and body messages, lack of commitment may be the overall impression left with participants. Also, if leaders say they want a spontaneous and relaxed atmosphere yet appear tense and uptight, their incongruent messages interfere with attaining their stated goal.

Disclosing personal experiences, showing involvement, and using humor are three important aspects of self-disclosure (McCarthy, 1982). Many leaders run lifeskills training groups in skills areas where they have had problems themselves. Disclosing your experiences may help participants feel that you understand their experiences—for example, coping with unemployment, coping with career as well as family, and overcoming substance abuse. As long as they are brief, to the point, and not overwhelming, such disclosures may engender feelings of universality, cohesiveness, and identification. On the other hand, leaders who keep talking about their experiences risk switching the focus of their group from the participants to themselves.

Self-involving disclosures are spontaneous and direct reactions to what participants say or do. There is a here-and-now quality about such reactions. Examples of self-involving disclosures are: "That's great," "I'm happy too," and "I'm sorry that he/she reacted that way." Sometimes self-involving disclosures are confrontations—for example, "You seem to think of yourself as a weak person, but I do not experience you that way" and "I really have to make an effort to keep listening when you start repeating yourself." Even negative self-involving disclosures can be constructive if they represent invitations to look at specific behaviors.

Humor provides a good vehicle for revealing your humanity and loosening up the emotional climate of a group. Humor can release the potential for fun in the group. British playwright Terence Rattigan, in his play about a schoolmaster *The Browning Version*, had the central character observe that boys learn much more from humor than earnestness. This observation probably also holds true for training-group participants. Humor need not necessarily block exploring deeper issues. Given the right relaxed atmosphere, participants may be more able and willing to expose themselves and to work for change.

Summarizing

In general, when facilitating training groups, it is undesirable to provide lengthy summaries of what individuals have said. Such summaries may block the processes of group interaction and learning. However, sometimes when leaders work with individual participants in front of the group, this rule may not apply. Leaders' summaries focused on individuals then may stimulate other participants to think differently about their problems.

Summaries focused on the group can take place at the beginning of, during, and at the end of sessions. At the start of a session, leaders can summarize the main learnings from the previous session. During a session, leaders can summarize the main learnings, feelings, themes, and emerging directions in the group. At the end of a session, leaders can summarize the session's main learnings. After summarizing, leaders can ask how accurate they have been and if participants have any further comments. A variation on the leaders' doing the summarizing is to ask participants to summarize either instead of or with the help of leaders.

Provided here is an evaluation questionnaire for assessing your use of facilitation skills in the initial stage of a training group. Many of these facilitation skills are highly relevant to leading other kinds of groups.

An Evaluation Questionnaire for Facilitation Skills in the Initial Stage
▾▾

This questionnaire has three purposes: (1) to guide you in preparing to use facilitation skills in the initial stage of training groups, (2) to assess your use of these skills, and (3) to allow others to assess your skills. You can answer the questionnaire either by placing a check for yes or a cross for no in the blank space by each item, or by responding to the items in your head, or by responding verbally in a learning or supervisory setting.

_____   I arranged the seating appropriately.

_____   I formulated and made a good opening statement.

_____   Where appropriate, I used getting-acquainted exercises well.

_____   I encouraged participation in the group.

_____   I encouraged participants to self-disclose relevant information.

_____   I encouraged participants to address each other.

_____   I gave permission to discuss fears about being in the group.

_____   I gave permission to discuss feelings of being different.

_____   Where appropriate, I supported individual participants.

_____   I fostered group rules conducive to participating in the group.

_____   I encouraged participant self-assessment in the targeted skills area(s).

_____   I encouraged participants to formulate and state personal goals.

_____   I helped the group work through resistances to participation.

_____   I demonstrated empathic understanding.

_____   I used questions well.

_____   I used facilitative confronting well.

_____   Where appropriate, I disclosed personal information.

_____   Where appropriate, I expressed feelings.

_____   Where appropriate, I used humor.

_____   I used good summarizing skills.

Exercise 11 provides some practice at facilitating the early stages of a lifeskills training group. The first part of the exercise is designed to give you practice at formulating and making opening statements. The second part of the exercise focuses on facilitating group interaction. Like many of the subsequent leader skills exercises, this exercise can be done either on your own or with others as part of a group leadership course or practicum.

Exercise 11 Develop Facilitation Skills for the Initial Stage
▼▼

1. Formulate and make opening statements
   a. What are the important considerations for formulating an opening statement for the first session of a lifeskills training group?
   b. Choose a lifeskills training group that you might want to run. Draft an opening statement for it. Speak your opening statement into a cassette recorder as though you were making it to the group. Play back your statement and modify both your content and delivery as necessary. If you are in a group leadership skills practicum, you can deliver your opening statement either in a subgroup or before the whole group.
2. Facilitate group discussion
   This part of the exercise is best done in groups of six to eight. Each person acts as leader and facilitates a group discussion of thirty to

forty-five minutes in a lifeskills area of his or her choice that is also of relevance to the rest of the group. The facilitator's task is to help participants share their experiences, assess their skills strengths and weaknesses, and formulate at least one personal goal. The skills to be used by facilitators include the following:

Formulating and making an opening statement
Encouraging participation
Assisting self-assessment and setting personal goals
Handling resistances
Where appropriate, empathic understanding, use of questions, facilitative confronting, and self-disclosing
Presenting an end-of-session summary

At the end of each session, there is a brief feedback period focused on how well the leader has used facilitation skills. To allow participants to be fresh, the sessions may need to be spread over a period of days or weeks. There are many possible variations on this exercise. These variations include using smaller groups, say one facilitator and three members; using co-facilitators; and using the "fishbowl" format, in which the inner circle or horseshoe is made up of participants in the facilitation exercise and the outer circle or horseshoe is composed of observers. These observers can be invited to provide feedback at the end of the session, possibly based on the Evaluation Questionnaire for Facilitation Skills in the Initial Stage, and on other occasions can act as the inner group. Video recording and playback may add to the exercise's value.

Facilitation Skills for the Working Stage
▼▼

Most of the facilitation skills necessary for the initial stage are highly relevant to the working stage of lifeskills training groups. In the working stage the training-group leader needs to have both good facilitation and good didactic skills to be maximally effective. Elsewhere, I have suggested that the working stage of most counseling groups centers on two main modes of interactive work: first, working in the "here and now"—developing the skills of intimacy; and second, working in the "there and now"—developing the skills of managing problems (Nelson-Jones, 1988b).

Lifeskills training groups, with their limited focus, tend to have a less intense focus on intimacy than do counseling or psychotherapy groups. Nevertheless, in training groups a reasonable degree of inter-participant intimacy is important in order to achieve such therapeutic factors as group cohesiveness, interpersonal learning (input), interpersonal learning (output), universality, and catharsis. In addition, leaders who facilitate participants in helping others manage their problems also help achieve such therapeutic factors as altruism and guidance. However, facilitation in training groups has additional functions beyond those of counseling and psychotherapy groups. Training-group leaders facilitate task-oriented learning. The didactic role of leaders necessitates using facilitation skills in such areas as running structured learning experiences; reviewing homework and use of skills outside the group; and encouraging participants' ongoing self-assessments of their skills strengths and weaknesses. In reality, no clear distinction exists between using facilitation skills for didactic as contrasted with group interactive purposes. Facilitating group interaction can greatly assist the didactic process. The present section focuses mainly on the facilitation of group discussion.

Leaders need to be mindful that facilitating discussion in training groups may require more focus than in counseling or psychotherapy groups. To what extent does discussion support or impede attaining training goals? Discussion in the working stage of a lifeskills group can help participants integrate their learning experiences inside and outside the group. Experiential learning requires not just participation in structured experiences, but also the opportunity to give personal meaning to these experiences and share these meanings with others. Furthermore, discussions involving self-disclosure and feedback are crucial ways in which participants learn from one another. A fatal assumption for training-group leaders is that they are the only source of significant input. However, leaders always have to make choices about the balance between discussion and structured experiences. In addition, even when permitting discussion, leaders need to make choices concerning whether or not participants' self-disclosures are relevant to attaining group goals and, if not, whether and how to intervene.

Facilitate Self-Disclosure

A major reason for using facilitation skills in the initial stage of training groups is to build trust both between participants and between participants and their leaders. During the working stage even more than in the initial stage, leaders endeavor to get participants to drop their social masks and defenses. Much learning in lifeskills training groups takes place in public. Consequently, in addition to their private anxieties, participants have the additional anxieties of being expected to expose and work on their skills strengths and weaknesses in front of others.

Following is a list of some of the rules or norms relevant to participants' self-disclosure that a leader may try to establish in lifeskills training groups.

We're all here to learn.

Each of us is worthy of respect and acceptance as a human being.

We will help ourselves more if we take responsibility for our learning and honestly admit our skills weaknesses and strengths.

We will help each other more if we share our difficulties and successes.

It's okay to talk about feelings and personal meanings as well as about thoughts and actions.

When discussing our experiences, we try to use "I" statements and to be specific.

It's okay to make and admit mistakes. Significant learning involves setbacks and mistakes.

It's okay to take risks in revealing ourselves in this group.

To get the most out of our skills group we need to collaborate rather than to compete with each other.

Each of us has a right to "air time" in the group.

Each of us tries to make our participation in discussions relevant to the group's purposes.

We respect each other's right to confidentiality.

How do leaders encourage rules conducive to constructive self-disclosure? Almost all of the skills of encouraging participation in the initial stage are also relevant to encouraging self-disclosure. These skills include encouraging self-referent talk, linking statements, issuing invitations to participate, giving permission to discuss fears, supporting, fostering norms conducive to participation, and intervening to prevent restrictive solutions to problems about participation. In addition, leaders who offer good facilitation skills of empathic understanding, use of questions, and facilitative confronting, and who model self-disclosure create a climate conducive to honesty and openness.

Training-group leaders can openly stress the value of participants' disclosures. Leaders can mention some of the ground rules just listed and ask participants their opinions about them. Furthermore, leaders can use and withhold rewards to foster constructive self-disclosure. For example, leaders can say something like "I appreciate your openness" or "I admire your courage" when participants level with the group about an embarrassing skills weakness or experience. On the other hand, leaders can query disclosures that are focused on other people rather than being self-referent—for example, "I'm wondering what the relevance of that is to you?" Furthermore, if a participant starts monopolizing and the group seems to be either doing little about it or possibly colluding in it, leaders can intervene to broaden participation. Possible statements in such circumstances include: "Is there anyone else who would like to share an experience?" or "Is there anyone else who would like to tell the group how they assess their skills?"

Facilitate Open Mutual Feedback

In any group, rules develop about what participants notice and what they do not notice, and also about participants' giving feedback. Participants learn about themselves from feedback in such areas as how they come across to others, habits that annoy or please, and how they confuse through not communicating clearly. In addition, participants can give each other feedback about how they perform in the targeted skills—for instance, when they speak in public or when they assert themselves. A further important learning from receiving feedback is that participants may find they possess the strength to take it. Critical comments, however aggressively given, do not mean the end of the world. Because someone else defines their behavior in a certain way does not mean that they automatically have to define themselves that way. Instead, participants can assess the comments and try to sort out what is of value. Also, leaders can help participants to develop the communication skills of acknowledging and responding to feedback.

Ivey and his colleagues have identified a skill they call *direct mutual communication* (Higgins, Ivey, & Uhlemann, 1970; Ivey & Authier, 1978). When using this skill, two people in an interaction try to share how they experience interacting with the other. Egan calls this skill "you-me" talk (Egan, 1977). Egan (1990) distinguishes among three types of immediacy in helping: (1) *self-involving statements*—"present-tense, personal responses" (p. 224) to another; (2) *relationship immediacy*—your ability to discuss "where you stand in your overall relationship" (p. 225); and (3) *here and now immediacy*—your ability to discuss "what is happening between you in the here and now of any given transaction" (p. 226). Egan's three types of immediacy are applicable to how participants relate in training groups. Here the term *open mutual feedback* is preferred to *immediacy*. Open mutual feedback can refer to feedback about either an overall relationship, or any interaction in it, or any behavior in it. In lifeskills training groups, much participant feedback focuses on performance in the targeted skills rather than on relationships.

Open mutual feedback between participants is a complex skill containing a number of different components. These components include tuning in to one's own thoughts and feelings as well as understanding and showing sensitivity to another's thoughts and feelings. Leaders can help participants develop the skills of *giving* feedback. It is one thing to give feedback and another to have it listened to. In general, feedback is more likely to be effective if the speaker (1) frames it as an "I" statement starting with "I feel . . . " or "I think . . . " rather than a a "you" statement starting with "You are . . . "; (2) is specific and clear; and (3) invites discussion rather than is dogmatic.

Leaders can also help participants develop the skills of *receiving* feedback. Some participants may be unrealistically threatened by

feedback and require thinking more calmly about it. Such participants can tell themselves things like "I do not need everyone's approval," "I do not have to be perfect," "People who give me feedback
may be trying to help me," and "I do not have to accept everything
that is said about me. Instead I can evaluate it to see if I can learn
something useful from it."

In addition, participants can develop the action skills of *responding to* feedback and, where appropriate, *inviting* it. Responding-
to-feedback skills include reflecting it to make sure that you have
understood it and asking for more specific information. Inviting-
feedback skills include statements like "I wonder how I'm coming
across to other people in the group" and "How did you assess my
skills after this role-play?" Also, leaders can provide feedback to participants on how they block feedback—for example, by getting angry, not paying attention, dismissing it out of hand, belittling the
sender, or changing the subject.

Exercise 12 is designed to give you the experiences of (1) trying
to facilitate others in open mutual feedback, (2) giving feedback, and
(3) receiving and responding to feedback.

Exercise 12 Facilitate Open Mutual Feedback

▾ ▾

This exercise can be done in groups of three to six. With numbers
larger than six, it may be best to subdivide the group. Video recording and playback may add to the value of this exercise.

1. Person A acts as facilitator, person B as the recipient of feedback, and the remaining participants of the group as providers of
feedback.

2. Person A explains the concept of open mutual feedback to the
group, who are seated in a circle. Person A then invites group participants to give person B feedback about either their thoughts and feelings about him or her or their assessments of his or her strengths and
weaknesses in a previously agreed-upon lifeskills area. Each other
participant gives person B feedback. During the feedback, person B
is allowed to ask for greater specificity if he or she does not understand the feedback. Only at the end of everybody's feedback is person
B allowed to comment on his or her reactions to both the feedback
and how constructively it was given. The session ends with person A
debriefing both person B and the remainder of the group on what it
felt like to receive and give face-to-face feedback.

3. The exercise continues with a new person A and person B until each participant has had a chance to be both the facilitator and the
receiver of feedback.

4. At the end, in light of their experience of doing the whole exer-

cise, the group discusses the role in lifeskills training groups of leaders' facilitating participants in giving and receiving feedback.

Facilitate Helping Each Other to Manage Problems

As in counseling and psychotherapy groups, in training groups participants often share outside problems with the group. However, this sharing tends to be in areas relevant to the group's objectives. Sharing of problems involving targeted lifeskills may intensify as participants try out new behaviors. Often such sharing takes place either before or after homework focused on transfer of skills to the outside.

When participants bring in their outside problems for discussion, this is a form of sharing with the whole group and not just with leaders. Participants may gain both from helping and being helped by their peers. Participants can often obtain more insight into their own problems if they help others break down and understand how they sustain their problems. Furthermore, just as two heads may be better than one, many heads may be better than two. Consequently, group leaders as trainers often help participants develop the skills of helping each other. Following is a list of skills that facilitate this kind of discussion.

Facilitate interparticipant empathy: Leaders can intervene in ways that encourage participants to be sensitive to and accurately listen to what others think and feel as they share problems with the group. Leaders can identify and encourage skills of not just accurately understanding information, but also of showing speakers that one understands and cares.

Facilitate participants' self-disclosing: One way that participants can help each other to manage problems is to share their experiences and struggles with similar problems. Leaders may need to intervene to help participants make disclosures relevant to another's problems. Sometimes participants can help each other much more by the disclosing skills of sharing problems than by the listening skills of empathic responding and questions. Frequently, the combination of disclosing and listening is desirable.

Facilitate participants in making working definitions of each other's and their own problems: Leaders can help participants acknowledge and help each other acknowledge the importance of assuming responsibility for their skills weaknesses in sustaining problems. Leaders can help participants break down and help each other break down problems in such a way that thinking and action skills weaknesses sustaining problems are clearly identified.

Facilitate participants in helping each other set goals and develop action plans: Leaders can assist participants to understand the importance of translating insight into action. While keeping responsibility for outside actions clearly with individuals, leaders can encourage participants to discuss their goals in the group and how they plan to achieve them. Furthermore, leaders can help participants understand the steps of managing and solving problems (D'Zurilla & Goldfried, 1971; Egan, 1990; Nelson-Jones, 1990a).

Encourage the formation of constructive group rules and behaviors: Leaders need to influence the development of rules that help participants work together on managing problems from outside the group. Pressures for conformity, excessive dependency on group decisions, and intellectualizing about rather than working on problems are all rules to be discouraged. Avoiding restrictive rules can mainly be achieved by encouraging constructive ones.

Make links: Leaders can help participants to make connections between others' problems and their own. They can assist participants to acknowledge that problems are a part of living and to realize that they can develop problem-management skills not only alone, but also by observing and helping each other work.

The purpose of Exercise 13 is to raise your awareness of the need for training-group leaders to facilitate participants in helping each other manage problems. Leaders who can successfully release their groups' helping potentials foster cohesiveness.

Exercise 13 Facilitate Participants in Helping Each Other Manage Problems
▼▼▼

This exercise can be done in groups of three to six. With numbers above six, it may be best to subdivide the group. Video recording and playback may add to the value of this exercise.

1. The group is seated in a circle. Participants agree upon who is to be facilitator and who is to share a problem with the group. This problem should be in a lifeskills area of interest and relevance to most, if not all, participants.

2. The facilitator starts the group by saying that the group has twenty minutes to help the problem sharer to manage it better. The problem is then shared and the facilitator works with participants to assist them in helping the sharer. Toward the end of the twenty minutes the facilitator summarizes where the group appears to have arrived at in its helping. Then he or she asks first the problem sharer and next the other participants for their reactions to the summary. The group finishes promptly after twenty minutes. Time follows for sharing and discussion focused on (a) feedback from the problem sharer regarding comments experienced as helpful or harmful to his or her managing the problem, (b) comments from the facilitator on issues in facilitating participant helping, and (c) comments from participants on any aspect of the session.

3. The twenty-minute sessions are repeated until each participant has had the opportunity to be both facilitator and problem sharer.

Set Limits on Discussion

Lifeskills training groups are working as well as talking groups. If anything, their task-oriented agendas take precedence over their relationship-oriented agendas. Because training groups mix discussion, presentation, and structured activities, leaders often have to set limits on the *amount* of discussion they facilitate. Sometimes leaders may allocate a set amount of time for discussion either in the whole group or in subgroups or pairs. For instance, leaders may allocate set amounts of time for discussing homework, getting reactions to lecturettes, and reviewing skills at the end of a session. On other occasions, leaders may allocate time for discussion based on the quality of the discussion, the amount of energy invested in it, and on what else requires attention. Leaders can also ask participants their views on the mix in a session between discussion, presentation, and structured activities.

Training-group leaders may also have to set limits on the *type* of discussion they facilitate. For instance, leaders in pain-management groups may allow participants some time to ventilate their negative feelings about being in pain, but then invite them to move on to look at ways of making the most of their lives despite their pain. Participants already know a lot about their pain. If this type of discussion were to go on week after week, leaders risk colluding in participants' getting stuck in unproductive self-pity rather than helping them to develop skills and coping strategies to manage pain better. In the working stage of effective lifeskills training groups, there should be a shift from descriptive discussion of difficulties to discussions in which participants show greater insight into the skills weaknesses that sustain them. Also, there should be an increase in participants' abilities to help each other.

Facilitation Skills for the Ending Stage
▼▼▼

Leaders use facilitation skills differently at the end of lifeskills training groups as contrasted with counseling and psychotherapy groups. Gazda (1989) observes that the group counselor's responsibility at what he calls the termination stage is "to reinforce the growth made by group members and to make sure that all group counselees have had the opportunity to work out their differences with the counselor and other group members before leaving" (p. 82). Training-group leaders tend to avoid words like *growth*, considering them insufficiently specific. In ending training groups, leaders are much more focused on reinforcing the specific self-help skills targeted as goals for the program than on sorting out unfinished relationship issues. The major agendas of the ending stage of training groups are consolidating participants' specific skills and facilitating their transfer, maintenance, and development outside.

Group leader skills in ending and evaluating lifeskills groups are covered more thoroughly later in this book. Suffice it for now to indicate that all the facilitation skills mentioned for the working stage also apply to the ending stage. However, there are differences in emphasis in how these skills are used in the two stages. For example, there may be a shift from facilitating self-disclosure about current problems in using the targeted skills to facilitating disclosure of anxieties about using the skills in the future without group support. Open mutual feedback will likely be focused on end-of-group assessments of each other's skills as well as on personal farewells. Also, when leaders facilitate participants in helping each other, the agenda may be the problem of how best to maintain and develop individuals' skills after the group ends. Leaders can help participants look at issues of reentry into their "home" environments and how to get support for their skills development. Furthermore, leaders can facilitate participants' discussing whether and how best to support each other after the group ends.

Ten *Must's* That Interfere with Group Facilitation
▼▼

Group facilitation, be it of counseling and psychotherapy or of lifeskills training groups, requires leaders to possess good inner game, or thinking, skills and good outer game, or observable action, skills. Group facilitators can be severely hampered by thinking skills weaknesses, sometimes colloquially referred to as "stinkin' thinkin'." Here the focus is on unrealistic rules or what Ellis (1980, 1989) terms irrational beliefs as contrasted with rational beliefs. The unrealistic *must*'s, *ought*'s and *should*'s that leaders may bring to facilitation are not only important in their own right, but also because they can adversely influence other leader thinking skills, such as coping self-talk and perceiving.

Ideally, group facilitators possess what Gallwey (1974) terms relaxed concentration. They are alert and relaxed at the same time. However, facilitating a training group may be fraught with anxieties. For instance, leaders may feel very much on display and under pressure to get participants involved. Furthermore, because of their previous experiences, leaders may inadequately comprehend how to facilitate training groups. For example, former teachers may overemphasize teaching, former preachers may overemphasize preaching, and former encounter group facilitators may overemphasize participants' encountering each other. Consequently, for both emotional and prior learning reasons, leaders may sabotage their effectiveness as facilitators through how they think.

The following are ten unrealistic rules or irrational *must*'s that may interfere with leaders' offering good group-facilitation skills. Such unrealistic personal rules are self-oppressing rather than self-supporting (Nelson-Jones, 1990a). These inner pressurizers are the very stuff upon which uptight and inflexible facilitation is built.

1. *I must be the sole source of wisdom in the group.* Leaders who set themselves up as universal experts both grossly overvalue their own contribution and also grossly undervalue the contribution that participants can make to each other's skills development.

2. *I must be in control of the group at all times.* The structured focus of lifeskills training groups means that the initial contract has implicit in it a greater degree of leader control than generally found in counseling and therapy groups. However, this initial contract should not be taken as an excuse for leaders to monopolize and dominate groups. Even if leaders wanted to, they could not control all the different interactions that transpire. However, there are many other reasons why such a high degree of leader control is undesirable—for instance, infantalizing participants and eroding their motivation and energy.

3. *I must be aware of everything that goes on in the group.* Unlike in individual work, where helpers can possess a high degree of awareness concerning their clients, such a level of awareness is impossible in group work. Skilled leaders are relaxed, yet alert enough to catch most of the significant messages sent in the group. However, skilled leaders also accept their limitations. They realize that because of the size of the group and their own fallibility, they may miss some important messages. However, such messages may still be picked up by other participants or later by the leaders themselves.

4. *I must be liked all the time by all participants.* The demand for approval is one of the classic Ellis (1980, 1989) "mustabatory" beliefs. This belief can lead to a superficial niceness rather than a willingness to be authentic and genuine. Further negative outcomes stemming from this belief may be a heightened self-awareness that takes energy away from true awareness of others, a need to perceive others in ways that sustain possibly unrealistic aspects of your self-picture, and a heightened sensitivity to signs of aggression and rejection. Such a universal demand for approval needs to be disputed and reformulated. A possible reformulation is "Though I might prefer to have participants' approval all the time, I certainly do not need it. What is important is that I do my job competently and remain sensitive to how others perceive my behavior, without being controlled by them."

5. *I must always maintain a professional facade.* Leaders are at risk of conveying a spurious expertness that may mask underlying

insecurities and doubts about their competence. Participants can be highly sensitive to cues that a less-than-competent group leader is engaging in impression management. Even competent leaders may seem more competent if they can be authentic, spontaneous, and honest about their limitations and mistakes. Participants like group leaders to be human as well as competent (Rogers, 1970). Leaders can help participants feel as if they are in a negative social exchange if, unlike themselves, participants are the only fallible people in the group (Homans, 1961).

6. *I must pressure participants to self-disclose.* Carl Rogers (1970) writes of his experience in facilitating encounter groups, "From my experience I know that if I attempt to push a group to a deeper level it is not, in the long run, going to work" (p. 48). Inexperienced training-group leaders may want quick results. They may expect deep and meaningful disclosures before a climate of trust has been established. Pressing too hard too soon can create resistance to disclosure. Alternatively, it can lead to phony pseudo-disclosure where participants feel they have to catalog their sins and skills weaknesses. Sound leader facilitation skills can help participants to drop their social masks so that they disclose and work on more fundamental issues in their lives. Groups tend to vary in their willingness and the pace at which they are prepared to disclose. Clumsy leader pressure to disclose, possibly coupled with gimmicky games and exercises, may well do more harm than good.

7. *I must ensure that great attention is paid to relationship issues between participants.* This unrealistic rule has been included as a caveat for those at risk of not fully making the transition from facilitating counseling and psychotherapy groups to facilitating training groups. There are limits to how much leaders can allow participants to discuss relationship issues without jeopardizing the overall task of developing specific lifeskills. Sometimes leaders can use relationship problems between participants as here-and-now examples of their strengths and weaknesses in the targeted skills areas. However, leaders must beware of letting the group lose momentum by lengthy discussions of participants' feelings about one another, especially if unrelated to the skills focus of the group.

8. *I must always have an explanation or interpretation for everything.* Rogers (1970) mistrusted facilitators who frequently gave interpretations of the motives and causes behind group members' behaviors. He objected to labeling people with comments like "You certainly have a lot of latent hostility" (p. 67). Even if such interpretations were accurate, he felt such comments might arouse defensiveness and unnecessary feelings of hurt. For two important reasons, lifeskills group leaders do not need to have explanations for everything. First, when facilitating, leaders should keep quiet much of the time and let the group do the work. Second, as Rogers rightly observed, interpretations and explanations may not always be helpful.

However, sometimes leader explanations may be helpful—for example, to throw light on how participants sustain skills weaknesses.

9. *Facilitating a training group must be all work and no play.* Just because some of the content of a lifeskills training group may be serious does not mean that the group must be conducted in an atmosphere of self-negation and pain. All work and no play makes for dullness. Often pain, tragedy, and laughter are not far apart. Participants who can use humor constructively have a great asset with which to confront difficulties. Skilled leaders do not take themselves too seriously, but know when to be serious. In addition, groups where it is okay to reveal happy as well as sad feelings are much more likely to be human and welcoming places than those where participants and leaders must wear mandatory long faces. Life is too short always to be serious. Lifeskills groups can and often should be fun!

10. *I must always get the balance right between presentation, structured activities, and group discussion.* Such a *must* erroneously assumes that there is a single right balance between didactic input and group discussion. Furthermore, this *must* erroneously assumes that leaders should carry all the responsibility for the decision about balance and not involve participants in it. Inevitably, leaders are going to make on-the-spot decisions about balance depending on their assessments of the relevant variables at the time. Such variables include their session objectives, how long the presentations and structured activities take to do properly, whether group discussion at that stage is likely to enhance skill development, and whether or not the group needs the opportunity for the emotional release of participating in a discussion.

The preceding list makes the point that facilitating a lifeskills training group involves not only what you do, but also how rationally you think about what you do. How much at risk are you of harming your outer game of facilitating a training group because of weaknesses in your inner game of how you think about it?

▼ Chapter Highlights

▼ Training-group leaders use facilitation skills both for facilitating group discussion and for facilitating structured learning experiences.

▼ Whether they are being didactic or facilitative, training-group leaders always send and receive messages.

▼ Leaders send messages in five main ways: verbal, voice, body, touch, and action. It is important that leaders send congruent or consistent messages.

▼ Facilitation skills for the initial stage include arranging suitable seating; making opening statements; using getting-acquainted exercises; encouraging participation; assisting self-assessment and stat-

(continued)

▼ **Chapter Highlights** (continued)

ing personal goals; handling resistances; and further facilitation skills such as empathic understanding, use of questions, facilitative confronting, self-disclosing, and summarizing.

▼ Facilitation skills relevant to group discussion in the working stage include facilitating self-disclosure, facilitating open mutual feedback, and facilitating participants to help each other manage problems. In addition, leaders may need to set limits on the amount and type of discussion allowed.

▼ Facilitation skills for the ending stage include those for the working stage modified for the different concerns participants have when lifeskills training groups are about to terminate.

▼ Training-group leaders require good inner game or thinking skills as well as good outer game or action skills to perform both their didactic and facilitative functions.

▼ Leaders may possess unrealistic rules or irrational *must*'s that interfere with the relaxed concentration required for effective facilitation of lifeskills groups. Ten of these interfering *must*'s are identified and discussed.

7

How to Speak in Public

All the great speakers were bad speakers at first.

Ralph Waldo Emerson

Chapter Questions

How do training-group leaders give effective presentations?

What are some of the dimensions of speech anxiety?

How can leaders use thinking skills to manage speech anxiety?

What are some considerations in preparing systematic content for lifeskills presentations?

What are some of the main audiovisual aids that leaders use?

What are good delivery skills?

When giving presentations, what voice and body messages should leaders convey?

Introduction

Previous chapters have focused on assessing participants and facilitating training groups. The next three chapters specifically focus on the didactic role of training-group leaders. In this role, leaders tell, show, and do. Correspondingly, participants learn from hearing, observing, and doing. Table 7-1 depicts the training and learning modes employed in lifeskills groups. The notion of consolidation has been incorporated into Table 7-1 to highlight the importance of leaders' focusing throughout groups on issues of transfer, maintenance, and development of skills after the groups end.

This chapter reviews public-speaking skills, the *telling* mode. The next chapter covers demonstrating lifeskills, the *showing* mode. Then follows a chapter on managing structured activities, the *doing* mode. With varying degrees of success, many academic presenta-

Table 7-1. Modes of Training and Learning

Training Mode	Learning Mode
Assessment	Learning from self-evaluating and self-monitoring
Facilitation	Learning from interacting in the group
Telling	Learning from hearing
Showing	Learning from observing demonstrations
Doing	Learning from doing structured activities and homework tasks
Consolidation	Learning from developing self-help skills in all the above modes

tions emphasize learning by hearing. However, training people to integrate applied lifeskills into their repertoires is generally more effective if it adds learning by observing and by doing. Figure 7-1 schematically represents interrelationships among learning by hearing, observing, and doing. During lifeskills groups, these three training and learning modes influence each other. For example, when initially presenting a lifeskill, a leader may tell, show, and then do. As participants practice a skill, doing may be interspersed with hearing and observing.

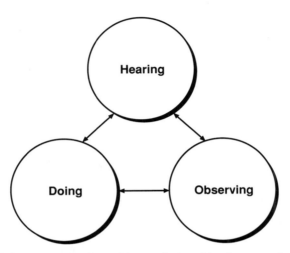

Figure 7-1 Representation of interrelationships between learning by hearing, observing, and doing.

Leaders, even those basing programs on training manuals, frequently present information. Following are examples of leaders with varying degrees of skill in the *telling* mode, or public speaking.

▾ Karima gives a presentation on saying no to unreasonable requests. Though Karima has prepared thoroughly, she handles her anxiety by reading her talk. Consequently, she fails to make contact with her audience.
▾ Jose gives a talk on identifying leisure interests. He has failed to structure his talk clearly. He further confuses his audience by using long and rambling sentences.
▾ Mary Beth introduces the topic of how to reduce parent–child conflict. She has thoroughly researched her talk. She then translates her notes into an interesting script with short and easily comprehensible sentences. She delivers her talk with good voice and body messages.

There is no magic about public-speaking skills. If you have observed polished speakers, you can be certain that they have worked hard to acquire their polish. They have learned to avoid inflicting on audiences what *New York Times* columnist Bill Safire describes as MEGO (My Eyes Glaze Over) (Valenti, 1982). Where appropriate, they use their hold over their audience's attention to influence them. Polished speakers may also have learned to avoid inflicting MATO (My Anxiety Takes Over) on themselves and their audiences. Thus, polished speakers possess the inner and outer game skills of effective public speaking.

In all lifeskills training sessions, there is a tension between the need for didactic and facilitative interventions. A balance is required, depending on the objectives of a particular session. The use of formal presentations can be overdone at the expense of learning by doing and group participation. Consequently, most often, leaders should give lecturettes of 5, 10, or 15 minutes rather than longer talks. Though these lecturettes often include skills demonstrations, here the focus is on public speaking.

Speech Anxiety
▼ ▼

Speech anxiety or "stage fright" is a very real affliction for many aspiring training-group leaders. Even famous actors, such as the late Laurence Olivier, suffer stage fright. Some anxiety prior to and during a performance can facilitate rather than debilitate (Alpert & Haber, 1960). However, too much or the wrong sort of anxiety interferes with competent task performance. Meichenbaum and his colleagues suggest that there are two general types of people suffering from speech anxiety: those for whom speech anxiety is part of a shyness response across a number of interpersonal situations and those for whom speech anxiety is only a problem in public-speaking situations (Meichenbaum, Gilmore, & Fedoravicius, 1971). Group leaders suffering from speech anxiety may fall into either category.

Following is a list of some considerations for defining speech anxiety and for assessing how much you suffer from it.

1. *Feelings*: Feelings associated with speech anxiety include tension, insecurity, bashfulness, embarrassment, confusion, fear, vulnerability, and inadequacy.
2. *Physical reactions*: Physical reactions associated with speech anxiety include feeling faint, nausea, blushing, perspiring, shaking, pounding heart, shallow breathing, butterflies in stomach, mind going blank, mouth going dry.
3. *Thoughts*: Negative self-talk and unrealistic personal rules are two thinking skills weaknesses contributing to speech anxiety.
   a. *Negative self-talk*: Negative self-talk is inner speech that is more negative than a realistic appraisal of the objective evidence

warrants. Some of this negative self-talk involves negative and catastrophic predictions. Negative self-talk statements include the following: "I'm no good"; "I'm going to make a mess of it"; "I can't cope with my speech anxiety"; "I lack the skills to hold my audience"; "My audience will think I'm incompetent"; "My audience is not interested in what I have to say"; and "My audience will think less of me because I am nervous."

    b. *Unrealistic personal rules*: Unrealistic personal rules cause speakers to put counterproductive pressures on themselves. Such rules, which may be at or just below awareness, include the following: I *must* be a good public speaker immediately; I *must* make the perfect speech every time; I *must* have my audience's total attention and approval; I *must* be the absolute master/mistress of my subject matter; I *must* be in control at all times.

4. *Verbal, voice, body, and action messages*: Illustrative verbal, voice, body, and action messages associated with speech anxiety include the following:

    a. *Verbal messages*: Being neutral and not stating your own opinions; being too ready to agree; using too many *um*'s and *er*'s; and using confused and rambling sentences

    b. *Voice messages*: Speaking quietly; speaking too quickly; stammering; and loudness that masks insecurity

    c. *Body messages*: Poor gaze and eye contact—for example, reading your talk; smiling too much; tight body posture; scratching your face; and shuffling papers

    d. *Action messages*: Avoiding public-speaking situations; only doing individual rather than group helping; speaking for as short a time as possible; avoiding time for discussion; leaving the speaker's position as soon as possible; and muddled use of audiovisual aids

5. *Defensive roles*: Some people handle public-speaking anxiety by wearing either social or professional masks. These masks may be viewed as defensive roles to the extent that they contain hidden agendas not directly relevant to the tasks at hand. Examples of defensive roles include pretending to be more of an expert than you are, acting more helpless and vulnerable than necessary, playing the clown, playing the cynic, playing the flirt, monopolizing, and being aggressive.

6. *Anxiety-evoking people*: You may experience speech anxiety more with some categories of people than others. Such people may include the following: strangers, authorities by virtue of their knowledge, authorities by virtue of their role, colleagues, the opposite sex, older people, children, resistant people, and reluctant people forced to attend.

7. *Anxiety-evoking situations*: Situations associated with speech anxiety include the following: participating in discussion groups;

leading discussion groups; situations involving formal assessment; a lifeskills talk before five to nine people; a lifeskills talk before ten to twenty people; a lifeskills talk before twenty-one to fifty people; a lifeskills talk before more than fifty people; answering questions after a lifeskills talk; having your lifeskills talk recorded on an audiotape or videotape; and going for an interview.

This section has developed some of the dimensions of speech anxiety. Some people may suffer from speech anxiety, but deny or dilute its extent. Awareness of a problem and breaking it down into component parts is a first step in coping with it. Exercise 14 is designed to raise your awareness of how you may suffer from speech anxiety.

Exercise 14 Assess Your Speech Anxiety
▼▼

Make a worksheet like the one following. For each of the dimensions fill in your assessment of how, if at all, you exhibit anxiety when you speak in public.

Feelings	
Physical reactions	
Negative self-talk	
Unrealistic personal rules	
Verbal messages	
Voice messages	
Body messages	
Action messages	
Defensive roles	

1. What kinds of people that you are likely to come across either evoke or might evoke anxiety in you when you speak in public?
2. What kinds of public-speaking situations that you are likely to face either are or might be anxiety-evoking for you?
3. Summarize how anxious you are when you speak in public and in what ways you experience and show your anxiety.
4. What are the consequences of any speech anxiety you possess for your effectiveness as a training-group leader?

Managing Speech-Anxious Thinking

How can lifeskills group leaders suffering from speech anxiety develop the skills of preventing MATO (My Anxiety Takes Over)? You can help to combat speech anxiety by learning, rehearsing, and practicing the skills of putting your talks together and delivering them in interesting ways. These composition and delivery skills are covered later. Here the focus is on learning to support rather than oppress yourself by how you think about speaking in public. Following is a list of nine broad areas of thinking skills, albeit overlapping, in which you may have either weaknesses or strengths or, most likely, both (Nelson-Jones, 1990a).

1. Owning your responsibility for being a chooser
2. Being in touch with your underlying feelings
3. Using self-talk constructively
4. Choosing realistic personal rules
5. Choosing to perceive yourself and others accurately
6. Accurately attributing cause
7. Making realistic predictions
8. Having goals that you articulate clearly and that reflect your values
9. Using visualizing to best effect

Each of these thinking skills is now reviewed in turn. The object is both to help those with speech anxiety to identify the skills weaknesses that maintain the anxiety and to suggest some ways of thinking more effectively.

Owning Your Responsibility for Being a Chooser

Some speech-anxious people may possess insufficient awareness that they are always choosers in their lives (Frankl, 1959; May & Yalom, 1989). For example, they may drift along in varying states of awareness that speech anxiety is a problem for them without ever trying to do much about it. Many people fail to realize their responsibility for making the thinking, feeling, and action choices that help them best realize their potential. They may possess illusions of assuming responsibility for their lives and yet not have the knowledge, skills, and discipline to do this effectively. People who avoid thinking about speech anxiety in terms of its component skills face a major stumbling block to working on their problems.

Being in Touch with Your Underlying Feelings

Being insufficiently in touch with your own feelings and valuing process may contribute to public-speaking difficulties in a number of ways. First, you may deny or dilute the extent to which you feel anxious about speaking in public. Insufficient awareness of the problem may impede taking corrective action. Second, you may lack a sufficient sense of your own identity. Because of this you may feel very exposed when giving public presentations. You may fear that people will perceive no substance under your surface. Third, you may overly focus on feelings of insecurity and anxiety and insufficiently focus on feelings of strength and competence. You are only in touch with part of your range of feelings. Fourth, you may place a value on perfectionist achievement in public-speaking situations that is a "hand-me-down" of someone else's values. Rogers has used the term *conditions of worth* to describe valuing yourself on the basis of another's beliefs rather than on your feelings and thoughts (Raskin & Rogers, 1989; Rogers, 1959).

Some people badly out of touch with their valuing process require counseling and psychotherapy. Self-help approaches include developing your skills of inner listening and focusing on aspects of your thinking in ways described in the following pages. Developing inner listening skills starts with acknowledging the importance of awareness of feelings (Gendlin, 1981). Feelings often appear first as feeling fragments rather than as full-blown emotions. You need to be able to identify and label these feeling fragments to be able to assess their significance. Sometimes you may need to clear a temporal and emotional space so as to spend quiet time focusing on your true feelings.

Using Self-Talk Constructively

Coping self-talk is another thinking skill for managing public-speaking anxiety (Fremouw & Zittler, 1978; Meichenbaum, 1983, 1985, 1986; Meichenbaum & Deffenbacher, 1988; Meichenbaum, Gilmore, & Fedoravicius, 1971). The idea is to replace anxious and task-irrelevant negative self-talk with more constructive self-statements. Kendall and Hollon (1989) have developed an Anxious Self-statements Questionnaire. Anxious self-statements include the following: "I can't take it"; "I can't cope"; I can't do anything right"; "Don't let me be crazy"; "I wish I could escape"; "Can I make it?"; and "I feel totally confused."

Coping self-talk involves replacing anxious and negative self-talk statements with helpful ones. In coping self-talk, calming and coaching statements tend to be interspersed.

Calming Self-Talk

Two important areas of calming self-talk are as follows. First, tell yourself to stay calm. Sample self-statements include: "Keep calm," "Relax," and "Take it easy." In addition, you can instruct yourself to "Take a deep breath" or "Breathe slowly and regularly." Second, tell yourself you can cope. Sample self-statements include: "I can handle this talk" and "My anxiety is a signal for me to use my coping skills."

Coaching Self-Talk

Coaching self-talk has three parts. First, specify your goals—for example, "I will give a talk lasting five minutes and speak at a comfortable rate for me and my audience." Second, break tasks down, thinking through the specific steps and tasks required for attaining goals—for example, "I need to maintain good eye contact with my audience."

Third, concentrate on the task at hand. You can instruct yourself like pilots talking themselves through to difficult landings. A small but important aid, self-instruction is easier if your external speech rate is not fast.

Coping Self-Talk for Before, During, and After

You can use coping self-talk before, during, and after public-speaking situations. Possible coping self-talk statements for *before* a stressful lifeskills talk situation include the following:

"I know I will feel less anxious if I am properly prepared."
"No negative self-talk. Just think rationally."
"Calm down. What is it I have to do?"

Possible coping self-talk statements for *during* a stressful lifeskills talk situation include the following:

"Relax. The audience is not expecting perfection so I don't need to expect it either."
"Stay cool. Take my time. Just aim for a steady performance."
"Hang in there. I'm using my coping skills and I'm doing okay."

Possible coping self-talk statements for *after* a stressful lifeskills talk situation include the following:

"My fears were not justified by how I felt once I got started."
"Each time I cope it seems to get easier."
"I'm proud of the way I'm learning to manage my fears."

Acquiring and using coping self-talk involves much work and practice. Those speech-anxiety situations in which leaders most need their coping self-talk skills are often the same situations where they are least likely to use them. Speech-anxious leaders need to identify the coping self-talk statements that work best for them. Then they need to rehearse and practice these statements both in real-life situations and in their imaginations. Imaginal rehearsal, in which you talk yourself through public-speaking situations as you visualize them, has many advantages. You are not restricted to requiring a live audience. You can anticipate and work through difficulties and setbacks. You can choose your rehearsal times and rehearse regularly.

Choosing Realistic Personal Rules

As mentioned in Chapter 2, your personal rules are the *do*'s and *don't*s by which you lead your life. Each of us has an inner rule book that guides our living. If your rules are self-supporting, they can motivate and help you to attain realistic goals. However, if your rules are self-oppressing, they leave you open to a triple dose of self-disparagement. Luis has a rule that he must be a good public speaker immediately. However, his first lifeskills talk does not go particularly well, so this activates his first dose of self-disparagement. His second dose of self-disparagement is because he then becomes anxious and depressed about his overall public-speaking ability. His third dose of self-disparagement comes about because now he starts devaluing not just his public-speaking ability but also his worth as a person.

Ellis (1980, 1989), as mentioned previously, has coined the term *mustabation* to refer to rigid personal rules characterized by *must*'s, *ought*'s, and *should*'s. He has developed a simple ABC framework (see Chapter 5) for showing how people's thinking affects their feelings and behavior (Ellis, 1962).

A = the activating event
B = your beliefs about the activating event
C = the emotional and behavioral consequences

Ellis regards the emotional and behavioral consequences as being determined by your beliefs relating to the activating event rather than by the activating event itself. Here the term *personal rules* is preferred to *beliefs*. Let us place the example of Luis into the ABC framework.

A Luis's first lifeskills talk does not go particularly well.
B Luis has the personal rule that he must be a good public speaker immediately.
C Luis's emotional consequences include anxiety and depression. Behavioral consequences for Luis may include either giving up or trying too hard next time.

Inappropriate feelings and actions may be signals that you possess one or more inappropriate personal rules. For example, if your speech anxiety is persistent and uncomfortable, you may be oppressing yourself through inappropriate personal rules. In addition, if you become aware that you behave inappropriately when giving a talk—for instance, speaking too much or being too gushing—again look at the realism of your rules. Earlier when describing speech anxiety, I suggested five unrealistic personal rules that may contribute to speech anxiety: I *must* be a good public speaker immediately; I *must* make the perfect speech every time; I *must* have the audience's total attention and approval; I *must* be the absolute master/mistress of my subject matter; I *must* be in control at all times.

Once you become aware that your underlying self-talk contains one or more unrealistic personal rules, what can you do about it? Disputing and reformulating these self-oppressing rules are two skills that can help you move toward self-supporting rules. Ellis (1980, 1989) considers the technique of disputing to be the most typical and often-used method of rational-emotive therapy. Disputing involves logically challenging the false assumptions that you may hold about yourself, others, and the world.

Barbara is a training-group leader who has the personal rule: I *must* give the perfect talk every time. Questions that Barbara might ask herself to dispute her self-oppressing rule include the following:

What evidence exists for the truth of my personal rule?
What is the worst that might happen if I give a less-than-perfect talk?
Do I demand the same standards of other people who give lifeskills talks as I demand of myself?
In what ways does giving a less-than-perfect lifeskills talk make me worthless as a person?
What are the costs and consequences to me and others of my demand that I must always give a perfect talk?
To what extent does my wanting always to give the perfect lifeskills talk represent my past learning history rather than the reality of my present situation and wishes?

You may need to dispute the same self-oppressing rules again and again. This is because such rules have become well-established habits. Ellis strongly emphasizes that people need to work hard to change. He regards most of his clients as "natural resisters who find it exceptionally easy to block themselves from changing and find it unusually hard to resist their resistances" (Ellis, 1987, pp. 370–371).

Reformulating involves substituting self-supporting for self-oppressing characteristics in specific personal rules. Some of the main characteristics of self-supporting personal rules are as follows:

Expressing preferences rather than demands: Though you would prefer to give a competent talk, it is not absolutely necessary for your survival.
A coping emphasis: You focus on managing or coping with your speech anxiety rather than being perfectionistic about mastering it altogether.
Being based on your own valuing process: Your public-speaking rules are not just rigid internalizations of others' rules.
Flexibility: Where appropriate, your rules are amenable to change.
Absence of self-rating: Your rules lead to a functional rating of your specific speaking skills for whether they help you attain realistic objectives. Your rules do not lead to rating your whole personhood.

Following are some possible self-supporting reformulations that Luis and Barbara, from our earlier examples, might use.

Luis

Self-oppressing personal rule: I *must* be a good public speaker immediately.
Self-supporting personal rule: Though I would prefer to be good immediately, this may not be realistic. I have to work and practice at developing my public-speaking skills. Setbacks are part of the learning process.

Barbara

Self-oppressing personal rule: I *must* give the perfect talk every time.
Self-supporting personal rule: Though my preference is always to give a polished talk, I may not always do so. If I give a less-than-perfect talk it is something with which I can cope, not a catastrophe, and I may learn something from it.

The outcome of identifying, disputing, and reformulating self-oppressing personal rules is that you should have less speech anxiety and perform better.

Choosing to Perceive Yourself and Others Accurately

People with speech anxiety may misperceive their speaking abilities both by negative self-labeling and by misperceiving others' reactions to their efforts. Here the ABC framework requires alteration to become:

A = the activating event
B = your perceptions
C = the emotional and behavioral consequences

The consequences for you of A are influenced by your perceptions of A at B. These consequences do not automatically follow from A. You have a choice of how you perceive at B.

Perceive Yourself Accurately

Negative self-labels are unrealistically negative perceptions either about yourself as a person or about your specific abilities, in this case public speaking. You may perceive yourself as a speaker to be deficient, incompetent, weak, pathetic, boring, inferior, and inadequate, to mention some labels. At best, such labels are overgeneralizations, since public speaking involves many subskills in each of which you may have different strengths and weaknesses. In addition, you may put yourself down by unthinkingly labeling your specific speaking skills in negative terms. While you may have weaknesses, you may also have strengths or areas that you can develop into strengths. Why keep focusing on your negatives? Instead, engage in what Ivey and his colleagues call "positive asset search" to identify your strengths (Ivey, Ivey, & Simek-Downing, 1987). When assessing both negative and positive characteristics, try to distinguish fact from inference and make your inferences reflect the facts as closely as possible. In this way you are likely to arrive at a more balanced, and possibly less negative, set of perceptions concerning your public-speaking abilities.

Perceive Others Accurately

If you are speech-anxious, the way you perceive situations may sustain your discomfort. Often people remain unaware that they jump to perceptual conclusions rather than saying to themselves, "Stop . . . think . . . what are my perceptual choices?" Beck observes that frequently people have *automatic* thoughts and perceptions that influence their emotions (Beck, 1976; Beck & Weishaar, 1989). Either they are not fully conscious of these thoughts and images or it does not occur to them that they warrant special attention. Beck collaborates with his patients in the scientific or detective work of identifying these self-oppressing perceptions or "what you tell yourself" (Beck, 1988; Beck & Emery, 1985; Beck, Rush, Shaw, & Emery, 1979). These perceptions are related to unrealistic personal rules. For example, if speakers have a rule, I *must* have my audience's total attention and approval, this is likely to sensitize them to look for signs of rejection.

Here is an example in the ABC framework for Manuel, who gives a lifeskills presentation.

A = Audience members Sally and Tarik have a brief word during Manuel's talk.
B = Manuel perceives: "Sally and Tarik are bored with my talk."
C = Manuel gets anxious and hurries through the rest of his presentation.

There are many other perceptions that Manuel might have had at B. These alternative perceptions include:

"Sally and Tarik often talk to each other no matter what is going on."
"Sally was telling Tarik not to sit so close to her."
"Sally and Tarik were passing complimentary remarks about my talk."
"Sally was making a remark to Tarik about someone else in the group."
"Tarik was asking Sally for some paper so he could take notes."

If, like Manuel, you are prone to jumping to negative perceptual conclusions when speaking in public, how can you combat this? First, become aware of your tendency. Second, monitor your thinking in

public-speaking situations and practice making the connections between upsetting perceptions and upsetting feelings. Third, question
your perceptions by logical analysis. This process involves engaging in
the following kinds of self-talk:

"Stop . . . think . . . what are my perceptual choices?"
"Are my perceptions based on fact or inference?"
"If my perceptions are based on inference, are there other ways of
    perceiving the situation that are more closely related to the fac-
    tual evidence?"
"If necessary, what further information do I need to collect?"
"What is the perception I choose because it represents the best fit in
    relation to the factual evidence?"

Let's assume that Manuel reviewed with his lifeskills group
supervisor why he started rushing his talk. The supervisor asked
Manuel to assess the evidence for his "Sally and Tarik are bored with
my talk" perception. On doing this he discovered that there were *no
facts* to support this conclusion and that it was an inference on his
part. Manuel then generated the alternative perceptions just listed.
He decided that "Sally and Tarik often talk to each other no matter
what is going on" was the best fitting perception. This perception did
not involve Manuel in putting himself down unnecessarily.

Accurately Attributing Cause

Attributions are the explanations, interpretations, or reasons that
people tell themselves for what happens. You may make attributions
both about your public-speaking anxiety and about the causes of your
success or failure in specific speaking situations. There are a number
of possible misattributions or faulty explanations for speech anxiety
that may weaken your motivation for change. Such explanations are
often partial truths: the mistake is to treat them as whole truths. Following are some possible misattributions concerning speech anxiety.

It's in my genes: This is the position that people are anxious by
nature rather than by nurture. However, a considerable part of
speech anxiety represents learned behavior that is sustained by
thinking and action skills weaknesses.

It's due to my unfortunate past: Many people, with or without professional help, have learned to overcome skills weaknesses caused by
their unfortunate pasts.

It's all their fault: Every time a talk of yours does not go down
well, you blame the audience. You get anxious because you do not
get the feedback you want, yet are unable to examine your behavior.

It's all my fault: You blame yourself for everything that goes
wrong when you give a talk. You may engage in black-and-white
thinking, whereby everything is either all right or all wrong. You may

fail to take into account that there are many situational and audience considerations related to the success of a talk.

I've tried before: You may have tried to overcome your speech anxiety before and been unsuccessful. However, this failure need not be your guide to the future. For instance, this time you can try harder, understand your speech anxiety better, possess better skills at managing it, know more about your subject, and possess better delivery skills.

My anxiety is the cause of my poor public speaking: Some people get anxious in speaking situations because they are not properly prepared. In this case their anxiety is a consequence of inadequate behavior and not antecedent to it.

These may not only be attributions of how you acquired speech anxiety but also of how you maintain it. Like unrealistic personal rules, such misattributions of cause require disputation by logical analysis, and reformulation. Following are some possible reformulations of the preceding misattributions.

"Though like many people I experience anxiety when talking before groups of people, my speech anxiety has largely been learned."

"Though others may have contributed to my speech anxiety, I currently sustain my speech anxiety through skills weaknesses that I can learn to overcome."

"Though others' behaviors may sometimes contribute to my talks not being a success, I also need to examine the ways in which my own behavior may have contributed."

"I am only responsible for my own behavior in public-speaking situations rather than accepting total responsibility for what happens."

"Though I've tried before, circumstances are different now. With more understanding of how I sustain my speech anxiety, I can develop new and better skills to overcome it."

"My speech anxiety may be the consequence of inadequate preparation. If so, I need to prepare my lifeskills talks more thoroughly."

Making Realistic Predictions

Predictions are thoughts and images about the probability of future events. When thinking of giving lifeskills talks, training-group leaders need to view the future realistically. They must avoid the twin dangers of overoptimism and undue pessimism. Leaders can set themselves up for disappointment by being overly optimistic and ignoring the realistic difficulties in giving training presentations. Adequate preparation geared to the needs of specific audiences is essential. Leaders who think they can survive on charm frequently get disillusioned.

Possibly more aspiring training-group leaders fall prey to undue pessimism than to unjustified optimism. They may fill their heads with catastrophic predictions about their own inadequate presentation skills, their audience's reactions, and their inability to cope with this feedback. Challenging negative predictions with logical analysis and working through the worst possibility are two skills for combating undue pessimism.

Challenge negative predictions with logical analysis: People can only make inferences about their futures since their futures have yet to happen. However, these inferences can possess varying degrees of relatednesses to existing facts. You can dispute your negative predictions about giving talks with logical analysis and reformulate them into more realistic predictions.

Work through the worst possibility: You can visualize the worst that could happen when you give a talk, assess how realistic this is, and think through whether and how you would cope (Emery, 1982). You may discover that not only is the worst possibility highly unlikely, but also that even if it occurred, you would have various personal and environmental resources to cope with it.

Having Goals That You Articulate Clearly and That Reflect Your Values

Training-group leaders who suffer from varying degrees of debilitating speech anxiety should clearly make managing speech anxiety a goal. Leaders may also contribute to their lack of confidence by setting their public-speaking goals too high. Such goals may reflect internalizations of others' rules rather than their own valuing processes. Frequently, beginning leaders contribute to their anxiety by attempting too much in a given time period. Then they get anxious about not finishing what they set out to do. This anxiety may contribute to a muddled and rushed presentation that in turn generates further anxiety. In brief, goals for both yourself as a public speaker and for each lifeskills talk should be realistic and manageable.

Using Visualizing to Best Effect

Visualizing has been mentioned already in regard to using coping self-talk as you imaginally rehearse upcoming speaking situations. In addition, mention has been made of the skill of confronting unduly negative predictions by visualizing coping with the worst possibility. Another use of visualizing is repeatedly to imagine yourself behaving competently in upcoming speaking situations (Lazarus, 1977). Getting a clear mental picture of yourself performing competently may help you to do so.

Visualizing can also be used both to mentally relax yourself before talks and as part of speech anxiety systematic desensitization procedures (Paul, 1968; Paul & Shannon, 1966; Wolpe, 1982; Zemore, 1975). Visual relaxation can be used either independently or in conjunction with muscular relaxation (Jacobson, 1938). Everyone probably has one or more scenes where they feel relaxed. Before giving a talk, sit in a comfortable chair or lie down and imagine a favorite scene. The following is an example of a visual relaxation scene:

> I'm lying on an uncrowded beach on a pleasant, sunny day enjoying the sensations of warmth on my body, There is a gentle breeze. I can hear the peaceful noise of the sea lapping against the shore nearby. I haven't a care in the world and enjoy my feelings of peace, calm, relaxation, and well-being.

Detailed descriptions of systematic desensitization are to be found elsewhere (for example, Goldfried & Davison, 1976; Wolpe, 1982). Briefly, it consists of three elements: (1) training in muscular relaxation; (2) the construction of one or more hierarchies of progressively more anxiety-evoking scenes—here around the theme of public speaking; and (3) presentation of the scenes to a person's imagination when relaxed. Originally, the idea was that people should feel no anxiety with a presented scene before moving on to the next one. An alternative approach is to view systematic desensitization as training in self-control. People are encouraged to "relax away" tensions as they build up (Goldfried, 1971; Goldfried & Davison, 1976). Self-desensitization, in which you go through the procedure without professional help, is a further variation of systematic desensitization.

Exercise 15 aims to develop your use of thinking skills to manage speech anxiety.

Exercise 15 Use Thinking Skills to Manage Speech Anxiety
▼▼▼

***Part A**: Use Coping Self-talk*

1. Identify and list anxiety-evoking and negative self-talk statements that contribute to your speech anxiety. One way to do this is to run through your mind in slow motion a public-speaking situation in which you have participated and get in touch with what you were saying to yourself.

2. Identify a specific public-speaking situation that you find stressful, if possible in relation to being a training-group leader. Write out at least three coping self-talk statements for each of (a) before, (b) during, and (c) after the situation. It may help if you write these statements on an index card for practice and use in emergency situations.

3. Rehearse and practice using your coping self-talk to help you manage speech anxiety. Even where you have access to actual public-speaking situations, rehearse and practice your coping self-talk as you imagine the situations in advance.

Part B: *Choose Realistic Personal Rules*

  1. Select a past or future public-speaking situation, preferably as a training-group leader, that you wish to work on.

A (the event) Describe the situation that contributed to or may contribute to your upset.

B (your personal rules) Looking out for *must*'s, *ought*'s, *should*'s, *have to*'s, and *got to*'s, list any demands you made or might make of yourself, others, or the situation.

C (the consequences) Describe how you felt and acted or might feel and act. Indicate which of your feelings and actions you consider to be inappropriate.

  2. Dispute each of the demands you made or might make in the situation.

  3. Reformulate one or more of your self-oppressing personal rules in the situation into self-supporting rules.

  4. What do you consider the effects of your new self-supporting rule(s) might have been or might be on your feelings and actions in and about the public-speaking situation?

Part C: *Choose How You Perceive*

1. *Generating different perceptions*: For each of the following public-speaking scenarios, generate at least three different perceptions.
   a. At the start of your lifeskills talk everyone in the group is not present.
   b. Halfway through your lifeskills talk someone gets up and leaves.
   c. You get feedback from one participant that your lifeskills talk was not good.
2. *Perceiving a specific speech anxiety situation differently*:
   a. Choose a situation in which you have experienced speech anxiety.
   b. Make up a worksheet with the following format:

Situation	Upsetting Perceptions	Different Perceptions

   c. Write down the situation and, in the Upsetting Perceptions column, any perceptions associated with your speech anxiety in that situation. Assess the realism of your upsetting perceptions by logical analysis.
   d. In the Different Perceptions column, write down as many different perceptions of the situation as you can generate. Then evaluate and star which one best explains the situation.

e. Assess the ways in which the emotional and behavioral consequences of your most realistic perception would have been
different from those of your original perceptions.

Part D: *Develop Thinking Skills to Combat Speech Anxiety*

1. *Assessment*: If you suffer from any level of debilitating speech anxiety, assess the contribution to this of any skills weaknesses you
may have in each of the following thinking skills areas.

Thinking Skills Area	Your Assessment
Owning responsibility for choices	
Being in touch with feelings	
Using coping self-talk	
Choosing realistic personal rules	
Perceiving accurately	
Attributing cause accurately	
Making realistic predictions	
Setting realistic goals	
Using visualizing skills	

Summarize and prioritize the key thinking skills that you need to
develop to help you manage your speech anxiety better.

2. *Change*:
   a. Make out a plan to develop your thinking skills in each of the
   areas you have targeted as in need of change. Your plan should
   include specific and realistic goals and state a time frame for
   changing each thinking skills weakness.
   b. Implement your plan and evaluate the effects of any changes in
   your thinking on your speech-related feelings and behaviors.

Preparing Systematic Content
▼ ▼

Speaking well is thinking clearly.
Speaking exceptionally well is thinking exceptionally clearly.
Jack Valenti

The previous section specifically focused on avoiding MATO (My
Anxiety Takes Over). This section and the following two sections

focus on putting your message together and conveying it to your audience in a way that avoids their reacting with MEGO (My Eyes Glaze Over). Thorough preparation can also help training-group leaders speak with confidence. In addition, such preparation is a necessity for a professional approach to imparting lifeskills information.

Leader presentations in lifeskills training groups are influence attempts designed to impart information relevant to building participants' skills. With their applied focus, lifeskills presentations differ from academic lectures in many ways. Lifeskills talks are most often fairly brief introductions to a skill. Demonstration of the skill is often incorporated into talks. A structured activity to encourage participation may also be included. Talks are usually followed by coaching, rehearsal, and practice. In short, lifeskills talks are part of skill-building sequences rather than ends in themselves. Following is a discussion of some of the component skills of preparing systematic content for your talks.

Setting Clear Goals

Lifeskills group leaders require clear goals for each talk they give. Considerations in goal setting include the following:

Be clear regarding the skill or subskill to be communicated: Some lifeskills talks get off to a poor start and never recover because leaders have inadequately thought through precisely what to convey. Muddled thinking leads to muddled speaking. Furthermore, some leaders have difficulty distinguishing between a descriptive discussion of a skill and a systematic "how-to" presentation of it. Clearly stating the specific behavior or behaviors targeted greatly enhances developing a systematic presentation. For instance, a goal like "Learning to use assertiveness skills to develop self-esteem" is too vague and general. The specific assertive behavior targeted requires clarifying—for instance, "Learning to identify, dispute, and reformulate unrealistic personal rules that make it difficult for you to say no." Even this is probably far too ambitious a goal for a lifeskills talk. It may be best approached in three separate talks: identification, disputation, and reformulation.

Set a realistic time limit: Many considerations influence the time allocated to a talk. These considerations include how much time is needed to do a proper introduction of a skill; how best to maintain the balance between talking and doing; and the attention span of the audience.

Have manageable objectives: As already mentioned, many aspiring lifeskills trainers try to do too much too quickly and succeed in doing nothing well.

Be sensitive to sequencing: All lifeskills talks take place within the context of overall programs and of individual sessions. The leader needs to take into account how the topic for each talk fits into the sequence of skills being developed over the group's life. Furthermore, the goals of talks must take into account what precedes and follows in individual sessions.

Be sensitive to your audience: Bernstein (1988) advises public speakers to think like listeners when preparing talks. The goals of lifeskills talks must take into account how well the audience relates to the learning sequence. For example, the learning sequence may be too advanced or too elementary.

Developing a Systematic Outline

It is essential for lifeskills talks to have a clear structure. Effective training is systematic rather than piecemeal. A clear structure introduces the skill in a logical and easily comprehensible sequence, preventing both speaker and audience confusion.

For example, a leader giving a presentation on the use of coping self-talk to manage anger might develop the following outline:

Goals of talk
Introductory definition of self-talk
    ABC framework
    What you say to yourself at B
    Negative self-talk and anger
    What is negative self-talk?
    Examples of negative self-talk
    Consequences of negative self-talk
    Becoming aware of negative self-talk
    Coping self-talk and anger
    Changing what you say to yourself at B
    Coping as contrasted with mastery
    Dimensions of coping self-talk
        Calming self-talk
        Coaching self-talk
    Coping self-talk in anger situations
        Before the situation
        During the situation
        After the situation
    Developing the skill of coping self-talk
        Coaching, rehearsal, and practice in the group
        Doing homework
    Summary and conclusions

In this example, the training-group leader would have the choice of whether to give the content of the outline in either a single presentation or a series of smaller presentations interspersed with structured activities and discussion. In addition, skilled leaders always look for ways to introduce demonstrations into presentations.

Using Language Effectively

With effective lifeskills talks, speakers make it easy for listeners to receive them "loud and clear." However, many factors can introduce "static" or "noise" into communication. Speakers may not have good skills at sending clear messages. They may heavily encode messages so that they require extensive decoding by listeners. Listeners may not have good skills at decoding messages. In addition, they may have their own agendas and unfinished business as they listen. Also, there may be contextual considerations—for instance, external noise—that interfere with communication.

With so many potential difficulties in having your messages received accurately, it is essential that you do not add to them by poor use of language. Following are some considerations in using language effectively.

Take the intelligence level and background of your audience into account: Just as good professional writers always write with specific audiences in mind, so skilled training-group leaders prepare their talks. Lifeskills training groups are not just for the college-educated. There can be enormous differences in educational level, socio-economic status, and other factors both among various participant groups and within the same group.

Use straightforward and unambiguous language: In general, where a simple word will suffice, avoid using a more complex one. Beware of psychobabble and jargon. In listening skills groups, even words like *empathy* may not communicate clearly. Instead of *empathy* you may use terms like *reflective responding*, *active listening*, or *listening with understanding*.

Use words economically: Shakespeare wrote in *Hamlet*, "Brevity is the soul of wit." Mark Twain observed, "As to the Adjective; when in doubt, strike it out." Too many words can block clear communication of meaning. Furthermore, being long-winded can take valuable time away from other elements in the skills-learning sequence, such as coaching and practice.

Avoid long sentences: Bernstein (1988) observes that the language of speech is different from written language. Sentence length is one of the main areas of difference. Bernstein writes, "Spoken English moves in a simple straight line—a sequence of short sentences" (p. 75). An important reason for using short sentences is that they add to audience comprehension. Referring to written language, the American Press Institute reports that sentences of as many as eight words will be understood by 100 percent of readers; as many as fifteen words, by 90 percent; as many as nineteen words, by 80 percent; and as many as twenty-eight words, by 50 percent (Goddard, 1989). With some groups of participants, short sentences may be a necessity. Remember, 50 percent of the population are below the average intelligence level! The remaining 50 percent may not be functioning too intelligently, either, in their areas of lifeskills weaknesses.

Address your audience directly: Prepare your content as though you are about to have a conversation with your audience. They are not just a sea of faces out there, but individual people with whom you will have a dialogue. Think of them as "you" and prepare as though "I" am about to talk with "you."

Being Practical and Focused on Participants' Needs

Skilled leaders enlist their audience's interest and motivation to acquire something of "take-away" value for outside the group. Lifeskills talks focus on the mechanics of how to perform a skill or subskill. They are the verbal equivalent of a skills manual. They are not academic discourses. Leaders should aim to present skills so that participants understand them well enough to be able to instruct themselves in them on their own. Skills of giving practical "how-to" presentations include breaking down tasks step by step; relating content to participants' own experiences; using good examples and case studies; giving clear demonstrations; and indicating the self-talk that participants might use when confronted with the need to use the skill in their daily lives.

Paying Attention to Beginnings and Endings

The suggestion that you pay attention to beginnings and endings is not meant to devalue the middles of presentations. However, unlike middles, where leaders always focus on imparting information, there are special considerations for beginnings and endings.

Beginnings

When you begin a talk you want to do at least three things: (1) create a relationship with the audience or, if you already have a relationship, nurture it; (2) stimulate their interest and attention; and (3) communicate the goals of your talk. Following are some suggestions on how to open talks. These methods can be used either on their own or in combination.

Make some linking comments: These linking comments may put your talk in the context of what has gone before in your work with participants.

State your goals and give the outline of your talk: Participants will appreciate knowing the structure of your talk from the start. Providing a clear outline can also indicate to participants that you know your material and have taken the time and trouble to prepare it properly.

Indicate why the topic is important: Participants are likely to be more motivated by leaders who communicate genuinely that their message is important than by those who do not. However, there is a danger of alienating participants by overselling.

Give an example: Giving an example is akin to telling a story that illustrates the point of your talk. You can give more than one example.

Tell a joke: You need to ensure not only that your joke is relevant, but also that it will be picked up accurately by your audience. To tell a joke properly, you need to have the requisite skills. You don't want to be like one British aristocrat of whom it was said "a joke in his mouth is no laughing matter" (Valenti, 1982).

Ask a question: You can ask a question that relates the content of your talk to participants' own lives.

Do a brief exercise: An introductory exercise should be designed to illustrate a major point in your talk. For instance, at the beginning of a presentation on coping self-talk you can invite the audience to close their eyes for thirty seconds and think of nothing. Most participants will become very aware that they are engaging in inner speech rather than thinking of nothing.

Often, formulating the introduction to your talk is best left until the end of your preparation. By then you know what follows.

Endings

The ending of lifeskills talks is often the start of practical work. There is much to be said for ending with a concise summary of the main points of your talk. Such summaries echo the advice often given to trainee teachers: "Tell them what you are going to say, say it, and then tell them what you have said." If you wish participants to consolidate the learnings from your talk by either reading a handout or by completing homework exercises, you may distribute these now. Many lifeskills talks end with time for questions and discussion. You may wish to end your talk this way too before moving on to coaching, rehearsing, and practicing.

Preparing a Systematic Script or Set of Notes

There are three main ways of giving verbal presentations: without notes, with notes, and from prepared scripts. The term *script* is used in preference to *text* to indicate that there are differences in writing for written and for verbal presentation. Giving a lifeskills talk without notes is not for beginners. Experienced training-group leaders may be able to carry in their heads the structure and content of their talks. Also, unlike many beginners, experienced leaders are unlikely to have debilitating anxiety interfere with recall. Nevertheless, at some stage, these leaders had to make the effort to develop systematic talks. This effort involved making either a good set of notes or a prepared script.

Giving talks from full scripts consumes much preparation time.

However, a word processor can save you time. When it comes to editing and making corrections, word processors offer much greater flexibility than handwriting. Leaders and aspiring leaders have to consider whether their talks merit the time for preparing scripts. Such an investment is desirable when leaders require the discipline of developing scripts to master material; are very nervous; and are likely to repeat the talk on many occasions. If you prepare a script, it will be easier to deliver if you type it double-spaced and with obvious gaps between paragraphs. Some scripts are written in the right two-thirds of a page with the left third being reserved for comments on delivery (Bernstein, 1988). Many leaders avoid prepared scripts since they are tempted to read them, and reading scripts blocks good audience contact.

Most training-group leaders give talks from notes of varying degrees of completeness. For some leaders, their outline, either on a sheet of paper or on a series of index cards, is all they require to cue them. Other leaders require fuller material.

Using Audiovisual Aids

Often skilled training-group leaders use audiovisual aids to reinforce spoken words. Accessing participants through their eyes as well as their ears can greatly assist holding attention and interest. Just putting up the outline of a talk on a whiteboard can make it easier for participants to assimilate the message. Following are descriptions of some audiovisual methods for accompanying and illustrating talks.

Whiteboard

Whiteboards are essential items in any training facilities. The availability of whiteboards can introduce flexibility into your presentations. In addition, you can work together with an audience as you put material up on a whiteboard. However, a disadvantage is that you must turn your back on your audience as you write. Also, you need to wipe off existing material if you wish to fill a whiteboard more than once. Whiteboards are much preferable to blackboards since audiences see cleaner images and leaders do not get chalky hands.

Overhead Projector

Along with whiteboards, overhead projectors are perhaps the other most essential visual aid. Advantages of overhead projectors include being able to make up transparencies in advance; use photocopies of existing printed material; move a piece of paper down over transparencies so that you progressively introduce material; add to or make up transparencies during your talks; switch the projectors on or off as you wish; and superimpose images over existing images. In addition, when using overhead projectors, leaders need not turn their backs on audiences since they can point out with pens or pencils items of interest on transparencies.

Leaders require some basic skills both in making up transparencies and in using overhead projectors. Skills for making up transparencies include not putting too much information on a single transparency, setting the information out clearly, writing it neatly and sufficiently large, and making it more interesting by using different colors. Skills for using an overhead projector include being able to turn it on and off, getting it in focus, and placing transparencies on it so that they are in the right position and with the right side up.

Flipcharts

Flipcharts have the big advantage of being able to show many prepared sheets in succession. Sheets can be thrown over the back of the easel as a talk progresses. The fact that the sheets may already be prepared does not preclude leaders from either adding to existing sheets or interspersing new sheets. A disadvantage of flipcharts is that the sheets are more cumbersome than overhead projector transparencies. Allied to flipcharts is the use of posters hung on walls to illustrate points. A merging of flipcharts and posters can be achieved by putting up individual flipchart sheets as posters as a presentation progresses.

Slides

Probably many more leaders use whiteboards and overhead projectors than slides. However, you can give polished presentations using well-prepared slides. On the other hand, as you know from viewing friends' travel slides, presentations built around slides can be very boring. The technology and repeated visual images can get in the way of the message. Flexibility and spontaneity can be lost. In addition, rooms may need to be darkened. Also, slide projectors may not function properly. Possibly you require more skills for using slide projectors moderately well than for using overhead projectors well. If you possess or are prepared to learn the requisite skills, then seriously consider using slides.

Film

Films can be shown as part of presentations. However, films have many disadvantages. Unless you keep a film library, films have to be hired. In addition, they require projectors and possibly projectionists. Another disadvantage is that they require darkened rooms. Advantages of film over videotape are greater clarity and larger images.

However, it is a rare training session in which films are shown that the technology does not become intrusive.

Videotape

Videotapes can be extremely useful for demonstrating skills. In large lifeskills groups, the drawback of a smallish video screen can be overcome by the use of two or three monitors. Videos do not require the room to be as dark as for films. Another advantage of videos is that most leaders are accustomed to using them. Furthermore, leaders can push the start, stop, or pause buttons as necessary. If you make your own videos, strive for as professional a result as possible. Some institutions, such as colleges and universities, have audiovisual centers where you can get advice and help in recording videos. If you have a large budget, you can hire an outside video firm to produce training material (Miles, 1988).

Photographs and Cartoons

Leaders may choose to integrate photographs and cartoons into presentations. For instance, in training groups on nonverbal communication, photographs may be worth the proverbial thousand words. In my thinking skills groups, cartoons of Mr. and Ms. Self-Oppression and Mr. and Ms. Self-Support are displayed with dialogue balloons to portray various thinking skills weaknesses and strengths (Nelson-Jones, 1990a).

Training Manuals and Handouts

Leaders can help participants consolidate their learnings either by referring them to the relevant sections in a training manual or by providing them with handouts. Always provide written instructions for any inside- or outside-class assignments.

Audio Cassettes

Audio cassettes can be useful for demonstrating skills. Sometimes audio cassettes may be preferable to videotapes. For example, in a group on public-speaking skills, audio cassettes may be preferable for illustrating voice message skills and videotapes for illustrating body message skills. Audio cassettes are also useful when demonstrating thinking skills since there are no distracting visual images. When making up audio cassettes, make sure to use a high-quality recording system so that your playback is of a professional standard. Poor-quality recordings introduce static into communicating your messages. Bernstein (1988) observes, "Audio aids work best when short, telling, and relevant. They work worst when the audience has to work hard at listening and when they take too long" (p. 134).

Exercise 16 Prepare a Systematic
Lifeskills Talk and Integrate Audiovisual Aids
▼▼▼

Part A: *Set Goals and Develop a Systematic Lifeskills Talk Outline*

Think of a lifeskills talk that you might wish to give either now or in the future.

1. Set yourself clear goals for your talk. Take the following considerations into account:
   a. clarity regarding the skill or subskill to be communicated
   b. a realistic time limit
   c. manageable objectives
   d. sensitivity to sequencing
   e. sensitivity to your audience
2. Write out a systematic outline for your talk using the example in the text as a guide.

Part B: *Prepare a Systematic Script and Set of Notes*

Either for the lifeskill you outlined in **Part A** or for another lifeskill:

1. Write out a fully prepared script for a ten- to fifteen-minute presentation, making sure to
   a. set clear goals
   b. use language effectively
   c. be practical and focused on participants' needs
   d. pay attention to beginnings and endings
   e. develop your content logically and systematically
2. Translate your fully prepared script into as many index cards as you require to be able to remember the main messages you wish to convey.

Part C: *Integrate Audiovisual Aids into Your Talk*

1. For the lifeskills talk for which you wrote out a systematic prepared script and developed a set of notes, consider which of the following audiovisual aids would be appropriate at the different stages of your talk:
   Whiteboard
   Overhead projector
   Flipcharts
   Slides
   Film
   Videotape
   Photographs and cartoons
   Training manuals and handouts
   Audio cassettes
2. Develop appropriate audiovisual material to accompany your lifeskills talk.

3. Incorporate into the notes for your talk instructions for when you intend to use audiovisual material. What effect is the inclusion of audiovisual material going to have on the length of your talk? Still try to observe the fifteen-minute time limit suggested in Part B.

Developing Delivery Skills
▼▼

I do not much dislike the matter, but
The manner of his speech.
William Shakespeare, *Anthony and Cleopatra*

It ain't what you say, but how you say it.
Anonymous

Think of your school teachers and college lecturers. How many of them either were or are skilled at getting their messages across? How many stimulated and held your interest? Apart from the adequacy of their content, what distinguished effective from ineffective performers? Training-group leaders can have great intellects, have prepared excellent content, and be largely in control of their nerves, yet still leave audiences with a bad dose of glazed-over eyes (MEGO). The missing ingredient is delivery skills.

Presenting a lifeskills talk necessitates giving a performance. You cannot just be your usual conversational self. Instead, you must put over your material in such a way that you build rapport with your audience and hold their interest. An analogy is that of making a stage performance. Good actors and actresses pay great attention to the skills of delivering their lines. Assuming that you have a coherent talk, you now need to put it across. Training-group leaders require awareness that preparing a talk does not stop at preparing its content, but incorporates putting time and energy into preparing its delivery. In particular, polished delivery entails sending effective voice and body mesages.

Sending Effective Voice Messages

Developing voice awareness is the first step in learning to use your voice as a delivery tool. Voice awareness entails breaking down voice communication into its principal component skills. You then possess a framework for assessing your own and others' strengths and weaknesses in these skills areas. Once you develop voice awareness you can make better voice message choices for polishing your training presentations. The components of sending effective voice messages are volume, articulation, pitch, emphasis, and rate. (You can remember these by the acronym VAPER.)

Volume

Volume refers to loudness or quietness. You need to speak at a volume that can be comfortably heard by all participants. Most lifeskills training groups are small enough that leaders can be easily heard with only moderate voice projection. However, if necessary, use a microphone and amplification. Speaking either too softly or too loudly are common mistakes. Perhaps more beginning leaders speak too softly than too loudly. Some leaders have the bad habit of fading, beginning either a sentence or their whole talk with adequate loudness and then letting their voices trail away.

Articulation

Leaders may speak with adequate loudness, but still be unintelligible. They must enunciate words clearly. Articulation or enunciation refers to the distinctness and clarity of continuous speech. Fischer (1972) writes: "A speaker is said to articulate correctly when his sounds and words are clearly made and easily understood, without their being overly precise" (p. 47). Mumbling and slurring words are examples of poor articulation. Some leaders with regional or foreign accents may have to work on their pronunciation so that they articulate words clearly. Leaders possessing excessively nasal, gutteral, or throaty voices that interfere with articulation might consider consulting speech therapists.

Pitch

Pitch refers to the highness or lowness of a voice. Voices can range from high-pitched and shrill to low-pitched and deep. In general, women's voices are higher pitched than men's. Also, when people are anxious, their voices may be higher pitched than when they feel calmer. Kruger (1970) observes that an optimum pitch range includes all the levels at which a pleasing voice can be produced without strain and that most good speakers vary their pitch within a range of at least an octave or two. Errors of pitch include being either too high-pitched or too low-pitched, with perhaps being too high-pitched the more common error (Bernstein, 1988). A further error is using too narrow a range of pitch.

Emphasis

Monotonous speakers use too little emphasis. Melodramatic speakers use too much emphasis. By emphasizing certain words you add variety, clarity, and rhythm to talks. The following sentence from John Kennedy's 1961 inaugural address as president of the United States would have been much less effective without his emphasizing the italicized words: "And so my fellow Americans—ask *not* what your country can do for *you*—ask what *you* can do for your country" (Valenti, 1982). By emphasizing certain words or phrases, you highlight your main points. In addition, by using emphasis you convey interest and commitment to your audience.

Rate

Speech rate or pace is often measured by words per minute. Kruger (1970) suggests that a rate of 140 to 180 words per minute is appropriate for average explanatory material that is neither too easy nor too difficult for average adult audiences. Speech rate depends both on how quickly words are spoken and on the frequency and duration of pauses between them. Many nervous people speak too quickly. Especially when beginning talks, it can be a good strategy to slow your speech rate down. Speaking more slowly may help you control your nerves and, thus, appear less nervous. A slower speech rate both gives you more time to think of what to say next and enables you to refer to your notes less often within a given time period.

Pauses are a form of vocal punctuation. Great actors and actresses are adept at using pauses to create clarity and emphasis in their speeches. They make pauses for effect and not just to breathe. John Kennedy used pauses to great effect in his 1961 inaugural address. Reread the sentence quoted above and note that the dashes indicate pauses.

In lifeskills talks, pauses can be used to give participants time to grasp your meaning, to relate what you say to their own experience, and to take notes. Pauses should be free of extraneous sounds, such as *um* and *er*. Other pause errors include having either too many or too few and making them either too long or too short. A further error is that of pausing in the wrong places.

Exercise 17 focuses on the voice message dimension of delivery skills.

Exercise 17 Be Aware of Your Voice and Send Effective Voice Messages
▼▼

Part A: Be Aware of Your Voice

This exercise is best done with a cassette recorder. You can record and play back the exercise in segments that have most meaning for your learning. Take the following sentence from John Kennedy's inaugural address: "And so my fellow Americans—ask not what your country can do for you—ask what you can do for your country." Imagine that you need to communicate this sentence to a lifeskills training group of eight participants.

1. *Volume*: First speak the sentence loudly, then speak it quietly, then try to arrive at a comfortable volume.

2. *Articulation*: First speak the sentence with poor articulation, then speak it with excessively precise articulation, then try to arrive at a comfortable yet clear level of articulation.

3. *Pitch*: First speak the sentence in a high-pitched voice, then speak it in a low-pitched voice, then try to arrive at a pleasing pitch.

4. *Emphasis*: Say the sentence emphasizing the "incorrect" italicized words: "And so my fellow *Americans*—ask not what your *country* can do for you—ask what you can do for your *country*." Then repeat the sentence emphasizing the "correct" italicized words: "And so my fellow Americans—ask *not* what your country can do for *you*—ask what *you* can do for your country."

5. *Rate*: First say the sentence quickly and without pausing, then say it slowly with many and frequent pauses, then try to arrive at a way of saying it that is effective in terms of speech rate and pauses.

6. Practice saying the sentence until you consider you have put all the voice message components together satisfactorily.

Part B: Send Effective Voice Messages

In Exercise 16 you wrote out a script for a ten- to fifteen-minute presentation and then put it on index cards.

1. Go through the introductory section of your talk and put dashes where you want to pause and underline words and phrases that you wish to emphasize. Practice delivering the introductory section of your talk into a cassette recorder until you are satisfied with your volume, articulation, pitch, emphasis, and rate.

2. Repeat the preceding for the middle and ending sections of your talk.

3. Deliver your whole talk from your prepared script into a cassette recorder until you are satisfied with your volume, articulation, pitch, emphasis, and rate.

4. Deliver the introductory section of your talk from notes into a cassette recorder, emphasizing effective voice messages. Critically evaluate your performance and, where necessary, alter it.

5. Repeat the preceding for the middle and ending sections of your talk.

6. Deliver your whole talk from notes into a cassette recorder until you are satisfied with your volume, articulation, pitch, emphasis, and rate.

Sending Effective Body Messages

Presenting a lifeskills talk is a performance. Leaders need to learn to make their body messages work for rather than against their overall messages. Leaders may send ineffective body messages both unconsciously and consciously. Nervous speakers may remain unaware or only partially aware of how they betray their lack of confidence through such mannerisms as inadequate eye contact, scratching their faces or heads, trembling arms or legs, excessive smiling, pacing up and down, and wooden and inappropriate gestures.

Training-group leaders can prepare and rehearse their body messages. Leaders require awareness of the power of body messages. By identifying subskills, leaders can gain greater control over body messages. The acronym GAME is used to help memorize some key body message components. GAME is shorthand for: gestures and facial expressions, appearance, movement and posture, and eye contact.

Gestures and Facial Expressions

Gestures are movements of parts of the body with the purpose of aiding in the expression of ideas and feelings. There are three main types of gestures (Fischer, 1972). First, there are *emphatic* gestures, such as pointing the finger, designed to make it clear that what is being said is important. Second, there are *descriptive* gestures—for instance, stretching your arms out when you say that marital partners are poles apart—designed to help illustrate your points. Third, there are *symbolic* gestures to which a commonly understood meaning has been ascribed—for instance, shaking the head in negation or the A-okay sign of a circle made by the thumb and forefinger to indicate success or approval. Gestures should have a purpose: be appropriate to the accompanying words, be made clearly, be used with and in moderation, and be used with sensitivity to cultural and regional differences (Argyle, 1986; Ekman, Friesen, & Bear, 1984).

Your facial expressions can also help illustrate ideas and feelings. Good facial expressions are congruent with speech. You can choose to control your facial expressions in the interest of your overall effectiveness. For example, if you are nervous when starting a talk, give your audience a pleasant smile rather than a deep frown.

Appearance

Appearance consists of a number of considerations, including how you dress, your hairstyle, and how well washed and groomed you are. When meeting groups for the first time, your appearance can either help you establish rapport or alienate some or all participants. For example, leaders' appearances may indicate that they are either rebels or conformers. The warmth of their subsequent receptions depends on the groups with whom they work. While needing to be true to themselves, leaders also require sensitivity to the effect of their appearance on others. Leaders should avoid drawing unnecessary attention to their appearance—for instance, by pulling at a cuff or picking lint off their clothes.

Movement and Posture

Some speakers move and stand in relaxed and comfortable ways, others in tense and rigid ways. Leaders' movements and postures can speak volumes about their relationships with themselves and their audiences. Do they rush around seemingly bound up in their own agendas or are they relaxed and accessible to their audience? Good speakers use movement to achieve their purposes. Poor speakers may use many distracting movements, such as pacing up and down or swaying from side to side. Good speakers use posture to show confidence and competence. Poor speakers may use their posture in ways that communicate sloppiness and anxiety.

Eye Contact

The importance of establishing relationships and keeping in touch with audiences by using good eye contact cannot be overemphasized. Whether through nervousness, lack of experience, or both, novice leaders frequently make poor contact with audiences because they rarely look at them. There is perhaps no quicker way to glaze over your audience's eyes (MEGO) than reading your talks with your eyes down. Look at the members of your audience as though you are conversing with them. Help each member of your audience feel that you are communicating directly with him or her. This kind of eye contact not only draws your audience into your talk, but also enables you to assess reactions. Do not look at the floor. Do not look at the ceiling. Do not look through your audience. Do not look only at one side of your audience or at just a few people. Make eye contact with each of them. Even if reading from a prepared script, develop the technique of looking down, memorizing a passage, and then looking up and delivering it directly to the audience.

Exercise 18 focuses on developing your skills of making eye contact and sending body messages when giving lifeskills talks.

Exercise 18 Make Good Eye Contact and Send Effective Body Messages
▼▼

Part A: *Make Good Eye Contact*

Preferably videotape yourself as you do this exercise. Failing that, do it in front of a mirror. Practice giving a lifeskills talk to an imaginary group of eight people while they sit in a horseshoe and you stand up front.

1. Deliver the preceding instructions for this part of the exercise to your audience. Look down and read each sentence to yourself

before looking up and delivering it out loud as you maintain eye contact with your audience. Evaluate your performance and try again if you are dissatisfied with it.

2. Memorize all four sentences of the preceding instructions and deliver them out loud to your audience as you maintain good eye contact with them. Repeat your delivery until you are satisfied that you have learned how to make good eye contact with your audience.

Part B: *Send Effective Body Messages*

Preferably videotape yourself as you do this exercise. Failing that, stand in front of a mirror. Practice giving your lifeskills talk to eight people while they sit in a horseshoe and you stand up front.

1. Prepare the introductory section of the talk you composed in Exercise 16, paying particular attention to how to integrate body messages, such as gestures, facial expressions, movement, and eye contact, into your talk. Rehearse giving the introductory section of your talk until you are satisfied with your performance.

2. Repeat the preceding for the middle and ending sections of your talk.

3. Deliver your whole talk, paying particular attention to sending effective body messages.

Put It All Together

The preceding sections have focused on managing speech anxiety, preparing systematic content, using audiovisual aids, and developing good voice and body message delivery skills. Use the accompanying Public-Speaking Skills Evaluation Questionnaire before and after talks to evaluate your preparation and delivery.

Public-Speaking Skills Evaluation Questionnaire
▼▼▼

This public-speaking skills questionnaire has three uses: (1) as a guide to preparing lifeskills presentations; (2) as a self-evaluation measure for after presentations; and (3) as a means for others to provide feedback to speakers. Respond to each item by putting either a check, a cross, or "yes" or "no" in the blank space.

Skills for managing speech anxiety

_____   I used coping self-talk

_____   I challenged unrealistic personal rules

_____   I accurately perceived my speaking strengths

_____   I accurately perceived my audience's reactions

_____ I accurately attributed cause for my speech anxiety
_____ I realistically predicted the consequences of my talk
_____ I set realistic goals for how well I might do
_____ I used visualized rehearsal and practice
_____ I used relaxation skills (such as breath management)

Skills for preparing systematic content
_____ I set clear and realistic goals
_____ I planned my talk with my audience in mind
_____ I developed a systematic outline
_____ I used language effectively
_____ I was practical and focused on participants' needs
_____ I covered the right amount of material for the time available
_____ I prepared a systematic script and/or set of notes
_____ I introduced my talk well
_____ I ended my talk by emphasizing my main points
_____ I conveyed self-instructions for implementing the skill(s)
_____ I used humor appropriately

Skills for using audiovisual aids
_____ I reviewed how best to use audiovisual aids
_____ I used good audiovisual material
_____ I rehearsed integrating audiovisual material into my talk
_____ I took my audience through my audiovisual material well

Skills for sending effective voice messages
_____ I was easy to hear
_____ I articulated words clearly
_____ I spoke fluently
_____ I spoke at a pleasing pitch
_____ I emphasized key words and points
_____ I communicated enthusiasm with my voice
_____ I spoke at a comfortable rate
_____ I used pauses effectively
_____ I rehearsed my voice as well as my verbal messages

Skills for sending effective body messages
_____ I spoke directly to my audience and made eye contact with them
_____ I made good use of gestures
_____ I avoided distracting mannerisms

_____ My facial expressions were appropriate

_____ My dress and grooming were appropriate

_____ I appeared relaxed

_____ My posture was good

_____ I rehearsed my body as well as my voice and verbal messages

Further skills

_____ I incorporated demonstration into my talk (covered in Chapter 8)

_____ I encouraged learning by doing (for example, with a structured activity, covered in Chapter 9)

_____ I allowed time for and invited questions

_____ I answered questions well

The need for thorough preparation has been either implicit or explicit throughout these discussions. The time has now come for you to give your lifeskills talk, integrating systematic content audio-visual aids, and voice and body messages. Exercise 19 asks you to rehearse giving your talk and then, if possible, to deliver it to a live audience.

Exercise 19 Make an Effective Lifeskills Presentation
▾ ▾

If possible, videotape and play back this exercise. Failing that, use a mirror and audio cassette recorder.

1. *Rehearse and practice*: Rehearse and practice delivering parts of the presentation and then the whole of the presentation for which you wrote out the content in Exercise 16. Work on giving a performance that successfully integrates systematic content, visual aids, and voice and body messages.

2. *Make a live presentation*: Where possible, make your lifeskills presentation to a live audience. Afterward hold a discussion and feedback session with the audience focusing on your public-speaking skills strengths and weaknesses, possibly using the Public-Speaking Skills Evaluation Questionnaire. Assess this feedback and, where necessary, set goals for change.

▾ Chapter Highlights

▾ Frequently, training-group leaders make short presentations as part of skills learning sequences.

   ▾ Successful leaders work hard to develop and maintain their

(continued)

▼ **Chapter Highlights** (continued)

public-speaking skills. They are aware of the necessity to prepare thoroughly both content and delivery.

▼ Speech anxiety can either facilitate, interfere with, or both facilitate and interfere with effective speaking.

▼ Thinking skills for managing speech anxiety include owning your responsibility for being a chooser, being in touch with your underlying feelings, using coping self-talk, choosing realistic personal rules, choosing to perceive yourself and others accurately, accurately attributing cause, making realistic predictions, having goals that you articulate clearly and that reflect your values, and using visualizing to best effect.

▼ Skilled training-group leaders prepare systematic content for their presentations. They use either prepared scripts or a good set of notes.

▼ Skills for preparing systematic content include setting clear goals, using language effectively, being practical and focused on the needs of participants, and paying attention to beginnings and endings.

▼ Leaders can use a range of audiovisual aids to help convey their messages. Such aids include whiteboards, overhead projectors, flipcharts, slides, films, videotapes, photographs and cartoons, training manuals and handouts, and audio cassettes.

▼ Effective delivery skills include being aware of and sending good voice and body messages.

▼ The components of effective vocal messages form the acronym VAPER: volume, articulation, pitch, emphasis, and rate.

▼ The components of effective body messages form the acronym GAME: gestures and facial expressions, appearance, movement and posture, and eye contact.

▼ Skilled group leaders manage their speech anxiety and put together their systematic content, audiovisual aids, and voice and body messages into well-prepared and coherent presentations.

8

How to Demonstrate Lifeskills

A picture is worth a thousand words.

Chinese proverb

Chapter Questions

▼▼

What is observational learning?

What are the main methods of demonstrating lifeskills?

What demonstrator characteristics should training-group leaders consider?

What demonstration characteristics should leaders consider?

How can leaders enhance the attention paid by observers?

How can leaders demonstrate thinking skills?

How can leaders demonstrate action skills?

How can leaders demonstrate action skills with accompanying self-talk?

Introduction

▼▼

The previous chapter focused on public-speaking skills, or the *telling* mode. This chapter focuses on demonstration skills, or the *showing* mode. The next chapter focuses on structured activity skills, or the *doing* mode. In teaching applied skills, showing provides an important bridge between telling and doing. *Observational learning* is another term for showing people what to do. Following are examples in life-skills training groups of observational learning from demonstrations.

▼ Parents of conduct-problem children, aged 3 to 8, observe video-taped programs demonstrating parenting skills (Webster-Stratton, Kolpacoff, & Hollinsworth, 1988).

▼ Chronically aggressive adolescents observe several examples of expert use of prosocial skills—for example, starting a conversation or dealing with an accusation, as part of an aggression-replacement training program (Glick & Goldstein, 1987).

▼ Institutionalized juvenile delinquents observe models handling situations such as during a job interview, dealing with the fact that they have a record; or coping with negative peer influence—for instance, not going along with the crowd and stealing a car (Sarason, 1976).

▼ Unassertive adults are asked to observe, in their imaginations, models behaving assertively in a range of situations (Kazdin, 1976).

▼ Trainee helpers are assisted in developing interview microskills by means of observing demonstration videotapes—for example, on how to demonstrate attention with your body messages (Ivey & Authier, 1978).

▼ Job Club members hear taped commentaries by former job seekers who were successful in obtaining employment (Azrin, Flores, & Kaplan, 1975).

▼ Young people participate in "work-shadowing" programs in which they follow a worker around for a period of time, observing the various tasks and components of his or her role (Herr & Watts, 1988).

▼ Children highly fearful of dentists observe videotapes of two children practicing controlled breathing and visualizing techniques to cope with their fears (Klingman, Melamed, Cuthbert, & Hermecz, 1984).

▼ Impulsive hyperactive children are asked to observe models instructing themselves out loud as they approach various tasks (Meichenbaum, 1977; Meichenbaum & Goodman, 1971).

Training-group leaders can use demonstration skills for imparting virtually every lifeskill. It should be normal rather than exceptional to include a demonstration when teaching a skill or subskill. Beginners in leading training groups may insufficiently acknowledge the power of good demonstrations. Frequently, they replicate methods of academic teaching rather than make the switch to methods of applied skills training.

What Is Observational Learning?

To explore what observational learning is, we will first define terms. Then we will look at the goals of observational learning and at how leaders and participants can serve as role models.

Defining Terms

Many terms are used to describe elements of learning from observation, including *imitating, copying, mimicking, following the example of, identifying with, modeling, showing,* and *demonstrating. Modeling* is perhaps the most commonly used of these terms in the psychology literature (for example, Bandura 1969, 1977). Perry and Furukawa (1986) define modeling as "the process of observational learning in which the behavior of an individual or group—the model—acts as a stimulus for similar thoughts, attitudes, or behaviors on the part of another individual who observes the model's performance" (p. 66). In acquiring and maintaining day-to-day behaviors, modeling is frequently both unintentional and also observed by people who are not fully conscious of its possible implications for their later behavior. For example, children copy some of their parents' vices as well as some of their virtues. This copying is without parents' ever consciously engaging in vice education programs nor children being aware that they are acquiring some negative behavior patterns.

In real life, much modeling is unintentional. However, in lifeskills training groups, leaders consciously promote observational learning of desired skills and subskills. *Demonstrating* is used here in preference to *modeling*. Unlike *modeling, demonstrating* is a word commonly used outside psychological circles. Leaders may intentionally either demonstrate or arrange for others to demonstrate skills. Both *model* and *demonstrator* describe the person demonstrating.

Goals of Observational Learning

Observational learning can be used in lifeskills groups to initiate new skills strengths; develop existing skills strengths; disinhibit existing skills strengths; and inhibit and weaken existing skills weaknesses. Observational learning is applicable to training participants in all lifeskills. Within this broad mandate, the goals of observational learning can be viewed in the following three categories:

Thinking skills: A demonstration focused on thinking skills might identify upsetting perceptions in a situation, assess their appropriateness through logical analysis, and generate and evaluate different perceptions to see if there are more accurate perceptions (Beck, 1976; Nelson-Jones, 1990a). The demonstrated thinking skills need not be related to any immediate observable actions.

Action skills: Action skills demonstrations focus on observable behaviors. An example of an action skills demonstration is one in which the demonstrator shows—focusing on verbal, voice, and body messages—how to handle aggressive criticism.

Action skills with accompanying self-talk: Here the demonstration focuses on both action skills and their accompanying self-instructions. Examples of teaching self-talk to guide behavior include training impulsive children to self-instruct their way through tasks (Meichenbaum, 1977; Meichenbaum & Goodman, 1971) and training test-anxious students in the self-verbalizations and principles for completing anagrams (Sarason, 1973).

These three categories of skills—thinking skills, action skills, and action skills with accompanying self-talk—can each be demonstrated in different parts of either the same session or an overall program. For example, in an anger-management training group, demonstrations can show how to reframe provocations (thinking skill), express anger by using "I" statements (action skill), and show appropriate behaviors in a specific anger-evoking situation with accompanying self-instructions (action skills with accompanying self-talk).

Leaders and Participants as Role Models

Apart from demonstrating or arranging for demonstrations of specific lifeskills, there are two other important aspects of observational learning in training groups: leaders as role models and participants as role models.

Leaders as Role Models

The importance of group leaders as role models is frequently stressed (for example, Bloch & Crouch, 1985; Corey, 1990; Corey, Corey, Callanan, & Russell, 1988; Yalom, 1985). Training-group leaders cannot *not* demonstrate behavior. Even when you are not consciously demonstrating a specific lifeskill, your behavior is always under the microscope and capable of influencing participants for good or ill. If leaders demonstrate commitment to program goals, participants are more likely to do so too. Leaders who arrive at sessions on time encourage participants to do the same. Leaders who listen well and show respect may unobtrusively help participants improve their skills in these areas. Leaders who are able to express feelings, be relaxed, show humor, and reveal appropriate personal information demonstrate these skills to participants. Leaders offering constructive feedback model this skill. Also, leaders set emotional climates in training groups as much by demonstration as by exhortation.

Participants as Role Models

Leaders can work to help participants demonstrate desirable behaviors for each other. These behaviors fall into at least three main interrelated categories: behaviors conducive to the group process, behaviors illustrating how to learn skills, and behaviors demonstrating various levels of performance of targeted skills.

By using group facilitation skills, leaders can assist participants in becoming role models for each other in the process factors conducive to successful group therapy (Bloch & Crouch, 1985; Yalom, 1985). For example, participants can demonstrate such therapeutic factors as the level of acceptance necessary for developing group cohesiveness, self-understanding, altruism, universality, being more trustful, and providing feedback on how people come across to them.

Leaders can help participants develop skills of being good lifeskills learners. These learning skills include owning responsibility for learning, adhering to any learning contract, setting personal goals, admitting mistakes, taking acceptable risks, fully participating in structured activities, working through setbacks, and completing homework assignments. The more leaders can help participants develop these learning skills, the more opportunity there is for participants to demonstrate them to each other.

A third way in which leaders can help participants become role models is to create good emotional climates for observational learning when participants acquire, rehearse, practice, and talk about targeted skills. This observational learning takes place in many ways. The leader can work on coaching, rehearsal, and feedback with an individual participant in front of the group. Participants can be broken into subgroups and then observe each other as they work on their skills.

Furthermore, participants can discuss either in pairs or larger units how they have progressed in using the skills outside of the group. In addition, former training-group participants can be invited back to give testamonials about their success in using targeted skills.

Considerations in Demonstrating Lifeskills
▼▼

Considerations in demonstrating lifeskills include the question of who demonstrates, demonstrator characteristics, methods of demonstration, characteristics of the demonstration, and ways to enhance observer attention. We'll examine each of these considerations in turn.

Who Demonstrates?

Options for who demonstrates include the following. These demonstrator options can be used singly or in combination.

Leaders: In their initial presentations of skills or subskills, leaders can systematically include formal demonstration by themselves. Also, during training groups, less formal leader demonstrations are almost inevitable.

Leaders' aides: Training-group leaders may be assisted by one or more aides who provide specific demonstrations. These demonstrations are sometimes performed together with leaders.

Participants: Participants can be demonstrators both for other participants and for themselves. Leaders can ask individual participants to take part in live or prerecorded demonstrations. In addition, participants can be asked to demonstrate skills for themselves. These self-demonstrations can be either in their imaginations (Kazdin, 1976) or by "self-as-model" edited videotapes of their own performances (Cormier & Cormier, 1985; Hosford & Johnson, 1983; Hosford, Moss, & Morrell, 1976).

Third parties: Numerous categories of people from outside the group can be used as demonstrators. Such people include actors or acting students who role-play scenes; participants from previous groups; associates of the leaders who volunteer their services; and those who take part in demonstration films and videotapes recorded elsewhere.

Puppets and cartoon characters: Puppets can be used as demonstrators, especially with children. For example, a survey found that 21 percent of all pediatric hospitals in the United States use puppet show presentations to prepare children for hospitalization and surgery (Peterson & Ridley-Johnson, 1980). Cartoon characters also can be used to present lifeskills. For instance, dialogue balloons can be drawn by characters' heads to demonstrate thinking skills.

Demonstrator Characteristics

This section particularly applies to characteristics of third-party demonstrators. Demonstrator characteristics are important in that they influence how much observers attend, retain, and are motivated. Characteristics to consider in selecting demonstrators include the following:

Similarity to observers: In general, the greater the similarity between demonstrators and observers, the greater the effect of the demonstration on subsequent observer behaviors (Kazdin, 1976; Perry & Furukawa, 1986). Demonstrators who are similar on characteristics such as age, sex, socioeconomic status, ethnic grouping, and race are more likely to be identified with and imitated than dissimilar demonstrators.

Prestige: The examples from demonstrators prestigious to observers may be followed more than examples from those not so prestigious. A caution is that observers may find it hard to identify with demonstrators who are so prestigious that they are unable to relate to demonstrators' behaviors (Perry & Furukawa, 1986).

Competence level: How competent should demonstrators be? Should they be seen to develop skills or should they show immediate mastery of skills? Kazdin suggests the advantage of demonstrators' showing behaviors similar to those of observers but then overcoming problems (Kazdin, 1976). Demonstrators who are seen to develop coping skills when dealing with problems may be more powerful influencers than those showing mastery or expert performance throughout.

Warmth and personal attractiveness: Bandura (1977) observes of everyday life: "Attention to models is also channeled by their interpersonal attraction" (p. 24). Models without engaging characteristics are either ignored or rejected. Observer attraction to demonstrators influences the outcomes of lifeskills demonstrations. For example, warmth and nurturance may enhance demonstration effects (Perry & Furukawa, 1986).

Methods of Demonstration

Training-group leaders have many options for how to present demonstrations. These options are not mutually exclusive. Demonstrations can take place in written, live, prerecorded, or visualized form, as summarized in Table 8-1.

Written

Much demonstration takes place through the printed page. Written demonstrations are possible for thinking skills, such as either changing negative into coping self-talk or reformulating unrealistic into realistic personal rules. Written demonstrations can be supplemented

Table 8-1 Methods of Demonstrating Lifeskills

Method of demonstrating lifeskills	Skills area		
	Thinking skills	Action skills	Action skills with self-talk
Written demonstration	✓	Difficult	Difficult
Live demonstration	✓	✓	✓
Prerecorded demonstration	✓	✓	✓
Visualized demonstration	Less suitable	✓	✓

by visual images such as cartoons. Written demonstrations can be stored and retrieved easily by participants. Another advantage is that written demonstrations can be introductory examples for subsequent written or live skills development exercises.

Live

Live demonstrations have the advantage of here-and-now communication. Observers can receive verbal, voice, body, and action messages as they actually happen. Models can be trained and rehearsed so the input of the demonstrations is carefully controlled. Live demonstrations also allow the possibility of spontaneity—for example, in front of groups, leaders can work with participants on current problems. Live demonstrations have the advantage that the demonstrator can interact with the audience and, if appropriate, show different or simpler ways to enact skills. However, live demonstrations have disadvantages too. Sometimes live demonstrations do not go according to plan: unlike in the case of prerecorded demonstrations, you cannot edit out mistakes. Also, depending on the size of the audience, it may be difficult to hear or see demonstrators. Furthermore, in settings such as schools where leaders may have discipline problems, unruly observers may interfere with the concentration of both demonstrators and interested observers (Nelson-Jones, 1986).

Prerecorded

Prerecorded demonstrations use films, videotapes, and audio cassettes. Demonstrators can be group leaders, participants, or third parties. Prerecorded demonstrations have some advantages. If you make the material yourself, you can carefully control input and edit out mistakes. Though demonstrators initially may be nervous in front of cameras or cassette recorders, unlike with live performances they have the opportunity to repeat demonstrations marred by anxiety. The process of making prerecorded demonstrations allows for successive attempts to rewrite scripts and improve role-plays. Successful demonstration tapes and cassettes can be stored for future use. Also, if you have access to funds for purchasing or renting films, videotapes, and audio cassettes, you can use professionally made products and be spared the work of developing your own materials. In addition, prerecorded demonstrations can be made or purchased in multiple copies. Consequently, individual participants can view or listen to copies either during training groups or when reviewing or rehearsing afterward. Another advantage of prerecorded material is that leaders can pause or rewind to emphasize points.

Training-group leaders also have to consider disadvantages of prerecorded demonstrations. Demonstrations may not be tailored to training requirements. Considerable time and expense may need to go into developing and recording material. Prerecorded material requires good equipment both when being made and when being shown. Good quality equipment may not be readily available. In addition, training tapes and films may get worn out with age and repeated use. Leaders who use prerecorded material may lose some of their flexibility in adjusting demonstrations to the level of attention and needs of their audience. For example, the recorded units may be longer or shorter than required. Furthermore, using playback equipment and possibly having to darken rooms may obstruct the smooth flow of learning sequences.

Visualized

In the psychological literature, visualized demonstration is called *covert modeling* (Cautela, 1976; Cormier & Cormier, 1985; Kazdin, 1976). Here leaders request that participants visualize the demonstration scenes that they describe. Depending on the instructions, participants either visualize themselves or third parties demonstrating the skills. Visualized demonstration has the advantage of flexibility. Different situations can be readily presented to participants' imaginations depending on their collective and individual needs and learning rates. Leaders have the choice of suggesting demonstrations either live or in prerecorded form. In addition, whether the initial suggestions were either live or prerecorded, participants can instruct themselves when rehearsing at home.

Visualized rehearsal can be used after live and prerecorded demonstrations. In such instances, visualized rehearsal can take place either immediately after the demonstration to help with memorizing skills or as a homework assignment to help with performing the skills.

Visualized demonstration has disadvantages. It is only appropriate for participants who have the capacity for visualizing scenes adequately. However, since scenes are never actually demonstrated, even for good visualizers there may be important slippages between what leaders describe and what they visualize. For example, in being asked to visualize assertiveness demonstrations, participants may miss important body messages depicted in live or prerecorded demonstrations.

Characteristics of the Demonstration

What are some of the other factors in setting up effective demonstrations for lifeskills training groups? Leaders still have numerous choices beyond selecting methods of demonstration.

Single or Multiple Demonstrators?

Generally it is much easier if there is just one demonstrator or pair of demonstrators for each skills sequence. Single demonstrators economize on leader time and effort. Also, it may be easier to control the verbal, voice, body, and action messages of single demonstrators. However, strong reasons exist for using multiple demonstrators if practical. Kazdin (1976) observes of covert modeling, "Generally, clients who have imagined several models show greater behavior change. . . . In view of the evidence from both overt (filmed) and covert modeling, the practicing counselor or therapist should employ different models over the course of therapy" (p. 484). Bandura (1976) has developed a participant modeling approach, consisting of demonstration followed by assisted performance of the demonstrated skill. In his approach, desired behaviors "are repeatedly modeled, preferably by different models" (p. 248).

Some of the reasons why multiple may be preferable to single demonstrators are as follows. In group approaches there are likely to be people with a range of characteristics. Multiple demonstrators increase the possibility of different paticipants' identifying with demonstrators. In addition, in the outside world, there are often a range of ways of dealing with situations. Multiple demonstrators are more likely to reflect the possible differences in implementing skills. This variability may increase the flexibility with which participants learn and perform skills. Furthermore, for performing feared tasks such as asking someone for a date, multiple demonstrators have the advantage of showing that a range of people can learn to overcome their fears and act appropriately. A risk in using multiple demonstrators is that little observational learning may occur if they are too inconsistent in their behaviors (Perry & Furukawa, 1986).

Scripted or Unscripted?

Whether or not to use prepared scripts is an issue for both live and prerecorded demonstrations. The main advantage of prepared scripts is that they lend themselves to systematic presentation of skills. Also, demonstrators can receive coaching feedback and practice for polished performance. However, in training groups there is also a role for unscripted demonstrations. For example, in anger-management groups, leaders can have participants show how they behaved in particular situations and then demonstrate alternative behaviors. Advantages of spontaneous demonstrations include that they are tailored to participants' problems and that they provide here-and-now feedback. In sum, for initial skills presentations, scripted demonstrations may be preferable to unscripted. However, for showing skills for application in individual participants' daily lives, unscripted demonstrations may be preferable.

Negative as Well as Positive Demonstration?

An issue in the demonstration literature is whether negative demonstrations should be provided as well as positive demonstrations (for example, Newman & Fuqua, 1988). Put more simply, should demonstrations of *don't*s be provided as well as of *do*'s? Ivey and Authier (1978), when developing microcounseling training videotapes, consider that observing ineffective models makes it possible to identify the behaviors that constitute skills weaknesses. They write, "Viewing these negative behaviors, then, makes it possible to develop positive models representing an antithesis" (p. 309). Sometimes great humor can be injected into lifeskills training by showing negative models—for instance, think of someone like comic actor John Cleese making outrageous mistakes.

Among reasons for only showing demonstrations of positive behaviors are the following. Demonstrating negative behaviors before showing positive ones takes additional time that may not be justified by results. Showing negative as well as positive behaviors may confuse rather than clarify the information leaders want demonstrated. Furthermore, sometimes negative demonstrations may worsen rather than improve participants' skills. For example, if a demonstrator overcoming a phobia showed an increase rather than a decrease in anxiety, the demonstration could backfire (Perry & Furukawa, 1986). To be of any help to phobic observers, the demonstrator should then show the skills of overcoming heightened anxiety.

No simple answer exists to the issue of whether to include negative demonstrations along with—and generally before—positive ones. Lifeskills training covers a huge variety of skills and populations. Leaders must use their judgments in individual instances. If in doubt, when initially introducing skills it is probably best to leave out negative demonstrations. Participants will likely have plenty of opportunity to observe negative models as they and their peers work in the group.

Graduated Demonstrations

Some skills may be so complex, difficult, or anxiety-arousing that leaders decide to present them by means of a series of demonstrations. For example, with a skill like speaking in public, the various verbal, voice, and body component subskills of effective public speaking may each be demonstrated and focused on separately prior to being reconstructed as a single overall skill. Graduated demonstration can be used in lifeskills programs to help participants overcome specific phobias. For example, people who are afraid of snakes can view models interacting with snakes in progressively more threatening scenes (Bandura, 1976). Graduated demonstration can also be used for the specific problems that participants bring into lifeskills training groups. For example, a young man with difficulty standing up to his father can observe the leader demonstrating how to handle a low-level confrontation before later observing a more difficult confrontation.

Rewards for Performance of Skills

Research into demonstration shows that observers who see demonstrators rewarded for a particular behavior are more likely to perform that behavior than if it is not rewarded (Kazdin, 1976). However, direct rewards have an even greater motivating effect in maintaining behavior over a period of time than do indirect or vicarious rewards (Bandura, 1977). Take the example of an observer watching a demonstration of the assertiveness skill of returning a defective purchase to a shop. Seeing the demonstrator rewarded for the assertive behavior by the salesperson's admitting the error and offering either a replacement or a refund is more likely to motivate the observer than if the assertive behavior is not shown to achieve the desired results. However, still more motivating is the observer's assertiveness being directly rewarded in real life.

Even if not externally rewarded, demonstrators can still demonstrate rewarding themselves for performing desired behaviors. If, in the earlier example, the demonstrator were unsuccessful in getting the purchase changed, he or she could say aloud to himself or herself, "Well done," for having performed the targeted assertive behaviors. Likewise, in real life, even if unsuccessful in achieving desired outcomes, participants can still reward themselves for using their skills.

Presenting the Rationale

Training-group leaders need to take care in how they introduce demonstrations. Observers can be given a rationale for the importance of learning from demonstration. For example, as part of the introduction for his demonstration program for juvenile delinquents, Sarason (1976) stated, "Having people watch others doing things and then discussing what has been done is a very important way and a very useful way to learn" (p. 58). For his covert modeling or visualized demonstration treatment, Kazdin (1976) stressed how people, by rehearsing situations in their imaginations, can alter their behaviors in real-life situations.

Giving Instructions

Leaders need to pay attention to the commentaries they provide for their demonstrations. Observers' attention to demonstrations can be increased by initial instructions both telling them what to look out for and also informing them that they will later be required to perform the demonstrated behaviors (Perry & Furukawa, 1986). Participant motivation can be further enhanced by making connections between the behavior to be demonstrated and its importance for their lives.

During prerecorded demonstrations, voice-overs can tell participants what specifically to observe. During live and prerecorded presentations, breaks can be interspersed in which instructional comments are made on what observers either will see or have seen or both. At the end of a demonstration, a summary of its main points can be provided. Furthermore, participants can be given written as well as spoken instructions about the content of demonstrations. These written instructions can be in handouts or sections of training manuals.

Elicting Observer Summaries

Observers can be encouraged to summarize the main points of demonstrations. Research studies indicate that observers who actively summarize the salient points of demonstrators' behaviors are better able to learn and remember this information (Bandura, Grusec, & Menlove, 1966; Perry & Furukawa, 1986). After a lifeskills demonstration, leaders can break down the group into pairs or other subgroups to allow each participant to have the opportunity to summarize.

Timing of Observers' Performance of Demonstrated Skills

The timing of observers' performing demonstrated skills can range from at the same time as the demonstration to not at all. An example of simultaneous performance is that of children highly fearful of dentists being asked to practice controlled breathing as they watch a film of a child model demonstrating the skill (Klingman, Melamed, Cuthbert, & Hermecz, 1984). Sometimes, as for instance in Bandura's participant modeling approach, demonstration and performance of skills are intermingled in progressively more difficult steps (Bandura, 1976). Within a single session, a skill is demonstrated and the observer is then assisted by the demonstrator to enact it, followed by further demonstration and enactment of a slightly more difficult skill, and so on. To date, participant modeling appears to have been used largely with individuals. However, depending on the skills involved, participant modeling might fruitfully be adapted to groups.

Most often, when demonstrations form part of initial skills presentations, enactment by participants follows shortly afterward. Though lifeskills can be acquired from demonstrations alone, they are more likely to be learned if demonstrations are followed by coaching, rehearsal, feedback, and practice (Bandura, 1976; 1977; Perry & Furukawa, 1986).

Ways to Enhance Observer Attention

Bandura (1977) writes, "People cannot learn much by observation unless they attend to, and perceive accurately, the significant features of the modeled behavior" (p. 24). How can leaders enhance observers' attention? At risk of repetition, following are some suggestions.

Pay attention to demonstrator characteristics: Demonstrator characteristics have been reviewed already.

Match demonstrations to observers' states of readiness: Take into account the intellectual levels and attention spans of observers. For example, Sarason (1976) approaches the problem of holding juvenile delinquents' attention by incorporating physical movement and a break for soft drinks into his modeling program. For all age levels, do not give lengthy and boring introductions to demonstrations and then expect wide-awake observers. Use appropriate language when making up scripts. Be prepared to use graduated demonstrations for skills that are complex or threatening.

Orient observers: Let observers know how, by watching demonstrations, they can help themselves achieve their goals. Without engaging in phony selling, convey enthusiasm for observational learning. Make sure that participants know what to look for in demonstrations. Let participants know that next it will be their turn to use the demonstrated skills.

Reduce debilitating anxiety: Anxiety can interfere with participants' abilities to attend and observe. Kazdin (1976) states that research on live and filmed demonstration suggests that training people to be relaxed facilitates observational learning. Relaxing participants may be especially appropriate for his covert modeling approach which relies on participants' visualizing scenes. However, Perry and Furukawa (1986) concluded that the role of relaxation across a broad range of modeling treatment programs has yet to be fully evaluated. Relaxation may prove helpful for unusually anxious observers. Other ways in which leaders can reduce participants' anxiety are by developing rapport with them and by fostering a group norm that in subsequent enactments of demonstrated skills, mistakes are okay.

Reduce extraneous distractions: Mention has already been made of dealing with within-group distractions caused by the different agendas of audience members. In addition, participants' attention can be badly disrupted by extraneous distractions. Such distractions include corridor noise and people coming into the room when demonstrations are in progress. Placing a sign on the door that says that a training group is in progress and that requests no interruptions and silence outside may be better than doing nothing.

Demonstrating Thinking Skills
▼▼

Training-group leaders subscribing to the cognitive-behavioral theoretical position are faced with the need to demonstrate not only action skills, or overt behaviors, but also thinking skills, or covert behaviors. Thinking skills are both lifeskills in themselves and are relevant to all specific lifeskill areas, such as relationships, leisure, work, and health. For example, the capacity to identify, dispute, and reformulate irrational beliefs or unrealistic personal rules is both a thinking skill in its own right and also a skill that can be applied to all areas in which such beliefs or rules occur (Ellis, 1989; Nelson-Jones, 1990a). Consequently, group leaders have the option of either teaching one or more thinking skills as such or teaching relevant thinking skills together with action skills for use in specific areas—for example, managing stress, job interviewing, or handling relationship conflicts.

Thinking is an inner process mostly involving self-talk. Therefore thinking skills lend themselves more readily to written and audio cassette demonstrations than do action skills. The visual images provided by videotapes or films are not required for thinking skills. Furthermore, visual images may interfere with demonstrating thought processes. Thinking skills can also be demonstrated live. Live demonstrations can be either when skills are initially presented or later as leaders endeavor to change participants' thinking both by repetition and also by working with material brought into the group.

Written Demonstration

Written demonstrations of thinking skills can come from published sources. However, here the focus is on building skills of developing your own demonstration materials. If you are a skilled cartoonist, you can draw dialogue balloons to illustrate points; if not, you will have to rely on the written word alone.

Written demonstrations often form part of instructional manuals or handouts. Leaders require clear goals for what they wish to achieve in each learning unit. Furthermore, they need to explain clearly the skill or subskill being demonstrated so that participants know what to look for both when introduced to the skill and when later rehearsing and practicing it.

Following is an example of an instructional handout for the thinking skill of coping self-talk. Meichenbaum and others have trained many different groups of people in coping self-talk. The life-skills they have targeted include managing anger, managing stress, being creative, curbing impulsiveness, managing pain, and controlling weight (Meichenbaum, 1977, 1983, 1985; Meichenbaum & Deffenbacher, 1988). The example of coping self-talk provided here is from a lifeskills program to train adolescents, college students, and others in the skills of managing shyness (Nelson-Jones, 1990b).

Sample Coping Self-Talk Handout

Coping self-talk is a useful thinking skill for managing feelings of shyness. The idea is that during your waking hours you continuously engage in an internal dialogue, or perform self-talk. The goals of coping self-talk are to calm your anxieties and to help you deal effectively with the task at hand. Thus, coping self-talk contains two major elements: calming self-talk and coaching self-talk. Coping self-talk is about coping or "doing as well as I can" rather than about mastery or "being perfect" and "having no anxiety." Coping is a much more realistic goal than mastery.

Coping self-talk involves replacing negative self-talk statements with helpful ones. Let's take the example of Kay and Sara going to a party. Note how Kay's self-talk oppresses her, while Sara's self-talk supports her.

Kay: "I know that I am going to find this party difficult. Everybody is looking at me. I feel unattractive. I don't want to make a mistake. I'm feeling tense and, when this happens, I know it will only get worse."

Sara: "I enjoy parties and meeting new people. Although I get a little anxious with strangers, I know I can overcome it. I have developed some good party skills and these usually work. All I have to do is my best."

Calming and coaching statements tend to be interspersed in coping self-talk.

Two important aspects of *calming* self-talk are as follows.

Tell yourself to stay calm: Simple self-statements include "keep calm," "relax" and "take it easy." In addition, you can instruct yourself to "take a deep breath" or "breathe slowly and regularly."

Tell yourself you can cope: Sample self-statements include "I can handle this situation" or "My anxiety is a signal for me to use my coping skills."

Coaching self-talk can help you to cope with shyness in the following ways:

Specify your goals: An example could be "I will go up and talk to a minimum of three new people at the party."

Break down tasks: Think through the steps needed to attain your goal.

Concentrate on the task at hand: You instruct yourself, as pilots do when they talk themselves through difficult landings.

You can use coping self-talk before, during, and after stressful social situations—for example, going to a party full of strangers or out with a new date.

Examples of possible coping self-talk statements *before* a stressful social situation include the following:

"This anxiety is a sign for me to use my coping skills."
"Calm down. Develop a plan to manage the situation."
"I know if I use my coping skills I can manage."

Examples of possible coping self-talk statements *during* a stressful social situation include the following:

"Take my time. Breathe slowly and regularly."
"Relax. I can manage if I just take one step at a time."
"I don't have to be liked by everyone. All I can do is the best I can."

Examples of possible coping self-talk statements *after* a stressful social situation include the following:

"Each time I cope it seems to get easier."
"I'm proud of the way I'm learning to manage my fears."
"I've shown myself I can do it now."

A few comments about the preceding written demonstration. First, written demonstration can be used in conjunction with other kinds of demonstration, such as audio cassette or live. In lifeskills training groups, written demonstration should rarely, if ever, be used alone. Second, both negative and positive demonstrations, namely Kay's and Sara's self-talk, were provided prior to breaking down the skills of coping self-talk and giving examples of specific coping self-statements. Kay's and Sara's statements were intended as attention-getters to help participants see the relevance of coping self-talk to their own lives. Third, this demonstration of coping self-talk for shy people lends itself to being followed up with an exercise, either in the group or as homework, to consolidate the skills being taught. For example, participants can be instructed to identify any negative self-talk contributing to their shyness and socially incompetent behaviors. Then, they can be asked to identify a specific social situation that they find stressful and to write out at least three coping self-talk statements for before, during, and after the situation. In addition, participants can be encouraged to use coping self-talk skills to manage shyness both inside and outside the group. Fourth, written demonstrations like the preceding can be easily stored and retrieved for revision and reuse.

Audio Cassette Demonstration

Self-help audio cassettes are often used in conjunction with psychological counseling (Yamauchi, 1987). For both individual and group use, audio cassette demonstrations of thinking skills have the advantage over written demonstrations that participants can hear how demonstrators think. People talk to themselves when they think. Audio cassette demonstrations much more closely replicate this self-verbalizing process than can written demonstrations. In addition, if they do not require copyright permission, audio cassette demonstrations are relatively inexpensive to reproduce. Accordingly, participants might receive copies for homework and revision purposes. Participants are likely to require much work and practice to change established patterns of thinking (Ellis, 1987, 1989). Consequently, a demonstration mode lending itself to repeated listenings has much to recommend it.

The initial audio cassette demonstration of a thinking skill is best recorded either by leaders or third parties. It is unreasonable to expect participants to demonstrate skills that they may not understand. However, leaders can encourage participants later in the learning process to make up their own demonstration cassettes. At the conclusion of lifeskills training groups, participants have to listen to their own self-talk without leaders. If participants are encouraged to use themselves as demonstrators of targeted thinking skills during groups, they may be more likely to maintain these skills afterward. Participants probably require repeated listenings to demonstrations for thinking skills to become part of their everyday repertoires.

Here the focus is on building skills of developing your own demonstration audio cassettes rather than encouraging you to use commercial ones. You can still decide to use other people's voices rather than your own. Audio cassettes provide the opportunity to pick up feelings from voice inflections. Consequently, audio cassettes may bring scripts much more to life than the printed page. However, even after playback, participants may not be able to memorize details of audio cassette presentations. In such cases you can also provide written scripts.

Following are two examples of scripts for audio cassette demonstrations. The instructions, left out in these examples, can be given live, put on the cassette, provided as a handout, or a mixture of these. For instance, leaders can stop their demonstration cassettes to highlight points and make comments. Leaders can also rewind and play again key sections of demonstrations.

The first thinking skill demonstrated is that of not jumping to unwarranted perceptual conclusions. The target audience is an adult lifeskills group on managing anger and conflict. The component subskills of not jumping to unwarranted perceptual conclusions include tuning in to upsetting feelings, logically analyzing their appropriateness, generating and evaluating different perceptions, and then selecting the best fitting perception. Kent is angry when his girlfriend, Jan, is half an hour late for a special meal he has cooked. However, rather than sulk, Kent decides to use the thinking skill of challenging his initial perception and seeing if there is a more accurate perception. The script for Kent demonstrating this thinking skill is as follows:

> I'm feeling mad because Jan has not arrived on time. Stop and think. What are my perceptual choices? Let's see if I am jumping to unwarranted conclusions. At the moment I'm thinking Jan has deliberately put me down. What is the evidence for that perception? When I stop to think, I know that Jan is very reliable and would not want to deliberately hurt me. She has never missed a special occasion before. Are there any other possible explanations? Let me think of a few. One possibility is that we did not make our arrangements clearly enough—I remember now that I had to rush off immediately after I gave the invitation. Another possibility is that something has happened to Jan on the way over—for instance, a flat tire. Still another possibility is that Jan was forced to work late and then got caught in the traffic. A further explanation is that Jan may have stopped off to collect something for me. Another explanation for my anger is that I am still too insecure in our relationship and am threatened by her lateness. This last perception seems to have the ring of truth about it. Consequently, when Jan comes I won't make a fuss over her lateness. I'm sure there is some good reason for it.

The second audio cassette demonstration script focuses on the thinking skill of identifying, disputing, and reformulating an unrealistic personal rule. The target audience is an adult group of executives and professional people attending a stress-management workshop. The script focuses on Li, a highly successful accountant, challenging her personal rule that life must be all work and no play.

> I haven't been eating or sleeping properly recently. Also, I'm feeling depressed and tense. I have to force myself to get through the day. Why do I keep pushing myself so hard? I seem to have this underlying personal rule that my life *must* be all work and no play. Let's try disputing this rule. Do I expect other people to sacrifice everything for their careers? Definitely not. I seem to have a double standard in

which I'm harder on myself than on other people. Do I need the extra money and status that come from working this hard? I want a good standard of living and for people to recognize my competence. However, I would still earn enough money even if I were to ease off a bit. Also, what I think of myself is more important than needing recognition from others all the time. I know I'm competent. Is the rule about all work and no play helping or harming me? The rule helped me when I was studying for my accountancy exams and getting started. I have just kept going at the same frantic pace ever since. My body and low feelings are telling me to watch my stress level. Also, I'm concerned that, in my early thirties and single, I'm having virtually no social life. There are also a lot of recreational activities I would like—for instance, I used to be a good tennis player. It would be fun to play again.

Let's try reformulating that personal rule about all work and no play into a rule that might work better for me at this stage of my life. Here's a try: "I want to earn good money and be respected for my competence as an accountant. However, I am likely to be a more successful person—and not necessarily a less successful accountant—if I lead a more balanced life and treat my social and recreational activities as though they are as important as my work." This new personal rule represents a drastic change from my current way of thinking. I will need to work hard to keep it in mind and also to change my behavior in line with it.

If possible, use highly sensitive recording equipment when you make up your audio cassettes. Aim for a professional standard of recording. Most home audio cassette recorders will not achieve the required level of clarity. Audio cassette recorders are on the market that eliminate virtually all motor noise and background hiss. You greatly lessen the effectiveness of audio cassette demonstrations if participants have to struggle with poor-quality recordings. Also, be prepared to rehearse and rerecord your efforts if necessary. Notable performers like Michael Jackson and Barbara Streisand go to these lengths when recording: perhaps you might too.

Live Demonstration

In live demonstrations of thinking skills, the demonstrators can be either training-group leaders or third parties. Third parties require careful coaching in how to present thinking skills. Many leaders may also have to work hard at preparing and delivering competent live demonstrations. However, if leaders are experienced in teaching about and demonstrating specific thinking skills, they may dispense with scripts and either make up demonstrations on the spot or demonstrate material used before. Competent impromptu demonstrations may come over as more real than those memorized from prepared scripts.

Whether intended or unintended, live demonstrations of good

and poor thinking skills happen much of the time in training groups. The group's focus does not have to be on thinking skills. When participants talk about virtually any subject, they demonstrate for each other thinking skills strengths and weaknesses. In groups focused on thinking skills, both leaders and participants can reinforce initial skills demonstrations with follow-up demonstrations. For example, participants can further demonstrate skills as they rehearse and practice them together. Also, leaders can use material generated in the group to illustrate effective thinking skills.

Exercise 20 aims to raise your awareness of and build your skills in demonstrating thinking skills. Readers wishing ideas for thinking skills on which they might focus are referred both to the section on managing speech anxiety in the previous chapter and also to *Thinking Skills: Managing and Preventing Personal Problems* (Nelson-Jones, 1990a).

Exercise 20 Demonstrate a Thinking Skill
▼▼

Work through the following sequence.

1. *Write out a demonstration*: Either as part of a lifeskills training group aimed at a specific thinking skill or as part of a group taking both a thinking- and an action-focused approach to a specific skill—for example, overcoming shyness or assertiveness—write out an instructional handout for a thinking skill or subskill that covers the following points:
   a. Your goal or goals for the learning unit
   b. The audience for your learning unit
   c. Clear instructions that identify for the audience the key points of the skill or subskill you aim to teach
   d. One or more demonstrations of the targeted thinking skill or subskill
   e. Some questions that enable your audience to practice the demonstrated skills either in the group and/or as homework
   Afterward, indicate how you might incorporate written demonstration into your overall presentation of your chosen thinking skill or subskill. For instance, would you plan to provide verbal as well as written instruction and demonstration?
2. *Audiotape a demonstration*: Either for the thinking skill you worked on in item 1 or for another thinking skill or subskill, make a demonstration audio cassette.
   a. Clearly state your goal or goals for a learning unit in which a specific thinking skill or subskill will be demonstrated.
   b. Identify your audience.
   c. Develop a script that demonstrates, using the first person singular, the use of your targeted thinking skill or subskill.

    d. Rehearse your script using either your own or other people's voices.

    e. When you are ready, make an audio cassette recording of your script.

    f. Play back your cassette, and modify it as many times as is necessary to attain a polished performance.

    g. Evaluate the likely effect of your final demonstration cassette in helping participants acquire your targeted thinking skill or subskill.

Think through how you might incorporate the audio cassette demonstration into your overall presentation of your chosen thinking skill or subskill. For instance, would you either provide all your instructions up front or stop the cassette to highlight points and provide commentary?

3. *Demonstrate live*: Either for the thinking skill or subskill for which you prepared a script in item 2 of this exercise or for another thinking skill or subskill, rehearse and give a live demonstration. If relevant, do not take part in the live demonstration, but coach and rehearse a third party to do it. Indicate how you might provide instructions for your live demonstration.

Assess the main advantages and disadvantages for lifeskills training groups of live over written and audiotaped thinking skill demonstrations.

Demonstrating Action Skills
▼▼

Action skills differ from thinking skills in that they are "outer game" skills that act on the environment rather than "inner game" skills involving thought processes. Action skills involve sending observable verbal, voice, body, and action messages. Another relevant distinction is that demonstrations of action skills frequently show two people interacting—for example, boss and worker—rather than the thinking or action skills of only one person. Consequently, with two-person demonstrations, leaders use confederates to play either or both roles. Methods of demonstrating action skills include using audio cassettes and videotapes, live demonstration, and using visualization.

Audio Cassette Demonstration

Audio cassettes are not recommended if training-group leaders wish to include a focus on body messages in skills demonstrations. However, if the main focus is on showing verbal and voice messages, audio cassette demonstrations of action skills may be appropriate. A focus on body messages can still be incorporated in different demonstrations. For example, in groups on public-speaking skills, demonstrating verbal and voice messages may come before showing the accompanying body messages.

Following is an example of a script for a brief audio cassette demonstration in which a teenager, Chrissie, returns a defective compact disc to a shop and requests that it be replaced. Within the overall goal of helping teenage participants become more assertive, the leader wishes to demonstrate the verbal message subgoals of using "I" statements, giving specific feedback, making clear requests, and reflecting resistances; and the voice message subgoals of speaking with good volume, firmly, at a moderate rate, and in a relaxed manner.

Chrissie: Hi.

Salesperson: Hi. What can I do for you?

Chrissie: Yesterday I bought this Prince compact disc and here is the receipt. When I got home I found that the disc was scratched. I request that the store replace it.

Salesperson: It's almost impossible for there to be anything wrong with CDs.

Chrissie: You feel that there is rarely anything wrong with CDs, but unfortunately I have found something wrong with this one.

Salesperson: Okay, you may be right in this instance. I'll change it. I know we still have others in stock. This time I will check it more carefully.

Chrissie: That's great. Thanks a lot.

In this example, the leader might role-play the salesperson and a teenage confederate of the leader might role-play Chrissie. Alternatively, the leader might coach people for both roles. Though only verbal messages have been provided in the preceding script, it is essential that the demonstrators are coached in appropriate voice messages. An assertive verbal message can be countermanded if it is given with either unassertive or aggressive voice messages (Alberti & Emmons, 1986). As with thinking skills, leaders making action skills demonstration cassettes must expect to polish initial efforts. In hearing the preceding example, the teenage audience may ask, "What happens if the salesperson persists in saying no?" The leader can either anticipate this question by placing a further demonstration on the cassette showing some skills of coping with this contingency or discuss the situation and possibly give a live demonstration in the group.

Videotaped Demonstration

Both filmed and videotaped demonstrations of action skills have the great advantage over audio cassette demonstrations that participants observe body messages. Many lifeskills training films and videotapes are already on the market. For example, the American Association for Counseling and Development has a film library. Since making demonstration films requires more resources than most group leaders readily have available, here the focus is on making training videotapes. When making training videotapes, leaders have to specify body message subgoals as well as verbal and voice subgoals. For instance, in the previous example of Chrissie returning a compact disc to a store, if the leader were to make a videotape he or she might also get Chrissie to demonstrate the body messages of adequate eye contact, erect posture, and good use of gesture.

In making training videos you have the choice of whether or not to do it on your own. If you decide to bring in outside resources, these may range from a professional videotape-making company to a central audiovisual unit in your institution or organization to a technician in your department. As with audio cassette recording, use the best available videotape-recording equipment and be prepared to retake scenes. If you make the videotape on your own, you may be restricted to one camera angle and not have the facility for editing. Also, your energies may be diverted into working the equipment rather than concentrating on the quality of the demonstration. With more resources, both human and technical, you can do a better job. However, the trade-off for a higher quality product may be unjustified time and expense.

In making training videotapes, group leaders act as movie directors and, as such, require many of their skills. For instance, leaders need to coach demonstrators in how to act their parts. During rehearsals and when shooting scenes, leaders may decide to rewrite scripts and emphasize targeted skills differently. Much trial and error goes into making polished demonstration videotapes.

Making demonstration videotapes may seem a daunting task to many training-group leaders. You have to concentrate on technical, teaching, and acting dimensions of videotapes. However, you are encouraged to persist. For many lifeskills, videotaped demonstrations add the vital visual dimension missing from audio cassette demonstrations. Even though your efforts may fall short of Steven Spielberg's, they are likely to be much better than no demonstration videotapes at all.

Live Demonstration

Training-group leaders can arrange for live demonstrations of action skills. Leaders can give these demonstrations themselves, either on their own or with other demonstrators. Alternatively, both roles in a dialogue can be enacted by others. If you only want to show a particular lifeskill once, you save time by demonstrating it live as contrasted with prerecording your demonstration. However, if on subsequent occasions you wish to repeat your live demonstration, you are faced with the extra time and trouble of working up further polished presentations. In addition, unless live demonstrations are taped, participants have no copies to watch on their own. Needless to say, repeating live demonstrations is easier if you are the only demonstrator than if others are involved too.

Some limitations of live demonstrations in initial action skills presentations have been mentioned. However, subsequently, live demonstrations can be extremely useful when rehearsing and practicing skills. For example, after initial presentations, leaders often demonstrate as they coach participants in targeted skills. In addition, leaders can demonstrate relevant coping skills when participants bring problems from their outside lives into groups. Prerecorded demonstrations do not have this flexibility.

Live demonstration can also be useful to leaders using Bandura's participant modeling approach. This approach has been used particularly to train those suffering from phobias (Bandura, 1976; Jeffrey, 1976). For example, participants can watch demonstrators perform progressively more threatening tasks in relation to feared objects such as snakes. After each demonstration, participants are given both guidance and ample opportunities to perform the demonstrated behaviors under favorable conditions. Examples of favorable conditions include both joint performance of subtasks with leaders and performing subtasks under protective conditions—for instance, touching snakes wearing gloves.

Visualized Demonstration

Visualized demonstration or covert modeling is used to demonstrate action skills in lifeskills training groups much less frequently than videotaped or live demonstration. Nevertheless, visualized demonstration is a useful leader skill. For example, it may be difficult to portray on prerecorded videotapes the range of scenes relevant to participants' problems. In addition, unlike in live demonstrations, all participants are actively involved as they imagine either demonstrators or themselves enacting suggested behaviors. Scenes in visualized demonstrations can be standard as well as individual (Cormier & Cormier, 1985). Furthermore, visualized demonstrations in training groups are good precursors to visualized rehearsal and practice outside the group.

In general, people visualize best when relaxed (Kazdin, 1976). Leaders can get participants to visualize neutral scenes as a way of confirming that they understand how to visualize. For example, participants may be asked to visualize someone eating dinner with them at home.

Three guidelines for developing visualized demonstrations are as follows:

Set the scene: Describe the situation in which targeted lifeskills are to be enacted in sufficient detail so that it it is easy for participants to visualize it.

Describe the action skill(s): Describe how the person enacts the targeted behaviors in the situation. The person visualized may be either a third party or participants themselves. Remember to describe clearly verbal, voice, and body as well as action messages. In brief, give full descriptions of any action skills you demonstrate.

Depict favorable consequences for using the action skill(s): Get participants to visualize the demonstrator's behavior being rewarded (Kazdin, 1976).

Following is an example of a visualized demonstration in a parent effectiveness training class. The targeted behaviors are active listening, sending an "I" message, and requesting a behavior change.

Set the scene: Picture a family consisting of father, mother, and two 9-year-old twin girls sitting at their dining room table. The meal has just started. Mom asks Dad how his day has gone and Dad starts to reply. Before he has had a chance to finish, one of the girls, Luisah, interrupts and asks if he will take her to her dancing lesson tomorrow. Dad, who has had a hard day at work, feels himself tense up at the interruption.

Describe the action skill(s): After the interruption, Dad turns to Luisah, catches her eye, and says in a warm but firm voice, "Honey, I know that it is important for you to get to your dancing lesson. However, I haven't finished answering Mom's question yet. Please let me finish and then we can talk about your concern." At no stage does Dad raise his voice or give his daughter an angry look. Rather, he calmly asserts his right to respect when he talks.

Depict favorable consequences for using the action skill(s): Luisah says in a relaxed voice and without sulking: "I'm sorry, Dad. I'll wait." Luisah does not feel put down by Dad's response. Dad feels good that he has set a limit on her interrupting.

Training-group leaders can develop different visualized demonstrations around targeted skills. These visualizations can be graduated by threat or difficulty. In addition, leaders can get participants to visualize a variety of people coping in the scenes. Visualized demonstration has the further flexibility that leaders can get participants to visualize themselves enacting appropriate behaviors in problematic scenes taken from their own lives.

Exercise 21 provides you with the opportunity to try out different ways of demonstrating action skills.

Exercise 21   Demonstrate an Action Skill
▼ ▼

Work through those parts of the following sequence that you find useful for your circumstances.

1. *Audiotape a demonstration*: Select a lifeskills training group to whom you might want to demonstrate the verbal and voice dimensions of a specific action skill or subskill. If possible, your demonstration should involve dialogue between two people. Depending on whether or not you participate in the demonstration, you will need one or two other demonstrators. Perform the following tasks:

   a. Within the context of your overall goal, set clear verbal and voice message subgoals for your demonstration audio cassette.

   b. Develop a relatively brief script that demonstrates the verbal skills you want to convey. In the margin indicate appropriate voice messages.

   c. Coach and rehearse your demonstrator(s) in the verbal and voice aspects of your demonstration.

   d. Make up at least one pilot audio cassette and then, if necessary, keep altering and rerecording your audio cassette until you are satisfied with it.

   e. Indicate how you might incorporate instructions in your demonstration audio cassette so that participants know what to look for—for instance, will you prerecord your instructions?

2. *Videotape a demonstration*: Follow the instructions for item 1 to make a videotape focused on the body message as well as the verbal and voice message dimensions of an action skill or subskill.

3. *Demonstrate live*: Either for the action skill or subskill you worked on in item 2 or for another action skill or subskill, rehearse and give a live demonstration. If relevant, do not take part in the live demonstration, but coach and rehearse third parties to do it.

4. *Use visualized demonstration*: Select a lifeskills training group to whom you might want to demonstrate the verbal, voice, and body message dimensions of a specific action skill or subskill by means of visualized demonstration. Perform the following steps:

   a. Develop a visualized demonstration containing at least two people. The demonstration should set the scene, describe the appropriate action skill, and depict favorable consequences for using the action skill.

   b. Make at least one pilot audio cassette and then, if necessary, keep altering and rerecording your cassette until you are satisfied with it.

   c. Find another person and ask him or her to visualize your scene as you describe it live. Afterward, get feedback regarding how realistic the person found your demonstration to be.

   d. Indicate how you might incorporate instructions in your visualized demonstration. For instance, would you provide instructions when your audience has their eyes open or shut?

   e. Think through how you might use visualized demonstration in any lifeskills group you lead now or might lead in the future.

Demonstrating Action Skills with Accompanying Self-Talk

▼▼

Training-group leaders may often want to demonstrate action skills with the self-talk that accompanies them. Ultimately, participants have to instruct themselves through action skills sequences. There is much to be said for building relevant self-talk into demonstrations. Perhaps increasingly, lifeskills demonstrations will be viewed as deficient if they do not contain both action skills and also accompanying self-talk. Arranging for demonstrations that show both action skills and self-talk can present an interesting challenge to a training-group leader's ingenuity.

Demonstrating self-talk along with action skills can be done in written form, live, prerecorded on either audio cassette or videotape, or in conjunction with visualized demonstration. To avoid repetition, we won't deal with each of these methods again. Rather, some ways to build self-talk into any of these forms of action skills demonstration are described.

Thinking Aloud

One way to add self-talk to a demonstration is to have demonstrators pause every now and then to verbalize relevant self-instructions out loud. Thinking aloud is less intrusive in individual demonstrations than in demonstrations where two or more persons are involved. For example, the thought processes of a demonstrator who looks at a test paper for the first time can be shown in such a way that the relationship between thinking skills and action skills seems comfortable. However, in a dialogue demonstration—for instance, with partners attempting to manage a conflict—it may seem artificial if each demonstrator thinks aloud before responding. In live demonstrations, thinking aloud is the only way of showing both action skills and self-instructions. In audio cassette and videotaped demonstrations, think-aloud segments can be interspersed before each action-skill segment.

Voice-Overs

With demonstration videotapes and films, voice-overs of the demonstrator's self-talk can be edited in. Voice-overs are less disruptive to the flow of the demonstration than alternating between self-talk and action. However, voice-overs have some disadvantages. A technical disadvantage is that the process of recording voice-overs may be beyond the available resources of many leaders. Another problem is that where demonstrations include much dialogue, finding appropriate openings for voice-overs may be difficult. A possible educational disadvantage is that voice-overs may confuse observers who are trying to learn self-talk and action skills. Participants may find it easier to concentrate first on self-talk and then on the relevant action skill rather than focus on both simultaneously.

Subtitles

Subtitles normally reflect visual images. However, in demonstrating self-talk, subtitles demonstrate relevant inner rather than outer talk. There are two advantages of subtitles over voice-overs. First, in demonstrations involving dialogue, they do not add possibly distracting sound. Second, subtitles can be left on the screen longer than verbal messages. This extra time may make it easier for participants to assimilate the self-talk being shown.

Thought Balloons

Thought balloons are often found in comic strips. Relevant self-talk can be placed in balloons next to demonstrators' heads. Thought balloons are for written, filmed, and videotaped demonstrations. They require much technical competence to superimpose on moving images. In such circumstances, thought balloons are probably best left to expert animators of Walt Disney caliber.

An Example Demonstration

Following is an example of an action skills plus self-talk demonstration in a college test-taking skills group. The demonstrator, Bernice, has the characteristics of an exam-anxious student. She tries to cope with anxiety and stay focused on the task at hand when looking at a test paper for the first time. Imagine that this is a videotaped demonstration. The *self-talk* subgoals for the demonstration are the use of calming statements ("Calm down"); focusing statements ("Think, what is it I have to do?"); self-reward statements ("I'm coping well so far"); specific task-oriented instructions ("I need to read the test paper instructions carefully"); and statements that combat unrealistic personal rules ("All I have to do is the best I can"). The *action skills* subgoals are the use of both anxiety-reduction skills (for example, breathing slowly and regularly) and test-taking skills (for example, reading the test's instructions carefully). Bernice's action skills plus self-talk demonstration is based on the work of Meichenbaum and his colleagues (for example, Meichenbaum & Goodman, 1971). Bernice intersperses think-aloud self-talk with performing action skills.

> Okay, I'm feeling pretty uptight. My anxiety is a signal for me to use my coping skills. Calm down. Breathe slowly and regularly. [Bernice breathes slowly and regularly.] Think, what is it I have to do? I need to read the test's instructions carefully and look out for how the marks are distributed and how many questions I have to answer. [Bernice reads the instructions carefully.] Then I must survey all the questions. [Bernice surveys the questions.] I'm coping well so far. Keep taking it easy. Next I must plan how to spend my time—in which order to do the questions and how much time to allocate to each question. Let's pick an easy question first. Remember to leave

time for checking my answers at the test's end. [Bernice drafts a plan.] I don't have to answer the questions perfectly—all I have to do is the best I can. I know I can keep calm and use my time sensibly. Now let's see what is really wanted in the first question I've chosen to answer. [Bernice starts working on the first question.]

All too often, leaders, when demonstrating action skills, forget that participants then have to instruct themselves in learning sequences outside the group. For example, leaders of stress-management groups can demonstrate the talk that accompanies muscular relaxation in either leader-centered or participant-centered ways. With leader-centered talk, leaders give instructions from outside—for example, "Now close your eyes and get yourself comfortable." With participant-centered talk, leaders demonstrate the instructions as though participants were instructing themselves—for example, "Now I close my eyes and get myself comfortable." Demonstrating participant-centered rather than leader-centered talk is a small but important difference when a goal of the stress-management program is to train participants to use relaxation skills on their own.

Exercise 22 gives you the opportunity to demonstrate an action skill with accompanying self-talk.

Exercise 22 Demonstrate an Action Skill with Accompanying Self-Talk

▼▼▼

Select a lifeskills group to whom you might want to demonstrate an action skill or subskill with accompanying self-talk. Assume that this is an individual demonstration in which the demonstrator talks himself or herself through an action skills sequence that does not involve other people. Perform the following tasks:

1. Within the context of your overall goal, set clear action skill and self-talk subgoals for your demonstration.
2. State the characteristics of your demonstrator.
3. Develop an action skill plus self-talk demonstration along the lines of the example in the text.
4. If possible, make a pilot videotape of your action skill plus self-talk demonstration and then, if necessary, keep altering and rerecording your videotape until you are satisfied with it.

▼ **Chapter Highlights**

   ▼ Demonstrations should be the rule rather than the exception in training-group skills presentations.
      ▼ Observational learning can be used in training groups to

initiate skills strengths, develop skills strengths, disinhibit skills strengths, and inhibit and weaken skills weaknesses.

▼ Three important areas for observational learning are thinking skills, action skills, and action skills with accompanying self-talk.

▼ Demonstrators of lifeskills can be training-group leaders, leaders' aides, participants, and third parties.

▼ Demonstrator characteristics that influence learning are similarity to observers, prestige, competence level, and personal attractiveness.

▼ Methods of demonstration include written, live, prerecorded, and visualized.

▼ Considerations in preparing for a demonstration include whether to use single or multiple demonstrations, whether or not to use a script, whether to provide negative as well as positive demonstrations, graduated demonstrations, demonstrator reward, presenting the rationale, giving instructions, eliciting observer summaries, and timing of observers' performing the skill.

▼ Methods by which leaders can enhance observers' attention include orienting them to the relevance of demonstrations, telling them in advance what to look for, and trying to reduce debilitating anxiety.

▼ Thinking skills can be demonstrated either in writing, by audio cassettes, or live. Visual images are unnecessary for demonstrating thinking skills.

▼ The verbal and voice message components of action skills can be demonstrated by audio cassette. However, visual images are necessary for demonstrating body messages.

▼ In making training videotapes, group leaders act as movie directors and require many of their skills—for instance, coaching demonstrators, developing and altering scripts, and retaking scenes.

▼ Live demonstration of action skills may be particularly useful in coaching participants after the initial presentation of a skill and in showing participants coping skills for use outside the group.

▼ Visualized demonstration, getting participants to imagine themselves or a third party performing action skills competently, is a useful skill in the group leader's repertoire.

▼ To develop a visualized demonstration, leaders must set the scene, describe the appropriate action skill, and depict favorable consequences for using the action skill.

▼ Participants will have to instruct themselves through action skills sequences once training groups end. Thus, where possible, relevant self-talk should be built into demonstrations.

▼ Self-talk can be provided to accompany action skills demonstrations by the use of thinking aloud, voice-overs, subtitles, and thought balloons.

9

How to Manage Structured Activities

What we have to learn to do,
 we learn by doing.

Aristotle

Chapter Questions

▼▼

What are structured activities?

What facilitation skills are relevant to managing structured activities?

How do leaders coach participants after initial skills presentations?

What methods exist for rehearsing behaviors?

What leader skills are necessary for preparing, directing, and processing action role-plays?

What are the different sources of feedback for participants?

What might leaders consider in designing exercises and behavior-change experiments?

How can leaders enhance participants' motivation to complete between-sessions homework tasks?

Introduction

▼▼

Learning by doing is essential to lifeskills training groups. Knowledge gained by hearing and by observing gets clarified and consolidated when participants learn by doing. Training-group leaders need to have the skills of promoting and managing learning by doing. You do not learn to drive a car without driving. Likewise, participants acquiring and strengthening specific lifeskills need relevant activities that help them improve the skills and integrate them into their daily lives.

Following are some examples of learning by doing in training groups. Note that in some of the examples, learning by doing focuses on thinking skills as well as on action skills.

▼ Adolescent job-seekers being trained in persuasion skills role-play job interview situations with others in their classes (Wild & Kerr, 1984).
▼ Management trainees play a training board game, *Stop Sexual Harassment*, whose purpose is to clarify some of the concepts and issues regarding sexism, sexual harassment, and sexual politics in the workplace (Wehrenberg, 1985).
▼ Couples in a Knowledge Increases Sexual Satisfaction (KISS) group do four exercises to improve sexual communication: initiating and refusing sexual activities, increasing their sexual vocabulary, giving instantaneous sexual feedback, and sharing sexual preferences and fantasies (Cooper & Stoltenberg, 1987).
▼ Participants in a group for divorced women imagine and then con-

front and challenge irrational beliefs about divorce in eight belief areas in which they report discomforting thoughts: children, finances, daily hassles, parents and in-laws, former husband, failure of marriage, rejection, and relationships with others (Graf, Whitehead, & LeCompte, 1986).

▼ Patients with chronic low back pain attend weekly lifeskills sessions focused both on progressive muscular relaxation and on identifying maladaptive thoughts connected with negative emotions related to pain and replacing them with more adaptive thoughts (Turner & Clancy, 1988).

▼ Trainee helpers, to develop their cross-cultural awareness and skills, participate in scripted role-plays in which they are interviewed by people from Arab cultures (Merta, Stringham, & Ponterotto, 1988).

These are just a few examples of structured activities in lifeskills training groups. Especially during the working stage, sessions are incomplete if they do not include learning by doing.

Like demonstrations, structured activities can focus on thinking skills, action skills, or action skills plus self-talk. Sometimes the structured activities are integrated with the learning sequence containing the initial demonstration. For example, coaching, rehearsal, and feedback take place immediately after a skill demonstration. On other occasions, structured activities are less planned as leaders help participants develop and apply skills to situations outside the group.

What Are Structured Activities?
▼▼▼

I hear, I forget.
I see, I remember.
I do, I understand.
Chinese proverb

No helping or training group is entirely unstructured. Even person-centered encounter groups operate within frameworks. However, there are degrees of structure both within and across groups. Learning activities that are consciously chosen in advance by leaders constitute an important way in which structure is built into training groups. As a leader you do not leave participants' skills development to chance. Instead, you intentionally set up and manage activities that allow participants to understand, rehearse, and practice targeted skills.

Following is a list of some of the main kinds of structured activities used by training-group leaders.

Self-monitoring forms: Participants can be encouraged to monitor their out-of-session behaviors, which can be feelings, thoughts, or actions, as well as their consequences for self and others. Such self-monitoring is used not only to collect initial assessment data, but also to help participants evaluate their progress throughout a group's life. Self-monitoring forms require both adequate introduction and adequate processing once data are collected.

Coached performance: Coaching consists of providing instructions, tips, hints, and rules for enacting skills. Before participants rehearse skills, they are likely to require coaching on specific points. Learning by hearing and observing are usually insufficient to enable participants to perform skills properly. Consequently, after demonstrating, leaders take participants through coached performances of skills.

Behavior rehearsal: Behavior rehearsal can be either covert, as with thinking skills, or overt, as with action skills, or both, as with action skills plus self-talk. Behavior rehearsal can be scripted or ad-libbed.

Role-play: There is no clear dividing line between behavior rehearsal and role-play. Role-plays can be used to consolidate initial presentation and demonstration of skills. Another use of role-plays is in assessing participants' outside behaviors and in developing skills to manage external problem situations.

Feedback: Leaders can systematically arrange for participants to obtain feedback on their skills strengths and weaknesses. Feedback can come from other participants and from audio cassettes and videotapes as well as from leaders.

Exercises: Exercises are activities specially designed to give participants practice in developing and performing targeted skills. For example, in listening skills groups, participants may do exercises on identifying speakers' internal frames of reference and on making reflective responses. Exercises can be written as well as action-oriented. Written exercises are especially common for thinking skills; examples are Ellis's rational-emotive self-help forms focused on identifying and disputing irrational beliefs (Ellis, 1989) and my series of Thinksheets (Nelson-Jones, 1990a). Exercises broadly defined include activities like games, feedback, and task assignments.

Games: Depending on the extent to which they involve play, exercises may be called games. Sometimes lifeskills board games are commercially produced (Wehrenberg, 1985). On other occasions, leaders develop their own games. For instance, in relationship skills groups, an exercise about sending "I" messages is turned into a game by having senders toss a ball along with an "I" message to their receivers. Try speeding this up and it becomes even more of a game!

Task assignments: Groups or subgroups can be given specific tasks and instructed to come up with solutions. Alternatively, subgroups can be given subtasks of overall tasks. For example, in training groups on team building, participants are given a problem to solve. Then they are asked to evaluate the processes of trust building and decision making that occurred in their group when solving the problem (Johnson & Johnson, 1987).

Critical incidents: Training groups can be given brief scenarios for situations relevant to the targeted skills. Then participants are invited to think through the relevant issues and skills. Hopson and Scally (1981) give the example scenario of a teenage girl going to a disco, arriving home two hours later than agreed, and finding her father waiting up for her. The group's attention can be directed to answering such questions as what each protagonist in the scene may think and feel, what thoughts and behaviors each needs to avoid, and what skills each could use to attain her or his goals.

Case studies: Case studies tend to give more detail and to present a longer-term problem situation than do critical incidents. Case studies are frequently used at business schools to train students in managerial and supervisory skills. However, the use of case studies need not be restricted to business. For instance, case studies can be introduced into parent education or couples education groups. A case study for a parent education group might be based on a videotape that invites participants to look at helpful and harmful communication patterns in a specific family.

Computer-assisted learning: Increasingly, training-group leaders are likely to explore computer learning. Already, computers have been used in such areas as helping sophomore and junior high school students explore career options (Johnson, 1985) and simulating job interviews to improve the decision-making skills of hirers (Ganger, 1989).

Behavior-change plans: Structured activities for obtaining targeted lifeskills goals can be performed outside as well as inside groups. An important leader function is the design of outside-the-group structured activities. Such activities enhance the transfer and maintenance of skills and their integration into participants' daily routines. Participants can be encouraged to develop plans to change their behavior and achieve their goals. Behavior-change plans can be worked on both within and outside lifeskills sessions. Plans should be realistic, clearly stipulate the goals, outline how they are to be achieved, and state a time frame. Plans are a notable feature of both Glasser's reality therapy groups (Glasser, 1965, 1984b) and cognitive-behavioral self-management programs (Kanfer & Gaelick, 1986).

Behavior-change experiments: In conducting experiments, participants make behavior-change hypotheses, implement them, and then evaluate the consequences for themselves and others of their changed behaviors (Beck & Emery, 1985; Nelson-Jones, 1990b). Even though the implementation of experiments is performed as homework, their design and some of the subsequent evaluation take place inside groups.

Homework tasks: As well as experiments, a range of other structured activities can be designed and assigned as between-sessions homework tasks. Outside practice is important for extending the learning opportunities provided by groups. Filling out self-monitoring forms, rehearsing and practicing behavior, doing exercises and games, and working through case studies and critical incidents are all structured activities to assign as homework in one session and process in the next.

Facilitating Structured Activities
▾ ▾

Training-group leaders need to have the skills to facilitate structured activities as well as group interaction. Even at the best of times, participants enter groups with varying levels of commitment and motivation. Much learning in training groups is public. Consequently, in addition to any anxieties they possess about developing specific skills, participants may have further anxieties about developing them in public. Many participants feel exposed, vulnerable, clumsy, and awkward when performing structured activities. They may get frustrated at their comparatively slow rate of learning. The skills on which participants work may be in sensitive areas. In addition, some structured activities, such as role-plays, may seem strange to them. Group leaders cannot assume that participants will automatically cooperate in structured activities. They may resist such activities for many reasons, including lack of a trusting group atmosphere, not seeing the point of particular exercises, shyness, trying to one-up the leader, and not wishing to work if others do not work too.

How can training-group leaders enhance participants' motivation and commitment to learning from structured activities? Here are some suggestions. First, leaders can create a safe and trusting emotional climate in which participants are prepared to take risks. Such risks may entail disclosing problems, admitting mistakes, and volunteering to work in front of the group. All the facilitation skills mentioned in Chapter 6 are relevant to building a safe emotional climate. In addition, by competently presenting and demonstrating lifeskills, leaders enhance their credibility and trustworthiness.

Second, leaders can allow performance fears to be aired and explored. Leaders can show sensitivity to participants' being uneasy about having to work in public. Leaders can make comments like "It's okay to feel uneasy about engaging in activities in front of the group" and "It's okay to make mistakes when learning any new skill." Participants can be invited to share any fears or anxieties they may have about learning by doing in public or about participating in specific activities. Such invitations to air performance fears may be by way of comments made to the whole group or, alternatively, by means of a "round" in which each participant is invited to speak (Jacobs, Harvill, & Masson, 1988). In addition, leaders can reassure participants that they will not be coerced into divulging private material or doing any exercise with which they persistently feel uncomfortable. Leaders should ensure that all participants have equal opportunity to work on their skills and problems in the group. Certain participants may be less resistant to working if they know their turn will inevitably come.

Third, leaders can ensure that reasons for doing each structured activity are clear. Participants are more likely to perform structured activities if they see connections between the activities and targeted skills. Leaders should clarify reasons for structured activities whose purposes are unclear. Sometimes it is a good idea to check out with a group which activities work best for them. Later in a group's life, such checking out may have more meaning than earlier: participants by then have experienced a range of structured activities.

Fourth, leaders can enhance participants' motivation and commitment by helping them process their experiences about doing structured activities. Working participants are defined as those who do behavior rehearsals, role-plays, or other structured activities in front of groups. Working participants may have thoughts and feelings both about the structured activities and about the material they present. Leaders who conduct structured learning activities should not be cold and impersonal. Often structured activities provide opportunities for valuable emotional and cognitive insights. Leaders can help participants to share and work through these insights. Nevertheless, always present is the problem of how to balance individual work with the group's needs. Time spent helping working participants access significant thoughts and feelings may help others too. Leaders can use working participants' contributions as springboards for encouraging others to work.

Fifth, leaders can encourage involvement in structured activities by facilitating feedback. Peer feedback can be very valuable to working participants. Leaders can create a group norm that says, "It's okay to give and receive constructive feedback. We are all here to learn." Leaders can give permission to the group to provide feedback—for example, "Does anyone have any comments they would like to make about how Cary handled that situation?" Invitations to the group can be by way of "rounds" in which each participant is given the opportunity to provide feedback. Leaders can refrain from giving their feedback until the group has had its opportunity. In addition, leaders can notice participants reacting to a specific activity and give them an "opener" to speak—for example, "Judy, I noticed you reacting pretty strongly when Brad did his role-play about standing up to his boss. Is there anything you would like to share with the group?"

Sixth, leaders can encourage involvement in structured activities by using different formats. Just as structured activities can be done in pairs, threes, or other small groups as well as in the overall group, so leaders can allow some of the processing of activities to be done in subgroups. Training-group leaders are managers of learning. They do not have to do everything themselves. Rather, they need to create learning environments and opportunities. By subgrouping, they facilitate participants in sharing personal meanings and giving and receiving feedback. In a given time period, more people have the opportunity to be working participants and offer feedback in subgroups than in full groups.

Coaching Participants in Skills
▼ ▼

Here coached performance refers to coaching taking place immediately after an initial skills presentation and demonstration. Then participants require "how-to" coaching in the skill. Learning from hearing and observing must be translated into learning from doing. Also, unless leaders as coaches watch participants perform skills, they cannot know whether participants have properly grasped the skills.

Following is a discussion of some of the considerations that group leaders need to take into account when coaching participants to perform lifeskills that have just been presented and demonstrated.

Consider Who Coaches

Different ways of approaching the task of coaching include the following. First, a training manual can be the coach. Participants can be referred to a written coaching manual that gives specific instructions and illustrations of how to enact skills. Second, the training-group leader can coach. This is the most common model in lifeskills training. Third, leaders' aides can coach. Even if done in small groups, coaching ultimately should look at how individual participants perform skills. Small group and individual attention is labor-intensive. Consequently, leaders' aides can be valuable additional coaches.

Fourth, other participants can coach. All participants have just heard and seen the skill's initial presentation and demonstration. Learning may be enhanced if they become coaches. Participants can coach either in front of leaders and the full group or in pairs or subgroups where leaders may be absent. Self-coaching is a fifth method of coaching. Working participants can be encouraged to instruct themselves through the performance of a skill. Last, there are various possible mixtures of the preceding coaching methods. Perhaps the main distinction is whether the mixture contains self-coaching as well as coaching from others.

Balance Facilitative and Didactic Coaching

In *didactic* coaching, an external source, probably the leader, gives a series of explicit instructions to learners on how to perform skills. The leader's comments take the form: "First, you do this. Then you do that. Then you do that," and so on. The leader is the expert taking beginners through sequences of performance choices.

In *facilitative* coaching, leaders have two important objectives: first, to draw out and build upon learners' existing knowledge and skills, and second, to help them acquire the skills of self-coaching, not just for now but for after the group. Leaders' initial comments can take the form: "Now you have had the initial presentation and demonstration of the skill. What has it told you about how to do it?" "Where are your strengths and weaknesses?" and "Assume that I am the other person in the situation. Now you show me how to use the skill just presented."

When coaching, training-group leaders need to be both facilitative and didactic. For example, leaders might start with trying to build on the existing knowledge and skills of learners, but then intersperse didactic prompts when learners get stuck. On the one hand, it can be wasteful of everybody's time to rely solely on drawing out participants' learning potential. On the other hand, coaching without using facilitative skills lessens the likelihood of targeted skills' being owned and integrated into participants' daily routines. Also, didactic coaching alone can create counterproductive resistances.

Other Considerations

When you've considered who will coach and resolved to achieve a balance between facililative and didactic coaching, you can focus on the details of the coaching process. Considerations include the following:

Give clear instructions: The previous two chapters have emphasized clear goals for each lifeskills learning sequence. These goals and subgoals can be in the areas of thinking skills, action skills, or action skills plus self-talk. When participants are coached through "how-to" performances of targeted skills, goals and subgoals need to be translated into clear and precise instructions.

Break tasks down: Leaders have to consider whether to further break skills and subskills down when initially getting participants to perform them. Leaders, when coaching participants after initial presentations and demonstrations, may still decide to break skills down further. Leaders need to consider how much participants can assimilate in each learning trial. For example, with a teenager wishing to return a compact disc to a shop, one trial might focus on verbal messages, another on voice messages, another on body messages, and another on putting it all together.

Use graded steps: Cumulative learning is built into well-designed lifeskills programs. When coaching participants in specific areas, leaders may decide to break the learning trials down to include successively more difficult steps. Participants can be asked to volunteer areas in which they find it either easier or more difficult to apply the targeted skills.

Use demonstration skills: Demonstrations can be a vital part of coaching. For example, where participants make assertive requests in weak voices, leaders can mirror those voice messages and then demonstrate more appropriate voice messages.

Use feedback and reward skills: Feedback and reward skills are covered in much more detail later in this chapter.

Decide on scripted or unscripted performance: There are advantages to leaders' using prepared scripts when initially coaching participants to perform skills. As with theater or movie scripts, prepared scripts can contain directions about voice and body messages. Participants asked to generate how they should behave may not highlight the points being taught. Coaching participants using prepared scripts can be a useful stepping-stone to coaching participants when they use their own material. Participants need not always memorize scripts. However, they should memorize the main rules, concepts, and points illustrated in scripts.

Use checking-out skills: Skilled leaders not only try to convey the main points on which they coach participants before and during performances, but also check out at the end whether participants have fully understood what they performed. For example, at the end of coaching trials, leaders can ask working participants to summarize the main learning points.

Decide on number of trials: How many coaching trials do participants require before they perform a skill or subskill competently? Coaching for initial skills acquisition overlaps with behavior rehearsal and practice. With or without graded steps, participants may require many attempts before they perform skills well within, let alone outside, their training groups.

Consider individual or group coaching: To what extent and in what ways can leaders coach more than one participant at a time? Some lifeskills, such as progressive muscular relaxation (Jacobson, 1938), lend themselves to group coaching. Inevitably, much coaching is with individual participants in front of groups. Leaders can also break groups down into subgroups and coach within them; and participants can be asked to make up video cassettes and audio cassettes to play back in groups or subgroups for coaching purposes.

Consider visual and written prompts: Prompts are interventions that direct participants' attention to required behaviors (Karoly & Harris, 1986). Apart from verbal instructions from leaders and participants, other prompts include cue cards, posters, handouts, and training manuals.

Consider fading: Fading means the gradual removal of external sources of instruction and prompting. Participants require coaching to the point, and sometimes beyond the point, where they can perform skills competently on their own. Coaching should emphasize ways in which participants can help themselves—for instance, clear self-instructions. Self-directed behavior rehearsals and practice can help participants build up skills so that leaders can withdraw external sources of instruction and prompting.

Exercise 23 aims to give you practice in coaching another person or persons to perform a lifeskill competently.

Exercise 23 Coach a Lifeskill
▼▼

1. Imagine that you have just given a verbal presentation followed by a demonstration of a specific skill or subskill to a lifeskills training group of your choice. You are now about to coach participants in how to perform the skill. How might you take each of the following considerations into account?
   a. Consider who coaches
   b. Balance facilitative and didactic coaching
   c. Give clear instructions
   d. Break tasks down
   e. Use graded steps
   f. Use demonstration skills
   g. Use feedback and reward skills
   h. Decide on scripted or unscripted performance
   i. Use checking-out skills
   j. Decide on number of trials
   k. Consider individual or group coaching
   l. Consider visual and written prompts
   m. Consider fading
2. If possible, work with another person or persons. Give them a verbal presentation that includes demonstration of a specific lifeskill or subskill. Do not attempt too much. Afterward, coach them to the point where, within the limits of this exercise, they competently perform the skill.
3. Repeat the second part of this exercise until you have coached another person or persons in (a) an action skill, (b) a thinking skill, and (c) an action skill plus self-talk.

Conducting Behavior Rehearsals and Role-Plays
▼▼

Learning by doing generally requires repeated performances of targeted skills. Behavior rehearsals can be of thinking skills, action skills, or action skills plus self-talk. Behavior rehearsals can involve enacting specific skills and subskills as part of a sequence of presentation, demonstration, coached performance, and rehearsal. Behavior rehearsals can take place either immediately after initial coached performance of skills or later as participants apply targeted skills to material they bring to groups. Rehearsals can be either coached or self-instructed.

Following are some examples of training-group behavior rehearsals and role-plays.

▼ Culturally disadvantaged high school students are helped to develop skills for entry into the post-secondary world by means of mock interviews with prospective employers followed by videotaped feedback (Hamilton, 1984).

▼ Students in a high school group on "Planning Your Future" role-play talking over vocational choice ideas with their parents (Mahler, 1969).

▼ Participants in a "Coping with Depression" class spend two sessions each on learning and rehearsing how to (1) relax, (2) increase pleasant activities, (3) change aspects of their thinking, and (4) improve social skills and increase positive social interactions (Brown & Lewinsohn, 1984).

▼ Participants develop skills in using the telephone by being divided into groups of three—caller, listener, and observer—and then being asked to play each role. The role-plays are of conversations of not more than two minutes on prearranged topics such as inquiring about a job or asking for a date (Priestley et al., 1978).

▼ Participants in an anger-management group visualize personal anger scenes, experience their anger, and then rehearse using cognitive and relaxation coping skills to manage it (Deffenbacher, Story, Stark, Hogg, & Brandon, 1987).

Methods of Behavior Rehearsal

The terms *behavior rehearsal* and *role-play* are often used interchangeably (for example, Goldfried & Davison, 1976). However, it is a simplification to equate behavior rehearsal with role-play. The one does not necessarily imply the other. Different methods of rehearsing behaviors include the following.

First, there is *live rehearsal*. Consider sports personalities like golfers or tennis players. When they wish to rehearse their shots, they go out and practice, either on their own or with others. Similarly, many lifeskills can be rehearsed live, with or without assistance either from others or from response aids (for instance, gloves for those afraid of snakes or furry animals).

Certain behaviors can be rehearsed live inside training groups. For example, participants in a group on making friends can rehearse basic conversational skills, such as self-disclosure, within as well as outside their group. Also, the skills of progressive muscular relaxation can be rehearsed both inside and outside stress- or anger-management lifeskills groups without the need for role-plays. However, when progressive muscular relaxation is rehearsed as part of a coping response to specific stressors or anger provocations, elements of role-play may be introduced.

Live rehearsal can assist practice either inside or outside of some training groups. For example, a within-group adaptation of Bandura's participant modeling approach would use assisted rehearsal and practice as participants have repeated trials in graded steps with stimuli such as snakes (Bandura, 1976; Jeffrey, 1976). In other training groups, such as for agoraphobics, assisted rehearsal might take place outside the central group meeting place as leaders or leaders' aides take participants either on their own or with others out into anxiety-evoking settings.

Action role-plays provide a second method of rehearsing behaviors. In action role-plays, participants rehearse observable behaviors in simulated or pretend situations. For instance, in the examples provided at the start of this section, training-group members rehearse interview skills, discuss vocational choices with parents, and try out telephone skills in mock settings. Throughout a group's duration, action role-plays can be used to assess skills weaknesses as well as to develop and rehearse skills strengths.

A third method for rehearsing behaviors is *mental rehearsal*. In mental rehearsal, participants rehearse and practice specific thinking skills—for example, either identifying and reformulating unrealistic personal rules or identifying upsetting perceptions and finding better ones. Mental rehearsal can be private or public. Private mental rehearsal involves repeatedly practicing a thinking skill on your own. Such private rehearsal may entail writing down your thought processes. Public mental rehearsal can be by thinking aloud in the group or sharing written answers to self-help "thinksheets."

Visualized rehearsal is a fourth method of rehearsal. Visualized rehearsal, otherwise known as imaginal or covert rehearsal, is a form of mental rehearsal involving pictorial images. The pictorial images in visualized rehearsal are usually of actual rather than role-played scenes. As such, visualized rehearsals are often stepping-stones to transferring skills rehearsed in action role-plays into live situations. After action role-plays you imagine yourself actually coping with an interview, talking to your parents about your vocational choices, or asking for a date on the telephone. You can also imagine yourself using appropriate calming and coaching self-talk. In training groups, visualized rehearsal is a common form of homework task.

A fifth method of behavior rehearsal is *action role-play with accompanying self-talk*. In a mixed action and thinking skills behavior rehearsal, leaders may intersperse asking participants to rehearse and verbalize relevant thinking before proceeding with action role-plays. For example, before Aaron role-plays asking a female college classmate to have coffee with him, the leader rehearses Aaron in calming and coaching self-talk. Unknown to Aaron, during the role-play, the confederate has been asked to indicate mild surprise as well as pleasure at being asked. When this happens, the leader calls for a pause in the role-play and asks Aaron to verbalize appropriate self-talk. The role-play ends with Aaron succeeding in getting his coffee date. Then the leader asks Aaron to verbalize appropriate self-talk that acknowledges he has attained his goal. The leader may also rehearse Aaron in a scene where his coffee date request is politely turned down and then ask him to verbalize coping self-talk.

Stage-Managing Role-Plays

Role-plays can be performed in front of whole groups, or groups can be subdivided—for instance, into triads of working participants, confederates, and coaches. This section assumes that the leader stage-manages or directs the role-play with the whole group present. Some leader skills for role-plays are preparing participants, selecting scenes and situations, directing, and processing.

Preparing Participants

The following skills are relevant to preparing participants to take part in role-plays.

Provide a rationale. When using role-plays for the first time in training groups, it is advisable to tell participants how this method can help them attain personal goals. Here is a rationale for the use of behavior rehearsal role-plays in a college dating skills group:

> You have just had a presentation and seen a demonstration of skills you might use in asking someone of the opposite sex for a date. Also, you have seen me coaching Aaron as he asked a classmate for a coffee date. Many of you have said that you don't act in these situations as well as you want to. Seeing other people enact the skills is okay, but you are unlikely to change your behavior unless you rehearse and practice using the skills. This group can provide a sheltered environment for you to take risks and try out new behaviors before you have to do it for real. I realize that this may feel awkward at first, but there is no substitute for learning by doing. Also, all of you are in the same boat. How do you feel about doing some role-plays like the one I did with Aaron?

This rationale attempts to enlist motivation and overcome resistances to role-playing in a number of ways, including showing enough respect for participants to explain why you want them to role-play, helping participants see the relevance of role-play to attaining personal goals, showing them you understand feelings of discomfort, letting them know that everybody is in the same boat, and allowing them to air reservations.

Ensure participants know targeted behaviors. If your goals were clear for your presentation and demonstration, most participants should have a good idea what is expected of them when their turn comes to role-play. Also, if you have coached one of the participants in front of the group, this further demonstration and your coaching comments should reinforce how to behave. Nevertheless, you may still need to keep reminding participants of the main learning points in their role-plays. One way to do this is to ask each participant, prior to playing the lead in a role-play, to summarize what is wanted. You may confuse participants if you have more than two or three learning points for any role-play.

Warm participants up. In psychodrama, leaders commonly use warm-up techniques to induce spontaneity prior to enacting dramas (Moreno, 1959). Training-group role-plays are briefer, more focused on developing specific skills, and less emotionally charged than psychodrama enactments. Nevertheless, some writers recommend using warm-up exercises prior to role-plays (for example, Goldfried & Davison, 1976; Wilkinson & Canter, 1982). Warm-up exercises in these circumstances should always be brief. Physical movement exercises are sometimes used to loosen participants up. Examples of physical movement exercises are running on the spot, flapping your arms like birds' wings, holding your hands together with fingers down, or keeping your legs together and hopping around the room like a kangaroo. Warm-up exercises can be related to later role-plays and possibly defuse some anxiety attached to them. For instance, in a dating skills group, participants can pair off as Romeo and Juliet and each be instructed to take turns at asking for a date in the most love-sick way imaginable. A major risk of such exercises is that they may be perceived as phony rather than amusing. Consequently, I only raise the possibility of using warm-up exercises prior to behavior rehearsal role-plays. You must exercise your judgment about their use.

Selecting Scenes and Situations

The following are three possibilities for selecting scenes for role-plays. First, leaders can take participants through *prepared scripts*. Earlier it was mentioned that prepared scripts have advantages in initially coaching participants to perform skills. With prepared scripts, leaders can ensure relevance and that learning points are highlighted. However, prepared scripts may lack the flexibility required in real life.

Second, leaders can use *prepared scenarios* and possibly also role descriptions, but leave participants to improvise dialogue. Prepared scenarios are more flexible than prepared scripts, yet leaders can still ensure relevance. As with prepared scripts, prepared scenarios allow leaders to introduce less complex and less anxiety-evoking rehearsals prior to more awkward ones. Following is an example of a prepared scenario that sets the scene in a college dating skills group.

> You are sitting on your own at a table in the student cafeteria when a male/female in one of your classes whom you find attractive asks if he/she can sit at your table.

A behavior rehearsal for this scenario might be broken down into four distinct sections: how to introduce yourself, how to converse, how to discern cues of interest, and how to request further contact. For each section, either verbally or by giving the actors written role descriptions, leaders can instruct participants in how to behave.

Third, leaders can work with *problem situations* that participants bring into groups. If anything, there is a development in training groups from role-plays in which leaders prepare much content in advance to more spontaneous role-plays. Especially as groups develop, behavior rehearsal role-plays focus on how best to handle problem situations in participants' outside lives. A major advantage of such role-plays is that they help participants integrate targeted skills into their daily routines. In some groups, participants are asked to keep diaries in which they record problem situations to discuss in the group. Training-group leaders must act as gatekeepers regarding the relevance of, complexity of, and amount of time spent on problem situation role-plays. For example, it is generally better to work with situations that have relevance for a number of participants rather than for only one. Also, if possible, work with simple and less anxiety-evoking situations before moving to more difficult ones.

Directing

Here the focus is on how training-group leaders go about directing behavior rehearsal role-plays for problem situations outside the group. Such role-plays owe much to Moreno's psychodrama approach (Blatner, 1989; Greenberg, 1975; Moreno, 1934; Moreno, 1959) The following parts are played in role-plays:

The director: The director is usually the group leader who stage-manages the role-play and ensures that it is used as a relevant learning experience.

The working participant: The working participant or protagonist is the person who either volunteers or is selected to role-play a problem situation.

The cast: The cast or *alter egos* are other participants who play roles in the situation described by the working participant. For instance, they may play boss, spouse, brothers and sisters, or even the family dog.

The audience: The audience is all those members of the lifeskills training group not in the role-play.

The candid camera: The candid camera is an optional extra that makes it possible to show videotaped feedback of role-plays.

Training-group leaders require director skills in the following, sometimes overlapping, elements of role-plays.

Select working participants. If leaders leave it for volunteers to emerge from groups, some people may never volunteer. Training groups require a norm that all participants act in role-plays. Within this framework, the following are options for selecting working participants. Leaders can do role-plays in early sessions with volunteers, but ensure that later everybody has a turn. Alternatively, leaders can ask the group to share problems and then pick a participant with an appropriate problem to illustrate the session's learning points. Where possible, leaders choose problems that have relevance to most participants. Another approach is to work with participants who seem either stronger or weaker in the targeted skills: stronger participants as models for their peers, weaker participants to help them catch up. Still another approach is to work with participants who have pressing concerns. Throughout this selection process, leaders need facilitative skills to deal with anxieties and resistances about role-playing.

Set the scene. Once working participants have been selected, leaders then work with them to set the scene. Leaders elicit information about the physical setting of proposed scenes, what other characters are involved, and how they behave. This information lays the basis for, within reason, altering the furniture in the room to establish a "stage" of, for instance, a family living room, a boss's office, or whatever. In addition, leaders assemble the cast either from volunteers or by request.

Assess current behaviors. Usually the extra time spent conducting assessment role-plays in which working participants demonstrate how they currently behave in problem situations is time well spent. Assessment role-plays can include reviewing participants' thoughts as well as actions. Training-group leader, working participant, cast, and audience each can assess the working participant's skills strengths and weaknesses. Also, assessment role-plays give the cast more information for understanding their parts in role-plays.

Formulate changed behaviors. Leaders assist working participants to formulate changed behaviors. For example, leaders may ask: "How would you like to behave differently in the situation from the way you did?" or "What are your goals in the situation and what skills would better enable you to attain them?" Leaders attempt to facilitate self-assessment prior to making suggestions. Together leaders and participants formulate changed ways of behaving that use targeted lifeskills yet feel comfortable. Leaders try to integrate the targeted skills into participants' existing interpersonal styles rather than impose something alien to them. In addition, leaders and working participants may identify self-oppressing patterns of thinking and re-formulate them into self-supporting thoughts. Leaders use many coaching skills, including demonstration, during this process of for-mulating changed behaviors.

Try out and rehearse changed behaviors. Once working participants are reasonably clear about their new roles, trial enactments or re-hearsals take place. Care should be taken to try neither too much nor anything too difficult too soon. Leaders can allow role-plays to run their course. Alternatively, leaders can intervene at one or more points along the way both to check out thinking processes and to coach. For the most part, this coaching focuses on how best to imple-ment the specific behaviors targeted in the group session. In addition, leaders can coach members of the cast in their roles. Video feedback can be used as part of coaching both during and after role-plays.

Behavior rehearsal role-plays are dry runs of how to behave in specific situations. A number of rehearsals may be needed to shape and strengthen a working participant's skills. Some of these rehears-als may involve the cast behaving in different ways. For example, a working participant asking for a pay raise might get it easily in one rehearsal, have to struggle to overcome a boss's reservations in a second rehearsal, and be refused in a third rehearsal.

Role reversal, mirroring, and the double technique are three psy-chodrama techniques that leaders can use (Blatner, 1989; Moreno, 1959). In role reversal, leaders get working participants to play the other person in interactions. The role reversal technique that forces participants some way into others' frames of reference is particularly useful for skills like negotiation and managing conflict. In mirroring, another participant is instructed to represent the verbal, voice, and body messages of the working participant. Working participants see themselves "as in a mirror" as others experience them. In the double technique, another participant is placed either behind or beside the working participant as a double of him or her. The role of doubles is to verbalize what working participants may really think and feel but not say.

Processing

Processing role-plays can be an important learning experience for both working participants and groups. Processing involves spending time dealing with emotions and thoughts generated by role-plays, discussing learnings from them, facilitating feedback, and making plans to transfer rehearsed skills outside. Generally, leaders process the feelings and reactions of the working participant first, the cast second, and the audience last.

Leaders can ask working participants processing questions like "How were you feeling in that role-play?" "How do you think that rehearsal went?" "What have you learned from that role-play that you can apply outside?" and "What difficulties do you anticipate in implementing your changed behavior and how can you overcome them?" Processing questions for the group include "Does anybody have anything they would like to feed back to [state working participant's name]?" and "What have you learned from that role-play that is useful for you?" After processing the previous rehearsal, group leaders can move on to the next rehearsal either with the same or another working participant.

Exercise 24 gives you practice stage-managing behavior rehearsal role-plays. The exercise also highlights some of the issues entailed in incorporating role-plays into training groups.

Exercise 24 Rehearse Behavior by Means of Role-Play
▾▾

This exercise should be performed either in a group of about five to eight persons or, failing that, with at least two others.

1. Discuss the advantages and disadvantages of leaders' incorporating each of the following methods of behavior rehearsal into lifeskills training groups:
   a. Live rehearsal
   b. Action role-plays
   c. Mental rehearsal
   d. Visualized rehearsal
   e. Action role-plays with accompanying self-talk
2. In a specific lifeskills area of your choice, implement a behavior rehearsal role-play for a problem situation presented by a working participant. Go through each of the following steps.
   a. Prepare participants
      1. Provide a rationale
      2. Ensure participants know the targeted behaviors
      3. Warm participants up (optional)
   b. Direct the role-play
      1. Select working participant
      2. Select role-play situation
      3. Set the scene
      4. Assess current behaviors
      5. Formulate changed behaviors
      6. Try out and rehearse changed behaviors
   c. Process the role-play
      1. With working participant
      2. With cast
      3. With audience

Each person in the group should have the opportunity to be both the director and the working participant. At the end of the exercise, discuss and process what you have learned for leading lifeskills training groups.

Providing and Encouraging Constructive Feedback

"How did I do?" and "How am I doing?" are questions that most learners ask of themselves and others. Participants require knowledge of the results and consequences of their attempts to develop specific lifeskills. Feedback can let them know if they are on the right track or whether and in what ways they need to alter behavior. Coaching by leaders involves feedback. However, leaders are not alone in providing feedback. Furthermore, there are many considerations in how leaders can best go about providing and facilitating others to provide feedback. Feedback can retard as well as enhance skills development.

Sources of Feedback

Effective lifeskills group leaders are managers of feedback to participants rather than always providing feedback themselves. The following are some of the sources of feedback available both to participants and to group leaders. First, there is *self-feedback*. Throughout lifeskills groups, leaders should encourage participants to develop the skill of giving themselves feedback. Leaders should assist participants to develop self-help skills of looking not only at how they behave, but also at their behavior's consequences for self and others.

Second, there is *leader feedback*. Leader feedback is essential because of their special knowledge of skills targeted by groups. A third source is *feedback from other participants*. Providing feedback can be a valuable learning process both for givers and receivers. Working participants can gain useful information about how their behavior is perceived. Participants giving feedback are forced to discriminate what constitutes effective behavior in targeted skills. Fourth, *audiovisual feedback* can be used both when assessing existing and developing new skills. The candid camera is especially useful for helping participants observe their body messages.

A fifth source is *feedback from outside-of-group aides*. Training-group leaders can enlist the assistance of others. For example, in conjunction with a group on making friends for elementary school children, leaders can train teachers and parents in how to provide support and constructive feedback. Sixth, participants can receive *feedback from third parties*. Participants inevitably receive much feedback from people with whom they interact daily. Sometimes leaders actively encourage participants to seek such feedback. For example, in shyness or assertiveness groups, participants speaking with quiet voices can be asked to check out how friends and relatives perceive their speech. Seventh, participants can receive *feedback from computers*. As part of some training groups, such as career exploration groups, computers analyze data given by participants and provide feedback.

Dimensions of Feedback

As managers of feedback, lifeskills group leaders need to bear a number of feedback dimensions in mind (Egan, 1990; Gazda, 1989; Hopson & Scally, 1981; National Training Laboratory, 1967; Osipow, Walsh, & Tosi, 1984). Some of these feedback dimensions are located in the receiver, some in the sender, and some in the process of giving feedback.

Self or External Feedback

Mention has already been made of the importance of leaders' encouraging participants to assess not only their behaviors, but also the consequences of their behaviors. As a guideline, after each structured activity, working participants should be the first to comment on their learnings and reactions. In addition, after other participants and the leader have given feedback, working participants should be given the further opportunity to comment on how they perceive the feedback.

Audiovisual Feedback

Audio cassette feedback is especially helpful when the focus is on verbal and voice messages. Videotape feedback is especially useful when the focus is on body messages. Audiovisual feedback lends itself to self-assessment by participants. Audiovisual feedback provides facts rather than perceptions and inferences. Playing and discussing audiovisual feedback of role-plays can provide valuable learning for everyone.

Audiovisual feedback also has potential disadvantages. Training-group leaders may get distracted by the technology of making video recordings. Furthermore, leaders require access to suitable equipment. Leaders may slow the learning process down by giving too much recorded feedback. Other participants may find this feedback boring. In addition, some participants may feel threatened by having to perform in front of audio cassette recorders or video cameras.

Behavioral or Emotional Feedback

A distinction exists between behavioral feedback, "how you behave," and emotional feedback, "I feel such and such about you or the way you have behaved" (Bloch & Crouch, 1985). Psychotherapy groups and experiential encounter groups contain much emotional feedback. In lifeskills training groups, behavioral feedback is emphasized. Not only should leaders both give and encourage behavioral feedback, they should also limit the amount of emotional feedback. Where possible, emotional feedback should be preceded by behavioral feedback: "When your behavior contains the following element(s), I feel such and such."

Specific or Nonspecific Feedback

Imagine a behavior rehearsal on how to ask someone for a date. Afterward the leader says to the working participant: "I don't think you did that very well" and leaves it at that. The leader has not provided specific feedback on how to improve, but instead has given negative feedback leading nowhere. Even worse would have been leader feedback that negatively rated the participant's personhood—for example, "I don't think you did that very well. It illustrates how weak you are." Feedback should always be specific and concentrate on targeted behaviors. For example, after a dating skills role-play, specific feedback to the working participant, Lou, might be: "Lou, when you asked Rachel for a date, I thought you did not make much eye contact with her and you spoke in a very quiet voice." If the behavior rehearsal had been videotaped, the leader could say to the working participant: "During the playback, I want you to notice how well you made eye contact with Rachel and how loudly you spoke to her." Here, the leader cues the participant on what specifically to look for during the video feedback. When giving specific feedback, try not to cover more than two or three points at any one time. Recipients suffer from and get confused by feedback overload.

Confirmatory, Corrective, and Motivating Feedback

Feedback can be confirmatory, corrective, or motivating (Egan, 1990; Gilbert, 1978). Confirmatory feedback lets participants know which specific behaviors they are developing along the right lines. Corrective feedback lets participants know which specific behaviors require altering and in what ways. Much feedback is both confirmatory and corrective—for example, "Lou, when you asked Rachel for a date you made good eye contact [confirmatory feedback]. However, I thought you spoke in too quiet a voice [corrective feedback]." Motivating feedback points out the consequences of good and poor use of skills and includes suggestions for improving performance: "Lou, the consequence of your speaking in a quiet voice was that you seemed diffident about wanting to be with Rachel; if you spoke louder she might take more notice [motivating feedback]."

Related to the dimensions of confirmatory, corrective, and motivating feedback are the dimensions of constructive or destructive feedback and of positive or negative feedback. Confirmatory feedback, as long as it is accurate, is likely to be both positive and constructive. However, corrective and even motivating feedback can be given in ways that are unnecessarily negative and destructive. A number of ways exist whereby leaders can detoxify feedback. First, leaders can work to establish trusting emotional climates in groups. The timing and strength of their feedback reflects the degree of trust. Second, leaders always can give participants the opportunity to share their reactions to corrective and motivating feedback. Third, where possible, confirmatory or positive feedback can precede corrective feedback. Fourth, inasmuch as possible, corrective feedback can be stated in positive terms. An example of corrective feedback stated in negative terms is: "Lou, your voice was too quiet when you asked Rachel for a date." A more positive statement of the same corrective feedback might be: "Lou, I think your voice should be louder when you ask Rachel for a date." Here corrective feedback takes on a characteristic of motivating feedback in that it suggests how to improve performance. Giving feedback in groups requires tact, not the least since it is usually both given and received in public.

"I" Message or "You" Message Feedback

Another way of detoxifying corrective and motivating feedback is to use "I" messages rather than "you" messages. Givers of feedback should always take responsibility and locate its source clearly in themselves. Locating the source of feedback in senders reduces the chance of its being received defensively. For example, the message "Lou, I think your voice should be louder when you ask Rachel for a date" is gentler and a more open invitation for discussion than "Lou, your voice should be louder when you ask Rachel for a date." The sender acknowledges that feedback reflects his or her perception. A further point is that "I" message feedback should always be given directly to the individual for whom it is intended.

Verbal or Demonstrated Feedback

Feedback can be given largely by means of words. However, often feedback can be communicated even more clearly and received even more accurately if verbal description is accompanied by demonstration—for instance, by videotapes or audio cassettes. Feedback can also be demonstrated without audiovisual aids. For instance, in the previous example either the leader or another participant could mirror Lou's voice messages when asking Rachel for a date. In addition, they could show Lou more appropriate behaviors.

Feedback or Confrontation

How can feedback be distinguished from confrontation? Much feedback is either in line with or reasonably close to participants' existing perceptions. Such feedback does not provide any major challenge or threat to their self-pictures. Confrontation is a category of feedback where participants' self-pictures are challenged. In training groups, confrontations can focus either on inconsistencies (for instance, between words and actions), on distortions of reality (for instance, selecting out inconvenient feedback), or on not owning responsibility for the consequences of one's behavior.

How as well as *what* leaders confront is important. Given the right trusting atmosphere, constructive confrontations have their place in groups. However, where possible, leaders should help speakers to confront themselves—for example, by asking them to search for evidence to back their statements. Also, leaders should use a minimum amount of "muscle." Although sometimes necessary, strong confrontations are generally to be avoided. Strong confrontations can create resistances. Also, always be mindful of the effects of confronting on observing participants.

Feedback or Reward

As well as specific feedback concerning how participants perform behaviors, leaders can also provide social rewards or reinforcers. Leader praise and encouragement are important sources of reward. Leaders can use reward to encourage desired group rules—for example, by saying "good" or "well done" when participants volunteer for behavior rehearsals. In addition, leaders can use reward when participants achieve targeted behaviors either inside or outside groups. Rewards can be nonverbal as well as verbal. Applause, head nods, smiles, and pats on the back are all examples of nonverbal rewards. In addition, forms of reward like money, soft drinks, candy, and exchangeable tokens are used in lifeskills training groups. Such rewards should be appropriate to the participants in question. Also, leaders need to beware of participants' only performing targeted behaviors under conditions of external reward rather than self-reward.

Sociocultural Feedback Considerations

Feedback needs to take into account the social and cultural milieu of participants. Leaders coming from different backgrounds from some or all of the participants require sensitivity to these differences. Leaders should be aware of differing rules governing feedback in other cultures and social groupings. Participants can be encouraged to relate how feedback is handled in their own cultures.

Feedback Training

Since much feedback in groups takes place between participants, leaders can train participants in basic skills of constructive feedback. Feedback skills include sending "I" messages, commenting on specific behaviors, and allowing receivers to react to feedback. Feedback training can be by brief instruction, initial and ongoing demonstrations, commenting on participants' feedback, and encouraging participants to comment on feedback they receive.

Using Exercises

▼▼▼

Lifeskills training groups tend to include many structured exercises. Most exercises are specifically designed to help participants develop targeted skills. Especially when working with children, leaders may choose to use exercises involving play. Whether designed for children or adults, exercises involving play are called games.

Exercises and games can be used in the initial, working, and ending stages of groups. In Chapter 6, many ice-breaking exercises were mentioned for use in initial sessions of lifeskills groups. Such ice-breaking exercises set an emotional climate for skills learning rather than develop specific targeted skills. Warm-up exercises used during the working stage of a group perform a similar function. Most exercises during the working stage of lifeskills groups focus on developing targeted skills. For example, leaders use skills manuals to get participants to perform relevant exercises as they work through the training program.

Kinds of Exercises

Exercises can focus on developing action skills, thinking skills, and action skills plus self-talk. The following six different kinds of structured activity fall into the broad category of exercises.

Action exercises: Action exercises involve physical movement—for example, role playing. Lifeskills training groups lay heavy emphasis on action exercises.

Written exercises: The instructions for most exercises are written, but written exercises require participants to write out their answers as well. Written exercises are often used for self-monitoring and assessment and to develop thinking skills.

Discussion exercises: Discussion exercises require the group to discuss specific topics—for example, in a group for dual-career couples, discussing sex roles for males and females.

Task exercises: Task exercises require the group to achieve or plan to achieve specific tasks.

Feedback exercises: Feedback exercises enable participants to receive comments or audiovisual feedback on how they perform in the targeted skills areas.

Games: Games are structured exercises involving play.

Design Considerations

There are two main sources of exercises and games: using other people's or making up your own. For this book I made up my own exercises. Using the relationship skills area as an example, existing sources of exercises include those in Egan's *You and Me* (1977), Johnson's *Reaching Out* (1986), my own *Human Relationships: A Skills Approach* (Nelson-Jones, 1990b), and the Pfeiffer and Jones series *Structured Experiences for Human Relations Training* (1969–85).

Other people's material may not be entirely appropriate for all or part of your training group. If so, you may need to construct some exercises. You are encouraged not only to use existing material, but also to tap your creativity and design some exercises for any training group that you run. The following are considerations in designing exercises and games:

Set clear, specific, and relevant goals: Participants should know the targeted skills that they are expected to work on by means of the exercise. Where possible, these skills should already have been presented and demonstrated.

Emphasize take-away skills: Training groups are about developing skills for daily living. Vague exercises unrelated to the development of specific take-away skills are to be avoided. Many trainee lifeskills leaders have difficulty putting sufficient practical emphasis into their exercises.

Make written instructions available: If instructions for the exercise are only given verbally, there is a greater chance of slippage between instructions and performance of the exercise than if the instructions are also written down.

Demonstrate the exercise: As well as written instructions, often the leader needs to demonstrate the exercise to ensure that participants know precisely what is expected. Since exercises are frequently performed in subgroups, leaders cannot always be present to correct misunderstandings.

Build in participation: When designing exercises for training groups, try to build in roles for most, if not all, participants. If necessary, break the group down into subgroups.

Coach and provide feedback: Pay attention to how participants obtain coaching and feedback on how they perform the exercise.

Process the experience: Participants should be given the opportunity to process with the group leader their experiences and learnings from the exercise.

Test the exercise: If possible, test your exercise beforehand to see if it works. If necessary, refine the exercise or even discard it and try again.

Exercise 25 is intended to help you become less dependent on others' exercises, by giving you the opportunity to design one of your own.

Exercise 25 Design an Exercise or Game
▼▼

This exercise can be done on your own, in pairs, or in a small group.

Pick a specific learning skill in a lifeskills training area of your choice that you wish to impart through learning by doing. If possible, familiarize yourself with the existing exercises and games in the area. Design and write out a handout for an exercise or game that helps a group of six to eight participants achieve your learning objectives. Take the following considerations into account as you design your exercise:

Set clear, specific, and relevant goals
Emphasize take-away skills
Make written instructions available
Demonstrate the exercise
Build in participation
Coach and provide feedback
Process the experience
Test the exercise

Designing Behavior-Change Experiments
▼▼

A major concern for all effective leaders is how best to help participants transfer trained skills to outside the group. Behavior-change experiments provide an excellent way to do this. Participants in conjunction with their leaders develop hypotheses about the consequences of using learned skills outside the group. Participants then implement their changed behaviors and evaluate their consequences. Whereas exercises can be done either inside or outside groups, experiments always provide a direct bridge to developing outside skills.

Most training-group leaders assign homework. Participants are asked to perform exercises and other tasks between sessions. Often participants are given a general instruction to try using their new skills outside the group and monitor how they get on. Behavior-change experiments provide a way of tightening up this general into a more specific instruction.

Experiments focus on the use of targeted skills in specific situations. There are six main steps in designing, conducting, and evaluating behavior-change experiments:

1. *Assess*: Existing behaviors in the problem situation are identified and assessed with special reference to targeted skills.

2. *Formulate changed behaviors*: Participants and leader work out how to behave differently in the situation using targeted skills.

3. *Make an "If . . . then . . . " statement*: The "If . . . " part of the statement relates to rehearsing, practicing, and then using your specified changed behaviors. The "then . . . " part of the statement indicates the specific consequences you predict will follow from the changes in your behavior.

4. *Rehearse and practice*: Participants need to rehearse and practice their changed behaviors to give themselves a reasonable chance of implementing them properly.

5. *Try out changed behaviors*: Participants try out their changed behaviors in actual problem situations.

6. *Evaluate*: Initially, participants should evaluate their changed behaviors on their own. This evaluation should focus on such questions as "How well did I perform the changed behaviors?" "What were the positive and negative consequences of using the targeted skills, for myself and for others?" "Have my predictions been confirmed or disconfirmed?" and "Do I want to use my changed behaviors, either without or with modification, in the future?" Later on leaders can help participants process, in the group, learnings from their experiments.

Following is an example of a behavior-change experiment taken from my book *Human Relationships: A Skills Approach* (Nelson-Jones, 1990b, pp. 165–166).

What happens when I am more open about sharing my feelings in a relationship?
▼ ▼

I. Expressing Positive Feelings

Part A: Assessment

1. Think of a relationship you think you could improve if you shared more of your positive feelings toward the other person.

_____

2. For an appropriate period, say three days, monitor how you send positive and negative messages to the other person.

_____

_____

_____

3. List all the positive feelings that are left unspoken in your relationship.

_____

_____

Part B: Make an "If . . . then . . ." Statement

Make an "If . . . then . . . " statement along the lines of "If I express these positive feelings [specify], then these consequences [specify] are likely to follow."

_____

_____

Part C: Try Out and Evaluate Your Changed Behavior

Try out your changed behavior. Assess its positive and negative consequences for yourself and the other person. Have your predictions been confirmed or disconfirmed? Has this experiment taught you something about the power of expressing positive feelings rather than leaving them unsaid? If so, what?

_____

_____

_____

II. Expressing Negative Feelings
   If appropriate, carry out the above experiment, but this time focus on expressing a negative rather than a positive feeling. Follow the guidelines for expressing feelings about another person.

_____

_____

_____

Exercise 26 encourages you to find out about the use of behavior-change experiments in training groups by conducting an experiment on yourself. You are then asked to act as group leader and help another person design an experiment to change her or his behavior.

Exercise 26 Design, Conduct, and Evaluate Behavior-Change Experiments
▼▼

1. Select a specific lifeskill on which you wish to work. Conduct and write up an experiment in which you change your behavior. Make sure to adequately cover each of the following six steps:

a. Assess
b. Formulate changed behaviors
c. Make an "If . . . then . . . " statement
d. Rehearse and practice
e. Try out changed behaviors
f. Evaluate

2. This part of the exercise should be done in pairs. Partner A acts as training-group leader and helps partner B, the participant, design and rehearse a behavior-change experiment for a particular life-skill. Together the partners go through the first four steps of the six steps for behavior-change experiments. After discussing what they have done together, partners reverse roles.

Emphasizing Homework
▼ ▼

Training-group leaders plan for participants to perform structured activities between sessions. Such homework activities include self-monitoring, behavior rehearsals, exercises, experiments, and more general practice of targeted skills. There are two main reasons why leaders assign homework. First, homework can speed up the learning process. Second, homework helps transfer trained skills to outside life. In their initial program presentations, leaders can let participants know why they attach great importance to participants' completing homework tasks. Some leaders make commitment to completing all homework tasks a clause in formal group contracts.

Participants are more likely to complete homework tasks if the following conditions apply. First, the *task requirements are clear*. To avoid misunderstandings, participants should receive handouts of homework assignments and of any worksheets they are expected to complete. Second, the homework tasks *are relevant*. The tasks are not only seen by leaders as relevant but also perceived by participants as relevant. Third, the homework tasks *consolidate earlier learning*. The homework builds on earlier learning by hearing, observing, and doing within the previous session or sessions. Fourth, the homework tasks are of an *appropriate level of difficulty*. The tasks take into account participants' levels of readiness. Where appropriate, graded steps are used. Fifth, a *realistic amount* of homework is assigned. Leaders can work out with participants what is a realistic amount of between-sessions homework. Sixth, leaders conduct *progress reviews*. At the start of the next session, leaders review how participants have fared in their homework. Such reviews have numerous functions: reward, feedback, coaching, support, targeting difficulties, and collecting information with which to plan future sessions. Seventh, leaders encourage *constructive group norms* regarding homework. Such norms include the expectation that all participants will do all of the homework, open discussion of successes and failures, and encouraging effort rather than ridiculing mistakes.

Numerous reasons exist why participants fail to do homework. For instance, in a school or college setting, an ungraded lifeskills group may have to compete for homework time with graded academic subjects. Sometimes participants attend training groups compulsorily rather than voluntarily. Also, homework may entail risks in trying new behaviors outside the group. As a group leader, you have to acknowledge and deal with any such difficulties and resistances as best you can.

▼ Chapter Highlights

▼ Learning by doing is essential to lifeskills training groups. Leaders structure activities to help participants develop targeted skills.

▼ Structured activities include self-monitoring forms, coached performance, behavior rehearsal, role-play, feedback, exercises, games, task assignments, critical incidents, case studies, computer-assisted learning, behavior-change plans, behavior-change experiments, and homework.

▼ Training-group leaders require good skills at facilitating structured activities. Such facilitation skills include creating a safe and trusting emotional climate, allowing performance fears to be aired and explored, helping participants process significant experiences, and facilitating peer feedback.

▼ After the initial presentation and demonstration of any skill, leaders coach participants through a performance of it. Coaching skills include facilitating self-coaching, providing clear instructions, breaking tasks down, using graded steps, demonstrating, and checking out participants' understanding of the skill.

▼ Behavior rehearsals can take place either immediately after the initial coached performance of a skill or as participants bring problem situations from their lives into the group.

▼ Methods of behavior rehearsal include live rehearsal, action role-play, mental rehearsal, visualized rehearsal, and action role-play with accompanying self-talk.

▼ Skills for leading action role-plays include preparing participants, selecting scenes and situations, directing, and processing.

▼ Skills for preparing participants include providing a rationale, ensuring that participants know the targeted behaviors, and warming participants up.

▼ Role-plays can be based on prepared scripts, prepared scenarios, or on problem situations in participants' lives.

(continued)

▼ **Chapter Highlights** (continued)

▼ Skills for directing role-play include selecting working partici-pants, setting the scene, assessing current behaviors, formulating changed behaviors, and trying out and rehearsing changed behaviors.

▼ Processing entails facilitating participants in dealing with thoughts and feelings generated by role-plays, discussing learnings, giving and receiving feedback, and making plans to transfer re-hearsed skills outside the group.

▼ Training-group leaders are managers of feedback rather than always providing feedback themselves.

▼ Dimensions of feedback include whether it is self or external; audiovisual; behavioral or emotional; specific or nonspecific; con-firmatory, corrective, or motivating; "I" message or "you" message; verbal or demonstrated; confrontational; and rewarding. Socio-cultural considerations and training participants in feedback skills are also important.

▼ Training-group leaders can either use other people's or make up their own exercises.

▼ Considerations in designing exercises include setting clear, specific, and relevant goals; emphasizing take-away skills; making written instructions available; demonstrating the exercise; building in participation; coaching and providing feedback; processing the experience; and testing the exercise.

▼ Behavior-change experiments are an excellent way of help-ing participants transfer targeted skills into their daily lives.

▼ Behavior-change experiments consist of six steps: (1) assess, (2) formulate changed behaviors, (3) make an "If . . . then . . ." statement, (4) rehearse and practice, (5) try out changed behaviors in real life, and (6) evaluate.

▼ Training-group leaders should emphasize the importance of participants' completing structured homework activities between sessions. Leaders must take care to design and introduce homework tasks so that participants are motivated to do them.

10

How to Prepare For and Lead a Session

A teacher should have maximal authority
and minimal power.

T. S. Szasz

Chapter Questions

▼▼

What skills are needed to prepare for an individual session?

How might leaders outline a session?

What skills does a leader need for managing the initial, working, and ending stages of a session?

How can a session be evaluated?

Introduction

▼▼

Lifeskills training sessions are microcosms of overall programs. Each session has its preparatory, initial, working, and ending stages. Training-group leaders are managers of learning. For any given session, the leader's function is to design and implement learning experiences to help the group attain targeted skills. The leader may perform numerous roles: energizer, facilitator, support, public speaker, information giver, demonstrator, coach, role-play director, disciplinarian, timekeeper, assessor, technician, and resource person, among others. Throughout any session, there will always be tension, as well as sometimes harmony, between the leader's didactic and facilitative roles. There is no such thing as the perfect group session. Leaders are constantly making choices between conflicting demands regarding both content and process.

The Preparatory Stage

▼▼

Training-group leaders who do not thoroughly prepare for sessions risk performing poorly in them. Leaders cannot just arrive and rely on their charm and facilitative skills plus the group's contribution. Lifeskills training sessions require careful planning and preparation.

Plan the Session

Effective leaders arrive at training-group sessions with well thought through session or "game" plans. Such leaders acknowledge that numerous things can go wrong in lifeskills sessions. They try to anticipate problems. The purpose of a session plan is to clarify objectives and to arrange a series of learning experiences to attain them. In this context, a session includes the period of time up to the start of the next session. If working with a co-leader, always try to plan sessions together. Following are some important considerations in planning for a session.

State Clear, Relevant, and Manageable Goals

Leaders need to be crystal clear about specific goals for each session. Vague goals lead to vague session plans. Irrelevant goals waste everyone's time. Goals that are not manageable lead to frustration on the parts of both leaders and participants. Often beginning leaders try to cover too much ground. As a consequence, they may either do a little well and then find they have insufficient time for the remainder of their material or they may do everything superficially. A good guideline when planning sessions is that a little done thoroughly is preferable to much done superficially. Quality is preferable to quantity.

Attend to Sequencing of Content across Sessions

Different design objectives and considerations are required for a group's beginning, middle, and ending sessions. Sessions are not isolated events. Each session should be designed in relation to what comes before and after. Much of the sequencing of session content comes from the overall or "master" plan of the lifeskills training group. This overall plan is the program plan as contrasted with the session plan. Program plans are designed before the first session, though they may be revised during a group's life. Most often, program plans contain outlines of individual session plans. An assumption in making program plans is that learning takes place in an orderly and cumulative sequence. Leaders need to carefully consider the implications of any large deviations from what was outlined for each session in their program plans.

Start from Where Participants Are

In planning sessions, leaders may have to deviate from original program plans in response to the starting points and rates of learning of the group participants. Furthermore, if there clearly are fast and slow learners in a group, leaders can design their sessions to take these differences into account—for instance, either by giving slow learners a chance to learn from fast learners or by grouping slow and fast learners separately for some activities. Leaders should always tailor the language, teaching materials, and activities they use to a group's learning level.

Consult with Participants

At one extreme, training-group leaders can be authoritarian and make all decisions about session agendas and processes themselves. At the other extreme, leaders can be professional "nice guys" or "nice gals" who, when making decisions, are oversolicitous of the wishes of the group and thus abrogate much of their leadership function. Effective leaders are neither tyrants nor wimps. They have clear learning objectives for the group, but nevertheless are willing to consult with participants about both content and process. An added bonus from consulting is that participants may work harder if they have voices in making decisions (Johnson & Johnson, 1987). The group becomes theirs as well as their leader's. Leaders can engage in systematic consultation at the end of sessions to check individuals' perceptions of their progress, their satisfaction with the group, and their ideas about the next session.

Emphasize Self-Referent Learning

There is an old saying: "Nobody loves yourself as much as yourself." Effective leaders take care to plan sessions so that participants are able to relate content to their own lives. Participants may quickly tune out of sessions either too intellectual or too focused on the needs of others rather than themselves. Participants have personal goals and reasons for being in groups. Though sometimes seemingly ambivalent about their acquisition, participants want specific takeaway skills to apply to specific life situations. Leaders who do not build on individuals' healthy interests in improving their lives are likely to elicit boredom, apathy, and other resistances.

Involve Participants in Learning Processes

One way of enhancing participants' involvement and motivation for learning is to make session content self-referent. A related way is to get participants involved in the learning process. Effective leaders are skilled at drawing participants into the processes of the group, be they either discussions or structured activities. In making session plans, leaders should ensure that participants are actively involved in their own learning rather than either being treated as passive objects by "having stuff thrown at them whether they like it or not" or being infantilized through spoon-feeding.

Balance Learning by Hearing, Observing, and Doing

The previous three chapters have stressed learning by hearing, observing, and doing. Leaders need to ensure that all three modes are incorporated in their session plans. Group size permitting, all sessions should have a high doing-to-talking ratio. Demonstrations should accompany both initial presentations and subsequent learning by doing.

Balance Facilitation with Didactic Input

When planning sessions, leaders must remember that they are not the sole source of learning in groups. Participants need time to share and discuss reactions to what transpires. Leaders should build in time for discussion and for processing of structured activities. Participants rushed through a learning sequence without care for their thoughts and feelings may become resistant. However, too much time spent on discussing and processing can also have negative outcomes—for instance, boredom because the group moves too slowly.

Attend to Sequencing and Variety

The distribution of time within a session needs to be such that the main learning points receive most attention. Adequate time should be allowed for each activity. The sequencing of material needs to be logical. For example, presentation and demonstration precede coaching and behavior rehearsal. Easy or less anxiety-evoking exercises precede more difficult and threatening ones. Variety is another consideration. If learners are passive the same teaching and learning methods quickly become boring. Sometimes variety can be introduced by breaking learning units down and interspersing presentation and demonstration with rehearsal and practice.

Think Through How to Start

Effective leaders think through how best to start their sessions. Some beginning-of-session questions that leaders can pose for themselves are: How do I link this session with the previous one? How do I let the group know what we are going to do this session? How can I help create an emotional climate whereby participants are glad to be back in the group? Do I need to help participants warm up? If homework was assigned at the end of the last session, how should I go about checking on whether and how it was done? and What do I do about people who missed the last session? Introducing a session requires careful planning. Participants can sense if you are poorly prepared. Also, you lower your confidence if you are unable to start a session competently.

Think Through How to End

Effective leaders do not end sessions in the middle of an activity by looking at their watches and saying, "Gosh, I'm sorry, I've lost track of the time. We've got to end now." Ending a session well is a critical part of leading a session well. Leaders can see that the main learnings of the session are summarized either by themselves or group members. Participants can be consulted on how they thought the session went and the agenda for the next session can be discussed. Time needs to be spent to clarify and possibly to formulate homework tasks. In short, how you end training sessions requires careful planning.

Design Homework

Training-group leaders should think of each session as including the period prior to the next session. Consequently, they must plan how participants best can use between-session time to attain their own and the group's goals. Usually, planning a session includes designing relevant homework. Leaders need not only ask themselves questions about the content of the homework, but also questions about how best to introduce it. If sufficient time is not set aside for introducing, formulating, and clarifying homework, it may be done poorly, if at all.

Decide on Between-Sessions Contact

Apart from contact with a co-leader, between-sessions contact can be between leader and participants and among participants. Also, leaders can seek between-sessions contact with third parties. Whether or not leaders encourage between-sessions contact may influence how they distribute time within a session. For example, leaders available to participants between sessions may consider they need to spend less time explaining homework than if not available. Also, when designing sessions, leaders can consider whether and how much to encourage participants to work with and support each other between sessions. Furthermore, leaders may plan to contact third parties cooperating in the training program. For instance, leaders can systematically contact teachers helping children make friends or managers helping supervisors develop skills. Purposes of such leader contact include monitoring how third parties support participants in their home settings and obtaining feedback on participants' progress.

Anticipate Difficult Participants

Difficult participants can be defined in two ways: participants experiencing difficulties developing the targeted skills and participants whom the leader experiences as difficult. Effective lifeskills group leaders are sensitive to individual differences, rates, and styles of learning. Leaders who have observed participants with learning blocks can think in advance whether and how best to approach them. In addition, leaders can prepare strategies for coping with participants who are difficult. For example, if Tomas and Fay make a habit of whispering to each other, the leader could go into the next session prepared with some options for handling them appropriately. In addition, if disciplinary problems involve many participants, as is common in schools, leaders can use the time between sessions to think through what to do and, if necessary, consult colleagues.

Prepare Audiovisual Materials and Equipment

If leaders are planning to use audiovisual materials, such as videotapes, they need to make sure that the training materials and equipment are both available and in good condition. If leaders are going to make their own audiovisual material, this requires even more advance planning. When preparing a session, you have to make sure that even simple aids, like whiteboards and overhead projectors, are available when wanted.

Consider the Availability of Written Training Materials

What written material is to be used in conjunction with a session? If the lifeskills group uses a training manual, is this readily available to all participants? Often handouts are useful adjuncts to lifeskills training sessions. Handouts can contain such items as session goals, session outlines, main learning points of sessions, homework tasks, and any worksheets required either during sessions or for homework. Participants can either be given or asked to purchase binders for keeping handouts. A practical tip is that handouts are more likely to end up in binders if they contain prepunched holes. If participants are being asked to read an article or articles in conjunction with sessions, leaders need to arrange for the articles to be available. Also, if participants are referred to library books, leaders should see that they are in the library.

Allow for Flexibility

Nothing is absolutely certain in training groups. Each session is different and provides different challenges. All the time leaders make choices concerning what to do, how to do it, what to say, when to be quiet, when to move on, how to divide their attention, and so on. In addition, the pace of individual and group learning varies. Different participants have different weaknesses within a skills area and different blocks to developing skills. Also, you cannot predict what pressing problems participants may bring into sessions. Furthermore, if participants feel you have a stopwatch and are moving them rigidly through your session plan, your rigidity is an invitation to noncooperation. When designing session plans, leaders need to be conscious of the varying degrees of importance of session items. Thus, if necessary, they know what items to sacrifice.

Make a Session Outline

Making a session outline is a necessary part of planning a session. A session outline presents the session's structure. Numerous considerations influence the session outline—for instance, targeted skills, group size, and whether it is a training group's beginning, middle, or ending session. Following are examples of session outlines for a first and a middle session. The time indicated for each item is a guideline rather than a straitjacket.

Example 1: First Session

Outline for the first session of a ten-session, two-hour, weekly stress-management group for twelve adults:

Welcome, outline of session	5 minutes
Warm-up exercise: moving around and intro-ducing self as if at party	10 minutes
Process warm-up exercise	5 minutes
Round: introduce self and say what you want from group	10 minutes
Leader outlines program	15 minutes
Group discussion of program and of "contract"	15 minutes
Lecturette on dimensions of stress	20 minutes
Dyad exercise: participants assess how they ex-perience stress on each dimension	20 minutes
Process exercise in whole group	10 minutes
Summarize; assign and discuss homework on self-monitoring and assessment of stress; consult about next session	10 minutes

Example 2: Middle Session

Outline for the fourth session of an eight-session, two-hour, weekly assertiveness training group for eight college students (four males and four females):

Welcome, brief outline of session	3 minutes
Warm-up in dyads: experiences of assertiveness and nonassertiveness in the past week	7 minutes
Process homework	10 minutes
Lecturette/ video demonstrations: making as-sertive requests for behavior change	20 minutes
In front of group, coached performance of a participant using prepared script and video feedback	10 minutes
Triad exercise: role-plays based on prepared scripts	15 minutes
Process exercise in group	5 minutes
Behavior rehearsal role-plays with video feed-back in whole group based on common problem situations	40 minutes
Summarize; discuss, formulate, and clarify homework; consult about next session	10 minutes

Formulating a session outline helps leaders clarify how to approach each session. Leaders still need to prepare material and ensure that needed equipment is available for the different parts of sessions, such as lecturette/demonstrations. Exercise 27 gives you practice at designing session outlines.

Exercise 27 Design Session Outlines
▼▼▼

For a lifeskills training group of your choice, complete the following sequence.

1. Specify the basic characteristics of the group: for instance, targeted skills, group size, number of sessions, and session length.
2. Specify your goals for the group's first session. Design a session outline to attain your goals. As well as your outline, what additional preparatory work is required to increase the likelihood of success for the group's first session?
3. Specify your goals for a middle session of the group. Design a session outline to attain your goals. As well as your outline, what additional preparatory work is required to increase the likelihood of success for this middle session?
4. Summarize your learnings from this exercise in regard to preparing future training-group sessions.

A Checklist for Preparing for Training Sessions

Leaders have so much to consider when planning lifeskills sessions that it is easy to overlook important things. Consequently, a checklist for preparing training-group sessions is provided here. Also, the checklist can be used for evaluating completed sessions.

A Checklist for Planning a Lifeskills Training Session
▼▼

_____ Do I have clear, relevant, and manageable goals?

_____ Am I paying adequate attention to the sequencing of content across sessions?

_____ Am I starting from where participants are?

_____ Have I consulted adequately with participants?

_____ Am I sufficiently emphasizing self-referent learning?

_____ Does the session contain sufficient involvement through participation?

_____ Is there a good balance of learning by hearing, observing, and doing?

_____ Am I adequately balancing facilitation with didactic input?

_____ Is the sequencing of items within the session appropriate?

_____ Is there sufficient variety within the session?

_____ Is the start of the session adequately planned?

_____ Is the ending of the session adequately planned?

_____ What homework is to be assigned?

_____ What, if any, between-sessions contact should I be either encouraging for participants or planning for myself?

_____ How can I help participants who have specific learning difficulties?

_____ What coping strategies can I use with participants who are difficult?

_____ What audiovisual material do I require?

_____ What written training materials do I require?

_____ Am I sufficiently flexible in how I approach the session?

_____ Have I designed an adequate session outline?

The Initial Stage

▼▼

It is important for a session to get off to a good start. If the opening minutes are a "downer," this negative atmosphere may be hard to retrieve. There are a number of functions to be performed early in a training session. Leaders require the skills to perform these functions adequately.

Set a Positive Emotional Climate

Following are a few simple guidelines for setting a positive emotional climate at the start of a session. Effective group leaders strive for businesslike, yet friendly, atmospheres.

Arrive fresh: Leaders require sufficient energy to interact well with a group of participants over the whole session. If you start the session tired and out of sorts, not only may your own performance suffer, but you risk demotivating the group.

Arrive a few minutes early: If you arrive a few minutes early, you can sort out your materials and compose yourself. If you arrive late, you risk sending negative messages about the importance both of punctuality and the group's work.

Welcome participants: Another advantage of arriving early is that you can welcome participants as they arrive. A pleasant welcome to each participant helps create a positive emotional climate, reinforces punctuality, and enhances leader attractiveness.

Start punctually: Starting on time is one of the most effective ways of creating the norm that participants should come on time, if not early.

Show commitment when introducing sessions: Presumably, as a group leader you consider the work of the session important. Without being overwhelming, let your commitment to the work of the group show by means of positive verbal, voice, and body messages.

Provide a Session Outline

At the end of the preceding session, you may have discussed with participants the agenda for this session. Nevertheless, it is a good idea at the start of a session to state the targeted skills and to provide an outline of how time will be spent. Most participants like to know both where they are going and how the leader intends to help them get there. Outlining sessions may reduce anxieties and help participants see how the different items fit together. In addition to leaders' verbal statements, session goals and outlines can be written on a whiteboard or in a handout. When outlining sessions, be prepared to answer questions and clarify the group's understanding of them. In some instances, in light of group feedback, you may decide to renegotiate and alter parts of a session.

Actively Involve Participants

Early in each session, try to get participants actively involved. Effective leaders strive to avoid participants' passively sliding into their shells. For example, participants can be assigned to pairs or small groups and asked to review their behavior in the targeted skills area since the last meeting. Alternatively, the leader can ask each participant in turn what he or she wants from the upcoming session (Corey & Corey, 1982). Here the focus has been on getting participants actively involved by interacting either in the whole group or in dyads or subgroups. Alternatively, some leaders start sessions with physical warm-up exercises.

Review the Previous Session

Lifeskills training groups use cumulative learning. Sessions build on what has gone before. Leaders can provide brief reviews of the main learnings of the previous session. Alternatively, leaders can turn the review into a warm-up exercise in which participants pair off and summarize for each other their main learnings from the previous session. Reviewing the previous session is especially useful for those participants who were unable to attend it. In addition, nonattending participants should receive handouts from missed sessions. Furthermore, both leaders and those participants who missed sessions must think through how to make up lost ground.

Review Homework

An important starting task is to review homework. Gazda (1989) observes, "Homework is much the content of the session itself; therefore those who do not complete the homework cut down on their potential involvement in the group" (p. 435). Leaders need to be alert to whether or not and how well participants do homework. If homework is not being done satisfactorily, leaders should explore reasons for this. Often participants will want to discuss specific difficulties they experience with homework tasks and with practicing targeted skills. Some coaching and feedback from both the leader and the group can take place immediately. However, sometimes both leader and participants can defer working with outside-the-group material until later in sessions. For example, specific difficulties in implementing skills can be topics for later behavior-rehearsal role-plays.

Deal with New and Unfinished Business

Leaders need to be sensitive to new business that participants bring into groups and to unfinished business from previous sessions. Many things may have happened in participants' lives since the last session. Participants may bring new joys, hurts, and momentous events into sessions. Participants may come obviously emotionally distraught or on a high. In addition, participants may be faced with immediate pressing situations involving the use of targeted skills.

There are no simple answers to how to deal with new business brought into groups. Probably it is best for leaders to allow major emotions to be aired. Bottling up strong emotions can act as a block to participation and learning. Participants themselves may act as gatekeepers for relevance. For example, they may appreciate the chance to get support during a personal crisis, but be very sensitive about disrupting the group's skills learning. Furthermore, though not guaranteed, personal crises can be good material for illustrating and working on targeted skills. Sometimes, both participants and leader may have issues arising from previous sessions that they wish to bring up. Again, it is probably wise to allow such issues to be aired. Both leader and group can then decide how much attention these issues merit.

Exercise 28 is designed to raise your awareness of some issues and leader skills for the initial stage of training sessions.

Exercise 28 Start a Training-Group Session
▼▼

Carry out the following activities:

1. Make up a worksheet by drawing a line down the middle of a page and at the top of the left column writing *Harmful Activities* and at

the top of the right column writing *Helpful Activities*. Think back over any lifeskills training groups in which you have participated either as participant or leader. In the relevant columns list harmful and helpful activities when starting sessions.

2. Discuss the role and importance of each of the following skills in the initial stage of training sessions:
   a. Setting a positive emotional climate
   b. Providing a session outline
   c. Actively involving participants
   d. Reviewing the previous session
   e. Reviewing homework
   f. Dealing with new and unfinished business

3. If possible, work with colleagues and role-play starting a training-group session in the middle of a group's life. After the role-play, discuss the major learnings for when you lead training-group sessions in the future. If possible, give everyone a chance to be the leader in a different role-play.

The Working Stage

▼▼

Spoon feeding in the long run teaches us nothing but the shape
of the spoon.

E. M. Forster

There is no clear working stage to a lifeskills training session. The work of the group takes place in the initial and ending stages as well. Here the working stage is defined as the middle section of the session—say, after the first ten minutes and up to the last ten minutes. The working stage is the heart of the session. During this period new material is introduced and previous material worked over. Many leadership skills for the working stage have been discussed in previous chapters. Here the focus is on some further skills for the working stage.

Maintain a Skills Focus

Participants join lifeskills groups to acquire and develop specific skills: be they action skills, thinking skills, or both. These skills entail learning specific behaviors. Training-group leaders as managers of learning need to beware of allowing sessions to lose much, if not all, of their skills focus. Sometimes sessions are not planned with sufficient skills emphasis in the preparatory stage. For instance, leaders are insufficiently specific about targeted skills. In addition, leaders may have wrongly planned the balance between discussion and structured skills development.

Three ways in which leaders can dilute the skills focus of a session are overly focusing on feelings, on relationships, or on problems. In each instance the issue is likely to be one of balance rather than rightness or wrongness. In regard to overly focusing on feelings, take the example of a spouse in a managing-conflict group who comes to a session extremely agitated after a marital fight. One option is for the leader to focus only on feelings—for example, "Tell us more about how you felt in the situation." Another option is to focus only on behaviors—for example, "How did you behave in the situation and how could you have improved on it?" Still another option is to focus on both feelings and behaviors: "You are extremely upset. What was good and what was possibly not so good about the way you managed your feelings and behaved?" In the last example, the leader's response both reflects a feeling and focuses on feelings in the context of developing skills.

Leaders may overly focus on the relationships within the group. However, in lifeskills sessions, such relationships are important mainly to the extent that they enhance or obstruct the group's learning. If relationship issues within the group can be used to illustrate targeted skills, they may merit attention. Otherwise, leaders should resist turning training-group sessions into encounter group sessions. Also, when participants bring problem situations into sessions, leaders may focus too much on the emotions and details of problems rather on the application of targeted skills to problems.

Use the Group Creatively

Many training-group leaders either by choice or by necessity work in groups of over eight participants. These leaders are faced with trying to design learning experiences that overcome some of the disadvantages of large group size. One way of mitigating or getting around the problem of large group size is to use co-leaders or leaders' aides. However, bringing in extra leaders is not always possible. Another way is to use good audiovisual presentations. You can then use your energy for managing the group. A third way is to be creative in your use of the group. Varying its format is recommended even for small groups of six to eight.

Leaders can vary the tasks, numbers, and seating in their groups. Already, in the chapter on structured activities, suggestions have been made for varying the tasks in which the group engages. Numerical variations include working with the whole group or breaking it down into small groups, quartets, triads, dyads, or even singles. Leaders can make decisions on size of working groups either on their own or in consultation with participants. Leaders can also vary the seating pattern of the group from that of a horseshoe. Seating variations include circular, be it the whole group or subgroups; the fishbowl, with inner and outer rings; and having a "stage" for role-plays in some part of the room with the audience in a semicircle (the stage's location may depend on where a video camera is mounted). In addition, as in some ice-breaking exercises, participants can stand rather than sit.

Actively Involve Participants

Getting and keeping participants actively involved is a major skill of effective lifeskills group leaders. Participant MEGO (My Eyes Glaze Over) can set in at any stage and not just during leader presentations (Valenti, 1982). It is all too easy for participants' attention spans and motivation to falter during what may be a long working stage of over an hour or more. Already, some suggestions have been made for getting participants involved at a session's start. Throughout a session, breaking the group down in various ways can encourage involvement. Furthermore, judicious use of structured activities can provide excellent opportunities for participation. Following are some additional suggestions for getting and keeping participants actively involved.

Tune In and Check Out

Training-group leaders as managers of learning should pay close attention to whether items in a session work for participants. Leaders require empathy to perceive how learning experiences are understood and received. For instance, leaders who sense that participants are getting restless with a presentation can either try to be more stimulating or move on to something more active. Leaders also require checking-out skills. For example, leaders perceiving that participants show little energy or interest for specific structured activities can check out their perceptions with the group.

Tuning-in and checking-out skills also are applicable to working with individuals. Leaders require sensitivity to individual differences in learning styles and attention spans. On the other hand, leaders can distort the group's work if they pay too much attention to unrepresentative feedback from individuals. Nevertheless, helping individual participants through learning blocks may be good for both individuals and groups.

Ask Drawing-In Questions

Good training-group leaders rarely, if ever, allow participants to be passive for long periods of time. Active participation covers thinking as well as doing. Even when giving presentations, leaders try to keep participants' minds active. Leaders can ask questions that have the effect of drawing participants into sessions. Such questions can be either for anyone in the group to answer, or entail going around the group with each person answering, or be addressed to individuals—possibly those who have not participated much to date. The following are examples of drawing-in questions:

"Can anyone give me an example of . . . ?"
"Has anyone had an experience of . . . ?"
"What are your reactions to . . . ?"
"To what extent and in what ways is he/she taking responsibility for his/her behavior?"
"What skills does he/she need to manage the situation better?"
"Does the demonstration trigger off anything in how any of you might behave differently?"
"Does anyone have any specific feedback that they would like to give to [mention name] after observing that role-play?"

In all these instances, if leaders ask questions of the group, their body messages should match their intentions. For example, their eyes should scan the group rather than be fixed on one individual. Any arm movements should show openness to the group (for instance, a sweeping gesture) rather than close off options (for instance, by pointing at someone).

Reward Helpful Involvement

Leaders can literally encourage—give courage to—participants who share experiences, answer questions, and take part in activities. Leaders can give both verbal and nonverbal rewards. Examples of verbal rewards for active involvement include, "Thanks for volunteering for the role-play," "That's a good example," and "I appreciate your sharing that with the group." Sometimes, leaders can choose to reflect participants' answers to show and check out that they have heard them correctly. In addition, leaders can support participants as they take part in activities and exercises by showing consideration for their thoughts and feelings. Examples of nonverbal rewards for getting actively involved include head nods, smiles, pats on the back, and hugs.

Curtail Harmful Involvement

Participants singly or as a group can disrupt the leader and each other by interrupting, showing off, making a joke of the proceedings, being aggressive, being overly critical, arguing, being irrelevant, being boring, whispering, talking loudly to each other, and throwing paper darts, among other behaviors Sometimes destructive behaviors are best ignored by the leader. Either the behaviors will drop off of their own accord or other participants will deal with perpetrators.

If the disruptive behaviors persist in interfering with the learning of the remainder of the group, leaders must consider how best to intervene. Leaders must make their interventions appropriate to the behaviors they want to curtail. For instance, if participants ramble on vaguely, they can be asked to talk about specific behaviors. If participants are discipline problems, there are a number of options. Part of the skill of the group leader is to get potentially disruptive elements in the group "on-side" rather than "off-side." Consequently, leaders should use the minimum "muscle" necessary to achieve the desired results. Sometimes humor can defuse situations of potential conflict. Giving disruptive participants "the teacher's eye" may be sufficient to curtail their behavior. Also, leaders can help disruptive participants explore their resistances. Moving further up the hierarchy of "muscle," leaders can make behavior-change requests in a firmer voice and, if necessary, repeat them. In addition, leaders and the other participants can point out the consequences of the disruptive behavior for the learning environment. Leaders in some lifeskills groups, if unable to exclude certain participants, may be faced with ongoing disciplinary problems. In such circumstances, they have the difficult task of containing the disruptive elements at the same time as helping those wanting to benefit from the group.

Use Minibreaks

To "take five" can sometimes help keep participants actively involved. When working with juvenile delinquents, Sarason (1976) initially estimated that their attention span was twenty to thirty minutes. Consequently, about midway through a one-hour session, he provided a soft drink for each participant. Both having brief breaks or time-out periods and also providing coffee, tea, and soft drinks may be conducive to involvement. In addition, opportunity for fresh air and physical movement—not just calls of nature—may help.

Make Balancing Choices

During a session, training-group leaders are faced with numerous choices concerning what is a good balance between conflicting considerations. Some of the considerations leaders have to balance include the following: whether to be didactic or facilitative; whether to make decisions alone or share decisions with the group; presenting and demonstrating versus doing structured activities; how much to work with individuals; whether to work with the whole group or break it down; how much to focus on action skills or thinking skills; whether to adhere to or deviate from session plans; whether to allow discussion or cut it off; and whether to be serious or humorous.

Constant tensions between conflicting considerations exist in all training groups. Leaders can make some of these choices in advance. However, what actually happens depends on the choices they make during sessions. Leaders who decide in advance what their main session goals are, how they want the emotional climate in sessions to be, and what their own roles will be, are in stronger positions to make balancing decisions than those unclear about these issues. If leaders think they have got the balance between some of these considerations wrong, they can often retrieve situations either later in the same session or in subsequent sessions.

Keep the Session Moving

Training-group leaders need to keep sessions moving. Keeping a session moving does not mean pressuring participants all the time. Rather, assuming the time distribution has been well planned, leaders can keep the group moving at a comfortable pace to complete the session's various tasks. Providing an outline at the session's start can help keep it moving. As a result, participants should be clear about the ground to be covered. Also, the outline provides a positive context for the leader's transition statements. Such transition statements are not just cutting-off-and-moving-*from* statements, but also opening-up-and-moving-*to* statements.

Here are some possible transition statements:

"Well, that's the end of my initial presentation of how to generate and evaluate different perceptions in situations you find difficult. If there are no further questions, I would now like to coach one of you through the steps of this skill in relation to a specific situation in which you feel shy."

"Does anyone have anything pressing they would like to add before we move on to . . . ?"

"Does Theo have anything to add or does anyone else have anything that they would like to feed back to Theo before we move on to the next role-play?"

"Though this is an interesting discussion, we seem to be getting away from the skills-building purpose of this session. I suggest we curtail the discussion and move on."

"I seem to be picking up a lot of body messages that we have spent enough time on that activity and should be moving on. Do you agree?"

The Ending Stage

▼▼▼

Effective group leaders pay close attention to how they end sessions (Corey & Corey, 1982; Jacobs, Harvill, & Masson, 1988). Much of the work of lifeskills training groups goes on between sessions. Therefore, leaders have the added reason for ending sessions well of taking full advantage of between-sessions time.

Ending-Stage Tasks

Quite apart from calling a halt to the proceedings, a number of tasks may be performed in the ending stage of a session. These tasks include the following:

Summarize: The main points of the session can be summarized either by the leader or by participants. Leaders can check that participants know not only what to do, but also how to instruct themselves when using targeted skills.

Correct misunderstandings: If participants misunderstand some of the session's learnings, the leader may be able to put them right before the session ends. However, leaders must defer major corrective instruction and coaching to the next session.

Formulate and assign homework: Sometimes leaders will ask participants to complete prepared homework tasks. On other occasions, leaders may work with participants to design individual behavior-change experiments and other activities. Leaders need to ensure that participants are clear on what is wanted in homework tasks. Also, leaders can help participants identify and work through blocks to doing homework.

Obtain feedback: Leaders can check out with participants their reactions to the session—what seemed to work for them and what did not.

Consult: Leaders can share with participants their ideas for the agenda and activities for the next session. Participants can be asked for their reactions and suggestions.

Deal with unfinished business: With their emphasis on behaviors rather than emotions, training-group sessions tend to end with less unfinished business than interactional group sessions. Nevertheless, if there are feelings and hidden agendas that may interfere with the group's work, it is probably best for these to be aired. Leaders can then decide whether these emotions and agendas merit more attention either now or in the future.

Arrange for mutual support: Leaders can raise the issue of participants' supporting each other, perhaps on a buddy system, between sessions. For example, participants might phone their buddy at least once to discuss progress.

Indicate between-sessions contact with leader: Leaders can indicate what, if any, between-sessions contact they are prepared to have with participants. If a participant appears particularly distressed during the session, the leader might have a brief word with her or him afterward. Many leaders discourage participants from asking routine questions—for instance, concerning homework—between sessions.

They expect participants to stay alert and ask such questions during sessions.

Ending-Stage Skills

During the ending stage of sessions, leaders use numerous skills: facilitating, checking out, summarizing, and assigning homework, among others. Here are a few further skills specific to the ending stage:

End on time: It is a good discipline for both leaders and the group that sessions start and end on time. Ending on time has the following advantages for leaders: providing a firm limit on session content; letting leaders get away gracefully; and cuing participants to raise important issues during the session. Also, participants appreciate it if the contract on session length is kept and they can make arrangements accordingly.

Allow time for ending: When designing and managing sessions, leaders need to allow sufficient time to end the session well. Allowing sufficient time for ending means paying attention to timekeeping throughout the session so that there is not a buildup of work by the end. Depending on the length of the whole session and on what the leader aims to achieve in the ending stage, perhaps 5 to 20 minutes may be set aside for it.

Make a transition statement: When outlining the lifeskills training program at the first session, leaders can make it clear to participants that in each session there will be an initial, a working or middle, and an ending stage. Nevertheless, when the time comes for the ending stage in each session, leaders still need to make transition statements. Such transition statements shift the focus of the group to the work of the ending stage. Two possible transition statements are the following: "I realize that this is an important issue for you and perhaps we can come back to it. However, we have about ten minutes left now. I would like to spend this time to get the group to summarize its main learnings from the session and to clarify homework," and "We are coming to the end of the session now. The time has come to consolidate learnings, sort out homework, and look ahead to the next session."

Actively involve participants: During the ending stage of sessions, as in earlier stages, leaders can actively involve participants. For example, when summarizing, one format is for the leader to summarize; another format is for one or more participants to summarize. The listening participants can then be asked to either verify or correct the summaries. Also, leaders can ask questions to be answered by anyone in the group (for example, "Does anyone have any feedback they want to give about the session?") or do rounds in which each participant gets the opportunity to speak (for example, "I'm now going to give each of you the opportunity to comment on what, if anything, you've learned from today's session.'').

Strengthen commitment to between-sessions work: Leaders can encourage participants to use the time between sessions fruitfully. Completing homework tasks and using targeted skills outside the group should be presented in a positive light. The time between sessions is really an extension of the session in which participants get the opportunity to practice, develop, and consolidate skills. When devising homework tasks, leaders can check out that they have relevance to participants' personal goals. Sometimes leaders may need to help participants state homework goals specifically, realistically, and with a time frame. Leaders can also explore with participants the payoffs for doing homework and changing their behavior.

Exercise 29 Lead a Training-Group Session
▼▼▼

1. In regard to either your Exercise 27 middle-session training-group outline or to another middle-session outline, discuss how you might use each of the following skills for the *working* stage of your session:
   a. Maintaining a skills focus
   b. Using the group creatively
   c. Actively involving participants
   d. Making balancing choices
   e. Keeping the session moving
2. In regard to the same outline, discuss how you might use each of the following skills for the *ending* stage of your session:
   a. Ending on time
   b. Allowing time for ending
   c. Making a transition statement
   d. Actively involving participants
   e. Strengthening commitment to homework
3. If possible, work with colleagues and role-play leading the whole of a training-group session. After the role-play, discuss major learnings for when you lead training-group sessions in the future. If possible, give everyone a chance to be the leader in a different role-play (to save time, sessions may have to be co-led).

Evaluating a Session
▼▼▼

Leaders may ask themselves such questions as "How can I tell if the session worked?" or "Has the session achieved its objectives?" Leaders can evaluate the effectiveness of a session during it, between sessions, and at the start of the next session (Hopson & Scally, 1981; Rose, 1986). Leaders require clarity concerning evaluation criteria.

There are several ways of evaluating whether sessions are successful. First, leaders can *observe* from participants' verbal, voice, body, and action messages such things as whether or not they are actively involved in the session, whether or not they understand the session content, their rate of progress in developing targeted skills, and which parts of the session they enjoy and which parts they find boring. Second, leaders can *listen to their own feelings* and use these as a basis for thinking about what either is happening or has happened in a session. For instance, a leader may have a feeling of unease about a session and then reflect on why this is the case. Third, leaders can review if *the session outline has been completed satisfactorily*. Assuming a realistic outline, one criterion for a successful session is if leader and participants consider that they have covered its content adequately. Were all the main learning points and targeted skills communicated?

Verbal feedback provides a fourth way of gauging the success of sessions. Leaders can get informal feedback from casual comments either from participants, colleagues, or third parties concerning the success of a session. Such feedback may or may not be representative of what the group thinks. Leaders can also systematically seek verbal feedback—for instance, by a round in which all participants can have their say. *Written feedback* offers a fifth way of assessing sessions. Participants can be asked to provide ratings and brief comments at the end of each session. For example, participants could rate on a seven-point scale, ranging from 1 for highly dissatisfied to 7 for highly satisfied, what they felt about the session. In addition, they could be asked to comment on what they liked and disliked about the session. Also, participants can be asked to rate and comment on adequacy of their own contributions to sessions. Leaders can also evaluate sessions by means of *videotape feedback*. They can play back videotapes of sessions and assess both their own and participants' behaviors.

Two further ways of assessing the success of sessions are *attendance* and *completion of homework tasks*. If attendance is poor at the next session, this may give the leader pause for thought about the adequacy of the previous session. However, beware of paranoia. Numerous reasons explain why participants either do not attend or attend sessions late. Calmly collect evidence before inferring the worst. If participants either fail to complete homework or complete homework tasks poorly, this merits further exploration. Again, calmly collect evidence before attributing the worst. For example, genuine difficulties in their lives may have interfered with participants' completion of homework. Alternatively, when participants attempted the homework, they may have misunderstood what was wanted. Consequently, an accurate attribution of cause might focus on your skills in assigning homework in the previous session rather than on the inadequacy of your leadership of the whole session.

All training-group leaders evaluate sessions, albeit with varying degrees of awareness and thoroughness. Between sessions, you are encouraged to reflect on the success and learnings for you and the group from the previous session. Leaders as well as participants should do their homework!

▼ Chapter Highlights

▼ Each training-group session has its preparatory, initial, working, and ending stages. During each stage, leaders are managers of learning.

▼ Lifeskills training sessions require careful preparation and outlining to attain clear, relevant, and manageable goals. Each session should be planned in the context of what precedes and follows it.

▼ Skills for managing a session's initial stage include setting a positive emotional climate, providing an outline, actively involving participants, reviewing the previous session, processing homework, and dealing with new and unfinished business.

▼ Skills for managing a session's working stage include maintaining a skills focus, using the group creatively, actively involving participants, making balancing choices, and keeping the session moving.

▼ Ending-stage tasks include summarizing, correcting misunderstandings of session content, formulating and assigning homework, obtaining feedback, consulting, arranging for mutual support, and providing information about between-sessions contact with leaders.

▼ Skills for managing a session's ending stage include ending on time, allowing time for ending, making a transition statement, actively involving participants, and strengthening commitment to between-sessions work.

▼ Ways of evaluating training-group sessions include observing; listening to feelings; comparing what happened with the session outline; attending to verbal, written, and videotape feedback; and noting attendance and completion of homework assignments.

11

How to Consolidate Self-Help Skills and to End a Group

The final test of a leader is that he leaves behind
    him in other men the conviction and the will
    to carry on.

Walter Lippman

▲▲▲

Chapter Questions

Introduction

A critical issue for all lifeskills group leaders is "Will my group have any lasting effects?" Kendall (1989) emphasizes: "Training in a skill does not automatically mean that the skill will persist nor that it will appear in contexts meaningfully different from the one in which training took place" (p. 358). The "train and hope" approach to the transfer and maintenance of treatment gains is not reliable (Goldstein & Keller, 1987; Martin, 1990; Stokes & Osnes, 1989). Leaders require many strategies to increase the chances of participants' retaining their skills. As depicted in Figure 11-1, consolidating trained skills as self-help skills in preparation for a group's ending is at the heart of lifeskills training. Consolidation is the central integrating focus or hub of all leader training skills and participant learning endeavors.

Generalization, transfer, maintenance, and *development* are four important terms describing somewhat overlapping aspects of consolidating trained skills as self-help skills.

Generalization: Skinner (1953) observes, "Generalization is not an activity of the organism; it is simply a term which describes the fact that the control acquired by a stimulus is shared by other stimuli with common properties" (p. 132). Regarding lifeskills training groups, *generalization* refers to the possibility of skills' being used in response to nontrained situations or stimuli similar to those trained for in groups. Participants are flexible rather than rigid in how they apply targeted skills outside groups.

Transfer: It is wholly insufficient for participants to use targeted skills only in training-group settings. *Transfer* refers to the ability of participants to use trained skills in their daily lives.

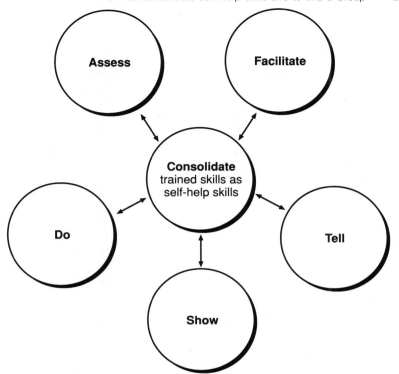

Figure 11-1 Consolidation of self-help skills as the central integrating focus of training groups.

Maintenance: *Maintenance* refers to participants' abilities to keep using trained skills after a group ends. Maintenance is not always consistent: participants may suffer periods of relapse. However, over time, despite relapses, they still maintain their skills. The opposite of maintenance is regressing to baseline or worse.

Development: When a group ends, some participants may not only maintain but also develop trained skills to higher levels. These participants are able to shift the balance of weaknesses and strengths in one or more skills areas still further in the direction of strengths.

Thinking Skills That Enable Consolidation

▼ ▼

Training groups have their endings built into them from their beginnings. Diligent leaders do not wait until a group's ending stage to help participants consolidate targeted skills as self-help skills. Effective leaders assist with consolidating self-help skills in the group's preparatory, initial, and working stages as well. Leaders wishing to help participants transfer trained skills into self-help skills must focus not only on relevant action skills, but also on relevant thinking skills (Nelson-Jones, 1990a). Furthermore, leaders need to focus on their own thinking skills as well as on those of participants.

Leader Thinking Skills

A group leader's thinking skills can help or hinder participants' attempts to develop lifeskills as self-help skills. Leaders intent on consolidating participants' self-help skills require the effective thinking skills of attributing cause accurately, possessing realistic rules, and predicting realistically.

Attributing Cause Accurately

Groups may be too leader-centered. This style of leadership weakens participants' motivation for assuming responsibility for their learning. The causes of learning in training groups are attributable to participants and leaders together, not just to leaders alone. In addition, leaders need to attribute cause accurately when explaining their own and participants' successes and failures. For example, leaders who fail to train for maintenance should not blame participants for skills relapses.

Possessing Realistic Rules

Leaders require realistic rules regarding the processes and outcomes of training groups (Ellis, 1980, 1989). Following are some unrealistic "mustabatory" rules that interfere with consolidating self-help skills:

"I must cure participants": Cure is a medical rather than a psychological concept. While leaders might prefer it if participants acquired and maintained perfect lifeskills, this is an unrealistic goal. Furthermore, the idea of the leader curing participants contributes to an excessively leader-centered approach to lifeskills training. A more realistic reformulation of the mustabatory rule is: "My job is, to the best of my ability, to train participants to acquire and maintain targeted lifeskills as self-help skills for when the group ends. Afterward, participants will still have to work hard to retain their skills."

"I must focus on acquisition training rather than on acquisition and maintenance training": Here the leader overemphasizes initial acquisition of skills at the expense of realizing that participants must maintain skills themselves. As Stuart (1980) observes of marital therapy, "Building skills of maintaining positive therapeutic outcome is fully as important as promoting change in the first place" (p. 367). Stuart's observation provides a more realistic reformulation of the preceding unrealistic rule.

"I must cover a lot of ground": Leaders can put pressure on themselves to cover too much material, both over the group's life and in individual sessions. A more realistic reformulation is: "My best approach is to allow sufficient time to teach each skill thoroughly so that participants learn it well enough to apply it on their own."

"I must have a standardized program": For many reasons, leaders may need to have much of their training program standardized. Nevertheless, ultimately participants have to use the skills in the specific situations of their own lives. Consequently, transfer and maintenance of skills may be enhanced if leaders provide opportunities to work on individual as well as on group concerns. Individual activities and behavior-change experiments can take place within the context of group approaches. A more realistic reformulation is: "Lifeskills training groups are composed of individuals with different learning styles, personal goals, and life circumstances. Consequently, I need to balance interventions for the whole group with those helpful to specific individuals."

"I must not be criticized": Leaders need to be open to participants' feedback regarding those aspects of the group that work and do not work for them. Leader defensiveness interferes with participants' both acquiring and maintaining skills. A more realistic reformulation is: "Though some participants' comments may be destructive, probably most feedback is meant constructively. I need to listen carefully to feedback to see how I can improve this and future groups."

Predicting Realistically

Leaders need realism in predicting what can be achieved in a training group, be it six or twenty sessions long. Jacobson (1989), writing of marital therapy, concluded: "Nevertheless, in retrospect it seemed almost embarrassingly naive of us to have expected a treatment program lasting six months to have a lasting impact on most couples" (p.329). Training-group leaders must beware of harboring similar naiveté themselves and of passing it on to participants. As shown in Chapter 2, most participants enter training groups with long histories of maintaining lifeskills weaknesses in targeted areas. They also have confidence and thinking-skills problems that interfere with change. Many participants will require further individual and group interventions to develop their skills. A simple analogy is that of a group of beginners who complete a series of tennis lessons. They have acquired some new skills and must practice to retain them. However, to move beyond the beginner's stage, they must make a commitment to more coaching and practice. Becoming even better requires still more coaching and practice. Quick fixes are rarely the answer in acquiring and maintaining lifeskills.

Participants' Thinking Skills

Though it is often underemphasized in the maintenance literature (for example, Goldstein & Keller, 1987; Stokes & Osnes, 1989), training to consolidate self-help skills requires paying close attention to participants' thinking skills. The following are some thinking skills that may help participants maintain and develop targeted lifeskills.

Attributing Cause Accurately

Throughout training groups, leaders need to emphasize overtly and covertly that participants are personally responsible for making their lives through the quality of their choices. More specifically, participants are personally responsible for making the most of the learning opportunities provided during training groups. Also, participants have the responsibility for maintaining and developing their skills when groups end. Potential attributional errors that sustain skills weaknesses require exploration and, if necessary, correction. Such attributional errors include: "It's my nature," "It's my unfortunate past," "It's my bad luck," "It's my poor environment," "It's all someone else's fault," and "It's all my fault." In addition, leaders need to pay close attention to how participants attribute cause for setbacks. For example, participants should beware of making internal and stable attributions of failure when relapses occur (Kendall, 1989).

Possessing Realistic Rules

Participants may require assistance in reformulating unrealistic rules about learning lifeskills. Following are examples of unrealistic rules and their more realistic reformulations.

Unrealistic rule: "I must be cured."
Reformulation: "While I would prefer to have no problems in the future, the best I can do is improve my skills during the group and strive to maintain them afterward."

Unrealistic rule: "Change must be easy."
Reformulation: "I have not only to develop new and better skills, but also to unlearn bad habits. Consequently, I have to work hard to change during the group and also to persist in working hard afterward."

Unrealistic rule: "During and after the group I must improve all the time."
Reformulation: "Learning any new skill involves making mistakes, experiencing periods of uncertainty, and encountering setbacks. Ups and downs are inevitable. All I can do is to learn from mistakes and cope with setbacks to the best of my ability."

Unrealistic rule: "The leader must teach me."

Reformulation: "The leader is a resource person whose job is to assist me to develop self-help skills. I need to work together with the leader during the group and on my own afterward."

These are just a few of the unrealistic rules that participants may have about lifeskills learning. Leaders may identify and reformulate other unrealistic rules that either individuals or groups possess.

Self-Instructing

Leaders need to ensure that participants understand the sequences of choices in targeted skills well enough to instruct themselves. For example, when demonstrating skills, leaders can demonstrate self-instructions too. Also, leaders can get participants to summarize these self-instructions either in the group or by making up homework cassettes. Where skills are complex, leaders can instruct participants in the main rules guiding effective enactment—for example, communication rules for couples (Stuart, 1980).

Using Coping Self-Talk

Use of coping self-talk is highly relevant to maintaining as well as acquiring skills. Coping self-talk can be used when participants are faced with difficult situations in implementing skills—for example, public speaking, asserting oneself, or making a date. Coping self-talk can also be used by participants to deal with temptations such as food, alcohol, or drugs. Participants can make both calming and coaching self-talk statements to themselves before, during, and after difficult or stressful situations. Furthermore, participants can be helped to talk themselves through setbacks when either learning or implementing skills.

Perceiving Accurately

Participants can be helped to perceive their skills strengths and weaknesses accurately. Developing the skills of accurate perception of strengths and weaknesses not only helps participants improve their skills during groups but also gives them the basis for correcting weaknesses afterward. Ways in which leaders can help participants see themselves accurately include assigning self-observation and assessment exercises, facilitating self-assessment, giving feedback, and providing the opportunity for others' feedback. Leaders can also work with specific tendencies that participants may have to perceive inaccurately—for example, engaging in negative self-labeling or failing to acknowledge progress. In addition, leaders can help participants to perceive others accurately—for instance, by encouraging them to provide evidence for questionable perceptions.

Predicting Realistically

Both during and after training groups it is important that participants predict the consequences of their behaviors realistically. Many participants are fearful of change and of taking risks. They may be unduly pessimistic. Leaders can help them develop the skills of adequately taking potential gains as well as losses into account when reviewing the future. Some participants may be overoptimistic. Here leaders can help them develop the skills of adequately taking potential losses into account. Also, leaders can help participants identify and work through specific anxieties about either learning or implementing targeted skills. Furthermore, leaders can assist participants in being realistic in predicting what they can achieve by the group's end and how hard they need to work to retain and develop skills.

Using Goal-Setting Skills

By imparting goal-setting skills, leaders can help participants make their futures both during and after groups. Personal goals in the targeted skills areas must be specific and realistic, and have time frames. Goals can be reviewed in light of experience and feedback.

Visualizing

Visualizing can be used by participants both to strengthen desirable and to weaken undesirable behaviors. For example, participants can visually rehearse and practice desired skills. In addition, participants can visualize the negative consequences of behaviors they wish to eliminate (Cautela, 1967; Lazarus, 1977).

Using Self-Reward

Participants can be trained to use self-reward to develop and maintain skills (Kanfer & Gaelick, 1986; Thoresen & Mahoney, 1974). Self-rewards can be external or internal. External rewards include (1) self-administration of new rewards outside the participant's everyday life, such as a new item of clothing or a special event; and (2) initial denial of some pleasant everyday experience and later administration of it contingent upon some desired action. Internal rewards include self-talk statements like "That's great," or "I did well," or "Terrific . . . I actually did it" that clearly indicate satisfaction with attaining a targeted action.

Positive self-reward programs require the following component skills:

1. Setting specific goals. Goals may need to be broken down so that participants reward themselves for attaining graded steps.
2. Self-observation and monitoring of targeted behaviors.

3. Identifying suitable rewards. Kanfer and Gaelick (1986) observe that, wherever possible, self-reward should be relevant to the target behavior. They write: "For example, the ex-smoker might select the purchase of new perfume or having teeth cleaned and polished, because such rewards emphasize the positive aspects of not smoking in terms of whiter teeth and increased sensitivity to smell" (p. 324).

4. Developing a behavior-change plan in the form of a contract with clear connections between achieving targeted behaviors and administering self-rewards.

5. Rehearsal and enactment of the behavior-change plan.

6. Review and evaluation of progress.

Using Relapse-Prevention Skills

Once on their own, participants are almost certain to experience relapses and setbacks as they implement targeted skills. Some trainers and therapists build relapse prevention (RP) into treatments (Marlatt, 1980; Marx, 1982). Marx has designed an RP worksheet that asks the respondent to choose an appropriate behavior to retain (Ivey, Ivey, & Simek-Downing, 1987). Respondents then assess strategies for anticipating difficult situations in relation to the targeted behavior; increasing rational thinking to regulate self-defeating thoughts and feelings; implementing action skills, such as assertiveness or relaxation, to support self-regulating behaviors; and monitoring and providing rewarding consequences for succeeding with new behaviors. Respondents are also asked to predict the circumstances of the first relapse, including people, places, times, and emotional states. Participants not only require the skills of relapse prevention, but also of dealing with their thoughts and feelings about any relapses that occur. Many relapse-prevention strategies are also retrieval skills for getting back on track.

Managing Problems

Participants can fail to retain lifeskills because of problems in the targeted skills areas. In addition, problems in other areas of participants' lives can impact on maintaining targeted skills. For example, Jacobson (1989) studied the maintenance of treatment gains after social-learning-based marital therapy. He found that for couples interviewed after their two-year follow-up assessment, stressful life events were by far the best predictor of relapse.

Elsewhere I have described in detail CASIE, a five-step framework for managing problems (Nelson-Jones, 1990a). The five steps are as follows:

C = Confront your problem
A = Assess and define your problem

S = Set goals and plan
I = Implement your plan
E = Evaluate the consequences of implementation

Leaders can teach participants the component skills for each of the five steps. Participants should understand that the framework is not intended as a straitjacket, but as a tool to be used flexibly. It can be used with varying degrees of formality and rigor, depending on how difficult and important the problem is. For many minor problems, participants may rightly judge it is not worth the bother of going through the five steps.

Retaining skills and preventing or overcoming relapses relies heavily on participants' using effective thinking skills once a group ends. Exercise 30 encourages you to examine how you might work with participants' thinking skills to consolidate trained skills as self-help skills.

Exercise 30 Consolidate Self-Help Skills: Work with Participants' Thinking Skills
▼▼

Make up a worksheet like the following one. In regard to a lifeskills training group of your choice, indicate how you might work with each of the listed thinking skills to help participants consolidate trained skills as self-help skills for when the group ends.

Thinking Skill	How You Might Work with It
Attributing cause accurately	
Possessing realistic rules	
Self-instructing	
Using coping self-talk	
Perceiving accurately	
Predicting realistically	
Using goal-setting skills	
Visualizing	
Using self-reward	
Using relapse-prevention skills	
Managing problems	

Summarize the main ways in which you might work with participants' thinking skills to facilitate consolidating self-help skills.

This exercise can also be done in a discussion format, either with or without individually completing the worksheet in advance.

Action Skills That Enhance Consolidation
▼▼

In addition to focusing on thinking, leaders can use other skills in the four stages of a group's life to help participants retain trained skills. These skills often have a thinking component. However, for the sake of simplicity, here they are categorized as action skills.

The Preparatory Stage

Leaders must be mindful of the need to consolidate self-help skills when they are designing programs and preparing groups. Following are some skills relevant to the preparatory stage.

Allowing for Overlearning

Goldstein and Keller (1987) state: "Overlearning involves the training of a skill beyond what is necessary to produce changes in behavior" (p. 116). Participants often require more than one or two trials using a skill to understand and use it properly. Then they may require homework and practice to integrate it into their repertoire of lifeskills. Consequently, when designing programs, it is important to allow for thoroughness in the number of trials for each specific skill. Program design strategies for overlearning include limiting the scope of the overall program, allowing for repeated skills demonstrations, emphasizing learning by doing, allowing for repeated trials, and ensuring adequate time and supervision for homework and practice.

Using Leaders' Aides in "Home" Environments

Though this strategy is not suitable for all groups, sometimes leaders can enlist the help of supportive people in participants' "home" environments and use them as leaders' aides. For instance, a leader running a friendship skills group in an elementary school can train teachers to understand, support, and reward children as they try using targeted skills in classrooms and playgrounds. Parents might also be enlisted as aides to help their children become more confident and better at using their friendship skills at home. Collaboration between leaders and outside group supports does not happen automatically. Leaders need to be systematic about creating roles for leaders' aides; contacting them; enlisting support; and, if necessary, training them in how best either to support participants or, at least, how not to do damage.

Advertising Realistically

Training-group leaders can realistically structure the expectations of prospective participants. For example, advertising can indicate that at most a group is a stepping-stone to acquiring and maintaining skills rather than a panacea. In addition, if and when conducting intake interviews, leaders can let potential participants know limitations as well as advantages of joining their groups. If an introductory group, most lifeskills will only be learned at a basic level. Even then, participants require continuous work and practice to prevent relapses and retain skills.

The Initial Stage

Structuring realistic expectations and developing participants' self-observation and assessment skills are two action strategies relevant to consolidating self-help skills that leaders can use in the group's initial stage.

Structuring Realistic Expectations

At the group's start, leaders can consolidate honest advertising and intake interviewing by stating the goals for the group realistically and not promising too much. Leaders can also emphasize the fixed length of the group so that it seems a positive opportunity for participants to make the most of the time. For example, a leader in a group on managing anger might say:

> We have ten sessions together. I know that all of you have been angry for much longer than that and are worried enough about the consequences of your anger to join this group. It requires a strong commitment on your part to develop some basic anger-management skills in ten sessions. During the group you will have to work hard to replace past unhelpful habits with new ways of thinking and acting. However, you should start seeing some positive results for yourselves and others from using your skills. After the group you will need to keep up the hard work to retain both your skills and also their benefits.

Developing Participants' Self-Observation and Assessment Skills

In the initial stage, if not before, leaders need to get participants assessing how they perform targeted skills. Such assessments provide a baseline against which participants can set personal goals and measure progress. Leaders can also help participants develop skills of self-observation and assessment and emphasize their importance for retaining lifeskills. Self-observation and assessment skills include making frequency counts and charting; devising and filling out either behavior logs or thinking, feeling, and behavior logs; asking for feedback; and openly acknowledging skills strengths and weaknesses.

The Working Stage

Group leader actions for consolidating self-help skills during the working stage include the following.

Using Leaders' Aides in "Home" Environments

Leaders' aides identified during the preparatory stage need attention during the group's working stage. Aides may require support, training, and assistance in how best to help participants. Also, leaders may get useful feedback from their aides on participants' progress.

Developing Participants' Self-Observation and Assessment Skills

Throughout groups, leaders need to maintain the emphasis on participants' becoming skilled observers and assessors of their own behavior. These skills are necessary both for evaluating progress and designing behavior-change plans.

Reminding the Group about its Finiteness

During groups, leaders can make statements that remind participants to work now for later benefits. For example, leaders might let participants know when it is their last opportunity in their group to work on a subskill. In addition, leaders may confront certain participants with the desirability of working harder and making more progress before the group ends. For instance, a leader might say, "What are going to be the consequences for you of maintaining your present level of skills after the group?"

Emphasizing Real-Lifeness

Paying attention in lifeskills groups to identical elements with natural settings means that the content of training possesses "real-lifeness" (Goldstein & Keller, 1987). The content of presentations and demonstrations should be tailored to real-life situations faced by participants. Behavior-rehearsal role-plays should resemble as closely as possible the real thing. Working in participants' natural settings—for example, in youth clubs—is another way to increase both relevance and also being perceived to be relevant. In addition, when participants learn skills in "home" environments, they are more likely to use them there afterward.

Training Diversely

Stokes and Osnes (1989) observe, "What has been frequently documented is the fact that focused training frequently has focused effects" (p. 345). Participants require flexibility when implementing lifeskills on their own. Leaders need to beware of narrow training. Regarding learning by observing, both multiple demonstrators and demonstrating the same skill in different scenes are strategies that enhance generalization and maintenance. Regarding learning by doing, participants can role-play using the same skill in different situations. Also, a single behavior-rehearsal role-play can have more than one trial, each with a different emphasis. For example, in a dating role-play, one trial can be with the date request being successful, another with the date request being questioned and then successful, and another with the date request being turned down.

Rehearsing Coping with Difficulties and Setbacks

Relapse prevention is not only a matter of thinking appropriately, but also of possessing appropriate action skills for coping with difficult situations. Action skills can be trained for in behavior-rehearsal role-plays. Participants can be "prepared for potential setbacks, unsympathetic relatives and friends, and unpredicted pressure through role-play of situations simulating [real-life] conditions" (Rose, 1986, p. 463).

Emphasizing Homework Tasks

Both leaders and participants require a commitment to homework as a bridge between learning and using skills. Homework should be a feature of all between-session periods. In the next session, participants should always have the opportunity to discuss their progress in homework tasks. Homework tasks can be assigned to give participants the opportunity to practice skills in diverse situations. In addition, difficulties and setbacks that participants experience can not only be discussed, but also be the focus of behavior-rehearsal role-plays.

Helping Participants Use Supports

Leaders and participants can work together on identifying people in "home" environments to support efforts to develop targeted skills. For example, supervisor trainees can seek out senior supervisors or managers to discuss how best to handle difficult situations such as underperforming workers. College students in study skills courses can seek out sympathetic faculty members who may help them develop specific skills, such as writing term papers or preparing for tests. Unemployed people can seek out friends and relatives who will not only provide them with emotional support, but also may be a source of job leads. Sometimes peer support is organized within training groups. Participants may adopt a buddy system in which they take an interest in each other's progress, for instance by phone calls. An inverse approach to support is to identify and avoid nonsupportive people. If these people are family members, avoiding them may be difficult. However, often people can choose their friendship and membership groups. For example, if juvenile delinquents want to change their ways it can be important for them to change the company they keep (Sarason, 1976).

Using Reward Strategies

Various reward strategies can be used by leaders to enhance skills transfer and maintenance (Goldstein & Keller, 1987; Stokes & Osnes, 1989). For instance, once a skill is initially acquired, leaders can reduce the regularity and frequency with which they reward participants for demonstrating it. In addition, prompts and reminders can be gradually faded. Leader aides can be trained in how to provide rewarding consequences for targeted behaviors enacted in participants' "home" environments. Also, participants can be taught how to recruit rewarding feedback tactfully. For example, they might ask friends or colleagues, "How's this?" or "How am I doing?"

Becoming a Consultant

As groups progress, leaders can alter the balance of how they play their roles. In a group's early stages, leaders may be more presenters, demonstrators, and coaches. In later stages, they may act more as consultants encouraging participants to work through how to think and act in specific situations. Leaders need to train participants in how to be effective on their own.

Exercise 31 is designed to get you thinking about how you might act in the preparatory, initial, and working stages of training groups to consolidate participants' self-help skills.

Exercise 31 Consolidate Self-Help Skills: Action Skills for the Preparatory, Initial, and Working Stages
▼▼

In regard to a lifeskills training group of your choice, indicate how you might use each of the following skills to help participants consolidate trained skills as self-help skills for when the group ends.

The preparatory stage

Allowing for overlearning
Using leaders' aides in participants' "home" environments
Advertising realistically

The initial stage

Structuring realistic expectations
Developing participants' self-observation and assessment skills

The working stage

Using leaders' aides in participants' "home" environments
Developing participants' self-observation and assessment skills
Reminding the group of its finiteness
Emphasizing real-lifeness
Training diversely
Rehearsing coping with difficulties and setbacks
Emphasizing homework tasks
Helping participants use supports
Using reward strategies
Becoming a consultant

Are there any other interventions you might use before the group's ending stage to consolidate self-help skills? If so, please specify.

The Ending Stage
▼▼

As indicated in the discussion on preparing for ending, in training groups there is no clear division between the ending stage and its preceding stages. The ending stage might start at the conclusion of the penultimate session with a homework assignment focused on self-assessment and postgroup plans for retaining and developing targeted skills. The ending stage concludes when all scheduled contact between participants and leaders finishes.

Formats for the Ending Stage

Some participants may drop out of training groups either because they are dissatisfied or because their life circumstances change. Here, the focus is on ending formats chosen by leaders. The following are possible formats:

Ending when individual goals have been attained: Ending on goal attainment implies open rather than closed training groups. Participants set themselves personal goals. They leave groups when they, together with their leaders, consider their targeted skills attained. Leaders running open groups tend to fill leavers' places from waiting lists. Open groups do not run forever. Therefore, some participants will be faced with specific cutoff points for developing skills by when a group ends.

Ending at the last regularly scheduled session: Many, if not most, training groups meet on a regular basis and terminate at the end of the last scheduled session.

Faded ending: Here the group's ending is gradual. For example, instead of meeting weekly, the group's final two sessions may be at biweekly or even monthly intervals.

Massed ending: Massed ending is the opposite of faded ending. The group, which may have been meeting weekly for two hours, ends with an all-day or a weekend marathon session.

Regular ending plus one or more follow-up group sessions: The follow-up sessions are not to teach new skills, but to assess participants' postgroup progress, motivate them, and help work through difficulties in translating trained skills into "home" environments.

Regular ending plus individual interview(s) or phone call(s) with leaders: The timing of individual interviews can vary. Some leaders conduct exit interviews to help participants set personal goals and develop strategies for consolidating self-help skills. These individual interviews may be as brief as fifteen to thirty minutes. Other leaders find it more valuable to schedule follow-up interviews three to six months after final group sessions. Leaders can also schedule follow-up phone calls with participants. In addition, leaders can indicate if and under what circumstances participants can initiate phone calls and interviews with them. Leaders may also contact participants and ask them to complete questionnaires evaluating postgroup progress.

Different permutations of the preceding: For example, massed endings could be followed either by booster sessions three to six months later or by one or more individual interviews with leaders.

Consolidating Self-Help Skills

The main leader task of the ending stage is to help participants further consolidate their trained skills as self-help skills. Many skills that leaders use during this stage build on skills used earlier in a group. Following are some skills for enabling consolidation in the ending stage.

Making Transition Statements

Mention has already been made of making reminder statements concerning a group's finiteness to encourage participants to make the most of meetings. One or more transition statements that introduce the ending stage can reinforce earlier reminders. The following are possible transition statements:

"Our next session is the final session. Maybe we should discuss how we can use the time we have left, including the time between sessions, to help you retain and build on the skills you've learned when the group ends."

"Since this is the start of the final session, in this session I want to focus on helping you integrate the skills you've learned in the group so that they become part of your daily lives. This integration includes assessing how much you have changed, identifying where you still need to change, and committing yourself to personal goals and to developing skills of dealing with setbacks.''

Summarizing

Approaches to summarizing include the following. During final sessions, the main learnings conveyed throughout groups can be summarized by leaders. Alternatively, participants might summarize the main learnings either in the whole group or in pairs or small groups. Summarizing is more personal if participants summarize the main learnings they personally found useful. Formulating a personal summary can be a homework assignment prior to final sessions. Participants might also be asked to record their summaries on cassettes as reminders for afterward. In addition, leaders may distribute handouts summarizing the group's main learnings. Leaders may use more than one of these ways of summarizing.

Facilitating Self-Assessment, Goal Setting, and Planning

During the ending stage, leaders continue to develop participants' skills of self-observation and assessment. Leaders can administer end-of-group self-assessment questionnaires. One option is to administer such a questionnaire in the final session. However, for a committed group, a better option may be to administer a questionnaire at the penultimate session as a homework task. The advantages of homework completion of questionnaires are that the questionnaire does not use up contact time; participants have more time to think about their answers; participants can assess progress if ending questionnaires are similar to beginning questionnaires; and participants have more time to think through postgroup personal goals and develop plans to attain them.

During final sessions, leaders and participants need to review assessments, personal goals, and plans to attain them. In addition, leaders can help participants devise ways of assessing themselves once groups end. For instance, leaders can hand out self-assessment worksheets for evaluating postgroup progress.

Giving and Facilitating Feedback

Feedback during final sessions can be useful for helping participants assess their progress over the group's life. Participants may receive leaders' and other participant's perceptions of their strengths and weaknesses, unhelpful ways of thinking and behaving, hopes for their future, ways to handle specific situations, and the adequacy of their personal goals and plans. Participants should be asked to give constructively critical as well as positive feedback. Constructive feedback gives participants further insights for goal setting and planning. Open acknowledgment by others of positive behavior changes motivates participants to keep working.

Reinforcing Effective Thinking Skills

Leaders can use the ending stage to reinforce thinking skills that help participants retain and develop trained skills. Effective thinking skills include those for attributing cause accurately, possessing realistic rules, self-instructing, using coping self-talk, goal setting, relapse prevention, and managing problems. Before the final session, leaders should introduce any thinking skills conducive to retaining targeted skills; the final session is almost too late. During the final session, leaders can review the use of previously presented thinking skills, both by way of summaries and also when dealing with participants' personal agendas.

Rehearsing Coping with Difficulties and Setbacks

Rehearsing coping with difficulties and setbacks should be a part of role-plays during groups, not an afterthought left until the final session. Nevertheless, in the final session, leaders can fruitfully take groups through some useful strategies for coping with difficulties, setbacks, and reentry problems. Leaders can emphasize that even though participants can only influence other people, they can have considerable power over their own behavior. Therefore, when in difficulty, looking at the adequacy of one's own thinking, behavior, and use of targeted skills is the best place to start. Participants can ask themselves such questions as "What are my goals and how is my behavior helping me attain them?" "What might I be thinking or doing that blocks my effectiveness?" and "How well am I using the skills I have learned and how can I improve?" Action strategies for dealing with setbacks vary considerably depending on the focus of the lifeskills training group.

Working with Leaders' Aides in "Home" Environments

At the ending stage, leaders can contact their aides to receive assessments of participants' progress outside the group. Leaders can also work with aides to identify ways in which they can support participants once programs end. Sometimes a three-way meeting between leader, participant, and aide is desirable. For example, at the end of a supervisory skills training program, leader, trainee supervisor, and manager could together plan how the supervisor might continue receiving appropriate learning experiences and feedback.

Helping Participants Use Supports

During groups, leaders should help participants identify and use supports for learning targeted skills. At groups' endings, leaders can help participants identify and use supports for maintaining and developing targeted skills. These supports may not be the same people who helped them during groups. For instance, some participants might continue the buddy system with partners they had worked with during a group. Alternatively, one or more participants might decide to enter peer self-help groups independent of their training groups.

Arranging for Follow-Up Leader–Participant Contact

Given the high probability of some degree of relapse in using targeted skills, leaders need to think through whether and how they might schedule follow-up contact with participants. Options include whole group booster sessions; individual interviews, either scheduled or at participants' request; phone calls, either scheduled or at participants' request; and follow-up questionnaires. In addition, groups may schedule social reunions during which progress and strategies for coping with difficulties are discussed. However, good attendance at reunions cannot be guaranteed.

Providing Information on Skills-Building Opportunities

Leaders can provide information on resources participants can use to improve skills. Sometimes, leaders refer participants for counseling help. Referral discussions are best conducted on an individual basis. Suggestions can be made of counselors and psychotherapists with a cognitive-behavioral orientation, preferably within a humanistic-existential framework. Also, leaders can discuss opportunities for further training groups, courses, or workshops, run by themselves or others. Leaders can review skills for choosing other lifeskills groups, including what to avoid.

Suggesting Further Reading and Audiovisual Material

If not using training manuals, participants may retain information by receiving session handouts and storing them in binders. In the final session, leaders can give out and go through annotated lists of further reading suggestions. Participants learn in different ways. Some benefit from having their postgroup attempts to learn reinforced by self-help reading. In addition, participants can be referred to appropriate self-help cassettes and videos.

Exercise 32 builds on Exercise 31 by encouraging you to think through ending-stage strategies for consolidating trained skills as self-help skills.

Exercise 32 Consolidate Self-Help Skills in the Ending Stage
▼▼

In regard to a lifeskills training group of your choice, indicate how, during the group's ending stage, you might use each of the following skills to help participants consolidate trained skills as self-help skills for when the group finishes.

Making transition statements
Summarizing
Facilitating self-assessment, goal setting, and planning
Giving and facilitating feedback
Reinforcing effective thinking skills
Rehearsing coping with difficulties and setbacks
Working with leaders' aides in participants' "home" environments
Helping participants use supports
Arranging for follow-up leader–participant contact
Providing information on skills-building opportunities
Suggesting further reading and audiovisual material
Other skills not mentioned previously

Summarize how you as a leader would aim, during your group's ending stage, to help participants consolidate trained skills as self-help skills.

Further Ending-Stage Tasks and Agendas

Along with the major task of consolidating self-help skills, there are other tasks for the ending stage of training groups. Leaders and the group can choose how much time and emphasis to allocate to each task.

Evaluating the Group

In the final session, participants can make unstructured comments about the group's degree of success and the reasons for their observations. Alternatively, leaders can initiate rounds in which each participant has the opportunity to share views. Leaders can also share their thoughts and feelings about the group's processes and outcomes. Another possibility is for participants to fill in end-of-group questionnaires, either before, during, or possibly after the final session. Training groups being researched may have extra time set aside for posttest evaluation. Also, rigorous researchers schedule follow-up evaluations.

Evaluating the Leader(s)

During training groups, all leaders receive informal feedback and some collect systematic feedback on how participants react to them and perceive their skills. The main focus at the group's end should be on participants' needs. However, leaders can also solicit feedback about themselves. One method is to ask an open-ended question: "Does anyone have anything they would like to feed back to me about the way I led the group?" Leaders can also encourage each participant to comment about their leadership, either in front of the group or by answering end-of-group questionnaires.

Dealing with Emotional Business

Training groups tend to be less emotionally charged than long-term counseling and psychotherapy groups. Nevertheless, participants may have feelings of sadness, anxiety, and possibly abandonment when the time comes for the group to end. Other participants may breathe a sigh of relief. Ideally, most participants will have a sense of accomplishment. Leaders can facilitate open discussion of feelings about the group's ending. Training groups spend much less time and effort than interactional groups on trying to work through unfinished emotional business either between participants or between participants and leaders.

Saying Goodbye

Leaders should pay close attention to how they close the group's final session. Much earlier good work can be undone through closing the session sloppily. Assuming the group has worked hard, leaders' verbal, voice, and body messages should communicate appreciation of this fact. If leaders have enjoyed working with the group, they can share this feeling. Last impressions as well as first impressions are important. In addition, participants want to say goodbye to each other and possibly exchange phone numbers and addresses. Some participants may want to go for an end-of-group drink or meal, either immediately after the final session or at a later date.

Ending Ethically

A number of important ethical issues surround how leaders terminate training groups. For example, if participants clearly have major unresolved personal issues at a group's end, leaders should offer individual interviews. Another issue is how much support to offer participants after the group. Leader support can be important for participants as they try out their skills. However, too much support can engender dependency. Still another ethical issue is that of being honest about the limitations of groups and not overselling them. As stressed throughout this chapter, participants need to be prepared for a continuous struggle to retain and develop skills. A further issue is that of confidentiality. Leaders can remind participants of their ethical obligation to keep confidences.

Concluding Comment

▼▼▼

Ending stages of lifeskills training groups represent beginnings too. The closure of the ending stage represents a commencement of the need for participants to consolidate trained skills on their own. This consolidation of trained skills as self-help skills is a lifelong endeavor. For those participants able to retain some or all of their trained skills, the rewards to themselves and others should justify the effort.

▼ Chapter Highlights

▼ Leaders should not "train and hope" that their group will have a lasting effect on participants. Instead, in all the group's stages, leaders must use strategies to help participants consolidate trained skills as self-help skills.

▼ Generalization, transfer, maintenance, and development are four important dimensions of consolidating trained skills as self-help skills.

▼ Leader thinking skills relevant to consolidating participants' self-help skills include attributing cause accurately, possessing realistic rules, and predicting realistically.

▼ Participant thinking skills relevant to consolidating self-help skills include attributing cause accurately, possessing realistic rules, self-instructing, using coping self-talk, predicting realistically, using goal-setting skills, visualizing, using self-reward, using relapse-prevention skills, and managing problems.

▼ Skills for leaders to use at the preparatory stage for consolidating participants' self-help skills include allowing for overlearning, using leaders' aides in participants' "home" environments, and advertising realistically.

▼ Skills for leaders to use at the initial stage for consolidating participants' self-help skills include structuring realistic expectations and developing participants' self-observation and assessment skills.

▼ Skills for leaders to use at the working stage for consolidating participants' self-help skills include using leaders' aides in participants' "home" environments, developing participants' self-observation and assessment skills, reminding the group of its finiteness, emphasizing real-lifeness, training diversely, rehearsing coping with difficulties and setbacks, emphasizing homework tasks, helping participants using supports, using reward strategies, and becoming a consultant.

▼ Different formats exist for the ending stage of lifeskills groups. These formats include follow-up contact with the leader in either group sessions or individual interviews.

▼ Skills for leaders to use at the ending stage for consolidating participants' self-help skills include making transition statements;

(continued)

▼ **Chapter Highlights** (continued)

summarizing; facilitating self-assessment, goal setting, and planning; giving and facilitating feedback; reinforcing effective thinking skills; rehearsing coping with difficulties and setbacks; working with leaders' aides in participants' "home" environments; helping participants use supports; arranging for follow-up leader–participant contact; providing information on skills-building opportunities; and suggesting further reading and audiovisual material.

▼ Further ending-stage tasks and agendas include evaluating the group, evaluating the leader, dealing with emotional business, saying goodbye, and ending ethically.

12

How to Evaluate and Research a Training Group

The whole of science is nothing more than a
refinement of everyday thinking.

Albert Einstein

Chapter Questions

What information might leaders collect when evaluating themselves and a training group?

What evaluative questions might leaders ask of participants?

What are the main variables to consider in researching a training group?

What designs are appropriate for researching a training group?

Introduction

This chapter on evaluating and researching a training group builds on the earlier discussions regarding designing a lifeskills program in Chapter 4 and assessment and helping self-assessment in Chapter 5. Effective training-group leaders monitor and evaluate throughout their groups. Participants, interested third parties, supervisors, and researchers are among others who evaluate training groups. Here, three approaches to end-of-group evaluation are reviewed: leader self-evaluation, participant evaluation, and evaluation by research.

Leader Self-Evaluation

By a group's end, leaders have many sources of information for evaluating themselves. These sources of information include recollections and impressions (Whitaker, 1985), session notes, journal entries (Corey, Corey, Callanan, & Russell, 1988), verbal feedback, written feedback, comments made at postgroup interviews, feedback from colleagues and interested third parties, video feedback, attendance, and compliance with homework tasks. Leaders need to evaluate their experiences soon after the group ends; otherwise, they risk forgetting valuable information.

Leader self-evaluation has numerous purposes. First, it can give leaders an opportunity to gain more perspective on their groups. Second, they can get a clearer idea of how successful their groups have been. Third, they can get affirmation that their efforts have made a positive difference. Fourth, leaders can identify processes and factors contributing to both positive and negative outcomes. Fifth, leaders can identify skills strengths to maintain and skills weaknesses on which to work. Sixth, they can clarify ideas for leading future groups.

Leader self-evaluation need not be a long and arduous process. Here is a series of questions that leaders can ask themselves to guide self-evaluation.

Leader Self-Evaluation Questions

1. To what extent did the group achieve its overall goal and broad subgoals? How do I know?
2. To what extent were individual participants satisfied that they had attained their personal goals as a result of the group? How do I know?
3. Where there any additional positive and negative outcomes from running the group?
4. Did I set sufficiently clear and realistic goals for the group?
5. Am I satisfied both with the program I used and with the way it was designed?
6. Am I satisfied with the group's size and composition?
7. Did I lay sufficient groundwork and consult adequately with third parties with an interest in the group?
8. Did I have a sufficiently clear contract with participants?
9. Am I happy with the ways in which I encouraged participants to assess themselves and to set personal goals?
10. Am I satisfied with the way I opened the group and conducted the initial session?
11. Under what circumstances and how well did I use facilitation skills during the group?
12. How satisfied am I with the written training material I used?
13. What were my public-speaking skills strengths and weaknesses?
14. What were my demonstration skills strengths and weaknesses?
15. What were my skills strengths and weaknesses in using structured activity?
16. How satisfied am I with how I used and monitored between-session homework?
17. How satisfied am I with the way I planned individual sessions during the group's working stage?
18. How satisfied am I with the way I conducted individual sessions during the group's working stage?
19. What strategies for consolidating trained skills as self-help skills did I use and how effective did they seem?
20. How well did I end the group?
21. How satisfied am I with the way I identified and handled ethical issues arising from the group?
22. Did I have adequate personal and professional support and supervision when leading the group?
23. What aspects of leading the group did I find rewarding and what aspects less rewarding?
24. What specifically did I learn about my style and skills for leading training groups?
25. What are my goals for improving my performance as a training-group leader?
26. Should I continue to lead training groups and, if so, in what life-skills areas?

When leaders evaluate themselves they need to beware of tendencies to perceptual distortion. Two important perceptual skills are the ability to distinguish between facts and inferences and to make your inferences lead logically out of the available facts. Some leaders may be so intent on validating their efforts that they selectively perceive positive feedback and weigh it too highly. At the other extreme are leaders who discount successes and excessively dwell on shortcomings. Other perceptual errors that interfere with self-evaluation include black-and-white thinking, such as deciding the group is either going extremely well or extremely badly; tunnel vision, focusing on only a portion of the available information in situations rather than taking into account all significant data; and self-rating, going beyond functional ratings of specific characteristics of your group leadership to devaluing yourself as a whole person (Beck, 1976; Beck & Emery, 1985; Beck & Weishaar, 1989; Nelson-Jones, 1990a).

Participant Evaluation
▼▼▼

Leaders can get participants to evaluate lifeskills training groups in two main ways. First, participants can evaluate what they learned from the group and how helpful it was for attaining personal goals. Second, participants can evaluate group processes and leader skills.

Self-Assessment

Participants can be asked to fill in self-assessment forms before or at the final session and at follow-up sessions. Here are some of the questions that might be asked.

Participant Self-Assessment Questions
▼▼▼

1. List each of your goals on joining this training group. How satisfied are you with your progress in attaining each goal?
2. In what specific situations, if any, are you coping better as a result of skills developed in the group?
3. With what specific people are you coping better as a result of skills developed in this group?
4. What kinds of difficulties and setbacks did you encounter when you tried to implement your skills outside the group?
5. What coping strategies did you find helpful when you faced difficulties and setbacks in implementing trained skills outside the group?
6. What kinds of feedback and support did you receive from significant people in your life when you tried to implement your skills?

7. What, if any, negative outcomes and consequences has your participation in the group had for you?
8. How actively did you participate in the learning process in the group?
9. How actively did you participate in homework tasks outside the group?
10. What are your goals for maintaining and developing your skills after the group?
11. How do you intend to assess your postgroup progress?
12. What difficulties and setbacks do you anticipate in implementing your skills after the group and how do you plan to cope with each?

Evaluation of Group

Leaders can also systematically collect participants' perceptions of how skillfully they led groups. An issue here is whether or not to allow the feedback to be anonymous. Gazda (1989) favors anonymous posttreatment questionnaires. Perceptions of group experiences may change over time, so follow-up data may be of interest. Simple end-of-group questionnaires can consist of four items:

1. A rating of the group on a scale of 1 (no good at all) to 7 (excellent).
2. "State as specifically as possible what you consider the strengths of the group to have been."
3. "Indicate as specifically as possible what areas of the group are in need of improvement."
4. "Make any other comments in the space below."

Participants can evaluate groups and leaders both in more detail and also more systematically than this. For example, participants could be asked to rate and provide comments on usefulness of sessions, effectiveness of each intervention, and dimensions of leadership such as acceptance, warmth, competence, attractiveness, cultural sensitivity, trustworthiness, and respect. Readers are referred to the section in Chapter 5 on devising assessment measures for further ideas on ways to design simple evaluation procedures.

Evaluation by Research

▼▼

The great tragedy of Science—the slaying of a beautiful hypothesis by an ugly fact.

T. H. Huxley

Dictionary definitions of research tend to use adjectives like *careful* and *systematic* and nouns like *study*, *inquiry*, and *investigation*.

Research into lifeskills training groups involves systematically studying their processes and outcomes. Training-group leaders can conduct research solely for their own benefits. Alternatively, leaders can publish and share research findings with others. Leaders can also invite third parties to conduct research into their groups. The fact that already a research literature on training groups exists gives researchers a base for designing further studies.

Research into lifeskills training groups can be of different degrees of methodological tightness. Training groups do not lend themselves to the kind of almost total environmental control sometimes achievable in the natural sciences. Also, many variables in training groups, such as leader empathy, do not lend themselves to precise quantification. Consequently, at best, training-group researchers are limited in the extent to which the content and outcomes of their studies will be reliable and valid. What training-group researchers must strive for is the maximum degree of tightness they can attain. Always, they need to be conscious of actual and potential sources of invalidity in their work. Furthermore, training-group researchers need to beware of misinterpreting and overinterpreting findings. In addition, they should always view their findings in the context of relevant findings from other studies.

Research Variables

Leaders require clear goals for any research they conduct into their groups. Research goals need to be formulated in the group's preparatory stage; otherwise, necessary baseline data may not be collected. What can be looked at in training groups? Following are suggestions of variables, sometimes interrelated, that might be explored.

Leader Variables

Leader variables include age, sex, race, culture, socioeconomic status, professional training, relevant background and experience, leadership style, theoretical orientation, facilitative skills, didactic skills, emotional well-being, thinking skills, attitudes and values, perceived trustworthiness, perceived attractiveness, perceived competence, nonverbal communication, access to support and supervision, and expectations (Beutler, Crago, & Arizmendi, 1986; Rose, 1986; Smith & Glass, 1977).

Participant Variables

Participant variables include age, sex, race, culture, socioeconomic status, education, occupation, emotional well-being, attitudes and values, expectations, commitment to the group, self-disclosure, nonverbal communication, thinking skills, group attendance, and homework compliance rates (Garfield, 1986; Rose, 1986).

Process Variables

Process variables consist of specific details regarding the content and management of training programs. Process variables include group size, pregroup training, type of group, focus of group, number of sessions, frequency of sessions, duration of sessions, use of training manual, balance of discussion and didactic input, verbal presentations, method and use of demonstrations, use of structured activities, use of homework tasks, and postgroup contact (Gazda, 1989; Matarazzo & Patterson, 1986).

Outcome Variables

The main outcome variables for training groups are participants' performances in targeted skills. Additional outcome variables include premature termination and level of satisfaction. Outcome variables may focus on individual as well as on group change. Methods of assessing outcomes were reviewed in Chapter 5. Assessment methods include participant self-observation and monitoring, observation in natural settings, psychological tests and lifeskills inventories, and leader-designed measures.

Training group researchers can explore relationships among these variables. For example, level of satisfaction with groups might be explored in relation to racial and cultural similarity between leaders and participants.

Research Designs

Basically, two main groupings of research designs exist for investigating lifeskills training groups: comparison group designs and single group designs.

Comparison Group Designs

The most common design in the group work literature is that based on a control group and an experimental group. Gazda (1989) reports that 70 percent of the group studies published in 1983–87 that he reviewed used some form of a control group. In the case of an assertiveness program, those undergoing the intervention would form the experimental group, whereas the control group would be a no-treatment condition. Comparison group designs can be more elaborate. For example, as well as the control group, there could be three experimental groups, each with a different focus. For instance, one assertiveness group could emphasize group discussion, another demonstration and structured activities, with the third combining group discussion with demonstration and structured activities.

A minimum requirement for comparison group designs is that of pretest and posttest administrations of evaluation or assessment measures. By administering pretests and posttests to experimental and control groups, researchers can then infer that positive changes in targeted skills found in experimental groups above those found in control groups are attributable to experimental interventions. With more than one experimental group, researchers not only investigate whether the experimental interventions make a difference over no treatment, but also which interventions are more effective than others.

Wherever possible, training-group researchers should administer follow-up measures. Follow-up data allow researchers to infer the extent to which trained skills are retained and consolidated as self-help skills. If a training group is designed with a postgroup booster session, follow-up data can be collected in conjunction with this session. However, the presence or absence of a booster session also lends itself to research. For example, participants may be more inclined to retain skills knowing there will be a booster session than if there is no booster session. Thus, not only is it important for training-group researchers to discover whether or not groups have lasting effects, but also to discover the processes whereby transfer, generalization, and development of skills can be enhanced.

Webster-Stratton and her colleagues provide an example of a life-skills group study using a control group, three treatment conditions, and collection of follow-up data (Webster-Stratton, 1989; Webster-Stratton, Hollinsworth, & Kolpacoff, 1989; Webster-Stratton, Kolpacoff, & Hollinsworth, 1988). Parents of conduct problem children were randomly assigned to either a waiting-list control group or to one of three treatment programs: (1) video modeling of parenting techniques plus group discussion focused on the videotaped vignettes; (2) group discussion of the same topics covered in the videotapes, but without seeing the videotapes; and (3) self-administered watching of the videotapes without group discussion. Research measures were completed at baseline, immediately after treatment, and at a one-year follow-up. These measures included mothers and fathers answering two checklists on their children's behavior and also a parenting stress inventory; teachers filling out a questionnaire on the children's behavior; mothers filling out a daily report on their children's behavior during the assessment periods; and direct observation of mother–child and father–child interactions in the home. In addition, a consumer satisfaction questionnaire was administered.

Some advantages of comparison group studies have already been indicated. Such studies are experimental in that they allow for intervention hypotheses to be tested against control-group performance. Also, they allow for comparisons to be made among various interventions. Disadvantages include the extra time and effort involved in measuring control groups. Most leaders find running lifeskills training groups time-consuming enough as it is. In addition, there are ethical issues entailed in withholding treatment from control groups. Such issues may be mitigated if control groups are waiting groups that receive the same training programs soon. However, providing training for control groups shortly after experimental groups end limits collection of comparative follow-up data. Comparison group designs may also be criticized on the grounds of paying insufficient attention to "moment-to-moment behavior changes or individual variations in responding" (Thoresen & Mahoney, 1974, p. 34). This criticism is not fully justified since, in comparison group designs, individual data can be analyzed and reported along with group data.

Single Group Designs

Gazda (1989) reports that 95 percent of the studies he reviewed from 1970 to 1976, 91 percent from 1976 to 1980, and 70 percent from 1983 to 1987 used some form of control group. He observes: "This decrease may be due in part to research utilizing a variety of experimental designs that do not necessitate a defined control group" (p. 318). Single case research designs are increasingly used in counseling and psychotherapy research (Kazdin, 1982, 1986; Tracey, 1983). Kazdin (1986) writes: "Single case experiments permit inferences to be drawn about intervention effects by using the patient as his or her own control. The impact of treatment is examined in relation to changes in the patient's dysfunction over time" (p. 39). He states that there are four main characteristics of single case experiments: clear specification of goals, use of repeated observations, the delineation of time periods in which different conditions (baseline, treatment) apply, and relative stability of data—the more variable the data, the more difficult it is to draw conclusions about intervention effects.

Single case designs and single group designs both overlap and differ. Single group designs allow for the analyzing and reporting of group data either with or instead of individual data. Useful inferences can be drawn from single group designs without satisfying each of Kazdin's characteristics of single case designs. For example, group data may still be of value despite Kazdin's condition of repeated observations, such as daily frequency counts of targeted behaviors, not being met. Also, in single group designs, if use is not made of repeated measures, Kazdin's characteristic of stability of data cannot be assessed. When designing any training-group study, researchers must always consider the advantages and disadvantages of collecting repeated-measures data in addition to data from pretest, posttest, and follow-up administrations.

These single group designs can be used for evaluating lifeskills groups:

Pretest/posttest design: Group data can be analyzed and reported with a pretest/posttest design. Pretest/posttest designs have the advantage of simplicity. However, pretest/posttest designs without control groups have the disadvantage that researchers cannot make rigorous inferences about cause and effect.

Waiting-list control design: A waiting-list control design entails a minimum of three measurements. Take the example of an eight-week weight-loss group. The first measure might be eight weeks prior to the start of the group, the second measure at the group's start, and the third measure at the group's end. The eight-week time interval before the group starts is a no-treatment control period. The waiting-list control design can be viewed as an experimental design. Researchers can compare changes taking place during the program with any change that may have taken place with no treatment. However, the notion of no treatment is contaminated by the fact that the expectancy of treatment may influence behavior.

Pretest/posttest/follow-up test design: In the pretest/posttest/follow-up test design, instead of the no-treatment period being before the program starts, it takes place immediately after the program ends. Again, the importance of collecting follow-up data is stressed. However, the use of a follow-up period for control purposes has distinct limitations. First, researchers cannot equate a no-treatment period with a withdrawal of treatment at the end of the group period. In the former, participants have had no treatment; in the latter, they have experienced the intervention. Second, many lifeskills training groups heavily emphasize consolidating trained skills as self-help skills for when groups end. This emphasis makes the assumption of equivalency between a pregroup and a postgroup control period even more problematic.

Waiting-list control/pretest/posttest/follow-up test design: Where possible, this is the optimum design for much single group research. This design has the twin advantages of a reasonably "pure" waiting-list control period and also the collection of follow-up data.

Reversal design: Inasmuch as the group intervention is withdrawn or reversed, the pretest/posttest/follow-up test design can be viewed as a reversal design. However, probably the most popular reversal design in single case research is the ABAB design (Thoresen & Mahoney, 1974). The ABAB design can be restricted to four administrations of measures: pretreatment, end of first treatment period, end of reversal period, and end of second treatment period. However, often the ABAB design entails also taking repeated measures. For example, in a management-of-smoking lifeskills group, repeated measures of smoking behavior might be taken during the following four periods: A, prior to the intervention; B, during the first administration of the intervention; A, during a period when the intervention is withdrawn; and B, during the period when the intervention is reinstated. The reversal to a no-treatment condition is meant to help show that any changes that take place are influenced by the treatment condition: their incidence falls off when treatment is withdrawn and increases when treatment resumes.

From a research viewpoint, there are limitations to ABAB reversal designs. For example, frequently performance does not reverse to baseline levels in the reversal phase. Indeed, the whole emphasis in lifeskills training groups is that it should not. Consequently, assuming reversibility in reversal control periods is questionable. Also, there are practical limitations to ABAB reversal designs. Training groups tend to be run continuously rather than on a start-stop-start-stop basis. Training groups with a no-treatment period in the middle may be difficult to organize and also contribute to participant dropout. Furthermore, even participants who remain may feel used as research guinea pigs and be resentful. Such resentment adversely affects the group's emotional climate and may create resistances to participation and learning. The use of repeated measures may be perceived by participants as more relevant for some training groups, such as weght loss and managing smoking, than for others, such as managing conflict. In any event, to gain compliance, requests for repeatedly filling in self-observations need to be sensitively made. In addition, there are ethical reservations about withdrawing and then reinstating treatment unless, in the long run, this is to participants' advantage.

Multiple baseline design: In multiple baseline designs, a minimum of two baselines are required. Thoresen and Mahoney (1974) give the example of baseline data being collected for four personal hygiene behaviors. First, nail biting is treated for several weeks, while the remainder of the behaviors remain untreated. Then toothbrushing is added to the currently-under-treatment category while the other two behaviors remain untreated. Ultimately, all four behaviors are treated. Multiple baseline designs seek to demonstrate that targeted behaviors change only when interventions are applied. There are a number of limitations to multiple baseline designs. First, the design assumes that the baselines are independent and that an intervention focused on one behavior will not change others. This assumption of baseline independence is not always tenable. Second, in training groups, it is often desirable to teach general rules and thinking skills in addition to targeting specific behaviors. For instance, at the start of personal hygiene programs, some general rules presented, such as the need to assume responsibility for health, are relevant to most, if not all, personal hygiene behaviors. It is poor pedagogic practice to target specific hygiene behaviors alone. Third, ethical issues exist in withholding treatment for behaviors subject to a prolonged baseline period.

Leaders and researchers can evaluate single group data in a number of ways. First, the data can be subjected to visual inspection. Changes and trends can be observed, both for groups and individuals.

Where individual as well as group data are reported, interesting observations may be made about presence or lack of individual progress that might be disguised in group data. Second, the data can be evaluated statistically. Statistical analyses may entail use of conventional t and F tests, time series analysis, and randomization tests. Third, the data can be evaluated in terms of their practical validity for leaders and participants. Do the data make practical and therapeutic sense? Fourth, attempts can be made to replicate data from training-group studies. Tracey (1983) uses Chassan's (1979) distinction between direct and systematic replication. In direct replication, leaders and researchers conduct and investigate second or third lifeskills training groups run like the first in as many ways as possible. In systematic replication, some variables of interest are changed in each subsequent single group study.

When designing and leading lifeskills training groups, all leaders should regard themselves as hypothesis makers and testers. Leaders should be applied scientists doing their best to learn from both past and current experiences. At the very least, all training-group leaders should engage in self-evaluation, invite participant evaluation of the group experience, and foster participant self-assessment. The degree to which leaders participate in more rigorous forms of evaluative research depends on numerous factors such as their current interests, the time available, their research skills, and what research support they can call on. Most leaders should be able to manage a straightforward single group pretest/posttest/follow-up test evaluative sequence in addition to collecting and analyzing less formal evaluation questionnaires. Exercise 33 has been designed to develop your skills of evaluating lifeskills training groups.

Exercise 33 Evaluate a Lifeskills Training Group
▼ ▼

Either for the lifeskills training group you designed in Exercise 6 or for another training group, answer the following questions:

1. *Leader self-evaluation*: What questions do you think it important to ask yourself to evaluate your work with the group?

2. *Participant evaluation*: What questions do you think it important to ask participants so they evaluate (a) their own progress, and (b) the group experience and your work as leader?

3. *Research evaluation*: Design a research study evaluating your lifeskills training group using either a comparison group or a single group design. Make sure to specify the goals for your research, what measures you intend using, when you will take measurements, and any scientific, practical, or ethical problems with your research design.

Concluding Comment

▼ ▼

A continuing need exists for well-designed and well-conducted research studies on lifeskills group processes and outcomes. Though much has been achieved, further creative and well-executed studies are still badly needed in all lifeskills training areas (Martin, 1990). Such studies are likely to go beyond the resources of most group leaders. Nevertheless, the need for high-quality applied research into training groups is great. Applied researchers and research funding bodies have a big role to play in creating a sound data base for future lifeskills training practice.

▼ Chapter Highlights

▼ Effective training-group leaders monitor and evaluate throughout their groups.

▼ Leader self-evaluation after a group ends has numerous purposes: gaining perspective, assessing the degree of goal attainment, receiving affirmation, identifying what interventions work, and assessing your own strengths and weaknesses in leading training groups.

▼ When self-evaluating, leaders must counteract tendencies to perceptual distortion.

▼ Leaders can encourage participants to evaluate their group experience in two main ways: first, evaluating what they learned from the group and how helpful it was for attaining personal goals; and second, evaluating group processes and leader skills.

▼ Leaders require clear goals for any research that they conduct into their groups.

▼ Clusters of variables that training-group researchers can investigate include leader variables, participant variables, process variables, and outcome variables.

▼ Two main categories of research designs for studying lifeskills training groups are comparison group designs and single group designs.

▼ As a minimum, a comparison group design requires pretests and posttests on both control and experimental groups.

▼ Variations in the basic comparison group design include adding follow-up tests and using comparison groups with treatment modifications.

▼ Single case research designs and single group research designs both overlap and differ. Single group designs allow for the analyzing and reporting of group data with or instead of individual repeated-measures data.

▼ The optimum design for much single group research is the waiting-list control/pretest/posttest/follow-up test design.

(continued)

▼ **Chapter Highlights** (continued)

   ▼ Single group data can be evaluated by visual inspection, statistical analyses, determining whether or not they make practical or therapeutic sense, and by attempts at replication.

   ▼ Researchers into training groups should always be mindful of any scientific, practical, and ethical limitations and issues in their studies.

   ▼ A continuing need exists for well-designed and well-conducted research studies on training-group processes and outcomes.

13

How to Maintain and Develop Training-Group Leadership Skills

The toe of the star-gazer is often stubbed.

Russian proverb

Chapter Questions
▼▼▼

What is the current state of your training-group leadership skills?

How can leaders consolidate, maintain, and develop lifeskills training skills?

Reassessing Your Training-Group Leadership Skills
▼▼▼

Throughout this book, you have explored your skills as a training-group leader. By now you have completed many, if not all, of the exercises. In addition, you may have practiced these skills either at work or in other settings, such as voluntary agencies. Exercise 34 asks you to reassess your training-group leadership skills. Exercise 34 is the follow-up or posttest corresponding to Exercise 2, your initial assessment. Once you have completed Exercise 34, look back at your answers to Exercise 2 and note any differences. You can use Exercise 34 as a reassessment exercise both now and in the future. Unlike the leader self-evaluation questions listed in the previous chapter, Exercise 34 can be filled in prior to conducting training groups as well as after. Take your time over the exercise. Accurate self-assessment is vital for pinpointing strengths and weaknesses. Once you have clearly identified weaknesses, already you are part of the way to correcting them.

Exercise 34 Reassess Your Strengths and Weaknesses as a Training-Group Leader
▼▼▼

Using the following format, make a worksheet for reassessing your strengths and weaknesses as a training-group leader. For more details about a skills area, see the relevant chapter.

Skills Area	My Strengths	My Weaknesses
Preparing training groups		
Designing lifeskills programs		
Assessment and helping self-assessment		
Facilitating training groups		
Speaking in public		
Demonstrating lifeskills		

Designing and implementing struc-tured activities		
Preparing and managing individual training sessions		
Consolidating self-help skills and end-ing training groups		
Evaluating and researching training groups		

Make a list of your main skills strengths. Then make a list of the specific skills weaknesses you most need to work on. Set yourself goals and make and implement a plan to improve your group leadership skills.

Consolidating, Maintaining, and Developing Your Training-Group Leadership Skills

▼ ▼

You have now acquired some skills for leading lifeskills training groups. How can you consolidate, maintain, and develop these skills? As with participants trying to consolidate trained skills as self-help skills, consolidating your leadership skills does not happen automatically. You still need to work hard on the thinking and action skills of being an effective group leader. Many factors can interfere with your effectiveness. You must cope with them as best you can. Some of these factors are internal, such as thinking skills weaknesses. Other factors are external, such as poor supervision or insufficient opportunity to lead groups.

Each reader will have come to this book with a different set of group leadership strengths and weaknesses, will have been exposed to different kinds of training, and will have had varying experiences as group leaders. Some may be either enrolled in or have completed practicum courses in group leadership. These courses may or may not have emphasized leading training groups. Others may be leading training groups without formal training. Still others may be both trained and experienced leaders. Whatever your current status, following are suggestions for how to consolidate, maintain, and develop your trainer skills.

Clarify Your Values

What are the values by which you choose to lead your life? What ultimately is of worth to you? How can you develop and sustain the inner strength to be an effective training-group leader? Some leaders may need to clarify their values before they can gain a genuine commitment to leading groups effectively. For example, instead of viewing training groups mainly in terms of either materialistic values ("How much money is there in it for me?") or needs for approval ("How can I be really popular in groups?"), some leaders may need to access more fundamental human values. Such values include a concern for developing participants' full humanness, prizing the uniqueness of each participant, being committed to working with participants for their sakes and not just for your own, and helping participants make their own choices. Some leaders find inner strength and guidance from religious beliefs. The more deeply centered leaders are in fundamental human values, the more they strive to consolidate and improve their training skills. Conversely, committed leaders are less likely to be sidetracked into superficial values and actions. Clarifying your values is partly a matter of self-help and of listening more deeply to yourself (Gendlin, 1981) and partly a matter of working with and learning from others.

Discipline Your Thinking

You need to discipline your thinking to keep growing as a training-group leader. Thinking skills to work on include attributing responsibility accurately for developing training skills, possessing realistic rules and avoiding perfectionism, accurately perceiving feedback, using coping self-talk when faced with difficulties and setbacks, predicting the future realistically, setting realistic goals for yourself and your groups, using visualization to rehearse and enhance strengths and cope with setbacks, and thinking yourself through difficulties rather than reacting impulsively (Beck & Weishaar, 1989; Ellis, 1989; May & Yalom, 1989; Meichenbaum & Deffenbacher, 1988; Nelson-Jones, 1990a). Like clarifying your values, disciplining your thinking is partly a matter of self-help and partly a matter of working with and learning from others.

Observe Skilled Leaders

In this book, I have emphasized learning by observing. Learn by observing skilled leaders. The groups you observe need not necessarily be lifeskills training groups. For example, you can learn much about group facilitation by observing well-led person-centered groups. A number of ways exist to observe skilled leaders. In all instances, participants should consent to being observed. There is less resistance to observers where participants understand that such observation is for group leadership training. However, participants require reassurance that observers will maintain confidentiality. The following are some arrangements, not necessarily mutually exclusive, for observing lifeskills training groups:

Be present: You may be allowed to sit in the room while a group is in progress. It may be easier for participants if you are unobtrusive. For instance, you can sit outside the horseshoe and not participate in discussions or structured activities.

Observe through a one-way mirror: Observers can watch groups from behind one-way mirrors. A microphone and speaker system can provide sound. One-way mirror observation has the advantages of relative unobtrusiveness and of enabling you to see proceedings both life-size and also as they happen.

View closed-circuit TV: A video camera can be connected to a monitor in another room. Disadvantages of closed-circuit TV include the obtrusiveness of a camera in group rooms and a lessening of visual detail through problems of camera angle and monitor size.

Make videotapes: Watching your own videotapes of groups has some of the disadvantages of using closed-circuit TV. In addition, participants may have more reservations about being recorded and observed than if only observed. However, videotapes have the advantage that leaders and observers can discuss and analyze them. Also, tapes can be stopped and played back to highlight specific *do*'s and *don't*s. Furthermore, videotapes can be reused for training purposes.

View videotapes and films recorded elsewhere: Observing videotapes and films recorded elsewhere is another way to learn leadership skills. Sources for purchasing films and videos include the American Association for Counseling and Development film library (5999 Stevenson Avenue, Alexandria, VA 22304, phone 703/823-9800); Psychological and Educational Films (3334 East Coast Highway, Corona Del Mar, CA 92625, phone 714/494-5079); and Brooks/Cole Publishing (511 Forest Lodge Road, Pacific Grove, CA 93950, phone 408-373-0728) who have available a video series featuring Irvin Yalom, entitled "Understanding Group Psychotherapy," (Yalom, 1990). An advantage of films and tapes recorded elsewhere is that often they are of well-known leaders who portray a range of skills. Disadvantages can include price, the there-and-then nature of material, and that observers do not view series of sessions.

Two important issues in observational learning are how many sessions observers watch and whether or not they engage in postgroup discussions with the leaders of observed groups (Yalom, 1985). Observing single sessions can be very valuable. Nevertheless, added benefits accrue from observing one or more complete lifeskills training groups. Observers may see leaders use different skills for initial, working, and ending stages. Also, observers may watch the development, or lack of development, of participants' skills. Where possible, observers should have the opportunity for postsession discussions with leaders. These discussions are best held shortly after group sessions when the sessions are still fresh in people's minds.

Obtain Supervision

Training-group leaders require practice to develop competencies. You can build your skills by receiving supervision. Since the skills of leading lifeskills groups are varied, different approaches to supervision may suit different skills. The following are some approaches to supervision that can be used either singly or together:

Discussing sessions as case studies: The preparatory, initial, working, and ending stages of each group you lead can be discussed with supervisors as case studies. Supervisors can help you design programs and develop presentations. In addition, supervisors can be sounding boards as you work through problems and issues from sessions. An added strength of the group case study approach is that supervisors can focus on cognitive group leadership skills (Biggs, 1988). A disadvantage is lack of videotaped evidence to support discussion of how you actually behaved.

Having supervisor view and then discuss live sessions: Your supervisor may view you leading sessions. Yalom states that an excellent supervision format, schedules permitting, is for supervisors to observe the last thirty minutes of psychotherapy group sessions and then hold supervisory discussions immediately afterward (Yalom, 1985). Live viewing followed by supervision has the advantage of immediacy. However, if only viewing part of a session, supervisors may not see the full range of skills you used. Also, apart from recall, there is no evidence to illustrate specific points.

Having supervisor view and discuss videotaped sessions: Viewing videotapes is much preferable to listening to audiotapes since trainee leaders and supervisors can pick up body as well as verbal and voice messages. Broadly speaking, there are two main approaches to viewing supervision videotapes: supervisor-centered and supervisee-centered. In the supervisor-centered approach there is an expert-neophyte relationship. Supervisors control the sessions and stop the video playback to point out good and poor use of skills. The supervisee-centered approach is represented by Kagan's interpersonal process recall method (Kagan, 1984). Here supervisees control the proceedings and stop the video playback when they want. The supervisor's role is to facilitate the supervisee's recall by making inquiries—for example, "What were you trying to do?" "What were you feeling?" and "Were there any risks for you?" Much supervision adopts a mixed model. A variation of the mixed model is to have supervisors control one session and supervisees control the next.

Co-leading with experienced leaders: One of the best ways to learn trainer skills is to co-lead groups with more experienced leaders. In such instances, the experienced leaders may not be your supervisors. Nevertheless, they can always perform a supervisory function as you prepare groups, plan sessions, work together during sessions, and discuss afterward how you performed.

What characteristics make for effective supervision? Supervisors need to have a sound knowledge both of the subject matter of your group and of how to put material across. The quality of the supervisory relationship is important. Supervisors are likely to be more effective if they demonstrate warmth, respect, and empathy. In addition, supervisors should provide specific rather than general feedback. Furthermore, immediate postgroup supervision is likely to be more effective than supervision delayed by several days (Matarrazzo & Patterson, 1986).

Arrange Peer Supervision

Practicing leaders should consider peer supervision in which you support, facilitate, and learn from each other. Co-counseling is one model of peer supervision. For instance, you may have thirty minutes each, reversing the supervisor/supervisee roles at the end of the first period. Furthermore, you can negotiate the role you wish your supervisor to play—facilitator, trainer, personal support, or such—so that you control your supervision. Groups are another model of peer supervision. The group can decide how best to use the talents and resources of participants. Again, individual participants who present material can state what kind of assistance they require.

Practice and Experiment

Training-group leaders can build their training skills and confidence by rehearsal and practice. Furthermore, if prepared to take calculated risks, leaders can extend both the range of their interventions and the areas in which they lead groups. Effective group leadership is not just a matter of being safe all the time. Good leaders are flexible and creative in preparing groups, designing interventions, and in responding to moment-to-moment session events. Also, leaders can increase the range of lifeskills groups they offer. Broadening their training range may both increase leaders' skills and also provide added stimulation and interest.

Participate in Groups

Participant experience is often useful for learning about both how to function in groups and how groups function (Corey & Corey, 1982; Rogers, 1970; Yalom, 1985). The accreditation committee of the American Group Psychotherapy Association has recommended a requirement of sixty hours of participation in groups (Yalom, 1985). There are two main, if overlapping, agendas for participating in well-led groups. First, there is the personal growth agenda. You may learn much about how you relate to people, including your defensive processes. You may also work through some of your anxieties about interacting in groups. Second, there is the professional growth agenda.

You may have much more empathy for what it feels like to be a participant in groups if you have participated yourself. Also, you may have more insight into the benefit of good facilitation if you have experienced it. Rogers (1970) states that in the person-centered group leadership program at La Jolla, about half of the program's 150 hours were given to direct experience as a participant in more than one small encounter group. In addition, you may have a better grasp of didactic skills of leading training groups if you have experienced and observed them in a number of lifeskills groups.

Obtain Counseling

Group leaders who are not at ease with themselves are likely to communicate tensions and anxieties to participants. An intensive group experience may not give the trainee leader sufficient help with exploring specific problems and coping styles. Having individual sessions with a competent and disciplined counselor may be necessary. Training-group leaders should be effective choosers who are in touch with their feelings, think effectively, and act appropriately. Leaders should have worked through much of the emotional baggage and unfinished business from their upbringings, including self-defeating ways of feeling, thinking, and acting. Such working-through is often difficult to achieve without competent help.

Attend Conferences, Workshops, and Courses

There are no hard-and-fast distinctions between conferences, workshops, and courses. However, training courses are usually spread out over a longer period, say a month or more, whereas workshops are ordinarily relatively intense experiences lasting from a day to a week. Some conferences are composed almost entirely of workshops. Other conferences have more of a focus on academic content. National professional associations in such areas as counseling, psychology, social work, teacher education, career counseling, nursing, personnel work, and business management are one source of information about lifeskills training courses and workshops. Also, professional associations may run sessions or workshops on group leadership at their conferences. Some associations focus specifically on group work—for example, the Association of Specialists in Group Work, a division of the American Association for Counseling and Development (address supplied earlier), and the American Group Psychotherapy Association (21 East 21st Street, 6th floor, New York, NY 10010, phone 212/477-2677). Other associations, without focusing exclusively on group work, may run events highly pertinent to developing lifeskills group leadership skills—for example, the Association for the Advancement of Behavior Therapy (15 West 36th Street, New York, NY 10018). Here is a checklist for assessing training courses and workshops.

Checklist for Assessing Training Courses and Workshops

▼▼

1. What are the goals?
2. What methods will be employed?
3. What is the pertinent training and experience of the group leader?
4. What is the size of the training course or workshop? Is there a screening process prior to entry?
5. When does the course or workshop start? How long is each session? Over what period will the course or workshop continue? Where will it be held? Are the facilities adequate?
6. What is the fee for the course or workshop, if any? Will it involve additional expenses?

If you are interested in building your group leadership skills in a particular area, you can also explore training opportunities in specialized agencies. For example, leaders wanting to direct role-plays can attend psychodrama courses or workshops run by psychodrama agencies. Leaders wishing to develop their group facilitation skills can attend courses and workshops run by experts in these skills. Developing your leadership skills involves making use of a variety of learning opportunities.

Keep Abreast of Relevant Literature

Effective group leaders keep up with the relevant literature. You can read books and journals about how to lead groups. By reading, you can increase your understanding of the theoretical and research underpinnings of group leadership. Furthermore, you can expand your understanding of the specific areas in which you lead groups—for example, pain-management skills or parenting skills.

How can you find out about relevant books and training manuals? Here are some sources of information:

Name and subject catalogs in libraries: Even if you do not know any names, you can still search for books under relevant key words, such as *groups* or *assertiveness*.

Publishers' catalogs: If possible, find out which publishers specialize in books on helper training and structured groups. For example, Brooks/Cole, the publisher of this book, has a number of other titles on group work (Brooks/Cole, 511 Forest Lodge Road, Pacific Grove, CA 93950, phone 408/373-0728). A well-known publisher of training material is University Associates (8517 Production Avenue, San Diego, CA 92121, phone 619/578-5900).

Book reviews in journals: You can subscribe to or get access to copies of *Contemporary Psychology*, a journal that publishes only book reviews. In addition, look up the book review sections in relevant professional and academic journals.

Master reference sources: In North America, the master reference to currently available books, authors, and publishers is the eight-volume *Books in Print* (1989). Again, if you do not know the names of authors, you can conduct searches using key words. The similar source for books available in Britain is *Whitaker's Books in Print* (1989). There is an *Australian Books in Print* (1989). If possible, always use the most recent edition of these sources.

Ask around: If necessary, be prepared to ask around about what books other people read and which training manuals they use. If you operate as part of a team or are in a network of group leaders, you can help keep each other up to date on reading suggestions.

You can also keep abreast of the literature by reading relevant professional and academic journals. Some journals focus specifically on group work—for example, the *International Journal of Group Psychotherapy*, the *Journal for Specialists in Group Work*, and *Group Relations*. Other journals include research articles on group approaches to the training of different lifeskills—for example, *Cognitive Therapy and Research* and *Behavior Therapy*. The main reference source for finding out about journals is *Ulrich's International Periodicals Directory* (1989). *Psychological Abstracts* is the main source of abstracts of psychological journal articles. A list of journals for articles relevant to leading lifeskills groups is provided as Appendix A.

Keep Abreast of Audiovisual Training Resources

Leaders also require keeping up with the latest training films, videotapes, and audio cassettes. Some journals now review audiovisual material as well as books. Publishers' catalogs are another source of information. Mention has already been made of such film and videotape distributors as the American Association for Counseling and Development and Psychological and Educational Films. Distributors of self-help audio cassettes include BMA Audio Cassettes (200 Park Avenue South, New York, NY 10003, phone 1-800/221-3966 or in NY 212/674-1900); Psychology Today Tapes (Dept 9101, Box 059073, Brooklyn, NY 11205-9061, phone 212/337-6759); and Research Press (Box 3177, Champaign, IL 61826, phone 217/352-3273). If interested, ask film, videotape, and audio cassette distributors to send you their most recent catalogs.

Keep Abreast of Relevant Information

Many training groups require leaders to have up-to-date information. For example, at the very least, leaders of career education groups should have knowledge about current sources of occupational information and about occupational trends. Other examples of leaders providing information include leaders of single mothers' groups providing relevant legal and welfare information; leaders of preretirement groups providing financial planning, occupational, and leisure information; and leaders of health education groups providing relevant health care information.

Avoid Burnout

Paraphrasing General MacArthur, "Old lifeskills group leaders never die, they burn out long before." Leading lifeskills groups can be stressful. When such stresses are added to other stresses they may face, group leaders can become excellent candidates for burnout or breakdown. Freudenberger (1980) defines burnout: "To deplete oneself. To exhaust one's physical and mental resources. To wear oneself out by excessively striving to reach some unrealistic expectation imposed by one's self or by the values of society" (p. 17). Maslach and Jackson (1981) assess burnout as having three major components: emotional exhaustion, depersonalization, and insufficient sense of personal accomplishment.

Many thinking and action skills weaknesses contribute to training-group leaders' feeling burned out. Relevant thinking skills weaknesses include having perfectionistic personal rules, misattributing cause, being unduly pessimistic, setting unrealistically high goals, and having undue need for approval. Action skills weaknesses include inability to set limits on work loads, poor time management, insufficient recreational outlets, and poor skills at looking after health and physical fitness.

Leaders who are punch-drunk with exhaustion lack energy to lead groups competently. When thoroughly run down, you are not at your best. Your emotional depletion communicates itself to participants. Training-group leaders have both professional and personal obligations not just to avoid burnout, but to be positively psychologically well. Skills for managing stress and burnout include negotiating a realistic work load, both with others and yourself; muscular and visual relaxation; adequate recreational outlets; networking with supportive people; effective thinking; being assertive; and assuming more responsibility for your health. Take steps to prevent burnout where possible.

Exercise 35 helps you assess methods of consolidating, maintaining, and developing your group leadership skills.

Exercise 35 Consolidate, Maintain, and Develop Your Training-Group Leadership Skills
▼▼

Listed here are different methods to consolidate, maintain, and develop your group leadership skills. Use the worksheet and assess both whether or not and how you might use each method.

Method	My Assessment of Whether and How I Can Use Each Method
Clarify my values	
Discipline my thinking	
Observe skilled leaders	
Obtain supervision	
Arrange peer supervision	
Practice and experiment	
Participate in groups	
Obtain counseling	
Attend conferences, workshops, and courses	
Keep abreast of relevant literature	
Keep abreast of audiovisual training resources	
Keep abreast of relevant information	
Avoid burnout	

Develop a plan to consolidate, maintain, and improve your training-group leadership skills.

Developing the Human Potential

▼ ▼

Nature is indifferent to the survival of the human species,
  including Americans.

Adlai Stevenson

Though nature may be indifferent to the survival of the human species, humans cannot afford this luxury. Furthermore, humans have the responsibility for making the most of their short sojourns on earth. Probably most people function well below their potential (Maslow, 1970). The lifeskills training movement represents an optimistic attempt to help people realize more of their potential. As a training-group leader, you are part of an exciting attempt to improve the amount of happiness and well-being on this planet. May you have strength and skill in your endeavors.

▼ Chapter Highlights

▼ Effective training-group leaders assume responsibility for consolidating, maintaining, and developing their skills.

▼ Leaders can periodically reassess their trainer strengths and weaknesses.

▼ Suggestions for consolidating, maintaining, and developing group leadership skills include the following: clarify your values; discipline your thinking; observe skilled leaders; obtain supervision; arrange peer supervision; practice and experiment; participate in groups; obtain counseling; attend conferences, workshops, and courses; keep abreast of relevant literature; keep abreast of audio-visual training resources; keep abreast of relevant information; and avoid burnout.

▼ The lifeskills training movement represents an optimistic attempt to help people fulfill more of their potential. As a group leader, you are part of this exciting endeavor.

Academic and Professional Journals

Here is a listing of some academic and professional journals to consult for articles relevant to leading lifeskills training groups.

North America

American Journal of Family Therapy
American Psychologist
Applied Cognitive Psychology
Behavior Modification
Behavior Therapy
Canadian Journal of Counselling/Revue Canadiènne de Counselling
Canadian Journal of Psychology/Revue Canadiènne de Psychologie
Canadian Psychology
Career Development Quarterly
Counselor Education and Supervision
Journal for Specialists in Group Work
Journal of Abnormal Psychology
Journal of Consulting and Clinical Psychology
Journal of Counseling and Development
Journal of Counseling Psychology
Journal of Marital and Family Therapy
Journal of Personality and Social Psychology
Journal of Vocational Behavior
Personnel Journal
Personnel Psychology
Psychology Today
The Counseling Psychologist

Asia

Asian Journal of Psychology and Education
Japanese Journal of Behavior Therapy

Australia and New Zealand

Australian Counselling Psychologist
Australian Journal of Psychology
Australian Psychologist
Bulletin of the Australian Psychological Society
New Zealand Journal of Psychology

Britain

Behaviour Research and Therapy
British Journal of Clinical Psychology
British Journal of Social Psychology
Counselling
Counselling Psychology Quarterly
Group Relations
Journal of Occupational Psychology
Journal of Social and Personal Relationships
The Psychologist

International

International Journal for the Advancement of Counselling
International Journal of Group Psychotherapy

In addition, academic and professional journals in such areas as teacher education, social work, nursing, and management may publish articles of interest to training-group leaders.

Abramowitz, I. A., & Coursey, R. D. (1989). Impact of an educational support group on family participants who take care of their schizophrenic relatives. *Journal of Consulting and Clinical Psychology, 57,* 232–236.

Acock, A. C., & Hurlbert, J. S. (1990). Social network analysis: A structural perspective for family studies. *Journal of Social and Personal Relationships, 7,* 245–264.

Alberti, R. E., & Emmons, M. L. (1986). *Your perfect right: A guide to assertive living* (5th ed.). San Luis Obispo: Impact Publishers.

Allen, J. P., & Turner, E. (1990). Where diversity reigns. *American Demographics, 12*(8), 34–38.

Allen, V. B., Sampson, J. P., & Herlihy, B. (1988). Details of the AACD Ethical Standards. *Journal of Counseling and Development, 67,* 157–158.

Allred, G. B. (1988). Sensitizing nursing home staff to residents' needs: A workshop. *Journal of Counseling and Development, 66,* 248–249.

Alpert, R., & Haber, R. N. (1960). Anxiety in academic achievement situations. *Journal of Abnormal and Social Psychology, 61,* 204–215.

Amatea, E. S., Clark, J. E., & Cross, E. G. (1984). Life-styles: Evaluating a life role planning program for high school students. *Vocational Guidance Quarterly, 32,* 249–259.

Amatea, E. S., & Cross, E. G. (1983). Coupling and careers: A workshop for dual-career couples at the launching stage. *Personnel and Guidance Journal, 62,* 48–52.

American Association for Counseling and Development. (1988). *Ethical standards.* Alexandria, VA: Author.

American Psychological Association. (1973). *Guidelines for psychologists conducting growth groups.* Washington, DC: Author.

American Psychological Association. (1981). Ethical principles of psychologists. *American Psychologist, 36,* 633–638.

American Psychological Association. (1985). *Standards for educational and psychological testing.* Washington, DC: Author.

American Psychological Association. (1987). General guidelines for providers of psychological services. *American Psychologist, 42,* 724–729.

American Psychological Association. (1990). Ethical principles of psychologists. *American Psychologist, 45,* 390–395.

Anastasi, A. (1988). *Psychological testing* (6th ed.). New York: Macmillan.

Arbuckle, D. S. (1976). Comment on A. E. Ivey's paper "The counselor as teacher." *Personnel and Guidance Journal, 54*, 434.

Argyle, M. (1983). *The psychology of interpersonal behavior* (4th ed.). Harmondsworth, Middlesex: Penguin.

Argyle, M. (1984). Some new developments in social skills training. *Bulletin of the British Psychological Society, 37*, 405–410.

Argyle, M. (1986). Rules for social relationships in four cultures. *Australian Journal of Psychology, 38*, 309–318.

Arlow, J. A. (1989). Psychoanalysis. In R. Corsini & D. Wedding (Eds.), *Current psychotherapies* (4th ed., pp. 19–62). Itasca, IL: Peacock.

Australian books in print. (1989). Melbourne: R. Thorpe.

Azrin, N. H., Flores, T., & Kaplan, S. J. (1975). Job-finding club: A group-assisted program for obtaining employment. *Behaviour Research and Therapy, 13*, 17–27.

Azrin, N. H., & Philips, R. A. (1979). The Job Club method for the job handicapped: A comparative outcome study. *Rehabilitation Counseling Bulletin, 23*, 144–155.

Bandura, A. (1969). *Principles of behavior modification*. New York: Holt, Rinehart & Winston.

Bandura, A. (1976). Effecting change through participant modeling. In J. D. Krumboltz & C. E. Thoresen (Eds.), *Counseling methods* (pp. 248–265). New York: Holt, Rinehart & Winston.

Bandura, A. (1977). *Social learning theory*. Englewood Cliffs, NJ: Prentice-Hall.

Bandura, A. (1986). *Social foundations of thought and action: A social cognitive theory*. Englewood Cliffs, NJ: Prentice-Hall.

Bandura, A., Grusec, J. E., & Menlove, F. L. (1966). Observational learning as a function of symbolization and incentive set. *Child Development, 37*, 499–506.

Barnette, E. L. (1989). A program to meet the emotional and social needs of gifted and talented adolescents. *Journal of Counseling and Development, 67*, 525–528.

Barrow, J. C., & Moore, C. A. (1983). Group interventions with perfectionist thinking. *Personnel and Guidance Journal, 61*, 612–615.

Beck, A. T. (1976). *Cognitive therapy and the emotional disorders*. New York: New American Library.

Beck, A. T. (1988). *Love is never enough: How couples can overcome misunderstandings, resolve conflicts, and solve relationship problems through cognitive therapy*. New York: Harper & Row.

Beck, A. T., & Emery, G. (1985). *Anxiety disorders and phobias: A cognitive perspective*. New York: Basic Books.

Beck, A. T., & Greenberg, R. L. (1974). *Coping with depression*. New York: Institute for Rational Living.

Beck, A. T., Rush, A. J., Shaw, B. F., & Emery, G. (1979). *Cognitive therapy of depression*. New York: Wiley.

Beck, A. T., & Weishaar, M. E. (1989). Cognitive therapy. In R. Corsini & D. Wedding (Eds.), *Current psychotherapies* (4th ed., pp. 285–320). Itasca, IL: Peacock.

Bem, S. L. (1974). The measurement of psychological androgeny. *Journal of Consulting and Clinical Psychology, 42*, 155–162.

Bem, S. L. (1981). Gender schema theory: A cognitive account of sex typing. *Psychological Review, 88,* 354–364.

Bernstein, D. (1988). *Put it together, put it across: The craft of business presentation.* London: Cassell.

Beutler, L. E., Crago, M., & Arizmendi, T. G. (1986). Research on therapist variables in psychotherapy. In S. L. Garfield & A. E. Bergin (Eds.), *Handbook of psychotherapy and behavior change* (3rd ed., pp. 257–310). New York: Wiley.

Biggs, D. A. (1988). The case presentation approach in clinical supervision. *Counselor Education and Supervision, 27,* 240–248.

Blanchard, M. (1989). Wellness programs produce positive results. *Personnel Journal, 68,* 30.

Blatner, A. (1989). Psychodrama. In R. J. Corsini & D. Wedding (Eds.), *Current psychotherapies* (4th ed., pp. 561–571). Itasca, IL: Peacock.

Bloch, S., & Crouch, E. (1985). *Therapeutic factors in group psychotherapy.* Oxford: Oxford University Press.

Bloom, D. E. (1986). Women and work. *American Demographics, 8,* 25–30.

Books in print. (1989). Vols. 1–8. New York: R. R. Bowker.

Bowlby, J. (1979). *The making and breaking of affectional bonds.* London: Tavistock.

Bradford, L. P., Gibb, J. R., & Benne, K. D. (Eds.). (1964). *T-group theory and laboratory method: Innovation in re-education.* New York: Wiley.

Brammer, L. M. (1985). *The helping relationship: Process and skills* (3rd ed.). Englewood Cliffs, NJ: Prentice-Hall.

Brehm, S. S., & Smith, T. W. (1986). Social psychological approaches to psychotherapy and behavior change. In S. L. Garfield & A. E. Bergin (Eds.), *Handbook of psychotherapy and behavior change* (3rd ed., pp. 69–115). New York: Wiley.

Brolin, D. E., & Gysbers, N. C. (1989). Career education for students with disabilities. *Journal of Counseling and Development, 68,* 155–159.

Brown, A. (1986). *Groupwork* (2nd ed.). Aldershot, England: Gower.

Brown, R. A., & Lewinsohn, P. (1984). A psychoeducational approach to the treatment of depression: Comparison of group, individual, and minimal contact procedures. *Journal of Consulting and Clinical Psychology, 52,* 774–783.

Bundy, M. L., & White, P. N. (1990). Parents as sexuality educators: A parent training program. *Journal of Counseling and Development, 68,* 321–323.

Butler, P. E. (1981). *Self-assertion for women.* New York: Harper & Row.

Carkhuff, R. R. (1971a). *The development of human resources: Education, psychology, and social change.* New York: Holt, Rinehart & Winston.

Carkhuff, R. R. (1971b). Training as a preferred mode of treatment. *Journal of Counseling Psychology, 18,* 123–131.

Cautela, J. R. (1967). Covert sensitization. *Psychological Reports, 20,* 459–468.

Cautela, J. R. (1976). The present status of covert modeling. *Journal of Behavior Therapy and Experimental Psychiatry, 6,* 323–326.

Chassan, J. B. (1979). *Research designs in clinical psychology and psychiatry.* New York: Wiley.

Christensen, C. P. (1989). Cross-cultural awareness development: A conceptual model. *Counselor Education and Supervision, 28,* 270–287.

Christoff, K. A., Scott, W.O.N., Kelley, M. L., Schlundt, D., Baer, G., & Kelley,

J. A. (1985). Social skills and social problem-solving training for shy young adolescents. *Behavior Therapy, 16,* 468–477.

Clifford, T. (1987). Assertiveness training for parents. *Journal of Counseling and Development, 65,* 552–554.

Combs, A. W., Richards, A. C., & Richards, F. (1976). *Perceptual psychology: A humanistic approach to the study of persons.* New York: Harper & Row.

Conn, M. K., & Peterson, C. (1989). Social support: Seek and ye shall find. *Journal of Social and Personal Relationships, 6,* 345–358.

Cook, J. P. (1986). Training: A five-step program that keeps training on target. *Personnel Journal, 65,* 106–114.

Cooper, A., & Stoltenberg, C. D. (1987). Comparison of a sexual enhancement and a communication training program on sexual and marital satisfaction. *Journal of Consulting and Clinical Psychology, 34,* 309–314.

Corey, G. (1990). *Theory and practice of group counseling* (3rd ed.). Pacific Grove, CA: Brooks/Cole.

Corey, G., & Corey, M. S. (1982). *Groups: Process and practice* (2nd ed.). Pacific Grove, CA: Brooks/Cole.

Corey, G., Corey, M. S., & Callanan, P. (1988). *Issues and ethics in the helping professions* (3rd ed.). Pacific Grove, CA: Brooks/Cole.

Corey, G., Corey, M. S., Callanan, P. J., & Russell, J. M. (1988). *Group techniques* (rev. ed.). Pacific Grove, CA: Brooks/Cole.

Cormier, W. H., & Cormier, L. S. (1985). *Interviewing strategies for helpers: Fundamental skills and cognitive behavioral interventions.* Pacific Grove, CA: Brooks/Cole.

Corrigan, J. D., Dell, D. M., Lewis, K. N., & Schmidt, L. D. (1980). Counseling as a social influence process: A review. *Journal of Counseling Psychology, 27,* 395–441.

Costley, D. L., & Moore, F. A. (1986). The subliminal impact and hidden agendas of training. *Personnel Journal, 65,* 101–105.

Daws, P. P. (1973). Mental health and counselling: Counselling as prophylaxis. *British Journal of Guidance and Counselling, 1,* 2–10.

Deffenbacher, J. L., Story, D. A., Brandon, A. D., Hogg, J. A., & Hazaleus, S. L. (1988). Cognitive and cognitive-relaxation treatments of anger. *Cognitive Therapy and Research, 12,* 167–184.

Deffenbacher, J. L., Story, D. A., Stark, R. S., Hogg, J. A., & Brandon, A. D. (1987). Cognitive-relaxation and social skills interventions in the treatment of general anger. *Journal of Counseling Psychology, 34,* 171–176.

Dorn, N., & South, N. (1986). Developing work-related education on alcohol and drugs. *British Journal of Guidance and Counselling, 14,* 88–96.

Downing, N. E., & Walker, M. E. (1987). A psychoeducational group for adult children of alcoholics. *Journal of Counseling and Development, 65,* 440–442.

Dyer, W. W. (1976). *Your erroneous zones.* London: Sphere.

D'Zurilla, T. J., & Goldfried, M. R. (1971). Problem solving and behavior modification. *Journal of Abnormal Psychology, 78,* 107–126.

Egan, G. (1977). *You and me: The skills of communicating and relating to others.* Pacific Grove, CA: Brooks/Cole.

Egan, G. (1990). *The skilled helper: A systematic approach to effective helping* (4th ed.). Pacific Grove, CA: Brooks/Cole.

Egan, G., & Cowan, M. A. (1979). *People in systems: A model for development in the human service professions and education.* Pacific Grove, CA: Brooks/Cole.

Eidelson, R. J., & Epstein, N. (1982). Cognition and relationship maladjustment: Development of a measure of dysfunctional relationship beliefs. *Journal of Consulting and Clinical Psychology, 50,* 715–720.

Ekman, P., Friesen, W. W., & Bear, J. (May 1984). The international language of gestures. *Psychology Today,* 64–69.

Elliott, S. N., & Gresham, F. M. (1987). Children's social skills: Assessment and classification practices. *Journal of Counseling and Development, 66,* 96–99.

Ellis, A. (1962). *Reason and emotion in psychotherapy.* New York: Lyle Stuart.

Ellis, A. (1980). Overview of the clinical theory of rational-emotive therapy. In R. Grieger & J. Boyd (Eds.), *Rational-emotive therapy: A skills-based approach* (pp. 1–31). New York: Van Nostrand Reinhold.

Ellis, A. (1985). *Overcoming resistance: Rational-emotive therapy with difficult clients.* New York: Springer.

Ellis, A. (1987). The impossibility of achieving consistently good mental health. *American Psychologist, 42,* 364–375.

Ellis, A. (1989). Rational-emotive therapy. In R. Corsini & D. Wedding (Eds.), *Current psychotherapies* (4th ed., pp. 197–238). Itasca, IL: Peacock.

Emery, G. (1982). *Own your own life.* New York: New American Library.

Feindler, E. L., Marriott, S. A., & Iwata, M. (1984). Group anger control training for junior high school delinquents. *Cognitive Therapy and Research, 8,* 299–311.

Fischer, R. L. (1972). *Speak to communicate: An introduction to speech.* Encino, CA: Dickenson.

Frankl, V. E. (1959). *Man's search for meaning.* New York: Washington Square Press.

Frankl, V. E. (1969). *The doctor and the soul.* Harmondsworth, Middlesex: Penguin Books.

Fremouw, W. J., & Zittler, R. E. (1978). A comparison of skills training and cognitive restructuring-relaxation for the treatment of speech anxiety. *Behavior Therapy, 9,* 248–259.

French, J., & Raven, B. (1959). The bases of social power. In D. Cartwright (Ed.), *Studies in social power* (pp. 150–167). Ann Arbor: University of Michigan Press.

Freud, A. (1936). *The ego and mechanisms of defense.* New York: International Universities Press.

Freudenberger, H. J. (1980). *Burnout: The high cost of high achievement.* London: Arrow Books.

Fukuyama, M. A. (1990). Taking a universal approach to multicultural counseling. *Counselor Education and Supervision, 30,* 6–17.

Gallwey, W. T. (1974). *The inner game of tennis.* London: Pan Books.

Ganger, R. E. (1989). Computer-based training improves job performance. *Personnel Journal, 6,* 116–123.

Garfield, S. L. (1986). Research on client variables in psychotherapy. In S. L. Garfield & A. E. Bergin (Eds.), *Handbook of psychotherapy and behavior change* (3rd ed., pp. 213–256). New York: Wiley.

Garis, J. W., & Niles, S. G. (1990). The separate and combined effects of SIGI or DISCOVER and a career planning course on undecided university students. *The Career Development Quarterly, 38,* 261–274.

Gazda, G. M. (1989). *Group counseling: A developmental approach* (4th ed.). Boston: Allyn & Bacon.

Gendlin, E. T. (1981). *Focusing* (2nd ed.). New York: Bantam Books.

Georges, J. C. (1989). The hard reality of soft-skills training. *Personnel Journal, 68,* 41–45.

Gilbert, T. F. (1978). *Human competence: Engineering worthy performance.* New York: McGraw-Hill.

Glasser, W. (1965). *Reality therapy.* New York: Basic Books.

Glasser, W. (1984a). *Control theory: A new explanation of how we control our lives.* New York: Harper & Row.

Glasser, W. (1984b). Reality therapy. In R. J. Corsini (Ed.), *Current psychotherapies* (3rd ed., pp. 320–353). Itasca, IL: F. E. Peacock.

Glick, B., & Goldstein, A. P. (1987). Aggression replacement training. *Journal of Counseling and Development, 65,* 356–362.

Glick, P. C. (1984). How American families are changing. *American Demographics, 6,* 20–25.

Goddard, R. W. (1989). Use language effectively. *Personnel Journal, 68,* 32–36.

Goldfried, M. R. (1971). Systematic desensitization as a training in self-control. *Journal of Consulting and Clinical Psychology, 37,* 228–234.

Goldfried, M. R., & Davison, G. C. (1976). *Clinical behavior therapy.* New York: Holt, Rinehart & Winston.

Goldstein, A. P., & Keller, H. (1987). *Aggressive behavior: Assessment and intervention.* New York: Pergamon Press.

Goldstein, I. L., & Gilliam, P. (1990). Training system issues in the year 2000. *American Psychologist, 45,* 134–143.

Gonzalez, G. M. (1990). Effects of a theory-based, peer-focused drug education course. *Journal of Counseling and Development, 68,* 446–449.

Gordon, T. (1970). *Parent effectiveness training.* New York: Wyden.

Graf, R. W., Whitehead, G. I., & LeCompte, M. (1986). Group treatment with divorced women using cognitive-behavioral and supportive-insight methods. *Journal of Counseling Psychology, 33,* 276–281.

Gratton, L. (1985). Assessment centers: Theory, research, and practice. *Human Resource Management Australia, 23*(3), 10–14.

Greenberg, I. A. (1975). Moreno: Psychodrama and the group process. In I. A. Greenberg (Ed.), *Psychodrama: Theory and therapy* (pp. 11–28). London: Souvenir Press.

Gregory, S., & Lee, S. (1986). Psychoeducational assessment of racial and ethnic minority groups: Professional implications. *Journal of Counseling and Development, 64,* 635–637.

Gresham, F. M., & Elliott, S. N. (1986). *How I act towards others.* Unpublished test, University of Louisiana, Baton Rouge.

Grieger, R. (1989). A client's guide to rational-emotive therapy (RET). In W. Dryden & P. Trower (Eds.), *Cognitive psychotherapy: Stasis and change* (pp. 99–120). London: Cassell.

Guerney, B., Stollak, G., & Guerney, L. (1971). The practicing psychologist as educator—An alternative to the medical practitioner model. *Professional Psychology, 2,* 276–282.

Hains, A. A., & Szyjakowski, M. (1990). A cognitive stress-reduction intervention for adolescents. *Journal of Counseling Psychology, 37,* 79–84.

Hamilton, L. S. (1984). Developing game plans for entry into the post-secondary world: An intensive teaching approach. *Vocational Guidance Quarterly, 33*, 82–88.

Hatch, E. J., & Guerney, B. (1975). A pupil relationship enhancement program. *Personnel and Guidance Journal, 54*, 103–105.

Havighurst, R. J. (1972). *Developmental tasks and education* (3rd ed.). New York: David McKay.

Haynes, L. A., & Avery, A. W. (1979). Training adolescents in self-disclosure and empathy skills. *Journal of Counseling Psychology, 26*, 526–530.

Heimberg, R. G., Dodge, C. S., Hope, D. A., Kennedy, C. R., Zollo, L. J., & Becker, R. E. (1990). Cognitive-behavioral group treatment for social phobia: Comparison with a credible placebo control group. *Cognitive Therapy and Research, 14*, 1–23.

Heppner, P. P., Neal, G. W., & Larson, L. M. (1984). Problem-solving training as prevention with college students. *Personnel and Guidance Journal, 62*, 514–529.

Herr, E. L., & Watts, A. G. (1988). Work shadowing and work-related learning. *Career Development Quarterly, 37*, 78–86.

Higgins, W., Ivey, A., & Uhlemann, M. (1970). Media therapy: A programmed approach to teaching behavioral skills. *Journal of Counseling Psychology, 17*, 20–26.

Holland, J. L. (1987). *Self-Directed Search: 1987 manual supplement*. Odessa, FL: Psychological Assessment Resources.

Homans, G. C. (1950). *Social behavior: Its elementary forms*. New York: Harcourt, Brace & World.

Homans, G. C. (1961). *Social behavior: The elementary forms*. New York: Harcourt, Brace, & Jovanovich.

Hopson, B., & Hough, P. (1973). *Exercises in personal and career development*. Cambridge, England: CRAC.

Hopson, B., & Hough, P. (1976). The need for personal and social education in secondary schools and further education. *British Journal of Guidance and Counselling, 4*, 16–27.

Hopson, B., & Scally, M. (1981). *Lifeskills teaching*. London: McGraw-Hill.

Hosford, R. E., & Johnson, M. E. (1983). A comparison of self-observation, self-modeling, and practice without video feedback for improving counselor interviewing behaviors. *Counselor Education and Supervision, 23*, 62–70.

Hosford, R. E., Moss, C. S., & Morrell, G. (1976). The self-as-a-model technique: Helping prison inmates change. In J. D. Krumboltz & C. E. Thoresen (Eds.), *Counseling methods* (pp. 487–495). New York: Holt, Rinehart & Winston.

Huey, W. C., & Rank, R. C. (1984). Effects of counselor and peer-led assertive training on black adolescent aggression. *Journal of Counseling Psychology, 31*, 95–98.

Ivey, A. E. (1976). Counseling psychology, the psychoeducator model, and the future. *The Counseling Psychologist, 6*, 72–75.

Ivey, A. E. (1987). Cultural intentionality: The core of effective helping. *Counselor Education and Supervision, 26*, 168–172.

Ivey, A. E., & Authier, J. (1978). *Microcounseling: Innovations in interviewing, counseling, psychotherapy, and psychoeducation* (2nd ed.). Springfield, IL: Charles C Thomas.

Ivey, A. E., Ivey, M. B., & Simek-Downing, L. (1987). *Counseling and psycho-*

therapy: Integrating skills, theory, and practice (2nd ed.). Englewood Cliffs, NJ: Prentice-Hall.

Jacobs, E. E., Harvill, R. L., & Masson, R. L. (1988). *Group counseling: Strategies and skills.* Pacific Grove, CA: Brooks/Cole.

Jacobson, E. (1938). *Progressive relaxation* (2nd ed.). Chicago: University of Chicago Press.

Jacobson, N. S. (1989). The maintenance of treatment gains following social learning-based marital therapy. *Behavior Therapy, 20,* 325–336.

Jeffrey, R. W. (1976). Reducing fears through participant modeling and self-directed practice. In J. D. Krumboltz & C. E. Thoresen (Eds.), *Counseling methods* (pp. 301–312). New York: Holt, Rinehart & Winston.

Johnson, D. W. (1986). *Reaching out: Interpersonal effectiveness and self-actualization* (3rd ed.). Englewood Cliffs, NJ: Prentice-Hall.

Johnson, D. W., & Johnson, F. P. (1987). *Joining together: Group theory and group skills* (3rd ed.). Englewood Cliffs, NJ: Prentice-Hall.

Johnson, R. G. (1985). Microcomputer career exploration. *Vocational Guidance Quarterly, 33,* 296–304.

Jones, J. E., & Pfeiffer, J. W. (1972–1981). *The annual handbook for group facilitators* (Vols. 1–10). San Diego, CA: University Associates.

Jourard, S. M. (1971). *The transparent self* (rev. ed.). New York: Van Nostrand Reinhold.

Kagan, N. (1984). Interpersonal process recall: Basic methods and recent research. In D. Larsen (Ed.), *Teaching psychological skills* (pp. 261–269). Pacific Grove, CA: Brooks/Cole.

Kalodoner, C. R., & DeLucia, J. L. (1990). Components of effective weight loss program: Theory, research, and practice. *Journal of Counseling and Development, 68,* 427–433.

Kanfer, F. H., & Gaelick, L. (1986). Self-management methods. In F. H. Kanfer & A. P. Goldstein (Eds.), *Helping people change: A textbook of methods* (pp. 283–345). New York: Pergamon Press.

Karoly, P., & Harris, A. (1986). Operant methods. In F. H. Kanfer & A. P. Goldstein (Eds.), *Helping people change: A textbook of methods* (3rd ed., pp. 111–144). New York: Pergamon Press.

Katz, A. H. (1981). Self-help and mutual aid: An emerging social movement? *American Review of Sociology, 7,* 129–155.

Kazdin, A. E. (1976). Developing assertive behaviors through covert modeling. In J. D. Krumboltz & C. E. Thoresen (Eds.), *Counseling methods* (pp. 475–486). New York: Holt, Rinehart & Winston.

Kazdin, A. E. (1982). *Single-case research designs: Methods for clinical and applied settings.* New York: Oxford University Press.

Kazdin, A. E. (1986). Research designs and methodology. In S. L. Garfield & A. E. Bergin (Eds.), *Handbook of psychotherapy and behavior change* (3rd ed., pp. 23–68). New York: Wiley.

Keefe, F. J., Caldwell, D. S., Williams, D. A., Gil, K. M., Mitchell, D., Robertson, C., Martinez, S., Beckham, J. C., Crisson, J. E., & Helms, M. H. (1990). Pain coping skills training in the management of osteoarthritic knee pain: A comparative study. *Behavior Therapy, 21,* 49–62.

Kendall, P. C. (1989). The generalization and maintenance of behavior change: Comments, considerations, and the "No-cure" criticism. *Behavior Therapy, 20,* 357–364.

Kendall, P. C., & Hollon, S. D. (1989). Anxious self-talk: Development of the

Anxious Self-statements Questionnaire (ASSQ). *Cognitive Therapy and Research, 13*, 81–93.

Keyser, D. J., & Sweetland, R. C. (1984–1987). *Test critiques* (Vols. 1–4). Kansas City, MO: Test Corporation of America.

Klingman, A., Melamed, B. G., Cuthbert, M. I., & Hermecz, D. A. (1984). Effects of participant modeling on information acquisition and skill utilization. *Journal of Consulting and Clinical Psychology, 52*, 414–422.

Kruger, A. N. (1970). *Effective speaking: A complete course.* New York: Van Nostrand Reinhold.

LaFromboise, T. D., Trimble, J. E., & Mohatt, G. V. (1990). Counseling intervention and American Indian tradition: An integrative approach. *The Counseling Psychologist, 18*, 628–654.

Lazarus, A. (1977). *In the mind's eye.* New York: Guilford Press.

Lazarus, A. (1989). Multimodal therapy. In R. J. Corsini & D. Wedding (Eds.), *Current psychotherapies* (4th ed., pp. 503–544). Itasca, IL: F. E. Peacock.

Leduchowicz, T., & Bennett, R. (1983). Improving trainer effectiveness. *Personnel Review, 12*, 19–25.

Lloyd, A. P. (1987). Multicultural counseling: Does it belong in a counselor education program? *Counselor Education and Supervision, 26*, 164–167.

Lovett, S., & Gallagher, D. (1988). Psychoeducational interventions for family caregivers: Preliminary efficacy data. *Behavior Therapy, 19*, 321–330.

Mahler, C. A. (1969). *Group counseling in the schools.* Boston: Houghton Mifflin.

Marlatt, G. (March 1980). Relapse prevention: A self-control program for the treatment of addictive behaviors. Invited address presented at the International Conference on Behavior Modification, Banff, Alberta, Canada.

Martin, J. (1983). Curriculum development in school counseling. *Personnel and Guidance Journal, 61*, 406–409.

Martin, J. (1990). Confusions in psychological skills training. *Journal of Counseling and Development, 68*, 402–407.

Martin, P. R., Nathan, P. R., Milech, D., & van Keppel, M. (1989). Cognitive therapy vs. self-management training in the treatment of chronic headaches. *British Journal of Clinical Psychology, 28*, 347–361.

Marx, R. (1982). Relapse prevention for managerial training: A model for maintenance of behavior change. *Academy of Management Review, 7*, 433–441.

Maslach, C., & Jackson, S. (1981). The measurement of experienced burnout. *Journal of Occupational Behavior, 2*, 99–113.

Maslow, A. H. (1962). *Toward a psychology of being.* New York: Van Nostrand.

Maslow, A. H. (1970). *Motivation and personality* (2nd ed.). New York: Harper & Row.

Masters, W. H., & Johnson, V. C. (1975). *The pleasure bond.* New York: Bantam.

Matarazzo, R. G., & Patterson, D. (1986). Research on the teaching and learning of therapeutic skills. In S. L. Garfield & A. E. Bergin (Eds.), *Handbook of psychotherapy and behavior change* (3rd ed., pp. 821–843). New York: Wiley.

May, R., & Yalom, I. D. (1989). Existential psychotherapy. In R. Corsini & D. Wedding (Eds.), *Current psychotherapies* (4th ed., pp. 363–402). Itasca, IL: Peacock.

McCarthy, P. R. (1982). Differential effects of counselor self-referent responses and counselor status. *Journal of Counseling Psychology, 29,* 125–131.

McDonald, P. (1988). Families in the future: The pursuit of personal autonomy. *Family Matters, 22,* 40–47.

Meichenbaum, D. H. (1977). *Cognitive-behavior modification: An integrative approach.* New York: Plenum.

Meichenbaum, D. H. (1983). *Coping with stress.* London: Century.

Meichenbaum, D. H. (1985). *Stress inoculation training.* New York Pergamon Press.

Meichenbaum, D. H. (1986). Cognitive-behavior modification. In F. H. Kanfer & A. P. Goldstein (Eds.), *Helping people change: A textbook of methods* (3rd ed., pp. 346–380). New York: Pergamon Press.

Meichenbaum, D. H., & Deffenbacher, J. L. (1988). Stress inoculation training. *The Counseling Psychologist, 16,* 69–90.

Meichenbaum, D. H., Gilmore, J. B., & Fedoravicius, A. (1971). Group insight versus group desensitization in treating speech anxiety. *Journal of Consulting and Clinical Psychology, 36,* 410–421.

Meichenbaum, D. H., & Goodman, J. (1971). Training impulsive children to talk to themselves: A means of developing self-control. *Journal of Abnormal Psychology, 77,* 115–126.

Merta, R. J., Stringham, E. M., & Ponterotto, J. G. (1988). Simulating culture shock in counselor trainees: An experiential exercise for cross-cultural training. *Journal of Counseling and Development, 66,* 242–245.

Miles, J. R. (1988). Selecting a video firm that produces results. *Personnel Journal, 67,* 114–118.

Mitchell, J. V. (Ed.). (1983). *Tests in print 111: An index to tests, test reviews, and the literature on specific tests.* Lincoln, NE: University of Nebraska Press.

Mitchell, J. V. (Ed.). (1985). *Ninth mental measurements yearbook* (Vols. 1 & 2). Lincoln, NE: University of Nebraska Press.

Moore, D., & Haverkamp, B. E. (1989). Measured increases in male emotional expressiveness following a structured group intervention. *Journal of Counseling and Development, 67,* 513–517.

Moracco, J. (1981). A comprehensive approach to human relations training for teachers. *Counselor Education and Supervision, 19,* 119–135.

Morawetz, D. (1989). Behavioral self-help treatment for insomnia: A controlled evaluation. *Behavior Therapy, 20,* 365–379.

Moreno, J. L. (1934). *Who shall survive?* Washington, DC: Nervous and Mental Disease Publishing Company.

Moreno, Z. T. (1959). A survey of psychodramatic techniques. *Group Psychotherapy, 12,* 5–14.

Morgan, C. (1984). A curricular approach to primary prevention. *Personnel and Guidance Journal, 53,* 467–469.

Morin, C. M., & Azrin, N. H. (1987). Stimulus control and imagery training in treating sleep-maintenance insomnia. *Journal of Consulting and Clinical Psychology, 55,* 260–262.

Morrill, W. H., Oetting, E. R., & Hurst, J. C. (1974). Dimensions of counselor functioning. *Personnel and Guidance Journal, 52,* 354–359.

Mosher, R. L., & Sprinthall, N. A. (1970). Psychological education in secondary schools: A program to promote individual and human development. *American Psychologist, 25,* 911–924.

Mosher, R. L., & Sprinthall, N. A. (1971). Psychological education: A means to promote personal development during adolescence. *The Counseling Psychologist, 2*(4), 3–82.

Murgatroyd, S. (1985). *Counselling and helping.* London: Methuen.

Murphy, A. I., Lehrer, P. M., & Jurish, S. (1990). Cognitive coping skills training and relaxation training as treatments for tension headaches. *Behavior Therapy, 21,* 89–98.

National Board for Certified Counselors. (1987). *Code of ethics.* Alexandria, VA: Author.

National Training Laboratory. (1967). *Feedback and the helping relationship.* Washington, DC: NTL Institute for Applied Behavioral Sciences (mimeo).

Nelson, R. O., Hayes, S. C., Felton, J. L., & Jarrett, R. B. (1985). A comparison of data produced by different behavioral assessment techniques with implications for models of social-skills inadequacy. *Behaviour Research and Therapy, 23,* 1–11.

Nelson-Jones, R. (1984). *Personal responsibility counseling and therapy: An integrative approach.* New York: Hemisphere, and Milton Keynes, UK: Open University Press.

Nelson-Jones, R. (1986). Relationship skills training in schools: Some fieldwork observations. *British Journal of Guidance and Counselling, 14,* 292–305.

Nelson-Jones, R. (1988a). The counselling psychologist as developmental educator. *The Australian Counselling Psychologist, 4,* 55–66.

Nelson-Jones, R. (1988b). *Practical counselling and helping skills: Helping clients to help themselves* (2nd ed.). London: Cassell, and Sydney, Australia: Holt, Rinehart & Winston.

Nelson-Jones, R. (1990a). *Thinking skills: Managing and preventing personal problems.* Pacific Grove, CA: Brooks/Cole, and Melbourne, Australia: Thomas Nelson.

Nelson-Jones, R. (1990b). *Human relationships: A skills approach.* Pacific Grove, CA: Brooks/Cole.

Newman, J. L., & Fuqua, D. R. (1988). A comparative study of positive and negative modeling in counselor training. *Counselor Education and Supervision, 28,* 121–129.

Nomellini, S., & Katz, R. C. (1983). Effects of anger control training on abusive parents. *Cognitive Therapy and Research, 7,* 57–68.

Office of Population Census and Surveys. (1987). Editorial: A review of 1986. *Population Trends, 50,* 1–12.

O'Hare, W. (1989). In the black. *American Demographics, 11*(11), 24–29.

O'Hare, W. (1990). The rise of Hispanic affluence. *American Demographics, 12*(8), 40–43.

Ohlsen, M. M. (1977). *Group counseling* (2nd ed.). New York: Holt, Rinehart & Winston.

Ohlsen, M. M., Horne, A. M., & Lawe, C. F. (1988). *Group counseling* (3rd ed.). New York: Holt, Rinehart & Winston.

Osipow, S. H. (1982). Counseling psychology: Applications in the world of work. *The Counseling Psychologist, 10*(3), 19–25.

Osipow, S. H., Walsh, W. B., & Tosi, D. J. (1984). *A survey of counseling methods* (rev. ed.). Homewood, IL: Dorsey Press.

Paul, G. L. (1968). Two-year follow-up of systematic desensitization in therapy groups. *Journal of Abnormal Psychology, 73*, 119–130.

Paul, G. L., & Shannon, D. T. (1966). Treatment of anxiety through systematic desensitization in therapy groups. *Journal of Abnormal Psychology, 71*, 124–135.

Peale, N. V. (1953). *The power of positive thinking*. Kingswood, Surrey: The World's Work (1913) Ltd.

Pease, A. (1981). *Body language: How to read others' thoughts by their gestures*. Sydney: Camel.

Pentz, M. A., & Kadzin, A. E. (1982). Assertion modelling and stimuli effects on assertive behaviour and self-efficacy in adolescents. *Behaviour Research and Therapy, 20*, 365–371.

Perry, M. A., & Furukawa, M. J. (1986). Modeling methods. In F. H. Kanfer, & A. P. Goldstein, (Eds.), *Helping people change: A textbook of methods* (3rd ed., pp. 66–110). New York: Pergamon Press.

Peterson, L., & Ridley-Johnson, R. (1980). Pediatric hospital response to survey on pre-hospital preparation of children. *Journal of Pediatric Psychology, 5*, 1–7.

Peterson, L., Schultheis, K., Ridley-Johnson, R., Miller, D. J., & Tracy, K. (1984). Comparison of three modeling procedures on the presurgical and postsurgical reactions of children. *Behavior Therapy, 15*, 197–203.

Pfeiffer, J. W., Heslin, R., & Jones, J. E. (1976). *Instrumentation in human relations training* (2nd ed.). La Jolla, CA: University Associates.

Pfeiffer, J. W., & Jones, J. (1969–1985). *Structured experiences for human relations training* (Vols. 1–10). San Diego, CA: University Associates.

Plesma, D., & Flanagan, M. (1986). Human relations training for the elderly. *Journal of Counseling and Development, 65*, 52–53.

Poole, M. E., & Evans, G. T. (1988). Life skills: Adolescents' perceptions of importance and competence. *British Journal of Guidance and Counselling, 16*, 129–144.

Pretzer, J. L., Fleming, B., & Epstein, N. (1983). *Cognitive factors in marital interaction: The role of specific attributions*. Paper presented at the World Congress of Behavior Therapy, Washington, DC.

Priestley, P., McGuire, J., Flegg, D., Helmsley, V., & Welham, D. (1978). *Social skills and personal problem-solving: A handbook of methods*. London: Tavistock.

Professional Affairs Board. (1980). Technical recommendations for psychological tests. *Bulletin of the British Psychological Society, 33*, 161–164.

Pryor, E., & Norris, D. (1983). Canada in the eighties. *American Demographics, 5*, 25–29, 44.

Ralph, A. (1988). Social skills training: How can we tell if it works? *Australian Psychologist, 23*, 305–314.

Raskin, N. J., & Rogers, C. R. (1989). Person-centered therapy. In R. Corsini & D. Wedding (Eds.), *Current psychotherapies* (4th ed., pp. 155–194). Itasca, IL: Peacock.

Ratigan, B. (1986). Counsellors and staff development: Models of tutor training in tertiary educational settings. *British Journal of Guidance and Counselling, 14*, 140–153.

Raue, J., & Spence, S. H. (1985). Group versus individual applications of reciprocity training for parent-youth conflict. *Behaviour Research and Therapy, 23,* 177–186.

Resnik, J. L., Resnik, M. B., Packer, A. B., & Wilson, J. (1978). Fathering classes: A psychoeducational model. *The Counseling Psychologist, 7*(4), 56–60.

Riordan, R. J., & Beggs, M. S. (1987). Counselors and self-help groups. *Journal of Counseling and Development, 65,* 427–429.

Robey, B. & Russell, C. (1984). Trends: All Americans. *American Demographics, 6,* 32–35.

Roessler, R. T. (1988). Implementing career education: Barriers and potential solutions. *Career Development Quarterly, 37,* 22–30.

Rogers, C. R. (1957). The necessary and sufficient conditions of therapeutic personality change. *Journal of Consulting Psychology, 21,* 95–103.

Rogers, C. R. (1959). A theory of therapy, personality, and interpersonal relationships as developed in the client-centered framework. In S. Koch (Ed.), *Psychology: A study of science,* Vol. 3, *Formulations of the person and the social context* (pp. 184–256). New York: McGraw-Hill.

Rogers, C. R. (1961). *On becoming a person.* Boston: Houghton Mifflin.

Rogers, C. R. (1969). *Freedom to learn: A view of what education might become.* Columbus, OH: Charles E. Merrill.

Rogers, C. R. (1970). *Encounter groups.* London: Allen Lane The Penguin Press.

Rogers, C. R. (1980). *A way of being.* Boston: Houghton Mifflin.

Rogers, G. T. (Producer). (1984). *My father's son: The legacy of alcoholism* [Film]. Skokie, IL: Gerald. T. Rogers Productions.

Rogoff, B., & Morelli, G. (1989). Perspectives on children's development from cultural psychology. *American Psychologist, 44,* 343–348.

Romano, J. L. (1984). Stress management and wellness: Reaching beyond the counselor's office. *Personnel and Guidance Journal, 62,* 533–537.

Rose, S. D. (1986). Group methods. In F. H. Kanfer & A. P. Goldstein (Eds.), *Helping people change: A textbook of methods* (3rd ed., pp. 437–469). New York: Pergamon Press.

Russell, C., & Exter, T. G. (1986). America at mid-decade. *American Demographics, 8,* 22–29.

Ryan, C. W., Jackson, B. L., & Levinson, E. M. (1986). Human relations skills training in teacher education: The link to effective practice. *Journal of Counseling and Development, 65,* 114–116.

Sacks, S., & Gaylord-Ross, R. (1989). Peer-mediated and teacher-directed social skills training for visually impaired students. *Behavior Therapy, 20,* 619–638.

Sampson, D. E., & Liberty, L. H. (1989). Textbooks used in counselor education programs. *Counselor Education and Supervision, 29,* 111–121.

Sarason, I. G. (1973). Test anxiety and cognitive modeling. *Journal of Personality and Social Psychology, 28,* 58–61.

Sarason, I. G. (1976). Using modeling to strengthen the behavioral repertory of the juvenile delinquent. In J. D. Krumboltz & C. E. Thoresen (Eds.), *Counseling methods* (pp. 56–66). New York: Holt, Rinehart & Winston.

Saskatchewan Newstart. (1973). *Life skills coaching manual.* Prince Albert, Saskatchewan: Department of Manpower and Immigration.

Savikas, M. L. (1990). The career decision-making course: Description and field test. *The Career Development Quarterly, 38,* 275–284.

Schlichter, K. J., & Horan, J. J. (1981). Effects of stress inoculation on the anger and aggression management skills of institutionalized juvenile delinquents. *Cognitive Therapy and Research, 5*, 359–365.

Schmidt, J. R., Brown, P. T., & Waycroft, A. M. (1988). Developing the individual: Life skills and family therapy. *British Journal of Guidance and Counselling, 16*, 113–128.

Skinner, B. F. (1953). *Science and human behavior.* New York: Macmillan.

Skinner, B. F. (1971). *Beyond freedom and dignity.* Harmondsworth, Middlesex: Penguin Books.

Smith, M. L., & Glass, G. V. (1977). Meta-analysis of psychotherapy outcome studies. *American Psychologist, 32*, 752–760.

Spanier, G. B. (1976). Measuring dyadic adjustment: New scales for assessing the quality of marriage and similar dyads. *Journal of Marriage and the Family, 38*, 15–28.

Spindler, I., & Spindler, G. (1958). Male and female adaptations in culture change. *American Anthropologist, 60*, 217–233.

Sprinthall, N. A. (1973). A curriculum for secondary schools: Counselors as teachers for psychological growth. *The School Counselor, 20*, 361–369.

Sprinthall, N. A. (1980). Psychology for secondary schools: The saber-tooth curriculum revisited? *American Psychologist, 35*, 336–347.

Sprinthall, N. A., & Scott, J. R. (1989). Promoting psychological development, math achievement, and success attribution of female students through deliberate psychological education. *Journal of Counseling Psychology, 36*, 440–446.

Steiner, C. M. (1974). *Scripts people live.* New York: Bantam Books.

Steiner, C. M. (1981). *The other side of power.* New York: Grove Press.

Stewart, C. G., & Lewis, W. A. (1986). Effects of assertiveness training on the self-esteem of black high school students. *Journal of Counseling and Development, 64*, 638–641.

Stokes, T. F., & Osnes, P. G. (1989). An operant pursuit of generalization. *Behavior Therapy, 20*, 337–355.

Strong, S. R. (1968). Counseling: An interpersonal influence process. *Journal of Counseling Psychology, 15*, 215–224.

Strong, S. R. (1978). Social psychological approach to psychotherapy research. In S. L. Garfield & A. E. Bergin (Eds.), *Handbook of psychotherapy and behavior change* (2nd ed., pp. 101–135). New York: Wiley.

Stuart, R. B. (1980). *Helping couples change: A social learning approach to marital therapy.* New York: Guilford Press.

Sue, S., & Zane, N. (1987). The role of culture and cultural techniques in psychotherapy: A critique and reformulation. *American Psychologist, 42*, 37–45.

Suinn, R. M., & Deffenbacher, J. L. (1988). Anxiety management training. *The Counseling Psychologist, 16*, 31–49.

Sullivan, H. S. (1953). *The interpersonal theory of psychiatry.* New York: Norton.

Swain, R. (1984). Easing the transition: A career planning course for college students. *Personnel and Guidance Journal, 62*, 529–532.

Swenson, C. A. (1990). How to speak to Hispanics. *American Demographics, 12*(2), 40–41.

Sweetland, R. C., & Keyser, D. J. (Eds.). (1986). *Tests: A comprehensive reference for assessments in psychology, education, and business.* Kansas City, MO: Test Corporation of America.

Thoresen, C. E., & Mahoney, M. J. (1974). *Behavioral self-control*. New York: Holt, Rinehart & Winston.

Thorne, B., & Da Costa, M. (1976). A counselling service as a growth centre. *British Journal of Guidance and Counselling, 4*, 212–217.

Thurman, C. W. (1984). Cognitive-behavioral interventions with Type A faculty. *Personnel and Guidance Journal, 62*, 358–362.

Thurman, C. W. (1985). Effectiveness of cognitive-behavioral treatment in reducing Type A behavior among university faculty—One year later. *Journal of Counseling Psychology, 32*, 445–448.

Toomer, J. E. (1982). Counseling psychologists in business and industry. *The Counseling Psychologist, 10*(3), 9–18.

Tracey, T. J. (1983). Single case research: An added tool for counselors and supervisors. *Counselor Education and Supervision, 22*, 185–196.

Troy, W. G., & Magoon, T. M. (1979). Activity analysis in a university counseling center: Daily time recording or time estimates? *Journal of Counseling Psychology, 26*, 58–63.

Turner, J. A., & Clancy, S. (1988). Comparison of operant and cognitive-behavioral group treatment for chronic low back pain. *Journal of Consulting and Clinical Psychology, 56*, 261–266.

Twentyman, C. T., & McFall, R. M. (1975). Behavioral training of social skills in shy males. *Journal of Consulting and Clinical Psychology, 43*, 384–395.

Ulrich's International Periodicals Directory, 1989–90. (1989). 28th ed., Vols. 1–3. New York: R. R. Bowker.

Valenti, J. (1982). *Speak up with confidence: How to prepare, learn, and deliver effective speeches*. New York: William Morrow.

Vobiezda, B. (1991, March 12). The U.S. melting pot takes on Asian, Hispanic flavors. Washington Post syndicated article reprinted in *The Melbourne Age*.

Waldrop, J. (1990a). Up and down the income scale. *American Demographics, 12*(7), 24–30.

Waldrop, J. (1990b). Shades of black. *American Demographics, 12*(9), 30–34.

Waldrop, J., & Exter, T. (1990). What the 1990 census will show. *American Demographics, 12*(1), 20–30.

Watkins, C. E., Lopez, F. G., Campbell, V. L., & Himmell, C. D. (1986). Contemporary counseling psychology: Results of a national survey. *Journal of Counseling Psychology, 33*, 301–309.

Webster-Stratton, C. (1989). Systematic comparison of consumer satisfaction of three cost-effective parent training programs for conduct problem children. *Behavior Therapy, 20*, 103–115.

Webster-Stratton, C., Hollinsworth, T., & Kolpacoff, M. (1989). The long-term effectiveness and clinical significance of three cost-effective training programs for parents with conduct-problem children. *Journal of Consulting and Clinical Psychology, 57*, 550–553.

Webster-Stratton, C., Kolpacoff, M., & Hollinsworth, T. (1988). Self-administered videotape therapy for families with conduct-problem children: Comparison with two cost-effective treatments and a control group. *Journal of Consulting and Clinical Psychology, 56*, 558–566.

Wehrenberg, S. B. (1985). Management training games: The play's the thing. *Personnel Journal, 64*, 88–91.

Wehrenberg, S. B. (1988). Learning contracts. *Personnel Journal, 67*, 100–102.

Weishaar, M. E., & Beck, A. T. (1986). Cognitive therapy. In W. Dryden & W. Golden (Eds.), *Cognitive-behavioural approaches to psychotherapy* (pp. 61–91). London: Harper & Row.

Weissman, S. (1985). Preparing incarcerated youth for employment. *Journal of Counseling and Development, 63,* 524–525.

Whitaker's books in print. (1989). Vols. 1–4. London: J. Whitaker & Sons.

Whitaker, D. S. (1985). *Using groups to help people.* London: Routledge & Kegan Paul.

Wilbur, C. S., & Vermilyea, C. J. (1982). Some business advice to counseling psychologists. *The Counseling Psychologist, 10*(3), 31–32.

Wild, B., & Kerr, B. A. (1984). Training adolescent job-seekers in persuasion skills. *Vocational Guidance Quarterly, 33,* 63–69.

Wilkinson, J., & Canter, S. (1982). *Social skills training manual: Assessment, programme design, and management of training.* Chichester, England: Wiley.

Wolpe, J. E. (1982). *The practice of behavior therapy* (2nd ed.). New York: Pergamon Press.

Wolpe, J., & Lazarus, A. A. (1966). *Behavior therapy techniques: A guide to the treatment of neurosis.* New York: Pergamon Press.

Wragg, J. (1986). Drug and alcohol education: The development, design, and longitudinal evaluation of an early childhood programme. *Australian Psychologist, 21,* 283–298.

Yalom, I. D. (1980). *Existential psychotherapy.* New York: Basic Books.

Yalom, I. D. (1985). *The theory and practice of group psychotherapy* (3rd ed.). New York: Basic Books.

Yalom, I. D. (1990). *Understanding group psychotherapy* [Video series]. Pacific Grove, CA: Brooks/Cole.

Yamauchi, K. T. (1987). Self-help audiocassette tapes: Adjunct to psychological counseling. *Journal of Counseling and Development, 65,* 448–450.

Zelko, H. P. (1986). Better seminars and workshops for both sponsor and participant. *Personnel Journal, 65,* 32–34.

Zemore, R. (1975). Systematic desensitization as a method of teaching a general anxiety-reducing skill. *Journal of Consulting and Clinical Psychology, 43,* 157–161.

Zimbardo, P. G. (1977). *Shyness: What it is and what to do about it.* Reading, MA: Addison-Wesley.

To the owner of this book:

I enjoyed writing *Group Leadership*, and I hope that you have enjoyed reading it. I'd like to know about your experiences with the book; only through your comments and the comments of others can I assess the impact of this book and make it a better book for readers in the future.

School: _____

Instructor's name: _____

1. What did you like *most* about the book? _____

_____

_____

_____

2. What did you like *least* about the book? _____

_____

_____

_____

3. How useful were the *annotated reading lists and activities* at the end of the chapters?

_____

_____

4. What class did you use this book for? _____

5. In the space below or in a separate letter, please tell us what it was like for you to read this book and how you used it; please give your suggestions for revisions and any other comments you'd like to make about the book; include, if you'd like, your own ideas for group techniques.

Optional:

Your name: _____ Date: _____

May Brooks/Cole quote you, either in promotion for *Group Leadership* or in future publishing ventures?

Yes: _____ No: _____

Sincerely,

Richard Nelson-Jones